Open the magical windows
of children's literature
and share stories that are
"good enough for children" while making

MORE CREATIVE CONNECTIONS

More Creative Connections

Literature and the Reading Program
Grades 4-6

Mary Lou Olsen

Library Services-
Curriculum Consultant
Buena Park, California

1993

TEACHER IDEAS PRESS
A Division of
Libraries Unlimited, Inc.
Englewood, Colorado

TEACHER IDEAS PRESS
A Division of
Libraries Unlimited, Inc.
P.O. Box 6633
Englewood, CO 80155-6633

Library of Congress Cataloging-in-Publication Data

Olsen, Mary Lou, 1937-
    More creative connections : literature and the reading program,
grades 4-6 / Mary Lou Olsen.
    xvii, 319 p. 22x28 cm.
    Sequel to: Creative connections. 1987.
    Includes bibliographical references and index.
    ISBN 1-56308-027-3
  1. Reading. 2. Children--United States--Books and reading.
I. Olsen, Mary Lou, 1937- . Creative connections. II. Title.
LB1050.045 1993
372.4--dc20   93-29971
                                CIP

To Mary Lorelei Olsen,
an elementary teacher in the San Diego Unified School District, who empowers her students to be successful. As an educator for more than 30 years, and in memory of my grandmother, Annie Lee Atkins Mason, who taught school for 50 years in Florida, I salute my daughter, who has chosen the most important profession of all, that of being a teacher. May you and your students always have fun in the pursuit of learning.

Contents

Through an Introduction to
Research Technology

By Exploring Great Books

Grade Five
OPINIONS

About First Americans Through
Legends and Stories

**Grade Six
CHOICES**

*Through a Survey of Myths
and Legends*

In the World of Fantasy

From the World of Arts and Letters

When People Disagree

Introduction

My teaching style is that of a combination showman and ringmaster. Kids are the performers and I am the guide responsible for *Magic School Bus* type field trips, ethnic food menus that taste good and help us understand our international neighbors, and literature strands integrated across the curriculum in content areas.

I have very positive memories of the Ringling Brothers Circus. The return to its winter home in Sarasota, Florida, was, at that time, an official school holiday for Bradenton and Sarasota students. All of us Bradenton kids were excited about the festivities, which involved getting up before daylight, being driven to various railroad crossings to see the slowly rolling train cars with the canvas covers lifted up and all the animals in full view. This is my tunnel vision memory of childhood. Circuses no longer are housed under a "big top" having been supplanted by modern convention and sports arenas.

Those days no longer exist, but we can still make learning exciting for kids. Throughout this book the following teaching strategies are used:

Cluster strategies may be used to introduce a book through a variety of descriptive words. For example, to introduce *Pyramid*, students can draw the figure of a pyramid and then write down words or phrases that would describe the tomb of Cheops. Second-grade GATE (Gifted and Talented Education) students once described a pyramid as being a tomb, treasure house, made of blocks, smelled dank, had a curse on it, was very old, was hot because of the desert, and was a place they would like to visit. After summer vacation, one of the students shared with me what she had learned about pyramids including the measure of their volume! Another student persuaded his parents to visit the pyramid over winter holiday! He came back and gave us a well-researched report.

Game boards develop students' synthesis skills. These games create a new way to present the information they have learned. A new game could be designed that correlates with *Ramona and Her Father*. The problems Ramona's family has to deal with are elements of the board. When students land on the spaces, they have to come up with solutions to certain problems.

Hot Seat is a television news simulation. You are a guest on "60 Minutes" or "Meet the Press." How do you respond to the interviewer when asked if you knew *Someone Is Hiding on Alcatraz Island*?

Mind mapping presents a series of pictorial images that are developed around a curriculum topic. In preparation for the introduction of *The Slave Dancer*, students can develop a mind map schematica that includes information that the students know about the subject of slavery. Students can begin their mind maps with the most important facts that they know for a thumbnail picture. Examples might include Abraham Lincoln, letters of the word prejudice spelled out, or perhaps Harriet Tubman. From these central ideas, other ideas would follow and become miniature pictures about slavery.

Mind maps may be reviewed at the end of the study. They may also be revised to reflect new information. This technique is appropriate for the introduction of sensitive topics such as slavery.

Outlines are structures that help students prioritize information. What is the most important heading? What other information would you like to know or include in your writing? There are many ways to introduce this research and writing skill as a process, not an isolated library media center activity that does not relate to any specific curriculum. Information needs to be based and organized from actual print and nonprint materials. This technique is an interesting way for students to bridge subjects like language arts and social studies, art and science, and math with geography.

Quick writes are exactly what they sound like. They are generally about a paragraph to a page long and are used to compile and organize information quickly. These can be brief entries about class discussion or independent reading assignments.

Time lines need to be related to students and must present challenges about the history of the past and an introduction to the technologies of today. What new technologies will be in everyday usage tomorrow? Get students involved with their parents on time line concepts. What changes have parents observed during their lifetimes?

Transparencies are used as a time-saving tool. Consider how long it would take students to design butcher paper scene changes for a play. Transparencies are effective when used for background art or to present visual information. Teacher-developed materials on transparencies are easy to store in a file drawer. Transparencies could be used as map overlays to show geographic changes over time or illustrate routes characters used in their travels.

I like to meet students at the door of the library media center because I not only want them to be interested in what we are going to do, but, more importantly, I also want them to know I welcome them to this special place.

Seize the interest of students by relating to their experiences. *More Creative Connections* has individual learning models. Do involve students in the learning model of the lesson. Check for understanding. Model the lesson and its components. Allow time for supervised practice and independent work. In teaching library skills, kids were excited when I told them that each one had to answer a question correctly or "Down You Go" to the end of the dismissal line. Alphabetizing last names of second graders was great fun for them when we made up an alphabet letter train and chugged around the library media center and back to class.

Kids are always delighted to be chosen for small group seminars. Seminars, or cooperative learning groups, may be enrichment or remedial and kids never feel like bluebirds or blackbirds. It is confirmation that they are special!!!

I would like to share a wonderful communication tool learned in staff development. Clam claps are a small, silent expressive means of student participation. For clam claps, ball your fingers so that they touch the palm of your hand and make little hand motions. Two finger claps are the epitome of good work. Turn your left hand palm up, hit the right two fingers to the left hand's index and middle fingers. Primary kids passing me in lunch lines have given me their best two finger claps without making a sound.

Select literature that is "good enough for kids." Students have a large appetite for various genres. Their cravings for good books and stories are insatiable. Plant the seeds, and they will bloom and blossom on their own! Several out-of-print books have been listed in the bibliographies that accompany each unit. These are included because they contain special information and are available in public library collections. Other titles have been selected to integrate independent reading activities and to serve as a quick list of current books and other materials including read-aloud cassettes and videos.

In conclusion, if *Creative Connections* (Libraries Unlimited, 1987) was a basic cookbook, *More Creative Connections* is a recipe index. Pick and choose activities that meet the learning prescription for your students. Allow time to birdwalk with panache and extend the learning in your classroom or library. Not all students bring rich experiences to our classrooms and libraries, many children have never been to a zoo or a museum. It is, therefore, important that we know ourselves and our neighbors through travel across geographical boundaries and international borders to meet and understand the peoples of the world. (Even Cuddles and Muddles, the bears in the photograph accompanying the "About the Author" page, enjoy dressing up and making appearances at schools and conferences.)

At the Washington-Oregon state library media conference, a participant in my all-day literature immersion workshop made this insightful statement:

"Integrated literature is the period at the end of the sentence."

Grade Four

COMMUNICATION

Around the World Through Storytellers

ANANSI THE SPIDER
A Tale from the Ashanti

Author: Retold by Gerald McDermott
Illustrator: Gerald McDermott
Publisher: Henry Holt, 1976
Suggested Grade Level: 4
Classification: Folktale
Literary Form: Picture book illustrated in a supergraphic style
Theme: Folktales and mythology prepare man for adult life and transform the ordinary into the magical.

ABOUT THE BOOK

STUDENT OBJECTIVES:

1. Retell Anansi's story to another student as a cross-grade tutor.

2. Compare and contrast Anansi the spider with another story about this famous trickster: Berry, James. *Spiderman Anancy.* Henry Holt, 1988.

3. Produce a short play about Anansi and his six sons for readers theatre or a video project.

SYNOPSIS: Anansi is a well-known character in West African folklore. Anansi is always busy. According to Gerald McDermott, Anansi has many adventures and "tumbles into many troubles. This is one of his adventures."

ABOUT THE AUTHOR-ILLUSTRATOR: Gerald McDermott, 1941- .
Gerald McDermott might well be described as a born artist. His parents recognized his special talents, and, at the age of four, they enrolled him in Saturday classes at Detroit's Institute of Art. For 10 years McDermott continued his art classes and gained knowledge about art museums and their collections.

As a student at Cass Technical High School in Detroit, Michigan, McDermott attended small classes for artistically talented students. His curriculum included the formal study of art and painting, as well as music and ballet. Later his special interest became film production. McDermott graduated from Pratt Institute, New York.

McDermott first created five animated children's films that were subsequently released as picture books. That is the opposite of what normally happens; most successful children's books are first published and then adapted to filmstrip or video production.

McDermott thought that it would be easy to transfer his film production of *Anansi the Spider* into a picture book. He had made some 4,000 drawings for the animated movie and thought he would sort through the materials to select 40 pages for the book. He was in for a surprise; it did not work out that way. The format of a book differs from that of a movie, and he needed to adapt the material to fit within a 40-page print-production setup.

McDermott incorporated in his work one of folklore's major themes: The main character is on a quest and needs to find fulfillment. Anansi goes on a search, meets danger, is involved in conflict, and achieves success at the end of the story. McDermott describes his literature as a "journey on the rainbow trail."

SELECTED ADDITIONAL TITLES:

McDermott, Gerald. *Arrow to the Sun: A Pueblo Indian Tale.* Viking, 1974.

———. *Daughter of Earth: A Roman Myth.* Delacorte Press, 1984.

———. *Magic Tree.* Holt, Rinehart & Winston, 1973.

———. *Papagayo—The Mischief Maker.* Harcourt Brace Jovanovich, 1992.

———. *Stonecutter: A Japanese Folk Tale.* Illustrated by Gerald McDermott. Viking, 1975.

———. *Sun Flight.* Illustrated by Gerald McDermott. Four Winds Press, 1984.

———. *Zomo—The Rabbit.* Illustrated by Gerald McDermott. Harcourt Brace Jovanovich, 1992.

Mayer, Marianna. *Aladdin and the Wonderful Lamp.* Illustrated by Gerald McDermott. Macmillan, 1985.

USING THE BOOK

Suggested Approach to the Book

Model Lesson

1. Describe the book's end papers. Why do you think this pattern is used? Where can this type of design be found today? Is reversing the pattern on the two pages effective? Why or why not?

2. Locate the country of Ghana on a world map. What are the areas adjoining the country like? Could the desert and rain forests have any effect on Anansi and his tales? Explain your answer.

3. Define prologue. Explain the prologue of this book.

4. Do you think the melodic use of African-language patterning is effective in this book? How would the words sound if they were in a traditional spoken-language sentence structure?

5. Can you explain the various symbols used to identify the six sons?

6. List reasons why people might wear masks.

Library Media Center Connections

1. Use the library media center catalog to locate the following subjects. Include in your research both print and supplementary nonprint materials, including prints, recordings, film, and video. Write down the call number for each selection found. List and locate the materials in the library. Which materials would be suitable to use in a report?

Anansi Book Titles	African Folktales
Books by Gerald McDermott	African Art and Music
Mythology, including African Mythology	African Masks
Geography of African Countries	Spiders

Computer Connections

1. Write a letter to a computer pal in another class, and give your opinion of the Ashanti tale of *Anansi the Spider*. Ask your pal to recommend one of his or her favorite books. (Note: Recommendations may be stored in a special file that all students may access to add a title or to browse. Teachers should add their favorite selections to the computer file.)

Instructional Materials Connections

1. Arkhurst, Joyce Cooper. *The Adventures of Spider*. Cassette. Little, Brown, 1992.

2. McDermott, Gerald. *Anansi the Spider*. Sound filmstrip. Weston Woods, n.d.

3. McDermott, Gerald. *Arrow to the Sun*. Sound filmstrip. Weston Woods, n.d.

4. *Evolution of a Graphic Concept*. Includes *The Stonecutter* book and filmstrip. Weston Woods, n.d.

5. Stewig, John Warren. *Reading Pictures: Exploring Illustrations with Children*. Four posters and study guides of the works of Gerald McDermott. Resourceful Educator, 2770 S. 171st St., P.O. Box 246, New Berlin, WI 53151-0248.

6. Multi-Cultural Mask-Making Kit. Museum Company, 1014 Brea Mall, Brea, CA 92621.

Theme Reading Connections: African Art and Legends

Aardema, Verna. *Bringing the Rain to Kapiti Plain*. Illustrated by Beatriz Vidal. Dial, 1981.

———. *Why Mosquitoes Buzz in People's Ears*. Illustrated by Diane Dillon and Leo Dillon. Dial, 1975.

Brown, Marcia. *Shadow*. Charles Scribner's Sons, 1982.

Corwin, Judith Hoffman. *African Crafts*. Franklin Watts, 1990.

Courlander, Harold, and George Herzog. *Cow-Tail Switch and Other West African Stories*. Henry Holt, 1988.

Greaves, Nick. *When Hippo Was Hairy and Other Tales from Africa*. Illustrated by David Bateman. Barron's Educational Series, 1988.

Grifalconi, Ann. *Flyaway Girl*. Little, Brown, 1992.

———. *Osa's Pride*. Little, Brown, 1990.

———. *Village of Round and Square Houses*. Little, Brown, 1985.

Haskins, J. *Count Your Way Through Africa*. Lerner, 1989.

Jacobs, Shannon. *Song of the Giraffe*. Illustrated by Pamela Johnson. Little, Brown, 1991.

Knutson, Barbara. *Why the Crab Has No Head*. Carolrhoda, 1979.

Lurie, Morris. *Twenty-Seventh Annual African Hippopotamus Race*. Illustrated by Richard Sawers. Simon & Schuster, 1959.

MacDonald, Susu. *Space Spinners*. Dial, 1991.

Musgrove, Margaret. *Ashanti to Zulu: African Traditions*. Illustrated by Diane Dillon and Leo Dillon. Dial, 1976.

Owoo, Ife Nii. *A Is for Africa*. Africa World Press, 1992.

Price, Christine. *Dancing Masks of Africa*. Charles Scribner's Sons, 1975.

Critical Thinking Question
What is the purpose of the story of *Anansi the Spider: A Tale from the Ashanti*? Does the author-illustrator, Gerald McDermott, succeed in his presentation? In your opinion, should he have won a Caldecott award for this book? List books that received the Caldecott or Caldecott honor awards that year. What is your favorite Caldecott winner? Why?

Student Activities to Connect Literature and Curriculum

FINE ARTS

1. Research and present a four-minute oral class report about the types of musical instruments that are used in Africa. Visual props should be integrated.

2. Draw a model plan of one African musical instrument and build a scale model of it.

3. Design and print stationery with representational African art.

4. A contest has been announced to select an interior designer and an architect for a new luxury resort in West Africa. Each cooperative learning group will present art renditions, dioramas, or model mockups appropriate for the lobby, restaurant, ballroom, swimming pool, or guest rooms.

5. Construct paper-bag puppets representing Anansi, his six sons, and Nyame.

6. *Anansi the Spider* is printed in bright, primary colors. Design a story board and illustrate the book with soft watercolors. Is the use of soft colors effective? Why or why not?

7. Construct a mankala game from egg cartons and beans. Teach a friend how to play it. List the rules on a large card that will be attached to the game.

8. Create climbing critters or spider in a web. A pencil is used to suspend a spider and its web. For instructions, see *Ranger Rick's Nature Scope—Wild and Crafty*, available from the National Wildlife Federation, 1400 16th St., Washington, DC 20036-2266.

9. Make menagerie pins from beads. Pattern and directions (*McCall's Creates Menagerie Pins*) and supplies may be purchased in fabric stores.

LANGUAGE ARTS

1. Spiders are classified as arachnids; they are not insects. How did they receive their name? Identify the mythological character for which they are named. Write and illustrate a book about spiders. This project is an appropriate assignment for cooperative learning groups.

2. When an object or animal is given human qualities, the technique is called personification. Compare and contrast the personification of Anansi with Charlotte in White, E. B., *Charlotte's Web*, illustrated by Garth Williams, Harper & Row, 1952.

3. Robert Kraus has written several books for young readers about spiders, including *How Spider Saved Halloween* (Scholastic, 1986) and *Spider's First Day at School* (Scholastic, 1987). Write and illustrate a Spider story in Kraus's style.

WRITING PROMPT

1. Write the first paragraph of the lead story for the evening television newscast. Begin with

> Gerald McDermott Wins 1973 Caldecott Honor Award for *Anansi the Spider: A Tale from the Ashanti*

MATH

1. More than 34,000 different kinds of spiders have been identified. Construct an illustrated chart that displays spiders in basic categories.

2. How many Caldecott winners have used Africa and its cultures as their central theme? Design a time line from the inception of the Caldecott award in 1938 until today. Add the title that was honored each year on the time line. Using a color marker, highlight the titles that relate to Africa. Compute the percentage of these books in relationship to the total number of Caldecott book awards. Use a bar or circle graph to present the findings.

SCIENCE

1. Create an oversize model spider from materials available in the classroom. On a large index card, list the following information: Descriptions of size, body, habitat, and possible effects of its bite.

2. In cooperative learning groups, develop a Spider Game. On card stock the size of playing cards, name and describe a particular type of spider. On the opposite side, picture the spider. Identification may be by picture or by text. The cards may also be used as flash cards.

SOCIAL STUDIES

1. Creepy, crawly creatures are a part of African cultures. Make bookmark figures of snakes, crocodiles, lizards, and spiders from felt decorated with ribbon, string, sequins, buttons, and other available materials.

2. Prepare an African menu and serve a special lunch to students, staff, and parent guests as a social activity. School food services are frequently able to provide this curriculum support. Include laminated place mats, table decorations, and a written menu.

GEOGRAPHY

1. Ghana's area of 92,098 square miles is nearest in size to what U.S. state? Using two overhead transparencies, draw outlines of the two areas, showing their physical locations in reference to neighboring countries and states. List under each the form of government, language, population, industries, and national resources. (See *World Almanac*.)

BEYOND THE BOOK

Guided Reading Connections Across a Learning Rainbow: Spiders

Back, Christine, and Barrie Watts. *Spider's Web*. Silver Burdett, 1986.

Bender, Lionel. *Spiders*. Franklin Watts, 1988.

Climo, Shirley. *Someone Saw a Spider: Spider Facts and Folktales*. Thomas Y. Crowell, 1985.

Craig, Janet. *Amazing World of Spiders*. Troll, 1989.

Dallinger, Jane. *Spiders*. Lerner, 1981.

Horton, Lenga, and Marriott. *Amazing Fact Book of Spiders*. Creative Education, 1987.

Levi, Herbert, and Lorna Levi. *Spiders and Their Kin*. Golden, 1990.

Martin, L. *Bird Eating Spiders*. Rourke, n.d.

————. *Black Widow Spiders*. Rourke, n.d.

————. *Fishing Spiders*. Rourke, n.d.

————. *Funnel Web Spiders*. Rourke, n.d.

————. *Spider Discovery Library*. Rourke, 1989.

————. *Tarantulas*. Rourke, n.d.

————. *Trapdoor Spiders*. Rourke, n.d.

Merrians, Deborah. *I Can Read About Spiders*. Troll, 1977.

Morris, Dean. *Spiders*. Raintree/Steck-Vaughn, 1987.

Parsons, Alexandra. *Amazing Spiders*. Eye Witness Junior series. Alfred A. Knopf, 1990.

Patent, Dorothy H. *Spider Magic*. Holiday House, 1982.

Penny, Malcolm. *Discovering Spiders*. Franklin Watts, 1986.

Petty, Kate. *Spiders*. Franklin Watts, 1985.

Podendorf, Illa. *Spiders*. Childrens Press, 1982.

Pringle, Laurence. *The Golden Book of Insects and Spiders*. Illustrated by James Spence. Western, 1990.

Schnieper, Claudia. *Amazing Spiders*. Carolrhoda, 1989.

Enriching Connections

1. Share additional Anansi stories with the class. Cooperative learning groups may choose different ways to present the stories including flannel boards, room murals, bulletin-board displays, plays, films, transparencies, or other teacher-approved activities.

    Aardema, Verna. *Anansi Finds a Fool*. Illustrated by Bryna Waldman. Dial, 1992.

    Arkhurst, Joyce Cooper. *The Adventures of Spider*. Little, Brown, 1992.

    French, Fiona. *Anancy and Mr. Dry Bone*. Little, Brown, 1991.

    Haley, Gail E. *A Story, A Story*. Illustrated by Gail E. Haley. Macmillan, 1970.

    Kimmel, A., retold by. *Anansi Goes Fishing*. Illustrated by Janet Stevens. Holiday House, 1992.

    ———. *Anansi and the Moss-Covered Rock*. Illustrated by Janet Stevens. Holiday House, 1988.

FROM ANOTHER POINT OF VIEW

Gleeson, Brian. *Anansi*. Rabbit Ears, 1992.

Parent-Student Connections

1. Mythology, which attempts to place people in their world, is common to all cultures. Many stories have been told and written to explain the phenomenon of the Moon. What ways can the presence of the Moon be explained? (See Berger, Barbara, *Father Twilight*, Putnam, 1986.)

2. Encourage reading as a family activity. Select other Anansi stories from the library to share as a family.

3. Paper-plate art is a creative activity using materials available in the home. Create Anansi's face on the plate. Attach a tongue depressor or popsicle stick for a handle, and a face mask is completed. Attach the six sons to the plate with thread, and a mobile is created.

❀　❀　❀

THE SNOW QUEEN

Author: Hans Christian Andersen, retold by Amy Ehrlich
Illustrator: Susan Jeffers
Publisher: Dial, 1982
Suggested Grade Level: 4
Classification: Hans Christian Andersen fairy tale
Literary Form: Picture book illustrated in pointillism style
Theme: Unplanned events can change lives; Kai's heart is pierced and frozen.

ABOUT THE BOOK

STUDENT OBJECTIVES:

1. Recognize pointillism in other art work, including illustrated children's books.

2. Retell the Snow Queen story, integrating today's transportation, housing, food, clothing, and technology.

3. Develop plans for an ice palace of fairy tales to be built as an attraction in your state. The palace will have the interiors and exteriors illuminated. Each room will portray a different fairy tale.

SYNOPSIS: This relatively unknown fairy tale by Hans Christian Andersen depicts the friendship between a young boy and girl. Kai is spirited away by the Snow Queen, and he becomes a prisoner in her ice palace. Gerda, his friend, begins a quest to free Kai and encounters many obstacles in her search.

ABOUT THE AUTHOR: Hans Christian Andersen, 1805-1875.

Hans Christian Andersen was born to poor parents, a laundrywoman and a cobbler, in Odense, Denmark. The Andersen's one-room home was sparse: The furniture included a workbench for his father and a bed for his parents. Andersen's bed pushed into the closet during the day so the family had room to walk. Because Andersen's father was too poor to buy toys, he made them for his only child. Andersen's father constructed a puppet theater that his son never tired of using. Perhaps these early adventures in the theater stimulated Andersen's future writing.

Andersen's mother sent him to an ABC school, but he did not succeed there. The schoolmaster hit Andersen with a stick when his attention wandered. He was expelled for spending too much time watching the classroom clock, which had tiny figures that popped out every hour. His efforts at various schools resulted in failure: The boy was a dreamer. All of the schoolmasters made fun of the tall, disconnected boy. His school-level achievement was that of a primary student.

"To Hans there was nothing more wonderful than singing and acting. He made up his mind to become a famous actor.... The grownups liked to have Hans sing and act for them. But no one thought he could ever be an actor.... He was too ugly. He was too clumsy." (Moore, Eva. *The Fairy Tale Life of Hans Christian Andersen.* Illustrated by Trina Schart Hyman. Scholastic, 1969.)

Andersen did attempt to become an actor and dancer, but he failed. Because Andersen had always liked to tell stories to children, he began to write them. As an author he finally became successful. He received invitations to read his fairy tales to rulers at their European courts.

In December 1867 his home village of Odense held a week-long celebration to honor the man who lived a life like one of his own fairy tales. Hans Christian Andersen died in 1875.

Today, many scholars study Andersen's books. They believe that his works are suitable for adults as well as children. His works include 167 fairy tales, 47 plays, 14 novels, and 23 travel books. The story of the ugly duckling is his self-portrait. He told his mother once that a person must suffer to become famous.

The Hans Christian Andersen International Medal was established in 1956 by the International Board on Books for Young People. It is presented every two years to an author and an illustrator who have made substantial contributions to children's literature. Americans who have received this award are Mildred DeJong, Maurice Sendak, Scott O'Dell, and Paula Fox.

ABOUT THE ILLUSTRATOR: Susan Jeffers, 1942- .

Susan Jeffers, as a children's book illustrator, is continuing to do the things she enjoyed while growing up. "When I was small my best moments were spent drawing pictures, reading stories with my parents, playing with friends, and experiencing nature's perfection" (Press release from Dial Books for Children).

Jeffers works in pen-and-ink and wash. She makes thousands of little lines to make forms. She creates many small drawings, revising them until they reflect what she wants.

Jeffers attended Pratt Institute in New York for four years. "It was eight hours a day of drawing, painting, and sculpture interspersed with English and psychology. This was heaven" (Press release). She gained additional experience in children's books by working at three publishing houses. She lives with her family, which includes a daughter, in Westchester County, New York, surrounded by nature and wildlife.

SELECTED ADDITIONAL TITLES: Hans Christian Andersen

Andersen, Hans Christian. *Dulac's The Snow Queen and Other Stories by Hans Christian Andersen.* Illustrated by Edmond Dulac. Doubleday, 1976.

———. *Emperor and the Nightingale.* Illustrated by James Watling. Troll, 1979.

———. *Emperor's New Clothes.* Illustrated by Virginia Burton. Houghton Mifflin, 1979.

———. *Emperor's New Clothes.* Illustrated by Anne Rockwell. Thomas Y. Crowell, 1982.

———. *Emperor's New Clothes.* Illustrated by Nadine Westcott. Little, Brown, 1984.

———. *Emperor's New Clothes.* Illustrated by Dorothee Duntze. Henry Holt, 1986.

———. *Fir Tree.* Illustrated by Nancy E. Burkert. Harper & Row, 1970.

———. *Hans Andersen: His Classic Fairy Tales.* Illustrated by Michael Foreman. Doubleday, 1978.

———. *Hans Christian Andersen's The Snow Queen.* Translated by Eva Le Gallienne. Illustrated by Ariech Zeldich. Harper & Row, 1985.

———. *The Little Mermaid.* Illustrated by Chihiro Iwasaki. Picture Book Studio, 1984.

———. *Michael Hague's Favourite Hans Christian Andersen Fairy Tales.* Illustrated by Michael Hague. Henry Holt, 1981.

———. *The Nightingale.* Translated by Eva Le Gallienne. Illustrated by Nancy E. Burkert. Harper & Row, 1965.

———. *The Nightingale.* Illustrated by Lisbeth Zwerger. Picture Book Studio, 1984.

———. *The Nightingale.* Illustrated by Demi. Harcourt Brace Jovanovich, 1985.

———. *The Nightingale.* Illustrated by Beni Montresor. Crown, 1985. o.p.

————. *The Princess and the Pea.* Illustrated by Paul Galdone. Clarion Books, 1978.

————. *The Princess and the Pea.* Adapted and illustrated by Janet Stevens. Holiday House, 1982.

————. *The Princess and the Pea.* Illustrated by Dorothee Duntze. Henry Holt, 1985.

————. *The Red Shoes.* Illustrated by Chihiro Iwasaki. Picture Book Studio, 1985.

————. *The Snow Queen.* Adapted by Naomi Lewis. Illustrated by Errol Le Cain. Penguin, 1982.

————. *The Snow Queen.* Illustrated by Richard Hess. Macmillan, 1985.

————. *The Steadfast Tin Soldier.* Illustrated by Paul Galdone. Clarion Books, 1979.

————. *The Steadfast Tin Soldier.* Illustrated by Alain Vaes. Little, Brown, 1983.

————. *The Steadfast Tin Soldier.* Illustrated by David Jorgensen. Alfred A. Knopf, 1986.

————. *The Steadfast Tin Soldier.* Illustrated by Georges Leomine. Creative Education, 1986.

————. *The Steadfast Tin Soldier.* Illustrated by. P. J. Lynch. Harcourt Brace Jovanovich, 1992.

————. *The Steadfast Tin Soldier.* Retold by Tor Seidler. Illustrated by Fred Marcellino. HarperCollins, 1992.

————. *Stories of Hans Christian Andersen.* Retold by Robert Mathia. Illustrated by Robin Lawrie. Silver Burdett, 1985.

————. *The Swineherd.* Translated by Anthea Bell. Illustrated by Lisbeth Zwerger. Picture Book Studio, 1982.

————. *The Ugly Duckling.* Illustrated by Maria Rius. Silver Burdett, 1985.

————. *The Ugly Duckling.* Translated by Ann Stewart. Illustrated by Monika Laimgruber. Greenwillow Books, 1985.

————. *The Ugly Duckling.* Illustrated by Robert Van Nutt. Alfred A. Knopf, 1986.

————. *The Wild Swans.* Translated by Naomi Lewis. Illustrated by Angela Barrett. P. Bedrick, 1990.

Greene, Carol. *Hans Christian Andersen—Teller of Tales.* Childrens Press, 1986.

Moore, Eva. *The Fairy Tale Life of Hans Christian Andersen.* Illustrated by Trina Schart Hyman. Scholastic, 1969.

SELECTED ADDITIONAL TITLES: Susan Jeffers

Andersen, Hans Christian. *Thumbelina.* Illustrated by Susan Jeffers. Dial, 1985.

————. *Wild Swans.* Illustrated by Susan Jeffers. Dial, 1981.

Field, Eugene. *Wynken, Blynken and Nod.* Illustrated by Susan Jeffers. Dutton, 1982.

Frost, Robert. *Stopping by the Woods on a Snowy Evening.* Illustrated by Susan Jeffers. Dutton, 1978.

Grimm, Jacob, and Wilhelm K. Grimm. *Hansel and Gretel.* Illustrated by Susan Jeffers. Dial, 1981.

Jeffers, Susan. *All the Pretty Horses.* Illustrated by Susan Jeffers. Scholastic, 1985.

————. *Brother Eagle, Sister Sky.* Illustrated by Susan Jeffers. Dial, 1991.

————. *If Wishes Were Horses: Mother Goose Rhymes.* Illustrated by Susan Jeffers. Dutton, 1979.

————. *Three Jovial Huntsmen: A Mother Goose Rhyme.* Illustrated by Susan Jeffers. Bradbury Press, 1973.

Longfellow, Henry Wadsworth. *Hiawatha.* Illustrated by Susan Jeffers. Dial, 1983.

Marzollo, Jean. *Close Your Eyes.* Illustrated by Susan Jeffers. Dial, 1981.

Mohr, Joseph. *Silent Night.* Illustrated by Susan Jeffers. Dutton, 1984.

Perrault, Charles. *Cinderella.* Illustrated by Susan Jeffers. Dial, 1985.

USING THE BOOK

Suggested Approach to the Book

Model Lesson

1. Examine the title page of *The Snow Queen.* What do you see? What season is it?

2. Name a well-known Danish fairy tale that has as its main character a troll who hides under a bridge and harasses a goat family. Read it to the class and share the various illustrators who have drawn their versions of the story. Which version do you like best? Why? Has your favorite illustrator had other art works published? List the illustrators in a library media center database of authors and illustrators.

3. What are "the white bees that are swarming"? (Page 7.) Who is their queen?

4. Describe Kai's reaction after mirror splinters enter his heart and eye.

5. Why does Gerda throw her new red shoes into the river? Why does she try to throw the shoes into the river a second time? What happens?

6. Explain why the artist depicted two different seasons on page 19.

7. How do the prince and princess help Gerda with her quest?

8. Describe the queen's ice palace.

Library Media Center Connections

1. Trolls are pictured on the opening page. Use print and nonprint materials from the library media center to prepare a one- to two-page report on these fairy tale characters. Transparencies may be used to illustrate the presentation.

2. Cooperative learning groups will develop a library media center display that highlights books written by Hans Christian Andersen. Create a 10-question quiz about the famous Danish author as one component of the display. Book marks are appropriate rewards for students who correctly complete the quiz.

Computer Connections

1. Design a flyer and banner inviting students to visit the Hans Christian Andersen library media center display. Print Shop is an easy-to-use computer graphics program.

Instructional Materials Connections

1. Cassette and video tapes of these stories are available from the publisher.

   Andersen, Hans Christian. *The Steadfast Tin Soldier.* Illustrated by David Jorgensen. Alfred A. Knopf, 1986.

   ———. *The Ugly Duckling.* Illustrated by Robert Van Nutt. Alfred A. Knopf, 1986.

2. Owen, Pat. *The Story of Bing and Grondahl Christmas Plates.* Viking Import Press, 1962.

3. Owen, Pat. *The Story of Royal Copenhagen Christmas Plates.* Viking Import Press, 1961.

Theme Reading Connections: Versions of The Snow Queen

Andersen, Hans Christian. *Dulac's The Snow Queen and Other Stories by Hans Christian Andersen.* Illustrated by Edmond Dulac. Doubleday, 1976.

———. *The Snow Queen.* Adapted by Naomi Lewis. Illustrated by Errol Le Cain. Penguin, 1982.

———. *The Snow Queen.* Illustrated by Richard Hess. Macmillan, 1985.

Critical Thinking Question

How did Hans Christian Andersen become a successful author and role model for storytellers and authors despite the difficulties he had with his own education? How did Andersen's learning disability hinder his work as a writer? Explain your answers. List other learning disabilities that make learning difficult for some students. Interview a special education teacher to learn more about problems faced by students who have learning disabilities.

Student Activities to Connect Literature and Curriculum

FINE ARTS

1. Experiment with sponge painting. Plan a winter scene. Use black butcher paper for the background. Sponge with blue paint followed by white paint. Using various types and sizes of sponges will provide a dramatic background. Illustrate various segments of the story, and display the art in sequential order as a storytelling technique.

2. Using color pencils or pens, make an example of pointillism.

3. Hans Christian Andersen lived between 1805 and 1875. Using a reference source like *The Timetables of History,* list other famous writers, artists, and musicians who lived or whose works were published during this time period. (Note: Be sure to include the Grimm Brothers and Lewis Carroll.)

4. Compare the use of roses as illustrations in *The Snow Queen,* illustrated by Susan Jeffers, and *Beauty and the Beast,* illustrated by Mercer Mayer. Which do you like the best? Why? How have the writers integrated roses into each of their plots?

5. Construct a model of an ice palace to be the new attraction for a theme park. Have each room emphasize a different fairy tale. Select one room that you would like to develop. What problems do you expect to solve before construction commences? What research should be done before construction begins? What is your visual perception of the finished room? Plan for music or an audio tape and special effects to set the mood for persons viewing the exhibit.

List in order of importance other parts of the attraction that must be built; costume design; decoration; and the type of facility needed in terms of size, heating, cooling, display area, and storage. (Note: Several cities, including St. Paul, Minnesota, have had ice palaces as special attractions during the winter. Ask the librarian for help in finding information about these unique attractions.)

LANGUAGE ARTS

1. Gerda and Kai returned home and found that they "were no longer children" (page 40). Develop a picture book showing when people today are no longer children. Becoming mature may be the result of life experiences or chronological aging.

2. Videotape an interview with Hans Christian Andersen today. Make up the questions before the interview and practice them. For example, "What children's book writer would you like to invite to lunch?" "Please tell about your best and worst days at school." "What kind of toys did you have?" "How would you have played with our toys when you were our age?"

3. Prepare a blank resume form. Ask students to fill in the form on behalf of Hans Christian Andersen so that he can find a position as a writer. Stage mock interviews for the job. Ask students to take turns being on the interview panel and to evaluate each other.

WRITING PROMPT

1. What type of activities would have been planned to honor Hans Christian Andersen in his hometown, Odense, Denmark? Publish a schedule of activities for his homecoming under the following headline:

> Odense Plans Hans Christian Andersen Celebration

MATH

1. Develop math word problems for Kai's flight with the Snow Queen. Estimate how fast the sleigh could have flown. How long did it fly? How many miles were flown? Which do you think is faster, the Snow Queen's sleigh or Santa Claus's sleigh? Why? How many snowflakes can be found in a one-inch square in the book's illustrations?

2. Using the folded-paper technique, cut snowflakes from white paper to add to the sponge-painting art project for a three-dimensional look.

SCIENCE

1. Kai and Gerda used scientific information that enabled them to see through the frosted windows. How did they do it? What other scientific questions could be asked after reading the story?

SOCIAL STUDIES

1. Present drawings of Danish city houses, the old woman's cottage, the royal palace, the Finnish woman's home, the robber's place, and the ice palace. Which one would you rather live in? Why?

2. Discover what foods are included in a Danish smorgasbord. Plan a Scandinavian lunch for the class. Foods might include miniature open-face sandwiches or a cheese board with Jarlsberg cheese and crackers imported from Scandinavia. Add Danish recipes from the luncheon to a computer database for a class cookbook to be published at the end of the school year.

GEOGRAPHY

1. Based on the book, construct a pictorial map of Gerda's journey to find Kai. Include Denmark, Finland, and the North Pole.

2. Research Odense, Denmark. Write a two- to three-paragraph description of the town, and include a map of its location in Denmark. Why is it important today? Compare the advantages and disadvantages of living in a small village to the advantages and disadvantages of living in a city.

BEYOND THE BOOK

Guided Reading Connections Across a Learning Rainbow: Beautifully Illustrated Fairy Tales

Brett, Jan. *Goldilocks and the Three Bears*. Illustrated by Jan Brett. Putnam, 1987.

Collodi, Carlo. *The Adventures of Pinocchio*. Illustrated by Diane Goode. Random House, 1983.

Irving, Washington. *Rip Van Winkle*. Illustrated by Thomas Locker. Dial, 1988.

Ormerod, Jan, and David Lloyd. *The Frog Prince*. Illustrated by Jan Ormerod. Lothrop, Lee & Shepard, 1990.

Watson, Richard Jesse. *Tom Thumb*. Illustrated by Richard Jesse Watson. Harcourt Brace Jovanovich, 1989.

Grimm, Jacob, and Wilhelm K. Grimm. *Rumpelstiltskin*. Retold and illustrated by Paul Zelinsky. Dutton, 1986.

Enriching Connections

1. Danish heritage and culture can be seen in the annual Christmas plates produced by Bing and Grondahl and Royal Copenhagen. These porcelain factories have been making the uniquely colored blue-and-white collector plates since 1895 and 1909, respectively. In a ceremony at the end of each run, all of the molds for the annual plates are broken. It is a special honor to be selected as the Danish artist for each holiday plate. Design a plate that could be this year's Christmas plate. In the manufacturer's accompanying leaflet, write a one-paragraph description of the plate's design and significance.

2. Invite a guest collector to the classroom to share a collection of holiday plates.

3. Why does scarcity tend to enhance the monetary value of an item? Postal stamps are collectible items and can increase in value. The United States Postal Service does not honor a person as the subject of a postage stamp until after that person's death. For example, the Elvis Presley commemorative stamp was released in 1993.

FROM ANOTHER POINT OF VIEW

Lewis, Naomi. *Hans Christian Andersen's The Snow Queen.* Illustrated by Angela Barrett. Henry Holt, 1988.

Parent-Student Connections

1. Help the students choose art books from the public library. For example, Andre Derain (French, 1880-1954) and Georges Seurat (French, 1859-1891) are good beginning references.

2. Read aloud stories by Andersen. Compare and contrast various Andersen stories, and examine the art of various illustrators who have contributed their own interpretations.

❀   ❀   ❀

BEAUTY AND THE BEAST

Author: Retold by Marianna Mayer
Illustrator: Mercer Mayer
Publisher: Four Winds, 1978
Suggested Grade Level: 4
Classification: Fairy tale
Literary Form: Picture book illustrated with rich, full-color paintings
Theme: The outcast of a family can become a princess, or, Beauty is in the eyes of the beholder.

ABOUT THE BOOK

STUDENT OBJECTIVES:

1. Plan, write, and produce a video play about Beauty and the Beast.

2. Create a Beauty and the Beast advertising program to accompany the video.

3. Produce a rebus retelling the story. (A rebus substitutes a picture for a word or part of a word.)

SYNOPSIS: The ageless story of Beauty and the Beast is enhanced with rich illustrations. Students will recognize the story's fairy tale themes, including mean sisters, a slavelike younger sister, a single parent, a magic castle, crime and its punishment, and the beast and the princess.

ABOUT THE AUTHOR: Marianna Mayer, 1945- .
   Marianna Mayer was born in New York City. She studied art in high school and later at the Art Students League. She earned a living as an artist and art director for an advertising agency. Later, her interests turned to writing children's books.

In researching materials about Pinocchio, Mayer discovered, to her dismay, that "the original tale was not Disney's story at all! I was very impudent as a kid. Like Pinocchio, I was always in trouble. Nobody could tell me how to do things better. It's the conflict in Pinocchio that makes him wonderful." (*Something About the Author,* vol. 32, p. 130.)

ABOUT THE ILLUSTRATOR: Mercer Mayer, 1943- .

Mercer Mayer was born in Arkansas but grew up in Hawaii, where he attended art school. While attending school with ethnic students from the Pacific Rim, he felt like an outsider.

Mayer, like most illustrators, held many different jobs before he was able to work full time on children's books. He once was a door-to-door salesman for fire alarms and vacuum cleaners. Mayer also served as an art director for an advertising agency.

Mayer has a definite, elegant style that is easily recognized. His richly colored paintings reflect strength but are tempered with glowing colors.

(Note: At a California Library Media Educators Association conference in San Diego, Mayer explained that he does not like to show his work while it is in process. Mayer told the audience that once he had allowed a woman to see his unfinished work; she liked the colors. However, at that moment Mayer was trying to decide what was wrong with the picture and immediately knew that it was the sky colors! This comment may be related to the statement, Beauty is in the eyes of the beholder.)

SELECTED ADDITIONAL TITLES: Marianna Mayer

Mayer, Marianna. *Aladdin and the Enchanted Lamp.* Illustrated by Gerald McDermott. Macmillan, 1985.

———. *Pinocchio.* Illustrated by Gerald McDermott. Four Winds Press, 1981.

———. *Unicorn and the Lake.* Illustrated by Michael Hague. Dial, 1982.

SELECTED ADDITIONAL TITLES: Mercer Mayer

Mayer, Mercer. *East of the Sun and West of the Moon.* Illustrated by Mercer Mayer. Four Winds Press, 1980.

———. *Favorite Tales from Grimm.* Illustrated by Mercer Mayer. Four Winds Press, 1982.

———. *Sleeping Beauty.* Illustrated by Mercer Mayer. Macmillan, 1985.

———. *There's a Nightmare in My Closet.* Illustrated by Mercer Mayer. Dial, 1968.

USING THE BOOK

Suggested Approach to the Book

Model Lesson

1. List the room furnishings and wall hangings shown in the first picture of the family. What is the father's reaction to bad financial news? How was his fortune lost? Can the wealthy lose their fortunes the same way today? Why or why not?

2. Compare and contrast the way the three sisters are portrayed as Beauty carries the water buckets. If you had lived at this time, could you think of any other way that water could be delivered to the country home?

3. In the picture showing the father's wrecked ship, a disease carrier is illustrated. Name it. Why are these animals dangerous? Where can they be found today? What kind of destruction do they cause? How are they eradicated?

4. Write a caption for the picture of the father arriving at the Beast's castle on a very cold night. Why does the father say, "I don't suppose I should help myself"? What would you have done in the same situation?

5. Why did the Beast become so angry after the father picked a rose for Beauty? Do roses bloom in the snow?

6. Describe the grand dining room.

7. Who does Beauty dream about? What warning does she receive? Explain the magic of the hand mirror.

8. Why does the Beast begin to die? Is Beauty partially responsible for the Beast's pain and sorrow?

Library Media Center Connections

1. Using the subject index of the library media center catalog, list other books written by Mercer Mayer. How many fairy tale books are listed in the card catalog? Do all of their call numbers begin with 398.2? Some of their call numbers may begin with FIC. Ask the librarian to explain to the class why some fairy tale books are shelved as nonfiction and others as fiction. This is a very difficult issue for catalogers.

    Books are sometimes credited to the writer retelling the story instead of the original author. For example, Hans Christian Andersen wrote many books, but contemporary writers and illustrators continue to adapt his work. Consequently, the book is not always shelved as a fairy tale by Andersen (398.2 AND), but as the work of the writer retelling the story. An example is *The Snow Queen,* written by Hans Christian Andersen and retold by Amy Ehrlich. The adaptation is cataloged as fiction with Ehrlich as the author (FIC EHR).

Computer Connections

1. Explain to the class how databases are assembled. Brainstorm uses for databases. Have students assemble an annotated database of recommended library media center books. Design a brief form to list the author and title of the book, with space for a several-sentence annotation to encourage other students to read the book. This database may be a year-long class or school library media center project.

Instructional Materials Connections

1. "What Manner of Beast." In *Image and Maker.* Edited by Harold Darling and Peter Neumeyer. Green Tiger Press, 1984. pp. 13-25. The section offers a definitive comparison of various illustrations for *Beauty and the Beast.*

2. Hearne, Betsy. *Beauties and Beasts.* Oryx Press, 1993.

3. Thomas, Bob. *Disney's Art of Animation from Mickey Mouse to Beauty and the Beast.* Hyperion, 1991.

4. Integrate David Macaulay's *Castle* video (Unicorn Projects, 1983) into the teaching unit.

5. Invite a toy-store retailer to share examples of fairy tale dolls with the class. As an alternative, use catalogs that illustrate dolls and stuffed fairy tale figures.

Theme Reading Connections: Beauty and the Beast

Pearce, Philippa, retold by. *Beauty and the Beast.* Illustrated by Alan Barrett. Thomas Y. Crowell, 1972.

Brett, Jan, retold by. *Beauty and the Beast.* Illustrated by Jan Brett. Clarion Books, 1989.

Beauty and the Beast. Illustrations selected and arranged by Cooper Edens. Green Tiger Press, 1989.

de Beaumont, Marie Leprince, retold by. *Beauty and the Beast.* Illustrated by Hilary Knight. Simon & Schuster, 1990.

Beauty and the Beast and Other Tales. Illustrated by Walter Crane. Thames and Hudson, 1982. (Note: Walter Crane, a Victorian artist, has been called the father of the illustrated children's book. His art may be found in the New York Metropolitan Museum.)

Critical Thinking Question
What is beauty?

Student Activities to Connect Literature and Curriculum

FINE ARTS

1. Examine the end papers used in various fairy tale books. Design and produce a book cover for a selected fairy tale using wood-block printing or gouache painting.

2. Construct a miniature stage set suitable for presenting fairy tales to the class.

3. Prepare a wall frieze retelling the story of Beauty and the Beast for the classroom.

4. To the story boards created for the play sequence described in the Language Arts unit below, add sound effects and music that can be integrated into the production.

LANGUAGE ARTS

1. Adapt the story of Beauty and the Beast as a classroom play to be videotaped. Use story boards to plan the sequence of the play.

2. Design a chart on which to record data about two versions of Beauty and the Beast. Compare and contrast the Mayer and Jan Brett versions.

3. Search fairy tale anthologies to locate additional versions of Beauty and the Beast. Collect the various editions for a classroom book display. Students may vote for their favorite version.

WRITING PROMPT

1. Write a brief newspaper story under the following headline:

Walter Crane's *Beauty and the Beast* Book Is Released

MATH

1. Design a graph using x and y coordinates illustrating either Beauty or the Beast. The graph will show a picture of Beauty or the Beast when all graph coordinates have been plotted and the dots/graph points have been connected.

SCIENCE

1. Examine the art work in the book and list the various trees, plants, and flowers painted by Mercer Mayer. Research your findings and explain what type of climate is necessary for the growth of the illustrated trees and plants. On a world map, indicate areas that would support the growth of these trees and plants. Where do you think the story is set? Why?

2. Diagram and label the parts of a rose.

3. How many varieties of roses exist? How are roses named? List some of their unique names. What are the necessary growing conditions?

4. Beauty and the Beast are planning a picnic in his beloved rose garden. Plan a nutritious menu for their meal.

SOCIAL STUDIES

1. What kind of items do you think were on the wrecked ships belonging to Beauty's father? Carefully examine the details in the picture of the shipwreck.

2. Construct a pop-up book or model ship like the one illustrated. Research what kind of cargo ships of this type carried. Refer to library media sources that relate to wooden sailing ships.

GEOGRAPHY

1. And so the Prince and Beauty were married, and lived with love and happiness. Like all newly married people, the royal couple began to plan their life together.

    Create a new kingdom. Suppose the Prince said he wanted the gardens to remain as-is because he liked the roses. He thought a new name for his country, as well as a country flag and national anthem, were important. What kind of government would be needed? What role would Beauty play?

    The government offices would not be in the castle; suppose Beauty planned to update the palace with better heat and running water, redecorate everything from the dungeon to the turrets, and modernize the kitchen. What role might Beauty have in the government?

    What natural resources—such as fuel, forests, and minerals—are available? Would the citizens be able to farm or develop small businesses? Would financial help from the royal treasury be needed? For whom and how long? Could tourism be promoted? Prepare short- and long-range plans.

BEYOND THE BOOK

Guided Reading Connections Across a Learning Rainbow: Castles

Althea. *Life in a Castle.* Illustrated. Cambridge, 1983.

Cairns, Conrad. *Medieval Castles.* Illustrated. Lerner, 1989.

Clark, Richard. *Castles.* Illustrated. Franklin Watts, 1986.

James, Alan. *Castles and Mansions.* Illustrated. Lerner, 1989.

Macaulay, David. *Castles.* Illustrated by David Macaulay. Houghton Mifflin, 1977.

Miquel, Pierre. *Castles of the Middle Ages.* Illustrated. Silver Burdett, 1985.

Montes, J. *The Great Book of Castles.* Illustrated. Rourke, 1990.

Odor, Ruth. *Learning About Castles and Palaces.* Illustrated by Lynn Halverson. Childrens Press, 1982.

Unstead, R. J. *See Inside a Castle.* Illustrated by Dan Escott et al. Warwick, 1986.

Enriching Connections

1. Compare Mercer Mayer's Beast with the Beast in the 1991 Walt Disney movie *Beauty and the Beast.* (Note: The Disney artist, in a television interview, explained the Disney Beast as encompassing the head of a buffalo; the eyes of a gorilla with deep, penetrating intensity; the tusks of an elephant; and the mane of a lion.)

FROM ANOTHER POINT OF VIEW

Beauty and the Beast. Illustrated by Michael Hague. Henry Holt, 1983.

Parent-Student Connections

1. Read aloud several versions of *Beauty and the Beast* and share the illustrations. Which version do you like the best? Why? How should Beauty and the Beast look? Critics say that the original story offers no information describing either of the main characters. There have been both dark-haired and blond Beauties. Considering the kind manner of the Beast, describe how he should look in the illustrations. How does this story differ from *Cinderella* in its portrayal of the mean sisters? Compare and contrast how the mean sisters fare in the endings of *Beauty and the Beast* and *Cinderella.*

❋   ❋   ❋

THE CRANE WIFE

Author: Retold by Sumiko Yagawa
Illustrator: Suekichi Akaba
Publisher: Morrow, 1979
Suggested Grade Level: 4
Classification: Nonfiction
Literary Form: Folklore
Theme: Respect the wishes of others.

ABOUT THE BOOK

STUDENT OBJECTIVES:

1. Organize an acting troupe to present readers theatre plays in other classrooms.

2. Demonstrate Japanese brush-stroke writing.

3. Compare and contrast the cultures of the United States and Japan through an international fair.

SYNOPSIS: Yohei, a simple, young peasant, befriends a crane that has been struck by an arrow. That evening a young woman appears at his door and begs him to marry her. She weaves three exquisitely beautiful bolts of fabric to sell. Yohei wishes her to continue the weaving, but she cannot.

ABOUT THE AUTHOR: Sumiko Yagawa, birthdate unavailable.
   The Crane Wife, retold by Sumiko Yagawa and later translated into English by Katherine Paterson, a well-known author, was first published in Japan. Unfortunately, information about the author is limited.

ABOUT THE ILLUSTRATOR: Suekichi Akaba, 1910- .
   Suekichi Akaba, illustrator and author of children's books, is a resident of Japan who has received numerous awards in both Japan and the United States. Akaba received the Hans Christian Andersen International Medal in 1980 for his works, which include the U.S. publication of *The Crane Wife* and *Suho and the White Horse: A Legend of Mongolia.*
   Akaba describes his versatility as an author and illustrator: "I illustrate other people's stories, but write and illustrate as well. My own books are mostly nonsense books with which I hope to give joy to children." (*Something About the Author,* vol. 46, p. 24.)

SELECTED ADDITIONAL TITLE: Suekichi Akaba

Otsuka, Yuzo. *Suho and the White Horse: A Legend of Mongolia.* Illustrated by Suekichi Akaba. Viking, 1981.

USING THE BOOK

Suggested Approach to the Book

Model Lesson

1. Why did the crane fly in front of Yohei? How would you remove an arrow from its wing? Remember that the arrow has a strong point.

2. Imagine a young woman coming to your door and asking you to marry her. What would you say? Why is it believable in folklore but not in today's literature?

3. Why do the Japanese use paper screens for privacy?

4. Give an example of when a person is not satisfied with what he or she has but wants more, more, and more? Why is Yohei described as simple?

5. Compare the three illustrations of the wife weaving behind the screen. How are they alike or different? What is the meaning of the word *symbolic*? Is the weaving an example of symbolism? Why or why not?

6. Why did Yohei's values differ from his wife's values? Why did she say three times, "For the sake of heaven, remember. Do not look in on me"?

7. What were the final words Yohei's wife said to him?

Library Media Center Connections

1. Research and share with the class several versions of the story of the birth or creation of Japan.

2. Using print and nonprint materials, prepare a comprehensive reference bibliography about Japan. If your school is planning an international fair, what kinds of material offer information that will relate to that project? Using cooperative learning groups, divide the research into subjects that include the following:

Customs	Food	Industry	Clothing
Art	Music	Geography	Architecture
Religion	Calligraphy	Fairy Tales	Postage Stamps

Computer Connections

1. Enter into the library media center or classroom computer database information on Japan from the preceding research assignment.

Instructional Materials Connections

1. Allen, Carole. *Japan—Traditions and Trends.* Illustrated by Ted Warren. Good Apple, 1992.

2. Fisher, Leonard Everett. *Alphabet Art.* Illustrated by Leonard Everett Fisher. Four Winds Press, 1978.

3. Fisher, Leonard Everett. *Number Art.* Illustrated by Leonard Everett Fisher. Four Winds Press, 1982.

4. Grafton, Carol Belanger. *Treasury of Japanese Designs and Motifs.* Dover, 1983.

5. Harbin, Robert. *Origami.* Hamlyn, 1974.

6. Haskins, Jim. *Count Your Way Through Japan.* Illustrated by Martin Skoro. Carolrhoda, 1987.

7. *Japan—A Coloring Book Of.* Bellerophon, 1971.

8. Ozaki, Yei, T., comp. *The Japanese Fairy Tale Book.* Charles Tuttle, 1970.

9. Sakade, Florence, ed. *Japanese Children's Favorite Stories.* Illustrated by Yoshisuke Kurosaki. Charles Tuttle, 1958.

Theme Reading Connections: Japanese Folklore

Dolch, Edward W., and M. P. Dolch. *Stories from Japan.* Garrard, 1960.

Hodges, Margaret. *The Wave.* Illustrated by B. Lent. Houghton Mifflin, 1964.

McDermott, Gerald. *The Stonecutter: A Japanese Folk Tale.* Illustrated by Gerald McDermott. Penguin, 1975.

Morimoto, Junko. *Inch Boy.* Illustrated by Junko Morimoto. Penguin, 1986.

Uchida, Yoshiko. *The Two Foolish Cats.* Illustrated by Margot Zemach. Macmillan, 1987.

Yamaguchi, Marianne. *The Sea of Gold and Other Tales from Japan.* Creative Arts, 1988.

> Critical Thinking Question
> What values do people derive from fairy tales, folklore, and mythology? Do people today place any value on these myths and stories? Why or why not?

Student Activities to Connect Literature and Curriculum

FINE ARTS

1. Use cardboard looms in a classroom weaving lesson.

2. Create a classroom mural of Yohei's village using the snow technique pictured in the book's opening pages. Use neutral colors accented with bright colors.

3. Prepare a library media center display of origami. Each student will submit five examples, including a crane.

4. Choose one of these craft projects to make:

   Pagoda   Japanese Lantern   Flying Kite   Paper Screen

LANGUAGE ARTS

1. Write and illustrate a book about Japan's Seven Gods of Good Fortune.

2. Design a Japanese calendar that lists the following Japanese holidays and observances. Illustrate each special day on the calendar. (See *American Japanese Holiday Coloring and Talking Book,* Charles Tuttle, 1972.)

   Shogatsu—New Year

   Setsubun—Bean Throwing

Hana-matsuri—Flower Viewing

Tango no Sekku—Boys Festival

Tanabata—Weaver Festival

Aki-matsuri—Fall Festival

Shichi-Go-San—Children's Festival

Toshi no Ichi—End of Year Festival

3. Compare and contrast the following stories with their Japanese versions. (See *American Japanese Story Heroes Coloring and Talking Book,* Charles Tuttle, 1971.)

American	*Japanese*
Tom Thumb	Issunboshi (Little One Inch)
Peter Rabbit	Inaba No Usagi (Inaba)
Cinderella	Anjuhima (Princess Anju)
Snow White	Hachikatsugihime (Princess with Bowl-on-Head)
Little Red Riding Hood	Sarutokanii (Monkey and Crab)
Three Little Kittens	Kintaro (Kintaro)

WRITING PROMPT

1. You have been asked to make a guest appearance on television to review your favorite Japanese folktale. Begin your feature with the following statement:

> It was such a long time ago on a bitter, windy night when I met...

MATH

1. Carry a notepad for one week. Write in it any Japanese-manufactured products that you see at home or at school. Predict how many items you expect to report. How many items did you actually record? Graph your estimate and your count.

SCIENCE

1. In the past, many Japanese products were considered inferior to American products. However, Japanese manufacturers have improved their technology and quality control standards. Today, the Japanese ship many excellent products, from autos to watches, to the United States. List Japanese imports. Determine which products are consistently well made. (See *Consumer Reports* or similar magazines.)

SOCIAL STUDIES

1. In Japan, each merchant or storekeeper cleans the area in front of his or her business. If this practice was followed in the United States, could city taxes be reduced? Why or why not? Would there be any other benefits to this practice? Have one student contact city hall to find out the cost of keeping the downtown area clean and the number of merchants in the area. What is the cost that could be assessed to each merchant and home owner? (Divide the cost

by number of merchants.) The same question could apply to street sweeping in residential neighborhoods.

GEOGRAPHY

1. Construct a large-scale floor map of Japan. Identify cities and historic sites as well as major rail and sea transportation routes.

BEYOND THE BOOK

Guided Reading Connections Across a Learning Rainbow: Cranes

Byars, Betsy C. *The House of Wings.* Illustrated by Daniel Schwartz. Penguin, 1982.

Horn, Gabriel. *The Crane.* Crestwood, 1988.

Patent, Dorothy H. *The Whooping Crane: A Comeback Story.* Photos by Williams Munoz. Clarion Books, 1988.

Roop, Peter, and Connie Roop. *Seasons of the Crane.* Walker, 1989.

Voeller, Edward. *The Red-Crowned Crane.* Dillon, 1989.

Enriching Connections

1. Create art work using feathers dipped in paint to make textured designs. Use the completed art as new end papers for books in the library media center or for the student-created books about the Seven Gods of Good Fortune (created in the Language Arts activity). Students should sign their work. Some art work may be very complex, and some might include the marbled technique that is used in expensive books.

2. Construct greeting cards using the Japanese *kosode* design, which is the predecessor of the kimono. Use a two-fold design, with the card opening in the middle center like a kimono. On the card face, picture a *kosode* that opens in the front. Use art designs based on examples from the Edo Period, 1615-1865. *Kosode* were richly decorated with beading, embroidery, tie-dying, weaving, and painting.

FROM ANOTHER POINT OF VIEW

Bang, Molly. *The Paper Crane.* Illustrated by Molly Bang. Greenwillow Books, 1985.

Parent-Student Connections

1. Attend an exhibit of Japanese art.
2. Examine books that illustrate Japanese floral art arrangements and explain their symbolism.

❀ ❀ ❀

YEH SHEN
A Cinderella Story from China

Author: Retold by Ai-Ling Louie
Illustrator: Ed Young
Publisher: Philomel, 1982
Suggested Grade Level: 4
Classification: Fairy tale
Literary Form: Illustrated picture book
Theme: The theme of Cinderella appears in all cultures around the world.

ABOUT THE BOOK

STUDENT OBJECTIVES:

1. Recognize that fairy tales are told around the world.

2. Retell the story of Cinderella from another point of view.

3. Write a contemporary Cinderella story.

SYNOPSIS: There are twists in the Chinese version of the Cinderella story, which predates the European version.

ABOUT THE AUTHOR: Ai-Ling Louie, birthdate unavailable.
Ai-Ling Louie first heard the story of Yeh Shen, based on an ancient Chinese manuscript, from her grandmother. Ai-Ling was born in the United States and taught school in Massachusetts. She resides with her husband and daughter in New Jersey.

ABOUT THE ILLUSTRATOR: Ed Young, 1931- .
Ed Young lived in Shanghai until he was 19. He attended college in the United States. Young, a Caldecott medalist for his illustrations in *Lon Po Po,* is known for his artistic style. His work reflects a mysterious air. "The art work of Yeh Shen was more than two years in the making, and Mr. Young made two trips to China to do his careful research into traditional costumes and customs of the people in the area in which this tale is set" (Book jacket).
The artist explains his philosophy of art as follows: "It is some sort of challenge now to produce pictures to communicate a story without, or with very few, words like a mime. Illustrators and writers only differ in their means to express themselves—each is limited by his talent and his means" (*Illustrators of Children's Books, 1967-1976.* Horn Book, 1978).

SELECTED ADDITIONAL TITLES: Ed Young

Fritz, Jean. *The Double Life of Pocahontas.* Illustrated by Ed Young. Putnam, 1983.

Hearn, Lafcadio. *The Voice of the Great Bell.* Retold by Margaret Hodges. Illustrated by Ed Young. Little, Brown, 1989.

Leaf, Margaret. *Eyes of the Dragon.* Illustrated by Ed Young. Lothrop, Lee & Shepard, 1987.

Lewis, Elizabeth. *Young Fu of the Upper Yangtze.* New ed. Illustrated by Ed Young. Henry Holt, 1973.

Scioscia, Mary. *Bicycle Rider.* Illustrated by Ed Young. HarperCollins, 1983.

Yolen, Jane. *The Emperor and the Kite.* Illustrated by Ed Young. Collins-World, 1967.

Young, Ed, trans. *Lon Po Po: A Red-Riding Hood Story from China.* Illustrated by Ed Young. Philomel, 1989.

———. *Moon Mother: A Native American Creation Tale.* Illustrated by Ed Young. HarperCollins, 1993.

USING THE BOOK

Suggested Approach to the Book

Model Lesson

1. Examine the cover art. What do you see? List five observations. Examine the reproduction at the front of the book to find *The Miscelleanous Record of Yu Yang,* which dates from the T'ang Dynasty (618-907 A.D.).

2. Describe the birth family of Yeh Shen. What happened to Yeh Shen's parents? What would happen to a child today who lost both parents?

3. Using a stair-step format, identify components of the traditional Cinderella story.

4. Why is the story written in panels?

5. How did the stepmother hurt Yeh Shen?

6. Should the story have an emperor instead of a king? Why or why not? How would you describe a palace? Are European palaces different from Chinese palaces? Explain your answer.

7. Analyze Ed Young's use of color in the book's illustrations. How does it enhance the story?

Library Media Center Connections

1. Based upon research about China, have cooperative learning groups orally present information about the following topics:

Art	Theater	Architecture
Food	Agriculture	Lunar Calendar
Clothing	Geography	Government
Cities	Landmarks	Dynasties
Customs	Fairy Tales	Revolutions

(Note: These topics may be compared and contrasted to those researched in the *The Crane Wife* unit.)

Computer Connections

1. Using a word processor, write a contemporary version of the Cinderella story.

2. Prepare a database about China based upon library media center reference projects.

3. Develop a database about versions of fairy tales classified by countries of origin. This information should be available to students and faculty in the library media center.

Instructional Materials Connections

1. Sierra, Judy. *Cinderella*. Oryx Press, 1992. (This is a guide to 24 versions of Cinderella.)

2. Modern clothing constructed from authentic antique kimonos, as well as a varied selection of ethnic jewelry, are available from Pacific Artifacts, Fashion Island, 1101 Newport Center Drive, Newport, CA 92660.

Theme Reading Connections: Cinderella

Cinderella. Illustrated by Paul Galdone. McGraw-Hill, 1978.

Cinderella. Retold and illustrated by Arthur Rackham. Penguin, 1978.

Cinderella. Retold by Patricia Daniels. Illustrated by Maggie Read. Raintree/Steck-Vaughn, 1980.

Cinderella. Retold and illustrated by Marcia Brown. Macmillan, 1981.

Cinderella. Retold and illustrated by Hilary Knight. Random House, 1982.

Cinderella. Retold by Amy Ehrlich. Illustrated by Susan Jeffers. Dial, 1985.

Cinderella. Retold by Patricia McKissack and Frederick McKissack. Childrens Press, 1985.

Cinderella. Retold by Barbara Karlin. Illustrated by James Marshall. Little, Brown, 1989.

Climo, Shirley. *Korean Cinderella*. Illustrated by Ruth Heller. HarperCollins, 1993.

Grimm, Jacob, and Wilhelm Grimm. *Cinderella*. Illustrated by Nonny Hogrogian. Greenwillow Books, 1981.

Perrault, Charles. *Cinderella*. Illustrated by Roberto Innocenti. Creative Education, 1986.

———. *Cinderella*. Illustrated by Errol Le Cain. Penguin, 1977.

Critical Thinking Question
Explain how the fairy tale *Yeh Shen* may have been brought to Europe from China. Why is the term *global population* used today, but was not used in the 1940s? What historical events and inventions have influenced today's global society?

Activities to Connect Literature and Curriculum

FINE ARTS

1. Use the fish motif to create an art project. The fish symbol may be used in gift-wrapping paper, tee-shirt design, sculpture, or another student project. Explore various art media techniques.

2. Compile a list of subjects used in Chinese art and illustrations. Are any special meanings attached to these items?

3. Create a mural representing China and its many faces.

4. Present the story of Cinderella or the Glass Slipper using color transparencies as the background for the production. Create a new wardrobe for the characters. What kind of art decisions do you need to make when you are using different art materials?

LANGUAGE ARTS

1. Outline a Cinderella story for another culture. How will you introduce the main characters? What will their occupations be? Where and in what style will they live? What will be the subject of the quest? What elements of a Cinderella story will you introduce? Explain conflict, crisis, and resolution. How will the tale end?

2. You have been selected chairperson of a special Caldecott committee to select the best illustrated fairy tale book or fairy tale collection. What will be the standards for selection? How many committee members will be selected? When will the committee decision be announced? How will this information be released to the publishers and press? What other decisions will the committee and chairperson need to consider?

WRITING PROMPT

1. Prepare a book review of *Yeh Shen: A Cinderella Story from China* for your community newspaper under the following headline:

> *Yeh Shen,* A Chinese Cinderella Story, Is Traced to Ancient Manuscript

MATH

1. Poll students to determine the style and size of shoes that girls wear. Graph the results. Would you be able to make recommendations on style and size to a manufacturer? Why or why not?

SCIENCE

1. Silkworms are an important element of the Chinese export economy. Prepare an illustrated transparency of the life cycle of the silkworm. List products that are manufactured from silk. What are the characteristics of silk fabric? How much do these items cost? How does the price of silk clothing compare to nonsilk clothing?

SOCIAL STUDIES

1. Imagine that you have just been hired by the Chinese Travel Bureau to stimulate travel to China. Design a brochure with text and illustrations to encourage travel to China. Or, in a cooperative learning group, produce a brochure encouraging trade between the United States and Chinese silk producers.

2. Plan a Chinese New Year celebration to take place at your school. List the schedule, activities, and food. What classroom activities are appropriate? How will this celebration unite your school and community?

GEOGRAPHY

1. What cultures have Cinderella stories? Prepare a chart listing your findings and pinpoint the locations on a world map. (Note: See various editions of Ireland, Norma, ed., *Index to Fairy Tales,* Scarecrow, 1973-1989.)

BEYOND THE BOOK

Guided Reading Connections Across a Learning Rainbow: Fiction from or About China

Beyond the Great Wall. Scholastic, 1988.

Brightfield, Richard. *Why Was an Army Made of Clay?* McGraw-Hill, 1989.

DeJong, Meindert. *House of Sixty Fathers.* Illustrated by Maurice Sendak. Harper & Row, 1956.

Fritz, Jean. *China Homecoming.* Photographs by Michael Fritz. Putnam, 1985.

Wenjing, Yan, et al. *Favorite Children's Stories from China.* China, 1983.

Enriching Connections

1. Research koi fish, which are members of the goldfish family. Present a brief, illustrated report using color transparencies. Are there any koi fish in your community?

2. Check out art books from the library media center to use in the classroom to illustrate Chinese arts and crafts. Be sure to include origami and paper cutting.

FROM ANOTHER POINT OF VIEW

Climo, Shirley. *The Egyptian Cinderella.* Illustrated by Ruth Heller. Thomas Y. Crowell, 1989.

Parent-Student Connections

1. Read for pleasure five versions of Cinderella, including several selections from the following list:

Chinese Cinderella	Korean Cinderella
Egyptian Cinderella	Indian Cinderella
Cinder-Maid	Golden Shoe
Jeweled Slipper	Glass Slipper
Brocaded Slipper	Algonquin Cinderella
Little Burnt-Face	Little Cinder Girl
Tattercoats	

❀ ❀ ❀

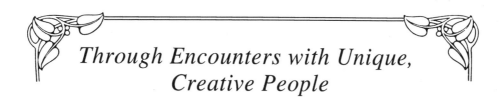

*Through Encounters with Unique,
Creative People*

LINNEA IN MONET'S GARDEN

Author: Christina Bjork
Illustrator: Lena Anderson
Publisher: Raben and Sjogren Books, 1987; distributed by Farrar, Straus & Giroux
Suggested Grade Level: 4
Classification: Art history and appreciation
Literary Form: Integrated picture book with silhouettes, photographs, and original art work by
   Monet
Theme: People express their creativity in many ways.

ABOUT THE BOOK

STUDENT OBJECTIVES:

1.   Identify works of art by Monet.

2.   Conduct scientific observations of plants growing in the classroom or at home.

3.   Organize an art exhibit of student works.

SYNOPSIS: Linnea develops a friendship with Mr. Bloom, a retired neighbor. Linnea and Mr. Bloom
   travel to Paris and to Monet's renovated home and garden at Giverney.
   (Note: Both the author and illustrator are Swedish. This book was first published in Sweden in
1985; it was translated and published in English in 1987.)

ABOUT THE AUTHOR AND ILLUSTRATOR: Christina Bjork, 1938- ; Lena Anderson, 1939- .
   Like the book's main character, Linnea, Christina Bjork and Lena Anderson were nature-loving
children in Stockholm. "The work of Christina Bjork and Lena Anderson reflects the Swedish love
and deep appreciation of nature in a society where laws protect the environment and all land is open
for anyone to walk along and pick the fruit of the land" (*Yellow Brick Road,* v. 6, n. 2 [November-
December 1990]).

Bjork and Anderson still share a home-studio in the city and continue to collaborate on children's books. A recent visitor to their studio explained that it was not difficult "to recognize that the charming 1710 pink wooden building belonged to someone connected to children's books. The windows were lined with stuffed animals of book characters."

The stories about Linnea are modeled after Anderson's daughter, who loved to plant seeds as a young girl. Linnea's name is taken from the flower *linnea borealis*, which was named for the famous Swedish botanist Carolus Linnaeus. During Bjork's childhood, all Swedish schoolchildren pressed flowers and had to learn their Latin names. Although this is no longer practiced, it gives the reader further insights into *Linnea in Monet's Garden*.

Bjork and Anderson have enjoyed a friendship for more than 30 years and intend to continue their research and travel in order to create children's books.

SELECTED ADDITIONAL TITLES: Christina Bjork and Lena Anderson

Bjork, Christina. *Elliot's Extraordinary Cookbook*. Illustrated by Lena Anderson. Raben and Sjogren, 1990.

———. *Linnea's Almanac*. Illustrated by Lena Anderson. Raben and Sjogren, 1984.

———. *Linnea's Windowsill Garden*. Illustrated by Lena Anderson. Raben and Sjogren, 1988.

USING THE BOOK

Suggested Approach to the Book

Model Lesson

1. What are a book's end papers? Describe the end papers in this book. What do you feel when you look at the art? What other art designs could be used? Why?

2. Describe Monet's pink house. How did Monet change his garden to provide growing examples of water lilies? Explain why Monet's water lilies are beautiful when viewed from a distance but, when examined up close, appear to be blobs and blotches of paint.

3. In Europe, dogs are allowed in public places, including cafes and restaurants. In the United States, this is not allowed unless they are Seeing Eye dogs for the blind. Discuss the merits of these two systems.

4. Why did art critics call Monet an Impressionist? Name some other Impressionists and describe their paintings. What are the Water Lily rooms? Where are they installed today? Examine Monet's four paintings of the Japanese bridge. How are they different?

5. What relationship exists between the second-oldest tree in Paris and America? Of all the flowers that Linnea saw, which ones are also found in America?

6. Why did Monet have to approve of the boys' professions and the girls' husbands?

Library Media Center Connections

1. The Esmeralda Hotel was built in 1640 as a home. Describe what an American home would have looked like in that year.

2. Using supplementary library media center materials, prepare brief reports about the following Impressionists:

Camille Pissarro	Auguste Renoir	Alfred Sisley	Berthe Morisot
Mary Cassatt	Édouard Manet	Edgar Degas	

Computer Connections

1. Using a word processor, compose a letter to a computer pal describing a proposed trip to Paris and Giverney.

2. Create a computer database about famous artists. Include painters, sculptors, musicians, and dancers. Design a database form to coordinate the entries.

Instructional Materials Connections

1. Balsamo, Kathy. *Exploring the Lives of Gifted People: The Arts.* Illustrated by Phyllis Johnson. Good Apple, 1987.

2. Frayling, Christopher, Helen Frayling, and Ron Van Der Meer. *The Art Pack.* Alfred A. Knopf, 1992.
   "A one-of-a-kind art book of pop-up examples using paper engineering ... use of color, line and composition ... and an audio guide to 20 greatest pictures of all time." Museum of Fine Arts, Catalog Sales, P.O. Box 1044, Boston, MA 02120.

3. Goode, Diane. *Where's Our Mama?* Dutton, 1991.

4. MacDonald, Fiona. *A Nineteenth Century Railway Station.* Illustrated by John James. Inside Story series. P. Bedrick, 1990.

5. Munro, Roxie. *The Inside-Outside Book of Paris.* Dutton, 1992.

6. *A Day in the Country: Impressionism and the French Landscape.* Video. Finley-Holiday Film Corp., Box 619, Whittier, CA 90608.

7. Kinghorn, Harriet, Jacqueline Badman, and Lisa Lewis-Spicer. *Let's Meet Famous Artists,* Denison, 1991.

Theme Reading Connections: Art

Cvach, Milos. *Robert Delaunay: The Eiffel Tower: An Art Play Book.* Abrams, 1988.

Galland, Sarah. *Peter Rabbit's Gardening Book.* Illustrated by Beatrix Potter. Warne, 1983.

Go In and Out the Window: An Illustrated Songbook for Young People. Henry Holt, 1987.

Lafferty, Peter. *Leonardo Da Vinci.* Pioneers of Science series. Bookwright, 1990.

Peppin. *Story of Painting.* Illustrated. Usborne-Hayes, 1980.

Rudstrom, Lennart. *A Home.* Illustrated by Carl Larsson. Putnam, 1974.

Sanchez, Isidro. *I Draw, I Paint Watercolor.* Childrens Press, 1991.

Stan, Susan. *Careers in an Art Museum.* Illustrated by Milton J. Blumenfeld. Lerner, 1983.

Striker, Susan. *Anti-Coloring Book of Masterpieces.* Henry Holt, 1982.

Sullivan, Charles, ed. *Imaginary Gardens.* American Poetry and Art for Young People series. Abrams, 1989.

Talking to the Sun: An Illustrated Anthology of Poetry for Young People. Henry Holt, 1985.

Tudor, Tasha, and Richard Brown. *The Private World of Tasha Tudor.* Little, Brown, 1992.

Turner, Robyn Montana. *Mary Cassatt.* Little, Brown, 1992.

Venezia, Mike. *Da Vinci.* Getting to Know the World's Greatest Artists series. Childrens Press, 1989.

———. *Mary Cassatt.* Getting to Know the World's Greatest Artists series. Childrens Press, 1990.

———. *Van Gogh.* Getting to Know the World's Greatest Artists series. Childrens Press, 1988.

Ventura, Piero. *Great Painters.* Putnam, 1984.

Critical Thinking Question
Would you have liked to live the life of Claude Monet? Would you make any changes? Explain. Would you rather be a great contemporary artist or a great artist at the time of Monet? Why?

Student Activities to Connect Literature and Curriculum

FINE ARTS

1. Prepare a three-dimensional model of the guest room at the Esmeralda Hotel as pictured in the book.

2. Use natural leaves to spatter paint or make crayon rubbings to decorate place mats. Lamination will preserve the mats for future use.

3. Prepare a scale model of the famous Japanese Bridge in Giverney.

LANGUAGE ARTS

1. Using *Linnea in Monet's Garden* as a source, write diary entries for Linnea's preparation for the trip, the visit to Paris, and her return home to Stockholm. This activity may be a cooperative learning assignment.

2. Linnea's diary in the preceding assignment can be written from an American viewpoint by describing the round trip from the student's home to Paris and Giverney.

3. Complete the following art critic's review of Monet's work. " 'Ooh, what a lot of blobs!' people said. They thought they looked messy, sloppy, and unfinished. And such loud colors!"

4. Using today's standards, write a critical review of one of Monet's works.

WRITING PROMPT

1. Research and write a three-minute television feature about recent sales of Monet's art works under the following title:

Monet's Art Works Bring Millions at Auction

MATH

1. Using a city map of Paris, explain the scale key. How large is the city in square miles? What is the Left Bank? How long is the route of the Seine River through the city?

2. What area of France is the coldest? Has the most rain? Is the warmest? Has the highest elevation? Prepare math word problems for these questions.

SCIENCE

1. Construct your own information book about plants by collecting, drying, mounting, and identifying both tree and plant leaves.

2. Monet's wife died of tuberculosis. What is tuberculosis? What steps are now taken for diagnosing and treating this illness? What do you think is the worst disease in the world today? Why?

SOCIAL STUDIES

1. Construct an illustrated time line of Monet's life using the What Happened When? information at the end of the book.

2. Diagram and illustrate your family tree.

3. Design travel brochures about Paris for your parents.

4. Compare and contrast the Fourth of July with France's Bastille Day (July 14).

GEOGRAPHY

1. Draw a map of Paris. Include the city's main boulevards, public buildings, museums, and train stations. Why do the train stations ring the city? Why doesn't the city have only one large train station? What areas of France does each station serve? Draw lines from each station to the area it serves.

2. Examine various forms of traditional railroad art, including Monet's Gare Saint-Lazare (1877).

3. Research information about the French flag and national anthem.

BEYOND THE BOOK

Guided Reading Connections Across a Learning Rainbow: Fiction Involving Art

Cameron, Eleanor. *The Court of the Stone Children.* Dutton, 1973.

Demi. *Liang and the Magic Paintbrush.* Illustrated by Demi. Henry Holt, 1988.

Konigsburg, E. L. *From the Mixed-Up Files of Mrs. Basil E. Frankweiler.* Macmillan, 1967.

Enriching Connections

1. Monet had several friends who were artists, including Auguste Renoir, Alfred Sisley, and Jean-Frédéric Bazille. Introduce them and their works.

2. Visit the public library to check out illustrated travel books about Paris and regions of France.

3. Serve a French meal to the class. In many schools, the food services department will make special meal presentations (including foreign language menus) for a class.

FROM ANOTHER POINT OF VIEW

Venezia, Mike. *Monet.* Getting to Know the World's Greatest Artists series. Childrens Press, 1990.

Parent-Student Connections

1. Grow vegetables at home from seeds or small, nursery-started plants. Use the vegetables in family meals.

2. From the school or public library check out art books to be shared at home.

3. In Sweden, all land is "open for anyone to walk along and pick the fruit" (*Yellow Brick Road,* v. 6, n. 2 [November-December 1990]). How would this policy work in the United States? What would be the benefits and drawbacks? Give examples.

4. French pastries can be made at home. Use a cookbook recipe for cream puffs or petit fours. Cream puffs are easy to make and may be filled with sweetened whipped cream or ice cream. Chocolate frosting may be swirled on the top of the puffs. A single-layer-cake recipe can be used to make petit fours. After the cake is baked and cooled, cut it into small squares or diamonds. Frost the petit fours on the top and all sides and decorate as desired.

❀ ❀ ❀

MARCO POLO

Author: Gian P. Ceserani
Illustrator: Piero Ventura
Publisher: Putnam, 1982
Suggested Grade Level: 4
Classification: Nonfiction social studies
Literary Form: Illustrated travel narrative
Theme: Knowledge about various countries results from cultural interchange.

ABOUT THE BOOK

STUDENT OBJECTIVES:

1. Write, develop, and present a classroom video of the book *Marco Polo*.

2. Present an illustrated time line of the life of Marco Polo.

3. Compare the adventures of Marco Polo with those of Neil Armstrong or another explorer. This exercise may be a cooperative learning activity, with reports given in a moderator-and-guest-panel format.

SYNOPSIS: The book chronicles the thirteenth century travels of the Venetian Marco Polo to Asia and his introduction to Chinese inventions, including spectacles, paper money, and firecrackers.

ABOUT THE AUTHOR: Gian P. Ceserani, birthdate unavailable.

Gian P. Ceserani has developed a detailed, informative writing style that is complemented by the illustrations of Piero Ventura. Ceserani's special interests are ancient architecture and monuments.

ABOUT THE ILLUSTRATOR: Piero Ventura, 1937- .

Piero Ventura was born and lives in Milan, Italy. Ventura has been long recognized for his quality illustrations. He has received the American Society of Illustrators Award for Excellence. Works that he has illustrated have been translated into 15 languages.

Ventura has a unique approach to illustrating children's books. He introduces his subject through miniature panoramas that detail clothing coupled with illustrations of home and work environments.

SELECTED ADDITIONAL TITLES: Gian P. Ceserani

Ceserani, Gian P. *Grand Constructions.* Illustrated by Piero Ventura. Putnam, 1983.

———. *In Search of Ancient Crete.* Illustrated by Piero Ventura. Silver Burdett, 1985.

———. *In Search of Troy.* Illustrated by Piero Ventura. Silver Burdett, 1985.

———. *In Search of Tutankhamun.* Illustrated by Piero Ventura. Silver Burdett, 1985.

SELECTED ADDITIONAL TITLES: Piero Ventura

Ventura, Piero. *Birth of a City: Venice.* Illustrated by Piero Ventura. Putnam, 1988.

———. *1492.* Putnam, 1992.

———. *Great Composers.* Illustrated by Piero Ventura. Putnam, 1989.

———. *Great Painters.* Illustrated by Piero Ventura. Putnam, 1984.

———. *Man and the Horse.* Illustrated by Piero Ventura. Putnam, 1982.

———. *Michelangelo's World.* Illustrated by Piero Ventura. Putnam, 1989.

———. *Piero Ventura's Book of Cities.* Illustrated by Piero Ventura. Random, 1975.

———. *There Once Was a Time.* Illustrated by Piero Ventura. Putnam, 1987.

USING THE BOOK

Suggested Approach to the Book

Model Lesson

1. Find Venice, Italy, on a world map. Why was Venice called "the Queen of the Seas" in the thirteenth century? Look at the illustration of Venice in *Marco Polo* under the heading "Venice—Home of Marco Polo." Describe the city through the artist's eyes.

2. Carefully examine the illustration under the heading "Merchants of Venice." What do you see? List 25 observations. How can your observations be grouped and classified?

3. Identify Kublai Khan and Genghis Khan. Why are they famous? How are Mongolian ponies different from other horses?

4. Explain why Marco Polo traveled farther than any other citizen of Venice. Why did the Polo brothers sail toward the Greek Wind? Describe the Gobi desert. Are there any deserts in your state?

5. Who is the Great Buddha?

6. Explain the expression *as dear as pepper*. What are some similar expressions used today?

7. How would you describe a palace? Are European palaces different from Chinese palaces? Explain your answer.

Library Media Center Connections

1. Research and prepare information to be orally presented by students in cooperative learning groups on the following topics:

   Chinese & Italian Food   Chinese & Italian Architecture

   Chinese & Italian Art   Chinese & Italian Customs

   Chinese & Italian Music   Chinese & Italian Fairy Tales

   Chinese & Italian Fashions   Chinese & Italian Toys

   Chinese & Italian Inventors   Chinese & Italian Historical Sites

   Chinese & Italian Currency   Chinese & Italian Tourism

Computer Connections

1. Create a database about Italy and China using research from the class projects.

Instructional Materials Connections

1. Artman, John. *Explorers.* Good Apple, 1986.

2. Everett, Felicity, and Stuart Reid. *Explorers.* Illustrated by Peter Dennis. Osborne, 1991.

3. Grant, Neil. *The Great Atlas of Discovery.* Alfred A. Knopf, 1992.

4. Use art books in the classroom to illustrate Chinese arts and crafts. Be sure to include origami and paper cutting. These books may be borrowed from the library media center.

5. Order silkworms from a science supplier. Follow the life cycle through scientific observation and analysis. Silkworms are available from Insect Lore Products. P.O. Box 1535, Shafter, CA 93263.

6. Ask students who have access to Italian and Chinese handcrafts and fabrics to share them with the class.

Theme Reading Connections: Marco Polo

Bruaneli, Vincent, adapt. *The Travels of Marco Polo.* Illustrated by Hieronimus Fromm. Silver Burdett, 1985.

Fritz, Jean, et al. *The World in 1492.* Henry Holt, 1992.

Greene, Carol. *Marco Polo: Voyager to the Orient.* Childrens Press, 1987.

Humble, Richard. *The Travels of Marco Polo.* Exploration Through the Ages series. Illustrated by Richard Hook. Franklin Watts, 1990.

Marco Polo, Christopher Columbus and Hernando Cortes. Age of Exploration series. Marshall Cavendish, 1989.

Marri, Noemi V. *Marco Polo.* Silver Burdett, 1985.

Reynolds, Kathy, ed. *Marco Polo.* Illustrated by Dan Woods. Raintree/Steck-Vaughn, 1986.

Rosen, Mike. *The Travels of Marco Polo.* Great Journeys series. Franklin Watts, 1989.

Critical Thinking Question
Kublai Khan sent Marco Polo's father and uncle to the Pope to request that 100 churchmen be sent to share their knowledge with his court. Unfortunately, the Pope was able to send only two friars. Because the trip was more dangerous than they had anticipated, the friars became frightened and scurried home. Can you explain how their fear might have influenced China's future opinion of the West over the long term?

Student Activities to Connect Literature and Curriculum

FINE ARTS

1. Prepare a diorama of Venice in the Italian art style.

2. Construct a scale model of a Mongolian settlement.

3. Compare Ventura's illustrations of the palace of Kublai Khan with the illustrations of palace art in Heyer, Marilee, *The Weaving of a Dream*, illustrated by Marilee Heyer, Viking Kestrel, 1986.

LANGUAGE ARTS

1. Retell the travels of Marco Polo in a classroom diary.

2. Prepare a list of questions that you would send with Marco Polo if you were Kublai Khan and wanted to learn more about how people lived, what they knew, and what they thought.

3. In two pages, compare and contrast the role of a thirteenth-century Venetian merchant with the role of a modern mall merchant.

WRITING PROMPT

1. Write a newspaper story detailing how travelers fear the Gobi Desert. Use the following headline:

> Travelers Fear Gobi Desert Evil Spirits Will Lure Them away from Their Party and Lead Them to Their Death.

MATH

1. Construct word problems describing Marco Polo's round trip to China with his father and uncle.

2. Draw an oversize floor map of Italy. Overlay the map with a grid. Have each student label and illustrate a section of the map.

SCIENCE

1. Prepare a set of illustrated transparencies that explain the life cycle of the silkworm.

2. Place 10 kitchen herbs and spices in 10 small, plastic, zip-lock bags. Label the bags by number or letter. Ask students to identify each herb or spice by smell and texture. Keep a record of correct answers, and present the research results to the class using a bar graph form.

SOCIAL STUDIES

1. Divide students into pairs. Each pair will construct an Italian gondola, "a long flat-bottomed boat that curves up with a smile at either end." Awards will be given based on the following criteria: most creative design, most unusual decoration, and most detailed model.

2. Construct a model of the most famous bridge in Venice. In what European country is a full-size replica of this bridge found?

GEOGRAPHY

1. Using the exploration map inside the front cover of *Marco Polo,* prepare an enlarged, illustrated map of Marco Polo's journey to China. Modernize the area cities and countries that exist today.

BEYOND THE BOOK

Guided Reading Connections Across a Learning Rainbow: Silk and Silkworms

Coldrey, Jenny. *The Silkworm Story.* Oxford, 1985.

Dineen, Jacquelin. *Cotton and Silk.* Oxford, 1988.

Johnson, Sylvia A. *Silkworms.* Illustrated by Isao Kishdia. Lerner, 1982.

Enriching Connections

1. Plan a special classroom luncheon using as many of the following spices as possible: cinnamon, pepper, cloves, nutmeg, ginger, and saffron. For each student, prepare a chart that has as its headings the spices used in the meal. Under each spice, have students list the dishes that they think are seasoned with the spice. Have students compare their charts with friends and rate their ability to identify spices in the food.

FROM ANOTHER POINT OF VIEW

Demi. *Chingis Khan.* Illustrated by Demi. Henry Holt, 1991.

Parent-Student Connections

1. Help your child use a cookbook to learn about the use of spices. Locate recipes using spices discovered by Marco Polo on his visit to China. Ask your child to identify some of the spices.

2. Plan a family meal using some of the spices introduced in class. Describe your family's reaction to each spice. What other spices does your family generally eat? Do the spices improve the taste of food? Why or why not?

❀ ❀ ❀

SING A SONG OF POPCORN
Every Child's Book of Poetry

Editors: Beatrice Schenk de Regniers, Eva Moore, Mary Michaels White, and Jan Carr
Illustrators: Marcia Brown, Leo Dillon, Diane Dillon, Richard Egielski, Trina Schart Hyman, Arnold Lobel, Maurice Sendak, Marc Simont, and Margot Zemach
Publisher: Scholastic, 1988, rev. ed.
Suggested Grade Level: 4
Classification: Poetry anthology
Literary Form: Anthology illustrated by nine Caldecott winners; revised edition published 14 years after the original
Theme: Nine thematic units of poetry explored through 128 selections.

ABOUT THE BOOK

STUDENT OBJECTIVES:

1. Select and read a favorite poem to the class.

2. Organize and illustrate classroom anthologies of poetry.

3. Analyze the careers and works of writers, painters, and musicians.

SYNOPSIS: A variety of poetry forms and subjects are presented in a beautifully illustrated volume. *Sing a Song of Popcorn* is a revised edition of *Poems Children Will Sit Still For*. According to the editors, "The volume would include sure-fire hits that a classroom filled with restless children would sit still for. From this concept, the three (original) editors created the anthology entitled *Poems Children Will Sit Still For*."

ABOUT THE ILLUSTRATORS:

Marcia Brown, 1918- .   Mostly Weather Theme
Caldecott medalist, *Cinderella*, 1955.
Once a Mouse, 1962.
Shadow, 1983.

Diane Dillon, 1933- ; Leo Dillon, 1933- .   Seeing, Feeling, Thinking Theme
Cadelcott medalist, *Why Mosquites Buzz in People's Ears*, 1976.
Ashanti to Zulu, 1977.

Richard Egielski, 1952- .   Mostly Nonsense Theme
Caldecott medalist, *Heh, Al*, 1987.

Trina Schart Hyman, 1939- .   Fun with Rhymes Theme
Caldecott medalist, *Saint George and the Dragon*, 1985.
Caldecott Honor medalist, *Little Red Riding Hood*, 1984.

Arnold Lobel, 1933-1987.   Mostly Animals Theme
Caldecott medalist, *Fables*, 1981.
Caldecott Honor medalist, *Hildilid's Night*, 1972.
Frog and Toad Are Friends, 1971.

Maurice Sendak, 1928- .   Story Poems Theme
Caldecott medalist, *Where the Wild Things Are*, 1964.
Caldecott Honor medalist, *In the Night Kitchen*, 1971.
Outside Over There, 1982.

Marc Simont, 1915- .   Mostly People Theme
Caldecott medalist, *A Tree Is Nice*, 1957.
Caldecott Honor medalist, *The Happy Day*, 1950.

Margot Zemach, 1931-1987.   Spooky Poems Theme
Caldecott medalist, *Duffy and the Devil: A Cornish Tale*, 1974.
Caldecott Honor medalist, *It Could Always Be Worse*, 1978.

SELECTED ADDITIONAL TITLES:

Marcia Brown

Andersen, Hans Christian. *The Snow Queen*. Illustrated by Marcia Brown. Macmillan, 1972.

Brown, Marcia. *Stone Soup*. Illustrated by Marcia Brown. Macmillan, 1986.

Beatrice Schenk de Reginers

de Regniers, Beatrice Schenk. *A Bunch of Poems and Verses.* Houghton Mifflin, 1976.

————. *It Does Not Say Meow.* Houghton Mifflin, 1972.

————. *Laura's Story.* Macmillan, 1979.

————. *May I Bring a Friend?* Macmillan, 1964.

————. *Picture Book Theater: The Mysterious Stranger and the Magic Spell.* Macmillan, 1975.

————. *Red Riding Hood.* Macmillan, 1977.

————. *So Many Cats.* Ticknor and Fields, 1985.

————. *This Big Cat and Other Cats I Have Known.* Crown, 1985.

————. *Waiting for Mama.* Harcourt Brace Jovanovich, 1955.

Diane Dillon and Leo Dillon

Aardema, Verna, retold by. *Who's in Rabbit's House?* Illustrated by Diane Dillon and Leo Dillon. Dial, 1977.

Greenfield, Eloise. *Honey, I Love: And Other Love Poems.* Illustrated by Diane Dillon and Leo Dillon. Harper & Row, 1986.

Hamilton, Virginia. *The People Could Fly.* Illustrated by Diane Dillon and Leo Dillon. Knopf, 1985.

Richard Egielski

Yorinks, Arthur. *It Happened in Pinsk.* Illustrated by Richard Egielski. Farrar, Straus & Giroux, 1983.

————. *Louis the Fish.* Illustrated by Richard Egielski. Farrar, Straus & Giroux, 1980.

————. *Sid and Sol.* Illustrated by Richard Egielski. Farrar, Straus & Giroux, 1977.

Trina Schart Hyman

Dickens, Charles. *A Christmas Carol.* Illustrated by Trina Schart Hyman. Holiday House, 1983.

Fritz, Jean. *Why Don't You Get a Horse, Sam Adams?* Illustrated by Trina Schart Hyman. Putnam, 1974.

————. *Will You Sign Here, John Hancock?* Illustrated by Trina Schart Hyman. Putnam, 1976.

Grimm, Jacob, and Wilhelm Grimm. *Rapunzel.* Retold by Barbara Rogasky. Illustrated by Trina Schart Hyman. Holiday House, 1982.

Thomas, Dylan. *A Child's Christmas in Wales.* Illustrated by Trina Schart Hyman. Holiday House, 1985.

Winthrop, Elizabeth. *The Castle in the Attic.* Illustrated by Trina Schart Hyman. Holiday House, 1985.

Arnold Lobel

Baker, Betty. *Little Runner of the Longhouse.* Illustrated by Arnold Lobel. Harper & Row, 1962.

Pretlusky, Jack. *The Headless Horseman Rides Tonight.* Illustrated by Arnold Lobel. Greenwillow, 1980.

Zolotow, Charlotte. *The Quarreling Book.* Illustrated by Arnold Lobel. Harper & Row, 1963.

Maurice Sendak

Sendak, Maurice. *Alligators All Around.* Illustrated by Maurice Sendak. Harper & Row, 1962.

————. *Chicken Soup with Rice.* Illustrated by Maurice Sendak. Harper & Row, 1962.

Marc Simont

Kuskin, Karla. *The Dallas Titans Get Ready for Bed.* Illustrated by Marc Simont. Harper & Row, 1986.

Lord, Bette. *In the Year of the Boar and Jackie Robinson.* Illustrated by Marc Simont. Harper & Row, 1984.

Sharmat, Marjorie. *Nate the Great.* Illustrated by Marc Simont. Harper & Row, 1972.

Margot Zemach

Grimm, Jacob, and Wilhelm Grimm. *The Fisherman and His Wife.* Translated by Randall Jarrell. Illustrated by Margot Zemach. Farrar, Straus & Giroux, 1980.

Zemach, Margot. *The Little Red Hen: An Old Story.* Illustrated by Margot Zemach. Farrar, Straus & Giroux, 1983.

USING THE BOOK

Suggested Approach to the Book

Model Lesson

1. On the board, write the names of the Caldecott medalists whose works are included in *Sing a Song of Popcorn*. Cluster students' thoughts about the artists and their works. Retain a copy of this information. At the end of the study unit, compare students' new thoughts about the artists and their works to the students' original impressions.

2. List the aesthetic criteria that should be used to determine quality art work in books for school library media centers. How should good quality poetry be determined? What is bad?

3. Read selections from the anthology to the class.

4. Ask students to note the nine thematic units in *Sing a Song of Popcorn* and to list titles of other poems that could be included in these categories. Ask students to determine if the categories in the collection are appropriate. Why or why not?

5. Read "Keep a Poem in Your Pocket," by Beatrice Schenk de Regniers, to students and recommend that they carry a poem in their pocket during this study. Offer students opportunities to recite their poems to the class or in pairs or small groups. A reward system for students who memorize special poetry selections may be integrated into lessons.

6. Discuss various forms of poetry, including rhyme and blank verse as well as haiku and cinquain. Define alliteration and onomatopoeia.

7. Mother Goose rhyme is one form of poetry. How many rhymes can students recite?

Library Media Center Connections

1. Introduce the Dewey Decimal classification system for poetry. How does the classification system for poetry differ from that for a novel?

2. List the titles of five poetry books in the school library media center. Which title looks the most interesting? Why?

3. Choose an illustrator from the following list, and identify 10 characteristics of the artist's works:

   Marcia Brown

   Trina Schart Hyman

   Richard Egielski

   Maurice Sendak

   Marc Simont

   Margot Zemach

   Leo Dillon and Diane Dillon

   Arnold Lobel

      (Note: For biographical information about these illustrators, see Olsen, Mary Lou, *Creative Connections,* Libraries Unlimited, 1987.)

Computer Connections

1. Using word processing and graphics programs, produce a class anthology of original poetry and illustrations. Store the poetry selections in a database.

2. Introduce specialized reference skills for poetry, including retrieval of poems by the first line of the work. Encourage students to organize a class database for poetry searches by first line.

Instructional Materials Connections

Hopkins, Lee Bennett. *Pass the Poetry Please!* Harper & Row, 1987.

Prelutsky, Jack. *The New Kid on the Block.* Cassette. Listening Library, 1986.

————. *Random House Book of Poetry.* Illustrated by Arnold Lobel. Random House, 1983.

Theme Reading Connections: Works of Caldecott Medalists

Brown, Marcia. *All Butterflies: An ABC.* Macmillan, 1974.

Conrad, Pam. *The Lost Sailor.* Illustrated by Richard Egielski. HarperCollins, 1992.

Hoffman, E. T. *The Nutcracker.* Illustrated by Maurice Sendak. Crown, 1984.

Hyman, Trina Schart. *Little Red Riding Hood.* Holiday House, 1982.

————. *Self Portrait: Trina Schart Hyman.* Harper & Row, 1985.

Kuskin, Karla. *The Philharmonic Gets Dressed.* Illustrated by Marc Simont. Harper & Row, 1986.

Lobel, Arnold. *The Book of Pigericks.* Illustrated by Arnold Lobel. Harper & Row, 1983.

———. *Ming Lo Moves the Mountain.* Greenwillow Press, 1982.

Price, Leontyne. *Aida.* Illustrated by Leo Dillon and Diane Dillon. Harcourt Brace Jovanovich, 1990.

Yorinks, Arthur. *Christmas in July.* Illustrated by Richard Egielski. HarperCollins, 1991.

Zemach, Margot. *It Could Always Be Worse.* Scholastic, 1986.

Zolotow, Charlotte. *Mr. Rabbit and the Lovely Present.* Illustrated by Maurice Sendak. Harper & Row, 1962.

Critical Thinking Question
Does the use of art by nine Caldecott medalists enhance the enjoyment of the poetry? Why or why not?

Student Activities to Connect Literature and Curriculum

FINE ARTS

1. Present a brief poem as an art lesson using illuminated letters and decorative page borders.

2. In cooperative learning groups, make an illustrated book of original poems.

3. Read unfamiliar poems to the class. Ask students to draw representational pictures of the poems; then show the original art that accompanied the poem. For an introductory lesson using this strategy, use Jack Prelutsky's *Ride a Purple Pelican* (Greenwillow, 1986), illustrated by Garth Williams. Williams is an artist noted for Laura Ingalls Wilder's Little House series as well as the classic novel, *Charlotte's Web* (Harper, 1952). Illustrated Mother Goose anthologies are other good sources for this exercise.

4. Provide opportunities for student groups to sing a poem. Encourage the use of wooden rhythm instruments, musical instruments, and recorded music.

5. Hold a competition to name a poet laureate for the class. Students may submit poetry, with or without illustrations, using collage or other art forms. Poetry will be judged by an independent committee with all entries blind. This activity works well in conjunction with a classroom or community Poetry Read-In.

LANGUAGE ARTS

1. Write rhyming poetry on the following subjects:

Colors	Animals	Holidays	Weather
Seasons	Trees	Flowers	Feelings
Relatives	Friends	Food	Monsters

2. Present readings of favorite poems during a special Poetry Break.

3. Write a letter to the publisher of *Sing a Song of Popcorn,* describing ways in which your class enjoyed the book and naming other Caldecott medalists whose art work you would like to see included. Address the letter to Publicist, Scholastic, Inc., 730 Broadway, New York, NY 10003.

WRITING PROMPT

1. Write a feature story for a children's bookstore newsletter under the following heading:

> Nine Caldecott Medalists Collaborate on Poetry Book

MATH

1. Write poems about popcorn, referring to Tomie dePaola's *Popcorn Book* for additional information. Distribute to each student a bag containing popcorn kernels. Have each student estimate how many popcorn kernels are in his or her bag. Weigh the popcorn before and after popping. On an area of the classroom floor, make a grid in one-foot-square sections. Place an electric popcorn popper in the center of the grid and estimate how many pieces will land in each square. Students should remain a safe distance from the popper.

2. Compose word problems using data from the preceding exercise.

3. Prepare a graph based on the following information from the *Popcorn Book*:

> Today Americans use 500,000,000 pounds of popcorn each year. Thirty percent is eaten at movies, circuses, ball games and county fairs. Ten percent is saved for seed while sixty percent is popped at home.

SCIENCE

1. Why is it best to keep popcorn kernels moist? If the corn becomes dry, how can it become moist again? What are "old maids?"

2. What uses of popcorn could be related to science? Invent additional uses for popcorn.

3. Estimate how far a student can pitch a piece of popcorn. Use a guideline on the floor or ground to mark the estimated and actual distances. Record the results on a grid chart using color marking pens.

SOCIAL STUDIES

1. Who discovered popcorn?

2. Where did archeologists find some popping corn that was 5,600 years old?

3. Explorers found popcorn kernels in Peru. How old were the kernels they found?

4. How did early people pop corn? What were the disadvantages of these methods? Compare and contrast these methods with popping corn in a microwave.

GEOGRAPHY

1. How can you present the following information about popcorn on a United States map?

> People in the Midwest buy more popcorn than people in any other part of the United States.

> Milwaukee and Minneapolis are the top popcorn-eating cities, followed by Chicago and Seattle.

BEYOND THE BOOK

Guided Reading Connections Across a Learning Rainbow: Poetry

Bauer, Carolyn F. *Windy Day: Stories and Poems.* Illustrated by Dirk Zimmer. Harper & Row, 1988.

Blishen, Edward, ed. *Oxford Book of Poetry for Children.* Illustrated by Brian Wildsmith. P. Bedrick, 1984.

Brooke, L. Leslie. *Rhymes from Ring O'Rosie.* Warne, 1987.

Ciardi, John. *You Read to Me, I'll Read to You.* Illustrated by Edward Gorey. Harper & Row, 1961.

Cole, Joanna. *New Treasury of Children's Poetry.* Illustrated by Judith Brown. Doubleday, 1984.

Foreman, Michael. *Michael Foreman's Mother Goose.* Illustrated by Michael Foreman. Harcourt Brace Jovanovich, 1991.

Frost, Robert. *Birches.* Illustrated by Ed Young. Henry Holt, 1988.

———. *Stopping by the Woods on a Snowy Evening.* Illustrated by Susan Jeffers. Dutton, 1978.

Hader, Berta, and Elmer Hader. *Picture Book of Mother Goose.* Illustrated by Berta Hader and Elmer Hader. Crown, 1987.

Kuskin, Karla. *Dogs and Dragons, Trees and Dreams: A Collection of Poems.* Illustrated by Karla Kuskin. Harper & Row, 1980.

Lindsay, Vachel. *Johnny Appleseed and Other Poems.* Buccaneer, 1981.

Livingston, Myra C. *Sky Songs.* Illustrated by Leonard E. Fisher. Holiday House, 1984.

Mayer, Mercer. *The Pied Piper of Hamelin.* Illustrated by Mercer Mayer. Macmillan, 1987.

Milne, A. A. *Now We Are Six.* Illustrated by Ernest H. Shepard. Dutton, 1988.

Nash, Ogden. *Custard and Company.* Illustrated by Quentin Blake. Little, Brown, 1985.

Opie, Iona, and Peter Opie. *Tale Feathers from Mother Goose.* Illustrated by Maurice Sendak. Little, Brown, 1988.

Petersham, Maud, and Miska Petersham. *The Rooster Crows: A Book of American Rhymes and Jingles.* Illustrated by Maud Petersham and Miska Petersham. Macmillan, 1987.

Prelutsky, Jack. *The New Kid on the Block.* Illustrated by James Stevenson. Greenwillow Press, 1984.

———. *Ride a Purple Pelican.* Illustrated by Garth Williams. Greenwillow Press, 1986.

Sendak, Maurice. *Seven Little Monsters.* Illustrated by Maurice Sendak. Harper & Row, 1977.

Seuss, Dr. *If I Ran the Circus.* Illustrated by Dr. Seuss. Random House, 1956.

Silverstein, Shel. *A Light in the Attic.* Illustrated by Shel Silverstein. Harper & Row, 1981.

————. *Where the Sidewalk Ends: Poems and Drawings.* Harper & Row, 1974.

Spier, Peter. *London Bridge Is Falling Down.* Illustrated by Peter Spier. Doubleday, 1989.

Viorst, Judith. *If I Were in Charge of the World and Other Worries.* Illustrated by Lynne Cherry. Macmillan, 1981.

Willard, Nancy. *A Visit to William Blake's Inn: Poems for Innocent and Experienced Travelers.* Illustrated by Alice Provensen and Martin Provensen. Harcourt Brace Jovanovich, 1982.

Wyndham, Robert, ed. *Chinese Mother Goose Rhymes.* Illustrated by Ed Young. Putnam, 1982.

Enriching Connections

1. Encourage students to read and share poems by various poets. Develop the aesthetics of art and poetry through identification of areas that held special interest to a poet or artist. (For example, in Robert Frost's *Stopping by the Woods on a Snowy Evening,* illustrated by Susan Jeffers, Frost has immortalized the woods on a snowy night and Jeffers has portrayed the same scene through pointillism.)

2. Develop classroom poetry games utilizing famous lines of poetry. Students may develop prototype games, including card and board games.

3. Present poetry through puppet theater.

4. If you had an opportunity to invite an artist or a poet home for dinner, who would you choose? Why? What menu would be appropriate?

5. Have members of cooperative learning groups play "hot seat." Have the student in the hot seat pretend to be a well-known poet. Interview the student in the hot seat. The student must answer each question.

FROM ANOTHER POINT OF VIEW

Koch, Kenneth, and Kate Farrell. *Talking to the Sun: An Illustrated Anthology of Poems for Young People.* Henry Holt, 1985.

Parent-Student Connections

1. Set aside several brief times each week to read aloud poems enjoyed by family members.

2. Teach your child how to pop corn. What safety steps should be observed?

❀ ❀ ❀

SIR FRANCIS DRAKE
His Daring Deeds

Author: Roy Gerrard
Illustrator: Roy Gerrard
Publisher: Farrar, Straus & Giroux, 1988
Suggested Grade Level: 4
Classification: Poetry
Literary Form: Picture book with unique watercolor illustrations
Theme: A retelling of the daring feats of the English explorer Sir Francis Drake.

ABOUT THE BOOK

STUDENT OBJECTIVES:

1. Present *Sir Francis Drake* as a mime play with several narrators reading the poetry.

2. Use student-prepared art transparencies as background scenery for the mime presentation.

3. Create a poetry book that describes the travels of another famous explorer. Experiment with decorative page borders.

SYNOPSIS: The story of Sir Francis Drake's exploration and battle is well told in poetry and illustrated in an unusual style.

ABOUT THE AUTHOR-ILLUSTRATOR: Roy Gerrard, 1935- .
Roy Gerrard is a resident of Stockpot, Cheshire, England. He has taught art, "a career which amazingly lasted some 20 years." His early works were oil paintings, which were never exhibited. Gerrard, thinking he was finished as an artist, destroyed all of his work in 1970!

Gerrard explains that he was injured in a climbing accident in 1972, and, in order to have something to do, he returned to painting. This time he chose a new medium. "My painting became obsessive and gradually took up all my spare time. In about three years I finally arrived at my true style of painting: small, highly detailed watercolours, remorselessly whimsical, and often Victorian/Edwardian in subject."

Explaining why he writes poetry instead of prose, he said, "I find it easier to sustain the pace and momentum of a story in rhyme rather than in prose, and I aim at the style of the Victorian/Edwardian popular monologue."

Visitors to London may be treated to exhibitions of his works at the Royal Academy or at private galleries. His works are also displayed in New Orleans. His works can be described as a "playful ballad of gallantry, devotion, and wisdom, mesmerizing in design and illustration" (*Kirkus Reviews*).

(Note: I felt privileged to receive a copy of Gerrard's biographical sketch from his New York publisher. The handwriting is elegant, rhythmic, and beautiful. His closing statement reflects a writer and illustrator who charts his own works in the publishing ocean. Finally he explains that "I hope this all makes sense. Feel free to edit, enlarge, amputate, lie openly or throw in the waste basket.")

SELECTED ADDITIONAL TITLES:

Gerrard, Jean. *Matilda Jane.* Illustrated by Roy Gerrard. Farrar, Straus & Giroux, 1983.

Gerrard, Roy. *The Favershams.* Illustrated by Roy Gerrard. Farrar, Straus & Giroux, 1983.

———. *Rosie and the Rustlers.* Illustrated by Roy Gerrard. Farrar, Straus & Giroux, 1989.

———. *Sir Cedric.* Illustrated by Roy Gerrard. Farrar, Straus & Giroux, 1984.

———. *Sir Cedric Rides Again.* Illustrated by Roy Gerrard. Farrar, Straus & Giroux, 1986.

USING THE BOOK

Suggested Approach to the Book

Model Lesson

1. Examine the buildings in the background on the first double-page spread. Where are the houses? What clues are presented in the text? Do you know something about the explorer that is not presented on these two pages? Explain.

2. Describe the ship that Drake boarded when he was ten years old. What kind of clothing were the sailors wearing? What clothing do sailors wear today? Describe the "grown up strong and straight" image of Drake.

3. What happened when Drake and his crew arrived in Mexico? Panama? South America? Why did Drake say, "They haven't heard the last of me"?

4. Compare Columbus's first journey to the New World with Drake's disastrous South American voyage.

5. How did Drake travel from a rain forest to a sea of ice?

6. Do you think Drake's ship was damaged when it slid off a rock? Why or why not?

7. Is the English city of Plymouth familiar? Who else set sail from Plymouth? Where did they land? Did either voyage change the course of history? Explain.

Library Media Center Connections

1. Prepare a documentary video about Sir Francis Drake and his mentor, Queen Elizabeth the Great.

2. Research the following topics:

English architecture	Spanish architecture
English and Spanish sailing ships	Atlantic and Pacific Oceans
English costumes and clothing	Spanish costumes and clothing
Queen Elizabeth I of England	King Philip of Spain
Spanish Armada	

Computer Connections

1. Begin a database on the following topics:

   International Architecture

   Sailing Ships

   Explorers

   Kings and Queens

2. Using a word processor, write a letter to Sir Francis Drake about how we explore outer space and the sea today.

Instructional Materials Connections

1. Anno, Mitsumasa. *Anno's Britain.* Illustrated by Roy Gerrard. Putnam, 1985.

2. Artman, John. *Explorers.* Illustrated by Kathryn Hyndman. Good Apple, 1986.

3. Goodall, John. *The Story of an English Village.* Illustrated by John Goodall. Macmillan, 1969.

4. Cherry, Lynne. *The Great Kapok Tree.* Illustrated by Lynne Cherry. Harcourt Brace Jovanovich, 1990.

Theme Reading Connections: Explorers

Adler, David A. *A Picture Book of Christopher Columbus.* Illustrated by John Wallner and Alexandra Wallner. Holiday House, 1991.

Ash, Maureen. *Vasco Nunez de Balboa: Expedition to the Pacific Ocean.* World's Great Explorers series. Childrens Press, 1990.

Clare, John D., ed. *The Voyages of Christopher Columbus.* Living History series. Harcourt Brace Jovanovich, 1992.

Codye, Corinn. *Queen Isabella I.* Raintree Hispanic Stories series. Illustrated by Rick Whipple. Raintree/Steck-Vaughn, 1990.

Foreman, Michael. *The Boy Who Sailed with Christopher Columbus.* Little, Brown, 1992.

Fradin, Dennis. *Explorers.* Childrens Press, 1984.

————. *Columbus Day.* Enslow, 1990.

Fritz, Jean. *Where Do You Think You're Going, Christopher Columbus?* Illustrated by Margot Tomes. Putnam, 1980.

Goodnough, David. *Francis Drake.* Troll, 1979.

Greene, Carol. *Christopher Columbus: A Great Explorer.* Childrens Press, 1989.

Greenwald, Sheila. *Rosie Cole Discovers America.* Little, Brown, 1992.

Hargrave, Jim. *Ferdinand Magellan: First Around the World.* World's Great Explorers series. Childrens Press, 1990.

Hook, David. *Sir Francis Drake.* Illustrated by Janet Caulkins. Franklin Watts, 1988.

Humble, Richard. *The Voyage of Magellan.* Exploration Through the Ages series. Illustrated by Richard Hook. Franklin Watts, 1989.

Hunter, Nigel. *The Expeditions of Cortes.* Great Journeys series. Franklin Watts, 1990.

Kent, Zachary. *Christopher Columbus.* World's Great Explorers series. Childrens Press, 1992.

Lauber, Patricia. *Who Discovered America?* Illustrated by Mike Eagle. Harper & Row, 1992.

Lomask, Milton. *Great Lives: Exploration.* Macmillan, 1988.

Marco Polo, Christopher Columbus and Hernando Cortes. Age of Exploration series. Marshall Cavendish, 1989.

Martin, Susan. *I Sailed with Columbus.* Illustrated by Tom La Padula. Overlook, 1991.

Matthews, Rupert. *Viking Explorers.* Beginning History series. Illustrated by Jack Keay. Bookwright, 1990.

Schlein, Miriam. *I Sailed with Columbus.* Illustrated by Tom Newsom. Harper & Row, 1991.

Simon, Charnan. *Explorers of the Ancient World.* World's Great Explorers series. Childrens Press, 1992.

Smith, Barry. *The First Voyage of Christopher Columbus.* Viking, 1992.

Stein, Conrad. *Hernando Cortes.* World's Great Explorers series. Childrens Press, 1991.

Wilkie, Katherine. *Ferdinand Magellan: Noble Captain.* Houghton Mifflin, 1963.

Williams, Brian. *Voyages of Discovery.* Tales of Courage series. Illustrated by Andrew Howat. Steck-Vaughn, 1990.

Yolen, Jane. *Encounter.* Illustrated by David Shannon. Harcourt Brace Jovanovich, 1992.

Critical Thinking Question

Why has Roy Gerrard received many awards for his books, including a *New York Times* Best Illustrated Book of the Year and a *Booklist* Children's Editors' Choice, but is not eligible for the annual Caldecott award? What are the requirements of the Caldecott award?

Student Activities to Connect Literature and Curriculum

FINE ARTS

1. Examine the background art used on page 4. Compare this repetitive use of design with an M. C. Escher design. Create new end papers for this book using a repetitive design and your choice of art media.

2. Construct a model of an English or a Spanish sailing ship.

3. Compare and contrast the art of British author-illustrator Roy Gerrard and U.S. illustrator Tomie dePaola. Could they be described as having unique, primitive styles? Why or why not?

4. Present life-size models of the English, Mexican, and Spanish flags. Explain the meanings of their designs.

5. Examine the pages with jungle art. Notice that the leaves on one type of plant were created using a technique called pointillism. Create a jungle scene using pointillism.

LANGUAGE ARTS

1. In cooperative learning groups, write a poem about explorers of the world. Use it as an example of choral reading, and enhance it with appropriate background sound effects.

2. Make an illustrated pop-up book about a favorite explorer. (See Moerbeek, Kees, and Dijs, *Six Brave Explorers*, Price Stern Sloan, 1988.)

WRITING PROMPT

1. Write the newspaper story for the following headline:

> Explorer Francis Drake Uses Two Ships as Fuel for Heat and Food Preparation

MATH

1. Graph the results of a student poll (see the first social studies activity) to name the most important explorer.

2. Trace the voyages of Drake and calculate the total mileage sailed. Which voyage was the shortest? Which was the longest? How long would it take to fly the routes today in a commercial airplane? How long would it take to travel the route by a motorized yacht?

SCIENCE

1. Identify the names of jungle plants illustrated in the book.

2. Create a classroom-size rain forest.

SOCIAL STUDIES

1. Conduct a poll to name the most important explorer.

2. What area of Earth should be explored today? Devise a cooperative learning plan based on the following premise:

> Imagine that you are making a one-year plan for 100 people to live on the ocean floor. Participants will not be able to leave the exploration area at any time.

What type of transportation is appropriate?

Design suitable housing.

What types of food are required?

Plan for recreational needs.

Design a wellness program.

What types of disaster plans might be needed?

GEOGRAPHY

1. On a world map, identify the following areas. Explain their importance today:

Mexico	Panama	Pacific Ocean	Atlantic Ocean
Antarctic	Plymouth, England	Cadiz, Spain	London

BEYOND THE BOOK

Guided Reading Connections Across a Learning Rainbow: Books by Jean Fritz

Fritz, Jean. *And Then What Happened, Paul Revere?* Illustrated by Margot Tomes. Putnam, 1973.

————. *Brady.* Illustrated by Lynd Ward. Putnam, 1960.

————. *Brendan the Navigator.* Illustrated by Enrico Arno. Putnam, 1979.

————. *The Cabin Faced West.* Illustrated by Feodor Rojankovsky. Putnam, 1958.

————. *Can't You Make Them Behave, King George?* Illustrated by Tomie dePaola. Putnam, 1982.

————. *The Double Life of Pocahontas.* Illustrated by Ed Young. Putnam, 1983.

————. *Make Way for Sam Houston.* Illustrated by Elise Primavera. Putnam, 1986.

————. *Shh! We're Writing the Constitution.* Illustrated by Tomie dePaola. Putnam, 1987.

————. *What's the Big Idea, Benjamin Franklin?* Illustrated. Putnam, 1982.

————. *Who's That Stepping on Plymouth Rock?* Putnam, 1975.

————. *Why Don't You Get a Horse, Sam Adams?* Illustrated by Trina Schart Hyman. Putnam, 1974.

————. *Will You Sign Here, John Hancock?* Illustrated by Trina Schart Hyman. Putnam, 1976.

Enriching Connections

1. On a chart, list in order of importance explorations and discoveries in space or in the ocean conducted for purposes of research or to locate sunken treasures. Instead of a list, the information may be presented as an illustrated time line.

2. Write and record a sea song suitable for Sir Francis Drake and his crew.

FROM ANOTHER POINT OF VIEW

Willard, Nancy. *The Voyage of the Ludgate Hill.* Illustrated by Alice Provensen and Martin Provensen. Harcourt Brace Jovanovich, 1986.

Parent-Student Connections

1. Ask the students to pick one significant news event they remember and explain why it is memorable. What were they doing at the time?

2. If it were possible to invite Sir Francis Drake to dinner at your home, what 10 questions would you ask him? List 10 things you would want to tell him about today's world. What food would you serve him? Why?

❀   ❀   ❀

HOANG ANH
A Vietnamese-American Boy

Author: Diane Hoyt-Goldsmith
Illustrator: Photographs by Lawrence Migdale
Publisher: Holiday House, 1992
Suggested Grade Level: 4
Classification: Nonfiction
Literary Form: Photo essay
Theme: It is important for all people to recognize and remember their heritage.

ABOUT THE BOOK

STUDENT OBJECTIVES:

1. Understand the culture of Vietnamese people living in the United States.

2. Share a New Year celebration with a Vietnamese family.

3. Retell a Vietnamese folktale.

SYNOPSIS: Meet Hoang Anh Chau, a Vietnamese refugee whose parents and family fled a war-torn country and eventually became U.S. citizens. Hoang, like most other kids, likes sports, pizza, and video games. He differs from other students in that he speaks Vietnamese at home and celebrates Tet, the Vietnamese New Year.

ABOUT THE AUTHOR: Diane Hoyt-Goldsmith, 1950- .
Diane Hoyt-Goldsmith, like a number of successful writers and illustrators, received her Bachelor of Fine Arts degree from Pratt Institute in New York. She is currently art director for Square Moon Productions, which she founded.
Totem Pole, her first published book for children, has been followed by five additional ethnic culture books. Subjects for her writings include totem poles, Pueblo storytelling, Inuit and Cherokee tribal activities, immigration of Vietnamese people to the United States, as well as African-American celebrations.

ABOUT THE PHOTOGRAPHER: Lawrence Migdale, 1951- .
Lawrence Migdale has collaborated on fine books with Diane Hoyt-Goldsmith. Migdale's special interest is photographing children in their environment.

SELECTED ADDITIONAL TITLES:

Hoyt-Goldsmith, Diane. *Arctic Hunter*. Photographs by Lawrence Migdale. Holiday House, 1992.

————. *Celebrating Kwanzaa*. Photographs by Lawrence Migdale. Holiday House, 1993.

————. *Pueblo Storyteller*. Photographs by Lawrence Migdale. Holiday House, 1992.

————. *Totem Pole*. Photographs by Lawrence Migdale. Holiday House, 1992.

Suggested Approach to the Book

Model Lesson

1. What decision did Hoang's parents make in 1977? Why? How did Thao Chau fool the communist government? How many Vietnamese did he help to escape?

2. What were some of the perils the refugees faced when they sailed to Malaysia? Describe the boat people.

3. Where was Hoang born?

4. How does the Vietnamese language differ from English?

5. Describe the Vietnamese New Year celebration, Tet.

Library Media Center Connections

1. Adapt and videotape the story *Everybody Cooks Rice* (Norah Dooley, Carolrhoda, 1991) or *Banh Chung Banh Day: The New Year's Rice Cakes* (Asia Resource, 1972) as a cooperative learning group project. Music, props, and visual effects should be included in the planning.

Computer Connections

1. Design a flyer and a written program for a school celebration of Tet.

Instructional Materials Connections

1. Nguyen-Dinh-Hoa. *Easy Vietnamese*. Charles Tuttle, 1966.

2. Huynh Quang Nhuong. *The Land I Lost*. Illustrated by Mai Vo-Dinh. Harper & Row, 1986.

Theme Reading Connections: Vietnam

Edwards, Richard. *Vietnam War*. Rourke, 1987.

Hauptly, Denis J. *In Vietnam*. Macmillan, 1985.

Lawson, Don. *An Album of the Vietnam War*. Franklin Watts, 1986.

————. *The War in Vietnam*. Franklin Watts, 1981.

Mabie, Margot. *Vietnam There and Here*. Henry Holt, 1985.

Tran-Khanh-Tuyet. *The Little Weaver of Thai-Yen Village*. Illustrated by Nancy Hom. Childrens Press, 1986.

Wright, David K. *The Story of the Vietnam Veterans Memorial*. Childrens Press, 1989.

———. *Vietnam*. Childrens Press, 1984.

———. *War in Vietnam*. Book 1, *Eve of Battle*. Book 2, *A Wider War*. Book 3, *Vietnamization*. Book 4, *The Fall of Vietnam*. Childrens Press, 1989.

> Critical Thinking Question
> What is communism? In your opinion, is it good or bad? What countries may be described as communist? What changes are effecting these countries to-day? What future impact do you foresee? Why?

Student Activities to Connect Literature and Curriculum

FINE ARTS

1. Copy the Vietnamese symbols for prosperity, wealth, and longevity.

2. Plan a multicultural photographic essay about the students in your school. How are students alike? How are they different? What do they do in their leisure time? What books do they read? Do they wear ethnic clothing? What food is served at home? Is a different language spoken at home?

LANGUAGE ARTS

1. Cooperative learning groups will create small, illustrated dictionaries of the English language that would help students who are new to the United States.

WRITING PROMPT

1. Write a feature story about the celebration of Tet for *Scholastic News*, a newspaper read by 3 million students in the United States. Begin the story with the following headline:

> Chuc Mung Nam Moi! (Happy New Year!)

MATH

1. How many people live in Vietnam? What is the land area of the country? If 24 percent of the land is readily arable according to the *World Almanac*, how many acres of land are available for farming? Compare the state of New Mexico and Vietnam, which are similar in geographic size.

2. What leisure activities do you like? List them in order of preference. What percentage of time do you devote to each activity? Present a bar graph or pie chart showing the percentage of time spent on each activity.

SCIENCE

1. Present an oral report about crabs or eels using transparencies as visual aids.

2. How do people in California conserve water? Has your community been forced to look for other sources of water because of the lack of rain or not enough snowpack melt? Present a water conservation plan for your home and community.

3. How do seasonal temperatures in Vietnam and your area differ?

SOCIAL STUDIES

1. Compare and contrast the celebration of the Chinese New Year and the Vietnamese New Year. What other special holidays are celebrated in Vietnam? Does the United States have holidays that are equivalent to those of Vietnam?

2. Plan a schoolwide observation of Tet as part of the multicultural curriculum. Ask food service to plan a special lunch menu for the day. With prior planning, community members may be invited to the festivities.

GEOGRAPHY

1. Locate the Mekong Delta in the southern part of Vietnam on a map of Southeast Asia. Can you find Hoang's former home, Kieng Giang? Plot the family's escape route to Malaysia and to Washington state. How many miles did they travel?

BEYOND THE BOOK

Guided Reading Connections Across a Learning Rainbow: Photography and Photographic Essays

Ancona, George. *Bananas: From Manolo to Margie.* Illustrated by George Ancona. Clarion Books, 1982.

———. *Freighters: Cargo Ships and the People Who Work Them.* Thomas Y. Crowell, 1985.

———. *Sheep Dog.* Lothrop, Lee & Shepard, 1985.

Blumenfeld, Milton. *Careers in Photography.* Lerner, 1979.

Fraser, Duncan. *Photography.* Franklin Watts, 1987.

Mitchell, Barbara. *A Story About George Eastman.* Carolrhoda, 1986.

FROM ANOTHER POINT OF VIEW

Waters, Kate. *Lion Dancer.* Photographs by Martha Cooper. Scholastic, 1990.

Enriching Connections

1. Explore Vietnam through photo and travel books.

Parent-Student Connections

1. Read Vuong, Lynette D., *The Brocaded Slipper and Other Vietnamese Tales*, Harper & Row, 1982; or Graham, Gail B., *The Beggar in the Blanket*, illustrated by Brigitte Bryan, Dial, 1988.

❀ ❀ ❀

THE GLORIOUS FLIGHT
Across the Channel with Louis Bleriot

Authors: Alice Provensen and Martin Provensen
Illustrators: Alice Provensen and Martin Provensen
Publisher: Viking, 1983
Suggested Grade Level: 4
Classification: Nonfiction
Literary Form: Picture book with richly detailed paintings that convey the wonderment of this historic event with authenticity.
Theme: Inventions require detailed planning and many modifications to the working model.

ABOUT THE BOOK

STUDENT OBJECTIVES:

1. Construct scale models of vehicles to be used for interplanetary travel in the future.

2. Construct a classroom diorama to display space-travel models. Select appropriate background music for the diorama display.

3. Enter information about five books you have read about inventors and inventions into a computer database.

SYNOPSIS: The story chronicles a step in the development of a flying machine. Louis Bleriot's pioneering cross-channel flight between France and England came 18 years before Charles Lindbergh's flight across the Atlantic Ocean from the United States to Paris, France.

ABOUT THE AUTHORS-ILLUSTRATORS: Alice Provensen, 1918- ; Martin Provensen, 1916-1987.
The authors and illustrators can be discussed jointly in terms of their careers. They were both born in Chicago and were illustrators before their marriage, which lasted 40 years until Martin's death. Alice worked for the Walter Lanz and Walt Disney movie studios; Martin worked for Disney. Alice worked on two Disney film classics: *Fantasia* and *Dumbo*.
The source of their background information was extensive travel. They never carried a camera but used a sketchbook for recording their ideas. The Provensens' philosophy was, "Publication of a book is in many ways similar to production of a movie or a play. It is not done by one person." The

Provensens' works include writing and illustrating a wide variety of subjects, including Bible stories, Greek myths, Mother Goose rhymes, Aesop's fables, and other subjects.

The animals on their farm in New York served as models for *The Year at Maple Farm, Our Animal Friends at Maple Hill Farm, A Horse and a Hound a Goat and a Gander,* and *An Owl and Three Pussycats.* The Provensens received the prestigious Caldecott medal for *The Glorious Flight.* They received a Caldecott Honor award for *A Visit to William Blake's Inn* written by Nancy Willard. *A Peaceable Kingdom,* also written by Nancy Willard and illustrated by the Provensens, was awarded the Newbery medal.

Alice Provensen summed up their careers: "Our profession is drawing and painting, our hobbies are drawing and painting. Our enthusiasms are drawing and painting. Outside of that, our interests are doing it better" (*Something About the Author,* vol. 9, p. 154).

SELECTED ADDITIONAL TITLES: Alice Provensen and Martin Provensen

Lawrence, D. H. *Birds, Beasts and the Third Thing: Poems.* Illustrated by Alice Provensen and Martin Provensen. Viking, 1982.

Provensen, Alice. *The Buck Stops Here: The Presidents of the United States.* Harper & Row, 1990.

Provensen, Alice, and Martin Provensen. *A Book of Seasons.* Illustrated by Alice Provensen and Martin Provensen. Random House, 1978.

————. *A Horse and a Hound a Goat and a Gander.* Macmillan, 1980.

————. *Leonardo Da Vinci: The Artist, Inventor, Scientist in Three-Dimensional Movable Pictures.* Viking, 1984.

————. *Our Animal Friends at Maple Hill Farm.* Illustrated by Alice Provensen and Martin Provensen. Random House, 1984.

————. *An Owl and Three Pussycats.* Illustrated by Alice Provensen and Martin Provensen. Macmillan, 1981.

————. *Town and Country.* Illustrated by Alice Provensen and Martin Provensen. Crown, 1985.

————. *The Year at Maple Farm.* Illustrated by Alice Provensen and Martin Provensen. Macmillan, 1978.

Willard, Nancy. *A Peaceable Kingdom: The Shaker Abecedarius.* Illustrated by Alice Provensen and Martin Provensen. Viking, 1978.

————. *A Visit to William Blake's Inn: Poems for Innocents and Experienced Travelers.* Illustrated by Alice Provensen and Martin Provensen. Harcourt Brace Jovanovich, 1981.

————. *The Voyage of the Ludgate Hill: A Journey with Robert Louis Stevenson.* Illustrated by Alice Provensen and Martin Provensen. Harcourt Brace Jovanovich, 1987.

USING THE BOOK

Suggested Approach to the Book

Model Lesson

1. Describe the Louis Bleriot family and its pets. Is the Bleriot family like an American family? Why or why not? Look at the Bleriot family portrait. What can you tell about where the family lives? Describe your family.

2. Describe the motorboat *L'Antoinette*. Why does it have a smokestack?

3. How did Bleriot learn to fly? How do people learn to fly today? Is there a government agency that qualifies flyers?

4. Describe the English Channel. Why is the destroyer *Escopette* waiting in the ocean below Bleriot's airplane? Did he have any previous flying accidents?

5. Why do the authors declare that it "truly was a glorious flight"?

Library Media Center Connections

1. Using library media center reference sources, prepare an illustrated time line of the history of flight.

2. Prepare a three-minute oral report that includes color transparency illustrations of the famous ocean flight of Charles Lindbergh from the United States to France.

3. Who are the pioneers of aviation? Are any women among them?

4. Why are the names Richard Rutan and Jena Yeager listed in the *World Almanac* under the heading "*Notable Around the World and International Trips*"?

Computer Connections

1. Design a database form to collect information about important inventions. Collaborative learning groups may be assigned to give input on 10 inventions that they consider significant.

2. Using a word processor, write a class letter to be placed in a time capsule that will be opened by students in 25 years. In the letter, describe the following: space flights, housing, food, transportation, school, technology, sports, recreation, and the five biggest problems facing mankind today.

Instructional Materials Connections

1. Bantock, Nick. *Wings: A Pop-up Book of Things That Fly.* Random House, 1989.

2. Endacott, Geoff. *Discovery and Inventions.* Illustrated. Strange and Amazing Worlds series. Viking, 1991.

3. Flight and Aerodynamics Kit is a hands-on course in how objects move through the air. This science kit, one in a series, is the result of an Alliance for Science partnership between the Museum of Science (Science Park, Boston, MA 02114) and the Nature Company (750 Hearst Ave., Berkeley, CA 94710).

4. Schools in Southern California may participate in Thomas Brothers Maps Educational Foundation activities, which encourage the study of geography. Classroom visits to the company may be scheduled, and teacher inservice seminars are offered. The company also makes available to area teachers surplus materials, including maps that may be used in craft projects, such as model airplanes, map picture frames, necklaces, and bracelets. The company maintains a library of reference materials, including lesson plans that integrate geography across the curriculum. The address is Thomas Brothers Maps Educational Foundation, 17731 Cowan, Irvine, CA 92714.

Theme Reading Connections: Flight

Ames, Lee J. *Draw 50 Airplanes, Aircraft, and Spacecraft.* Illustrated by Lee Ames. Doubleday, 1977.

Bendick, Jeanne. *Airplanes.* Rev. ed. Illustrated. Franklin Watts, 1982.

Berliner, Don. *Aeronautics.* Illustrated. Lerner, 1989.

———. *Before the Wright Brothers.* Illustrated. Lerner, 1989.

———. *Distance Flights.* Illustrated. Lerner, 1989.

———. *Flying Model Airplanes.* Illustrated. Lerner, 1982.

———. *Record Breaking Airplanes.* Illustrated. Lerner, 1985.

Boyne, Walter. *The Smithsonian Book of Flight for Young People.* Illustrated. Macmillan, 1988.

Braybrook, Roy. *The Aircraft Encyclopedia.* Illustrated. Messner, 1985.

Briggs, Carol. *Ballooning.* Illustrated. Lerner, 1985.

Chant, Chris. *Jetliner from Takeoff to Touchdown.* Franklin Watts, 1982.

Couper, Heather, and Nigel Henbest. *The Space Atlas: A Pictorial Atlas of Our Universe.* Illustrated. Harcourt Brace Jovanovich, 1992.

Curry, Barbara. *Historical Aircraft.* Illustrated. Franklin Watts, 1982.

Davoes, Eryl. *Transport on Land, Road and Rail.* Illustrated. Timelines series. Franklin Watts, 1992.

Embury, Barbara. *The Dream Is Alive: A Flight of Discovery Aboard the Space Shuttle.* Illustrated with photographs. Harper & Row, 1990.

Freedman, Russell. *The Wright Brothers: How They Invented the Airplane.* With original photographs by John and Orville Wright. Holiday House, 1991.

Jeffers, David. *Supersonic Flight.* Illustrated. Franklin Watts, 1989.

Lindbergh, Reeve. *View from the Air: Charles Lindbergh's Earth and Sky.* Photographs by Richard Brown. Viking, 1992.

Marriott. *Amazing Fact Book of Balloons.* Creative Education, 1987.

Nahum, Andrew. *Flying Machine.* Eyewitness Books series. Alfred A. Knopf, 1990.

Robbins, Jim. *Do You Know?: The Story of Flight.* Warwick, 1986.

Yolen, Jane. *Wings.* Illustrated by Dennis Yoland. Harcourt Brace Jovanovich, 1991.

> Critical Thinking Question
> What invention do you think has benefitted mankind the most? Why? What invention or discovery is needed the most today? Why?

Activities to Connect Literature and Curriculum

FINE ARTS

1. Draw and color your own family portrait.

2. Construct a model of Louis Bleriot's automobile using recycled materials, such as a milk carton.

3. Design a complete 1900s wardrobe suitable for Mrs. Bleriot.

4. Design two menu covers to commemorate Bleriot's and Lindbergh's flight. Suppose the covers will be used for in-flight menus on flights between England and France or between the United States and France.

5. Explain the design of the Caldecott medal, which is awarded to illustrators.

6. Develop a frieze for the classroom that includes original balloon art work.

7. Design a flip book to illustrate the flight of an object.

LANGUAGE ARTS

1. Write and enact a one-scene play depicting the Bleriot family auto trip. Use cardboard boxes and brown butcher paper for the backdrop and props.

2. Write dialogue to describe the flight of the airship over the city of Cambrai as well as the celebration in Papa Bleriot's cafe.

3. Design a quiz game for the class. Answers will be either Bleriot or Lindbergh. Each student will have a 2-inch by 10-inch color cardboard marker with the likeness of Louis Bleriot or Charles Lindbergh for answering the questions. This game may be played by two teams. Students hold up their markers to answer questions. Add or subtract points for correct or incorrect answers.

4. List some fairy tale or folk tale characters who were able to fly faster than the modes of travel available in their time.

WRITING PROMPT

1. Complete the story based on this Bleriot quote:

> "I, too, will build a flying machine," announces Mr. Bleriot.

MATH

1. The *London Daily Mail* English Channel competition offered a prize of £1000 for the winner of the coast-to-coast, nonstop Channel crossing in either direction. At today's currency conversion rate, how much money would the prize be worth? (Look in the financial section of the newspaper for this information.) Would £1000 purchase more today or at the time of Bleriot? Why?

2. It took Bleriot 36 minutes to fly to England. How long would the same flight take on a jet airplane? How fast do jet airplanes fly today?

3. Present a color bar graph listing the 10 busiest foreign or domestic airports in the world.

SCIENCE

1. Keep a scientific log of the development of Bleriot's flying machines.

2. Construct a model of a space bus that would provide transportation for future residents on the moon.

3. Build an airplane from paper, balsa wood, or styrofoam. Students can be awarded prizes for the following categories:

    Largest and smallest model planes that fly

    Most unique model plane design

    Airplane that remains in the air the longest

    Airplane that flies the farthest

    After awards have been given, students will return to collaborative learning groups to analyze the performance of the airplanes. How could these models be improved for another contest?

SOCIAL STUDIES

1. Plan an around-the-world flight that you would like to take. Label your planned stops on a world map. In sidebars, illustrate tourist attractions to be visited, such as monuments, museums, zoos, scenic stops, and fun zones.

2. In alphabetical order list countries that have launched manned space flights and the number of manned flights. (Use the *World Almanac* as your source of information.)

GEOGRAPHY

1. Plan and construct a physical map of England, France, and the English Channel.

2. Using color markers, define the routes of the airline companies Delta, SAS, and Air France from New York to Paris. Which airlines have direct routes? Are all of the routes direct? Why or why not?

3. What are time zones? How many are there? When it is noon in New York, what time is it in London and Paris? Where does the "first hour" start?

BEYOND THE BOOK

Guided Reading Connections Across a Learning Rainbow: Astronauts

Barnett, Norman. *Astronauts.* Illustrated by Mike Saunders. Franklin Watts, 1986.

Behrens, June. *Sally Ride, Astronaut: An American First.* Childrens Press, 1984.

Blacknall, Carolyn, *Sally Ride: America's First Woman in Space.* Dillon, 1984.

Briggs, Carol. *Women in Space: Reaching the Last Frontier.* Lerner, 1988.

Westman, Paul. *Neil Armstrong: Space Pioneer.* Lerner, 1980.

Enriching Connections

1. Discuss how people view the United States space program today. Should the program be expanded? Is the expense justified? How safe are the astronauts? What should the goals of space flight and exploration be?

2. Make a model airplane from old or outdated maps. Establish a launch area on the school playground. Designate five distances, marked by lines, for scoring. Each line may represent a town or location in your state, corresponding to the relative distance from your community (that is, the farthest line will represent the town farthest from your community). Point values may be assigned to each line; points are awarded as the airplane passes over the line.

3. Imagine the future. What part will space exploration and interplanetary travel play in everyday life?

FROM ANOTHER POINT OF VIEW

Burleigh, Robert. *Flight.* Illustrated by Mike Wimmer. Philomel, 1991.

Parent-Student Connections

1. Discuss something that you would like to invent. How would it be used? Who would it help? How much money would you need to develop and market the product? Would you expect to make a profit on the item? How many years of protection are granted by a patent?

   Look around your home. What inventions are labor-saving? Which do you consider absolutely necessary to maintain your quality of life? List items that you could do without.

2. Share the following books with your family:

   Duffey, Betsy. *The Gadget War.* Illustrated by Janet Wilson. Viking, 1991.

   Goode, Diane. *Where's Our Mama?* Illustrated by Diane Goode. Dutton, 1991.

   Munro, Roxie. *The Inside-Outside Book of New York City.* Illustrated by Roxie Munro. Putnam, 1985.

   ———. *The Inside-Outside Book of Paris.* Illustrated by Roxie Munro. Dutton, 1992.

   Scullard, Sue. *The Great Round-the-World Balloon Race.* Dutton, 1991.

❀ ❀ ❀

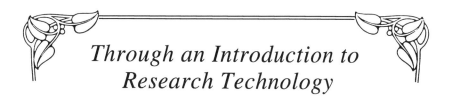

*Through an Introduction to
Research Technology*

THE MAGIC SCHOOL BUS
An Information Quintet

The Magic School Bus at the Waterworks, 1986.
The Magic School Bus Inside the Human Body, 1989.
The Magic School Bus Inside the Earth, 1987.
The Magic School Bus Lost in the Solar System, 1990.
The Magic School Bus on the Ocean Floor, 1992.

    (Note: Throughout this unit, these titles are designated as follows: WA-*Waterworks*; HB-*Human Body*; EA-*Earth*; SS-*Solar System*; OF-*Ocean Floor*.)

Author: Joanna Cole
Illustrator: Bruce Degen
Publisher: Scholastic
Suggested Grade Level: 4
Classification: Nonfiction, science
Literary Form: An introduction to science featuring a distinctive style of illustration and information
Theme: Science study is exciting, especially with Ms. Frizzle's hands-on teaching style.

ABOUT THE BOOK

STUDENT OBJECTIVES:

1. Organize, develop, and present a science fair based on the information in the Magic School Bus series.

2. Develop a premise for a television show entitled *The Magic School Bus*. Students will develop and analyze a plan for testing the hypothesis that *The Magic School Bus* program is needed and can be successfully marketed to schools throughout the United States. Analyze data from the survey to identify additional factors that need to be considered. Explore format presentations, possible filming problems, and supplementary materials that would be required.

SYNOPSIS: A dynamic, off-beat teacher, Ms. Frizzle, leads her students on wonderful, bizarre field trips to explore science.

ABOUT THE AUTHOR: Joanna Cole, 1944- .

Before becoming an author, Joanna Cole was an elementary-school teacher, a librarian, and a children's book editor. As a student, her favorite subject was science; she liked explaining things and writing reports. Like other successful writers, she earns her living doing things she enjoys. "Writing the Magic School Bus books is so much fun for me because I am able to combine the two things I love: science and humor" (Publicity pamphlet from Scholastic).

Based on many letters from students requesting other Magic School Bus books, she and Bruce Degen are in the process of developing some of these ideas into new books. Cole has her own system of coordinating with the illustrator. While she is writing the book, she pastes balloons containing information onto a dummy board. She does not want to unduly influence the artist's imagination.

Joanna Cole has more than 40 books to her credit, both fiction and nonfiction. She lives in Connecticut with her husband and daughter.

ABOUT THE ILLUSTRATOR: Bruce Degen, 1945- .

Bruce Degen likes to ask students what costumes Ms. Frizzle would enjoy wearing, particularly because he considers the teacher to be weird. He is often surprised by the enthusiasm of students in the schools he visits. "Sometimes I'll walk into a school, and the entire school will be decorated with bulletin boards and murals and mobiles hanging from the ceiling, with scenes and characters from my books. It's incredible" (Publicity pamphlet from Scholastic).

He feels fortunate to have had an elementary teacher who encouraged his talent for art. "She let me paint all the time. Even if there was a test, she'd say, 'You can answer the questions orally. Just stay back there and paint.' " Before becoming an illustrator, Degen earned his Bachelor of Fine Arts degree from Cooper Union Art School, New York, and his master's degree from Pratt Institute Graduate School of Art, New York.

Degen has illustrated more than 30 books. He lives with his wife and two sons in Connecticut, where he moved from Brooklyn, New York. Joanna Cole and Bruce Degen now live in the same town.

(Note: I had the pleasure of sitting with the guests of honor, Joanna Cole and Bruce Degen, at the author breakfast of the 1992 American Association of School Librarians convention in Baltimore. You could feel a sense of anticipation when the author and illustrator were introduced. The audience was not disappointed with their performance.

Sharing the presentation, Cole and Degen invited the audience to visit their work areas, via a slide presentation, and see how they collaborate on blending text and illustrations. Cole has an unparalleled love of science as evidenced by her first book, *The Cockroach*. Talking with her, you see a committed author who has a breadth of knowledge in her field as well as a strong commitment to science education based on her experience as a teacher and librarian.)

Degen enjoys creating art work portraying "The Friz." Asked how he would describe himself as an artist in regard to the format of the Magic School Bus series, he replied that he "was not a comic book illustrator but a children's book illustrator." The more audacious the field trip, the more outlandish is Ms. Frizzle's wardrobe. Degen and Cole are professionals who have worked hard behind the scenes to write and illustrate a best-selling series. The Magic School Bus will travel down the road, in the sky, or under the sea to expedite Ms. Frizzle's teaching plans.

The author and illustrator, with their publisher, Scholastic Press, anticipate innovative marketing plans for the Magic School Bus series. Incidentally, don't believe every clue that Degen presents to the reader; he is capable of tossing in a white or red herring! Examine the signal flags in *The Magic School Bus on the Ocean Floor*.

(Note: Please do not drop hints to students in the classroom, but if they are interested in the illustrations, encourage them to explore their meanings.)

SELECTED ADDITIONAL TITLES: Joanna Cole

Cole, Joanna. *Bony-Legs*. Illustrated by Dirk Zimmer. Four Winds Press, 1983.

————. *Cars and How They Go*. Illustrated by Gail Gibbons. Harper & Row, 1986.

————. *Cuts, Breaks, Bruises and Burns: How Your Body Heals*. Illustrated by True Kelly. Thomas Y. Crowell, 1985.

————. *New Treasury of Children's Poetry*. Illustrated by Judith G. Brown. Doubleday, 1984.

SELECTED ADDITIONAL TITLES: Bruce Degen

Bulla, Clyde. *Dandelion Hill*. Illustrated by Bruce Degen. Dutton, 1982.

Degen, Bruce. *Jamberry*. Illustrated by Bruce Degen. Harper & Row, 1983.

Sobol, Donald. *Encyclopedia Brown's Record Book of Weird and Wonderful Facts*. Illustrated by Bruce Degen. Dell, 1981.

————. *Encyclopedia Brown's Second Record Book of Weird and Wonderful Facts*. Illustrated by Bruce Degen. Delacorte Press, 1981.

Yolen, Jane. *Commander Toad and the Big Black Hole*. Illustrated by Bruce Degen. Putnam, 1983.

————. *Commander Toad and the Dis-Asteroid*. Illustrated by Bruce Degen. Putnam, 1985.

————. *Commander Toad and the Intergalactic Spy*. Illustrated by Bruce Degen. Putnam, 1986.

USING THE BOOK

Suggested Approach to the Book

Model Lesson

1. Think about your favorite class. What made it your favorite? List your reasons. Using the information, create an illustrated mind map. Display the student maps on a board. (Note: No names, please.) The teacher will assist the class in grouping and prioritizing the characteristics that were listed. Present the data as a Venn diagram. Ask students to name other ways that the data can be presented.

2. Show the five books to the class with their titles covered. Ask students to name each book based on the cover art. Keep the list of names until the end of the unit, then ask the class if the titles they selected were appropriate. Why or why not? What new titles would they choose now?

3. Ask students to examine the front flyleaf of each book without seeing the cover title. What clues to the book's title may be found in these illustrations?

4. Define geology, astronomy, ecology, anatomy, oceanography, physiology, and biology. Which book titles may be matched to these classifications?

5. What other special topics could be included in the Magic School Bus series?

Library Media Center Connections

1. The books in the Magic School Bus series may be studied in cooperative learning groups. Have students form groups based on which book they want to read. Provide sufficient copies of each Magic School Bus title so that groups can read the book as a whole unit. Each group may select a research topic appropriate to its book. Library personnel should be available to suggest additional materials on each topic, including films and videos as well as laser-disk and computer information.

2. The first hot-water vents in the ocean were discovered in the 1970s and 1980s. Develop an illustrated time line of oceanography research. (OF)

Computer Connections

1. Plan a Magic School Bus journey relating to a title selected for research. Produce a travel-agency brochure, including graphics, to promote the tour.

2. Using a word processor, send a class letter to Joanna Cole, the author, or Bruce Degen, the illustrator, giving a critique of a Magic School Bus book. Consider sending a Magic School Bus banner with Ms. Frizzle and her students seated on the bus. The letter should be sent to Scholastic Inc., 730 Broadway, New York, NY 10003. (Note: Most authors prefer a class letter instead of individual letters; they are more comfortable responding to one class letter than responding to 35 individual letters. Also, the class letter should not ask personal questions. Joanna Cole shared a letter from a young student in Florida with her Baltimore audience. The student wrote that Cole would not have any problem about dying, because this student would be able to take her place in the publishing world. The child's concern centered on who would be available when she herself needed a replacement! This provides an opportunity for the class to practice manners and develop letter-writing skills.

3. Ms. Frizzle requires her students to read five science books each week. Prepare a supplementary reading list for any of the Magic School Bus books and share it with other students. For each reference listed, write an annotation about the book and its value to the study unit. This reference list could be developed from a computer database located in the library media center or the classroom.

Instructional Materials Connections

1. Water conservation materials are usually available in class kits from the local water department. Speakers for school programs are available from some larger water departments.

2. Contact a local rock-hound club for speakers; usually they will coordinate their presentations with a display of rocks.

3. Local police departments can provide tobacco, alcohol, and drug abuse programs for students.

4. Many local dental associations have teeth-brushing kits and speakers available for class room visits.

5. Ask a local merchant to speak to students and demonstrate the use of a telescope for studying astronomy as contrasted to the limited capacity of the human eyes.

6. Center for Environmental Education Staff. *The Ocean Book: Aquarium and Seaside Activities and Ideas for All Ages.* John Wiley, 1989.

7. Conway, Lorraine. *Earth Science: Tables and Tabulations and Body Systems*. Good Apple, 1984.

8. Conway, Lorraine. *Marine Biology*. Good Apple, 1982.

9. Conway, Lorraine. *Oceanography*. Good Apple, 1982.

10. DeBruin, Jerry. *Young Scientist: The World of Water*. Good Apple, 1985.

11. Embry, Lynn. *Scientific Encounters of the Mysterious Sea*. Illustrated by Nancee McClure. Good Apple, 1987.

12. Deery, Ruth. *Earthquakes and Volcanoes*. Good Apple, 1985.

13. Fine, Edith, and Judith Josephson. *Water Wizard*. Learning Works, 1982.

14. Markle, Sandra. *Weather, Electricity, Environmental Investigations*. Learning Works, 1982.

15. Paige, David. *A Day in the Life of a Marine Biologist*. Photographs by Roger Ruhlin. Troll, 1981. Cassette also available.

16. Small geodes that have been cut in half and polished are available for a reasonable cost from The Nature Company, South Coast Plaza, 3333 Bristol St., Suite 2000, Costa Mesa, CA 92626.

17. An extensive selection of overhead transparencies and kits about earth history, astronomy, weather, energy, ecology, zoology, and the human body are available from Hubbard Scientific (P.O. Box 760, Chippewa Falls, WI 54729-0760 and Summit Learning, P.O. Box 493D, Ft. Collins, CO 80522).

18. The Astronomy Kit helps students explore the night sky, including stars. The kit answers questions like: How large are they? How far away? What keeps them going? Why are they always in the same position? This science kit is one in a series; it is the result of an Alliance for Science partnership between the Museum of Science (Science Park, Boston, MA 02114) and the Nature Company (750 Hearst Ave., Berkeley, CA 94710).

Theme Reading Connections

WATER AND ECOLOGY

Ardley, Neil. *Working with Water*. Franklin Watts, 1983.

Bright, Michael. *Pollution and Wildlife*. Franklin Watts, 1987.

Johnson, Tom. *Water, Water!* Gareth Stevens, 1988.

Lambert, Mark. *The Future for the Environment*. Franklin Watts, 1986.

McLaughlin, Molly. *Earthworms, Dirt and Rotten Leaves*. Macmillan, 1986.

Payne, Sherry. *Wind and Water Energy*. Raintree/Steck-Vaughn, 1982.

Seidenberg, Steven. *Ecology and Conservation*. Gareth Stevens, 1989.

EARTH AND GEOLOGY

Asimov, Isaac. *Earth: Our Home Base*. Gareth Stevens, 1988.

Ask About Volcanoes. Raintree/Steck-Vaughn, 1987.

Baylor, Byrd. *If You Are a Hunter of Fossils*. Illustrated by Peter Parnall. Macmillan, 1980.

Boyer, Robert B., and P. Snugs. *Geology Fact Book*. Hubbard Science, 1986.

Branley, Franklyn. *Earthquakes*. Illustrated by Richard Rosenblum. Thomas Y. Crowell, 1990.

———. *Mysteries of the Planet Earth*. Lodestar, 1989.

Cooper, Clare. *Earthchange*. Lerner, 1985.

Fradin, Dennis. *Disaster! Volcanoes*. Childrens Press, 1982.

Jacobs, Una. *Earth Calendar*. Silver Burdett, 1986.

Lauber, Patricia. *The Eruption and Healing of Mt. St. Helens*. Bradbury Press, 1986.

Osband, Gillian. *Our Living Earth*. Illustrated by Richard Clifton-Dey. Putnam, 1987.

Read, Brian. *Underground*. Silver Burdett, 1986.

Sipiera, Paul. *I Can Be a Geologist*. Childrens Press, 1986.

Symes, Dr. R. F., and Dr. R. Harding. *Eyewitness Books: Crystal and Gem*. Alfred A. Knopf, 1991.

Taylor, Paul D., *Eyewitness Books: Fossil*. Alfred A. Knopf, 1990.

HUMAN BODY AND HEALTH

Allison, Linda. *Blood and Guts: A Working Guide to Your Own Insides*. Little, Brown, 1976.

Arnold, Carolyn. *Pain: What Is It? How Do We Deal with It?* Morrow, 1986.

Berger, Melvin. *Why I Cough, Sneeze, Shiver, Hiccup and Yawn*. Thomas Y. Crowell, 1983.

Betancourt, Jeanne. *Smile: How to Cope with Braces*. Alfred A. Knopf, 1982.

Crump, Donald J., ed. *Your Wonderful Body*. National Geographic, 1982.

How and Why Activity Book of the Human Body. Scholastic, 1988.

Jennings, Terry. *The Human Body*. Childrens Press, 1989.

Lauber, Patricia. *What Big Teeth You Have!* Harper & Row, 1986.

SOLAR SYSTEM AND ASTRONOMY

Asimov, Isaac. *Ancient Astronomy*. Gareth Stevens, 1988.

———. *Space Garbage*. Gareth Stevens, 1989.

Astronomy Encyclopedia. Macmillan, 1989.

Branley, Franklyn. *The Sky Is Full of Stars*. Harper & Row, 1983.

Crump, Donald, ed. *Exploring Your Solar System*. National Geographic, 1989.

Darling, David J. *The Galaxies: Cities of Stars*. Dillon, 1985.

———. *The Stars from Birth to Black Hole*. Dillon, 1985.

Fradin, Dennis. *Astronomy*. Childrens Press, 1983.

Gallant, Roy. *The Macmillan Book of Astronomy*. Macmillan, 1986.

Kaplan, Sheila. *Solar Energy*. Raintree/Steck-Vaughn, 1982.

Simon, Seymour. *Galaxies*. Morrow, 1983.

————. *Our Solar System*. Morrow, 1992.

————. *Space Words: A Dictionary*. Illustrated by Randy Chewning. Harper & Row, 1991.

West, Robin. *How to Create Your Own Star World*. Carolrhoda, 1987.

MARINE ANIMALS, MARINE BIOLOGY, AND OCEANOGRAPHY

Arnold, Caroline. *A Walk on the Great Barrier Reef*. Illustrated by Arthur Arnold. Lerner, 1988.

Asimov, Isaac. *How Did We Find Out About Life in the Deep Sea?* Illustrated by David Wool. Walker, 1981.

Blair, Carol. *Exploring the Sea: Oceanography Today*. Illustrated by Harry McNaught. Random House, 1986.

Carwardine, Mark. *Water Animals*. Illustrated by Martin Camm. Garrett Education, 1989.

Dageling, Mary. *Monster Seaweeds: The Story of the Giant Kelps*. Dillon, 1986.

Exploring the Oceans. Silver Burdett, 1989.

Fine, John C. *Oceans in Peril*. Illustrated by John C. Fine. Macmillan, 1987.

Gilbreath, Alice. *The Continental Shelf: An Underwater Frontier*. Dillon, 1986.

————. *The Great Barrier Reef: A Treasure in the Sea*. Dillon, 1986.

————. *The Ring of Fire: And the Hawaiian Islands and Iceland*. Dillon, 1986.

Heller, Ruth. *How to Hide an Octopus*. Illustrated by Ruth Heller. Putnam, 1986.

Holling, Holling C. *Pagoa*. Illustrated by L. W. Holling. Houghton Mifflin, 1957.

Life in the Water. Silver Burdett, 1989.

Miller, Susanne S. *Whales and Sharks and Other Creatures of the Deep*. Illustrated by Lisa Bonforte. Messner, 1983.

Morris, R. *Ocean Life*. Illustrated by Ian Jackson, et al. Usborne-Hayes, 1983.

Myers, Arthur. *Sea Animals Do Amazing Things*. Illustrated by Jean D. Zallinger. Random House, 1981.

Parker, Steve. *Seashore*. Illustrated by Dave King. Alfred A. Knopf, 1989.

Pearce, Q. L. *Tidal Waves and Other Ocean Wonders*. Illustrated by Mary A. Fraser. Messner, 1989.

Poynter, Margaret, and Donald Collins. *Under the High Seas: New Frontiers in Oceanography*. Macmillan, 1983.

Rinard, Judy. *Amazing Animals of the Sea*. Edited by Donald Crump. National Geographic, 1981.

Roux, Charles. *Animals of the Seashore*. Silver Burdett, 1985.

Shale, David, and Jennifer Coldrey. *Man-of-War at Sea*. Gareth Stevens, 1987.

Sibbald, Jean H. *Homes in the Seas: From the Shore to the Deep*. Dillon, 1986.

————. *Sea Babies: New Life in the Ocean*. Dillon, 1986.

————. *Sea Mammals: The Warm-Blooded Ocean Explorers*. Dillon, 1988.

————. *Strange Eating Habits of Sea Creatures*. Dillon, 1986.

Simon, Seymour. *How to Be an Ocean Scientist in Your Own Home.* Illustrated by David A. Carter. Harper & Row, 1988.

Steele, Philip. *Life in the Sea.* Illustrated by Bob Bompton. Franklin Watts, 1986.

Updegraff, Imelda, and Robert Updegraff. *Seas and Oceans.* Creative Education, 1981.

Waldrop, Victor, H., ed. *Amazing Creatures of the Sea.* National Wildlife, 1987.

> Critical Thinking Question
> Evaluate the Magic School Bus series for teachers. Why should the books feature humorous illustrations? Are the books good enough for kids? Should the books be used in place of science books or with a science text?

Activities to Connect Literature and Curriculum

FINE ARTS

1. Write new words for one of the following songs: *Raindrops Keep Falling on My Head* or *Row, Row, Row Your Boat.* (WA) (OF)

2. After looking at Ms. Frizzle's classroom environment for the study of animal homes, duplicate the scene with the same teacher and students, but change the theme to earth study and geology. (EA)

3. Look at Ms. Frizzle's field-trip dress. Describe it. Continue reading the book. After Ms. Frizzle's class returns to school, design a new dress based on information from the field trip. (EA)

4. Each student, with the help of another student, prepares an outline of his or her body on brown butcher paper. Students enjoy tracing the outlines for each other. After the outlines are completed, each student draws in the parts of the body. (Note: Students cut out the body outlines, draw their faces on them, and seat the figures at their desks for a parents' back-to-school event or open house. They may dress the figures in clothing suitable for a field trip.) (HB)

5. Design a flannel-board presentation starring Ms. Frizzle after she has been selected the Best-Dressed Teacher of the Year. The presentation can integrate music, examples of her clothing, and a brief commentary about her unique teaching style.

6. Examine the illustrations carefully in the Magic School Bus series. What animal might be called Ms. Frizzle's mascot? List the characteristics of the art work produced by Bruce Degen. Did you know that his favorite book as a student was Ruth Gannett's *My Father's Dragon* (Random House, 1948)? Check it out from your library media center and see if you like it.

7. Hold a sand-castle art contest in the classroom. You do not need to go to a beach. Draw your designs; art will be judged solely on originality. (OF)

8. Construct a classroom oceanography mural to include sea life, the ocean floor, three kinds of coral reefs, and land formations, including islands. (OF)

9. Draw a cartoon introducing Lenny, the lifeguard. (OF)

LANGUAGE ARTS

1. Discover your own special rock and make it a pet rock. Write an essay about being a pet rock from the viewpoint of being on the ground and being able to look only up and ahead. (EA)

2. Produce a class newspaper with news about each science-fair entry. (See number 8 under Science.) An editor, news editor, feature editor, graphic artist, and composition editor are responsible for their own section or task. Each must help plan the edition and each should have reporters or assistants to help them. (Note: See the last page of SS for a hot news lead.)

3. Plan, produce, and present a filmstrip or video for one of the Magic School Bus field trips. Film with sprockets produced by U-Write film may be purchased from school supply stores.

4. As a culminating activity, hold a spelling-and-definition bee, with the class divided into teams. Words may include:

WATERWORKS

Vapor	Mist	Droplets	Cloud
Water Cycle	Sewage	Alum	Reservoir
Toxic	Evaporation	Filter	Globes
Impurities	Tank	Purification	Main
Chlorine	Fluoride		

EARTH

Rock	Crust	Minerals	Dirt
Soil	Sandstone	Shale	Limestone
Sedimentary	Fossil	Marble	Granite
Lava	Mantle	Basalt	Obsidian
Pumice	Volcano	Slate	Quartzite
Stalactite	Stalagmite	Igneous	

HUMAN BODY

Cells	Energy	Tongue	Digestion
Stomach	Esophagus	Villi	Blood
Plasma	Muscles	Molecules	Blood Vessel
Germ	Disease	Heart	Chamber
Platelet	Intestine	Oxygen	Circulate
Brain	Muscle	Digestion	Cerebral Cortex
Bones	Lungs	Nose	Spine
Liver	Cerebellum	Nerve	Kidneys
Heart	Ear	Eyes	

SOLAR SYSTEM

Orbit	Planet	Sun	Rotation
Gravity	Planetarium	Earth	Moon
Craters	Star	Mercury	Centigrade

Venus	Acid	Mars	Phobos
Deimos	Atmosphere	Canyon	Channels
Asteroid	Jupiter	Saturn	Graphite
Uranus	Autopilot	Neptune	Pluto

OCEAN FLOOR

Sea Urchin	Hermit Crabs	Jellyfish	Squid
Scallop	Limpets	Periwinkles	Mussels
Seaweed	Sea Stars	Shark	Crab
Lobster	Whelks	Continent	Coral Reef
Sea Pens	Plankton	Brain Coral	Reef
Barrier Reef	Atoll	Sea Fan	Skeletons
Octopus	Coral Polyps	Sea Hare	Moray Eel
Hot-water Vents			

WRITING PROMPT

1. Write a live radio report about a class field trip to the waterworks. (WA) Begin with the following statement:

> Our class is raining from the clouds like giant raindrops!

2. Prepare a television news release for the following bulletin. (EA)

> Magic School Bus Escapes Volcanic Eruption

3. Write an adventure story for the school newspaper about a class field trip through the human body. (HB) Use the following headline:

> Five, Four, Three, Two, One, Blast Off!

4. You are invited to a special White House banquet honoring Ms. Frizzle as Science Teacher of the Year. You have been selected by your class to introduce your teacher to the President of the United States. (SS) Please complete the following introduction:

> We are very glad that we were able to get Ms. Frizzle back safely from the solar system's asteroid belt.

5. Answer the following newspaper reporter's question for a feature story about *The Magic School Bus on the Ocean Floor*. (OF)

> Tell me, does your teacher always dress like that?

MATH

1. If two-thirds of your body is water, how much water accounts for your height (in inches) and your weight (in pounds)? (WA)

2. Explain the math formula that is carved into a wall:

   Limestone + Heat + Pressure + Time = Marble (EA)

3. Make up a math formula for soil. Using the formula, create soil as a science experiment. (EA)

4. How many bones are in the human body? List them. (HB)

5. Rank the planets according to their distance from the Sun. Next, order the planets by size, from the largest to the smallest. Is it possible to group the planets by color? (SS)

6. Construct other formulas for Magic School Bus field trips.

7. Poll students in grades three, four, and five to find out which of the Magic School Bus books is their favorite. Present the information in a graph.

SCIENCE

1. Construct a chart explaining the water cycle. (WA)

2. Assuming the average city loses one-fifth of its water to leaks, including leaks in the home, develop a water-conservation plan for your home. Ask your parents to look at the water bill before the plan begins and to compare the water use in your home after one month. Graph the data. Were you able to change the usage by 20 percent? What is the percentage difference? Are there any other ways to save water at home? Present your findings to the class on a bar graph. (WA)

3. In scientific terms, explain how the Magic School Bus is able to rise from a bridge and be inside a cloud. (WA)

4. "Soil is made of ground-up rock, mixed with clay, bits of dead leaves, sticks and small pebbles." Using this definition, collect samples of several kinds of soil. Samples might include garden soil, lawn soil, and dirt from a vacant lot. Record the location of the sample, a description of the location, and a soil analysis. Write a report based on your conclusions. (EA)

5. Define the term *striped rocks*. Have you seen any striped rocks before? Where? (EA)

6. What is a fossil? Where can fossils be found? Why?

7. With class members, conduct a blind taste test to identify food as sweet, sour, bitter, or salty. Keep records and graph the results of this experiment. Some foods that might be included are grapes, lemons, oranges, pretzels, crackers, chocolate, peanuts, olives, and bananas. (HB)

8. Plan a school science fair with exhibits from every classroom. Cooperative learning groups may work together on a science project.

9. Plan a cooperative picnic lunch for the class. Incorporate the major food groups. (HB)

10. Explain the following statements. Use a map or globe to support your explanations.

> All the oceans of the world are really one huge ocean. Earth is a watery planet—there is more water than land on Earth. Oceans cover almost three-fourths of the planet! (OF)

11. Conduct a classroom experiment. Make sea water using one cubic foot of water and adding two pounds of salt. How is it chemically different from faucet water? Why is ocean water salty? (OF)

12. Construct a food chain for ocean life. (OF)

13. Make scale models of different kinds of sharks, dolphins, seals, or walruses. (OF)

SOCIAL STUDIES

1. What is the source of the water in your area? Mark the water source on a map. How far does the water travel from the street to your home? To the kitchen sink? The bathroom? Present this information as a picture graph. (WA)

2. Construct flat models of the continents using salt dough. Recipes for the mixture may be found in Sattler, Helen Roney, *Recipes for Art and Craft Materials*, rev. ed., Lothrop, Lee & Shepard, 1987. (EA) (OF)

GEOGRAPHY

1. Construct an *active* volcanic model of Hawaii's Mauna Loa and Kilauea. (EA)

2. Using a world map, label all active volcanoes. (See the *World Almanac.*) (EA)

3. Construct a giant model or mobile of the solar system to hang in the classroom. Make the Sun and its nine orbiting planets to scale. (SS)

4. Develop a model of the continental shelf. (OF)

BEYOND THE BOOK

Guided Reading Connections Across a Learning Rainbow: Fiction

Cameron, Eleanor. *Stowaway to the Mushroom Planet*. Little, Brown, 1988. (SS)

Drury, Roger. *The Finches Fabulous Furnace*. Little, Brown, 1971. (EA)

MacGregor, Ellen, and Dora Pantell. *Miss Pickerell and the Supertanker*. McGraw-Hill, 1978. (WW)

Tomkins, Jasper. *The Hole in the Ocean*. Illustrated by Jasper Tomkins. Green Tiger Press, 1984. (OF)

Voyage of the Mimi. Bank Street College of Education, 1984. (OF)

Enriching Connections

1. Enjoy kitchen art. Use a paper plate to represent the solar system, add planets to create a kitchen mobile. (SS)

2. Ask the students to list and count the number of advertisements for body or health aids in a magazine. Compare the number of health-related advertisements in several different types of magazines, including news and food magazines. Can students rework any of the advertisements to target their age group? (HB)

3. Do a backyard dig. Dig a one-cubic-foot hole (12 inches by 12 inches by 12 inches). What did you find? How old do you think the buried things were? Why? What kind of things could be buried in the yard? Why? (Note: The following book's theme is how the surroundings of a house remain and change over an extended period of time: Pryor, Bonnie, *The House on Maple Street*, illustrated by Beth Peck, Morrow, 1987.) (EA)

4. Many communities must conserve water because of drought. How can your family save water? (WW)

5. Examine Ms. Frizzle's clothing at the conclusion of *The Magic School Bus on the Ocean Floor*. What book title do you think will be published next? Why?

6. Rent the video *Fantastic Voyage* (Twentieth Century Fox, 1966) for family viewing. This science-fiction film depicts a voyage in a miniaturized submarine through the human body. The trip includes a view of the lungs of a person who smokes. What other diseases and illness would be included if the movie were made today? (HB)

FROM ANOTHER POINT OF VIEW

Considering the Magic School Bus books as tall tales, compare them to other American folktales like Johnny Appleseed, Paul Bunyan, Pecos Bill, and Casey at the Bat.

Parent-Student Connections

1. Parents have many opportunities to discuss health issues with their children, including the goal of a wellness program, personal hygiene, growth and reproduction, and the need to avoid alcohol and substance abuse. (HB)

2. In the mid-1950s, the solar system was considered the last frontier. The United States has achieved many successes in its space program, but also witnessed the tragic explosion of a space shuttle lift-off that killed everyone on board, including the first teacher in space. Explain to children that, for many people, such events leave an indelible memory of what they were doing when they first heard the news. Relate what you remember about some of the space-program events.

3. Ask the students to begin a diary describing their feelings about important current events. This can be a very meaningful experience, and one that students may, in time, share with their own children to help them better understand our nation and world events. (EA) (WA) (SS)

4. Read aloud selections from *Blood and Guts: A Working Guide to Your Own Insides* by Linda Allison (Little, Brown, 1976). (HB)

❀   ❀   ❀

By Exploring Great Books

RAMONA AND HER FATHER

Author: Beverly Cleary
Illustrator: Alan Tiegreen
Publisher: Morrow, 1977
Suggested Grade Level: 4
Classification: Fiction
Literary Form: Novel
Theme: At some time, every family is confronted with unexpected problems and must make difficult decisions for the general welfare of everyone.

ABOUT THE BOOK

STUDENT OBJECTIVES:

1. Prepare a student budget for clothing, school lunches, supplies, and recreation. Calculate which items could be reduced or deleted in case of drastic cuts of 25-50 percent in income.

2. Understand that parents' income depends on various factors. Identify employers who depend on federal and state funding, and identify business factors, such as the cost of transportation, that affect tourism, farming, or manufacturing.

3. Recommend a new series title and story synopsis to follow publication of *Ramona and Her Father.*

SYNOPSIS: Members of a typical family are Mr. and Mrs. Quimby, their seventh-grade daughter, Beezus, and the family pest, Ramona, a second-grade student. Dad is laid off after a larger company buys his company. How does a family handle unemployment? The Quimbys will tell you how they faced the crisis.

ABOUT THE AUTHOR: Beverly Cleary, 1916- .
Beverly Cleary wanted to become a children's author when she was in grade school. Her teacher-librarian encouraged her to become a writer. Consequently, Cleary read stories with a critical eye. She was a poor reader in the early grades. In first grade, she realized that the groupings into

Bluebirds, Red Birds, or Blackbirds were based on reading ability. She was the only girl in the Blackbird group!

Cleary received degrees from Chaffee Junior College in Ontario, California; the University of California-Berkeley; and the University of Washington. Her professional career has included being a librarian.

Cleary has received many fan letters from children. The letters reflect her young readers' appreciation of her stories. One reader from a large city wrote, "I love to read your books because they make me feel so safe." Another child wrote, "I have a jumping feeling in my heart that you really mean what you say in your books" (Hopkins, Lee Bennett, *More Books by More People,* Citation Press, 1974). A 10-gallon mail box is sometimes needed for her daily mail, which can reach 150 letters in a day.

Cleary bases her books on her observations of children, including her own twins. She provides children with information they need, as in *Lucky Chuck*, a book about motorcycles. *Ramona and Her Father,* a 1978 Newbery honor book, addresses the issue of unemployment caused by hard economic times. *Dear Mr. Hinshaw,* a 1984 Newbery medal winner, describes a boy coping with divorce. Cleary writes about children, not problems.

Beverly Cleary calls herself "your basic middle-class housewife who has never done a thing of interest in my whole life—except write books that children read" (*More Books by More People*). She lives in northern California.

ABOUT THE ILLUSTRATOR: Alan Tiegreen, 1935- .

Alan Tiegreen, the illustrator of several children's books, is a professor at Georgia State University. One of his art projects was the decorating of the Hilton Hotel in Knoxville, Tennessee. His art has been displayed in private galleries as well as the Smithsonian Institution in Washington, D.C. Tiegreen's illustrations give life to several titles in the Ramona series.

SELECTED ADDITIONAL TITLES: Beverly Cleary

Cleary, Beverly. *Beezus and Ramona.* Illustrated by Louis Darling. Morrow, 1979.

———. *Beezus and Ramona Diary.* Illustrated by Alan Tiegreen. Morrow, 1986.

———. *Cutting Up with Ramona!* Illustrated by Jo Ann Scribner. Dell, 1983.

———. *Dear Mr. Henshaw.* Illustrated by Paul Zelinsky. Morrow, 1983.

———. *Ellen Tebbets.* Illustrated by Louis Darling. Morrow, 1951.

———. *Henry and Beezus.* Illustrated by Louis Darling. Morrow, 1952.

———. *Henry and Ribsy.* Illustrated by Louis Darling. Morrow, 1954.

———. *Henry and the Clubhouse.* Illustrated by Louis Darling. Morrow, 1962.

———. *Henry and the Paper Route.* Illustrated by Louis Darling. Morrow, 1957.

———. *Henry Huggins.* Illustrated by Louis Darling. Morrow, 1950.

———. *The Mouse and the Motorcycle.* Illustrated by Louis Darling. Morrow, 1965.

———. *Otis Spofford.* Illustrated by Louis Darling. Morrow, 1953.

———. *Ralph S. Mouse.* Illustrated by Paul Zelinsky. Morrow, 1982.

———. *Ramona and Her Mother.* Morrow, 1979.

———. *Ramona Quimby, Age Eight.* Illustrated by Alan Tiegreen. Morrow, 1982.

———. *The Ramona Quimby Diary.* Illustrated by Alan Tiegreen. Morrow, 1984.

————. *Ramona the Brave.* Illustrated by Alan Tiegreen. Morrow, 1975.

————. *Ramona the Pest.* Illustrated by Alan Tiegreen. Morrow, 1968.

————. *Ribsy.* Illustrated by Louis Darling. Morrow, 1964.

————. *Runaway Ralph.* Illustrated. Morrow, 1970.

USING THE BOOK

Suggested Approach to the Book

Model Lesson

1. What is a typical family? Describe your family in generic terms to the class. How many persons are in each student's family? Include brothers and sisters, as well as members of the extended family who reside in the house. Develop a statistical profile from the data. Keep the information on the board.

2. This book presents an opportunity to develop students' understanding of economics and family unity. What causes a recession or depression? Are there any safeguards that a family should have to minimize the frustrations and problems due to the loss of income and a job?

3. How does an American family differ from a Japanese family, a French family, or a Russian family?

4. In the book's opening, Ramona is planning her Christmas gift list. What items would be on your Hanukkah or Christmas gift list? Do presents reflect the religious aspect of the holidays? Why or why not?

5. Although Ramona often heard her mother say that house payments, car payments, taxes, and groceries seem to eat up money, Mrs. Quimby somehow managed to pay for all the family really needed, plus a little treat now and then (see p. 28). What other items should be included in a household budget? Why?

6. What effect does advertising have on students? Why? What television or radio advertisements do you like? What ads do you dislike? Do any ads offend you? Why or why not? Advertising agencies sometimes design an ad to be nerve wracking because such ads are effective: It is difficult to forget their message. How do you like the Whopper burger jingle on page 34?

7. Ramona thought she was being bright when she repeated this ad to her teacher: "Look, Mommy, the elephant's legs are wrinkled just like your pantyhose." Comment on her cleverness. Explain the old adage, You have hoof-and-mouth disease (or foot-in-mouth disease). List some other expressions that people use today.

8. What would you say to a friend whose father has just lost his job? Find out what unemployment benefits are. Does your state also offer or require disability benefits? What is the weekly benefit of each? How long may a person be eligible for either assistance in your state?

9. Have you ever done something dumb that had funny ramifications? Can the story be shared with the class?

Library Media Center Connections

1. *Ramona and Her Father* is one of several books that are part of a series. Using the library media center catalog or computer retrieval system, list other series that you like and would recommend to other readers. You may want to answer these questions regarding your recommendations: How far is the plot advanced in each book? Do the characters age and change? What makes the books interesting reading over a long period of time? Which is your favorite? Why? Do you know of any series that have declining reader interest today?

Computer Connections

1. Develop a database of popular, low-cost recipes. Include directions for preparation, a list of ingredients, and possible adjustments or substitutions of ingredients. Print out the recipes and include them in a class cookbook. Prepare a cover, table of contents, and index. With permission of the site administrator, the completed product could be a money-making project for funding the purchase of school library media center materials.

Instructional Materials Connections

1. *Better Homes and Gardens Step-by-Step Kids' Cookbook.* Better Homes and Gardens, 1984.
2. Cleary, Beverly. *Ramona and Her Father.* Cassette. Listening Library, n.d.
3. Cobb, Vicki. *More Science Experiments You Can Eat.* Illustrated by Giulio Maestro. Harper & Row, 1979.
4. Kyte, Kathy S. *The Kids' Complete Guide to Money.* Illustrated by Richard Brown. Alfred A. Knopf, 1984.

Theme Reading Connections: Family Life

Alcott, Louisa May. *Little Women.* Dell, 1987.

Blume, Judy. *Superfudge.* Dutton, 1980.

Byars, Betsy. *The Night Swimmers.* Delacorte Press, 1980.

Giff, Patricia. *Fourth Grade Celebrity.* Delacorte Press, 1979.

Jukes, Mavis. *No One Is Going to Nashville.* Illustrated by Lloyd Bloom. Alfred A. Knopf, 1983.

McLachlan, Patricia. *Sarah, Plain and Tall.* Harper & Row, 1985.

Critical Thinking Question

Is it possible to live comfortably with 50 percent fewer personal possessions? Why or why not? If you chose to give up one half of your possessions, what would they be?

Student Activities to Connect Literature and Curriculum

FINE ARTS

1. Prepare family portraits using different art techniques, including collage, paint, or photography.

2. Design paper stencils that may be used for carving pumpkins in October. Award prizes for the most unusual, the ugliest, and the most detailed faces.

3. Develop and construct a *Ramona* game board. Make the game board 12 squares on each side, including corner squares that deal with car payments, mortgage payments, groceries, and taxes. Devise game components in the class assignment. Make six players' markers representing Mr. and Mrs. Quimby, Ramona, Beezus, Picky-Picky (the cat), and Beverly Cleary. Develop a list of problems Ramona's family had to deal with and make a card for each problem. Mark "Problem" squares on the game board as well as "Lose a Turn" and "Take an Extra Turn." The player who lands on a "Problem" square will have to come up with a solution for the problem. The game will be played by rolling dice to determine the number of spaces a player will advance each time. Each trip around the board equals one month. Players start with $1,000 in savings. As players pass the start, they receive an unemployment payment of $500. Decide in advance how many months the game will involve.

4. Make a pair of stilts from tin cans. Have a contest to determine the best-decorated pair.

5. Using fabric art techniques, design a lamb costume that Ramona would be pleased to wear in the play.

LANGUAGE ARTS

1. Ramona wanted to earn additional money by babysitting. Draft a babysitting manual that gives safety advice and helpful suggestions to a beginning babysitter. What other information is needed?

2. Another of Ramona's money-making ideas is to make television commercials. Choose your favorite fast-food restaurant and design a television commercial with a script and story board.

3. Within cooperative learning groups, role-play the following scenes from the story:

   Mr. Quimby explaining to the family that he has become unemployed.

   The smoking "war" between Mr. Quimby and his two daughters.

   Ramona asking Mr. Quimby about his conference with Ramona's teacher.

   Ramona practicing her new commercial to be taped for television.

   Dinner at the Quimby home.

   The night Ramona woke up and heard strange noises downstairs.

4. Prepare a "quick write" from the viewpoint of a person involved in the one of the scenes listed in the preceding exercise. A quick write is a technique used to focus on brief writing samples generated through class discussion, which may include an outline of the assigned subject.

WRITING PROMPT

1. Make a list of questions that need to be asked by a reporter who is writing the story with the following headline:

> New State Report Shows Unemployment at 35 Percent

MATH

1. With a fixed income of $1,000 per month to pay for housing, food, transportation, personal necessities, recreation, and miscellaneous expenses, develop your own personal budget. Repeat this exercise twice, reducing spending by 25 percent and 50 percent. Using transparencies, give examples of the three budget levels.

2. Explain how to write a check. Include samples of checks and check registers.

SCIENCE

1. In the United States, people's reaction to smoking has changed over the years. Restaurants now have both smoking and nonsmoking areas. Smoking is not permitted on airline flights within the United States. Find one research study on smoking and report its findings to the class. What information is available now? What are the sources? Present the organized research to the class on transparencies. Predict what you think will happen in the future regarding this controversial subject. What other changes might be anticipated?

SOCIAL STUDIES

1. Poll students in the school to determine the number of different kinds of jobs held by parents. Give ballots to half of the students in each classroom and ask them to return the ballots unsigned. Ask the local Chamber of Commerce to supply information about occupations available in the area. Compare the school poll and the Chamber of Commerce data. Present the findings to the class. Are there any occupations that are unique to your particular area or community? Why?

GEOGRAPHY

1. Prepare a pictorial map of your state with special points of interest, centers of tourism, and recreational areas identified. Also include farming areas. Include a legend or key to explain the symbol used to denote each location.

BEYOND THE BOOK

Guided Reading Connections Across a Learning Rainbow: Fiction About Schools

Fitzgerald, John D. *The Great Brain at the Academy.* Illustrated by Mercer Mayer. Dial, 1972.

Fitzhugh, Louise. *Harriet the Spy.* Harper & Row, 1987.

Lenski, Lois. *Prairie School.* Harper & Row, 1951.

Shreve, Susan. *The Flunking of Joshua T. Bates.* Illustrated by Diane DeGroat. Alfred A. Knopf, 1984.

Stolz, Mary. *Bully of Barkham Street.* Illustrated by Leonard Shortall. Harper & Row, 1963.

Enriching Connections

1. Develop a Classroom Dollars system for rewarding academic achievement and classroom leadership. What will be the criteria for the awards? What type of prizes are appropriate? Will there be penalties or deductions? Would a student passport be a good idea? How would funding for awards be generated? What are some possible disadvantages to the program? What advantages do you foresee? Recommend a plan to the site administrator.

FROM ANOTHER POINT OF VIEW

Blume, Judy. *Tales of a Fourth Grade Nothing.* Dutton, 1973.

Parent-Student Connections

1. Teach your child simple cooking skills, including some "fun food" items for lunch or after-school snacks.

2. In confidence, discuss the family budget to give your child a realistic view of economics.

3. If possible, give your child more decision-making power over how his or her allowance is spent. Include specific chores to be performed to earn the allowance.

❊ ❊ ❊

FANTASTIC MR. FOX

Author: Roald Dahl
Illustrator: Donald Chaffin
Publisher: Alfred A. Knopf, 1986
Suggested Grade Level: 4
Classification: Fantasy
Literary Form: Novel
Theme: Human beings sometimes pursue a course of action that becomes a comedy of errors.

ABOUT THE BOOK

STUDENT OBJECTIVES:

1. Explain the components of a novel: plot, conflict, and resolution.

2. Produce an outline with chapter headings for a children's novel.

3. Make a book jacket with flaps, a story summary on the inside front flap, illustrator information on the inside back flap, and author information on the back cover.

SYNOPSIS: Mr. Fox and his family live in a tunnel beneath a tree on a hilltop. Mr. Fox forages for food at three nearby farms. The farmers decide to catch and kill Mr. Fox. The story features family protection, the need for food and shelter, and the farmers' need to be persistent to rid themselves of the thief, one way or another.

ABOUT THE AUTHOR: Roald Dahl, 1916-1990.
Roald Dahl was an honest man who felt it was important to tell the truth to his readers, be they adults or children. His publisher, Alfred A. Knopf, released a letter written by Dahl after he had earned a worldwide reputation for writing children's books (from which the quotes in this section

are taken). This pamphlet may be obtained from Alfred A. Knopf, Library Marketing, 225 Park Avenue South, New York, NY 10003.

Dahl's writing was affected by "eight major operations, three on the hips, five on the spine, and countless smaller ones." Extensive surgery on his hip included the placement of a "stainless steel spike with a ball hammered into the hollow of the thigh bone and glued into place." He explains that his body was most comfortable in a chair with a writing board and a suitcase under his feet.

Dahl wrote in a tiny brick hut not far from his English home. When he was there, he was oblivious to the mess or dirt around him. "My mind is far away with Willy Wonka or James or Mr. Fox or Danny or whatever else I am trying to cook up." He wrote with a pencil, not a typewriter. "I can't type," he explained.

Dahl was uncomfortable writing about himself, but he did write his autobiography in *The Wonderful Story of Henry Sugar.* (See the chapter entitled "Lucky Break.") Dahl undertook this work to answer the questions of his university students, who always wanted to know more about their famous teacher.

"I make good orange marmalade. I breed orchids and am a keen gardener. Vegetables are fun. Last year I grew 200 onions from seed and the average weight of each was 2 lbs."

Dahl was dismayed by changes in social mores and etiquette. "Forty years ago, a man would always give his seat to a woman in a bus or subway. Now, never. I still do it, hips or no hips."

Dahl felt that he drank too much (probably to escape his chronic pain). "Every day from 6 p.m. to 8 p.m. I drink whiskey."

SELECTED ADDITIONAL TITLES: Roald Dahl

Dahl, Roald. *The BFG.* Illustrated by Quentin Blake. Farrar, Straus & Giroux, 1982.

———. *Boy: Tales of Childhood.* Farrar, Straus & Giroux, 1982.

———. *Charlie and the Chocolate Factory.* Alfred A. Knopf, 1964.

———. *Charlie and the Great Glass Elevator.* Illustrated by Joseph Schindelman. Bantam Books, 1977.

———. *Danny the Champion of the World.* Illustrated by Jill Bennett. Alfred A. Knopf, 1975.

———. *The Enormous Crocodile.* Illustrated by Quentin Blake. Alfred A. Knopf, 1978.

———. *George's Marvelous Medicine.* Illustrated by Quentin Blake. Alfred A. Knopf, 1982.

———. *James and the Giant Peach.* Illustrated by Nancy Burkert. Alfred A. Knopf, 1961.

USING THE BOOK

Suggested Approach to the Book

Model Lesson

1. Discuss the autobiographical materials about Roald Dahl. How did poor health and multiple surgeries affect the author's life? How do people compensate for pain? Do you know anyone who suffers from chronic pain?

2. Show the cover to the class and ask what the book might be about. Why? Ask for information about foxes. Have students seen foxes in pictures or in zoos?

3. Why is the fox on the cover wearing clothes? Explain personification. List other stories that feature animals who dress and act like humans.

4. Explain the difference between fiction and nonfiction. Explain the difference between a novel and a picture book.

5. Introduce the characters in *Fantastic Mr. Fox*. After the introduction, have the students draw their impressions of the three main characters. This technique integrates auditory learning with an art lesson. Retain the papers until the unit is completed. After students have finished reading the book, ask them to compare and contrast their drawings with their impressions now. How accurate were their original impressions? Did anyone draw an outstanding illustration from the prereading?

6. To what animal is the fox related? (See *The Lincoln Writing Dictionary for Children*, Harcourt Brace Jovanovich, 1988.)

7. Why do most stories portray rats as bad and evil? How would you describe the rat in *Charlotte's Web* by E. B. White? How is he like the rat in *Fantastic Mr. Fox* (see pp. 50-51)?

Library Media Center Connections

1. Use the card catalog or online catalog to locate easy (E) books about animals. List the books by author, title, and subject.

2. Read to students several versions of Aesop's fables about foxes, including *The Fox and the Grapes*.

3. Farms and farmers have been the subjects of newspaper and television stories because of today's economic problems. Farming is a business and, unfortunately, many farmers have had financial trouble. Banks have auctioned farm properties to satisfy loan debts. What role does farming play in your area? How many farms are in your state and how much acreage do they encompass? What other information about agriculture, farming, farm products, and exports can be located through reference research using the *World Almanac*?

Computer Connections

1. Design a database form for the subject Animals. What information is important? Enter information into the database during language arts, social studies, and science study about animals. Make the information available to the library media center for use by other classes and students.

2. Add student evaluations to a database reading list about authors and their works.

Instructional Materials Connections

1. *Aesop's Fables.* Selected and illustrated by Michael Hague. Holt, Rinehart and Winston, 1985.

2. Aesop. *Aesop's Fables.* Illustrated by Heidi Holder. Viking Kestrel, 1981.

3. O'Mara, Lesley, comp. *Classic Animal Stories.* Illustrated by Angel Dominguez. Arcade, 1991.

4. Dahl, Roald. *Charlie and the Chocolate Factory.* Cassette. Caedmon, 1975.

5. Dahl, Roald. *Fantastic Mr. Fox.* Cassette. Caedmon, 1978.

6. Dahl, Roald. *James and the Giant Peach.* Cassette. Caedmon, 1977.

Theme Reading Connections: Foxes

Anders, Rebecca. *Ali the Desert Fox.* Translated by Dyan Hammarberg. Carolrhoda, 1977.

Berrill, Margaret. *Chanticleer.* Illustrated by Jane Bottomley. Raintree/Steck-Vaughn, 1986.

Braithwaite, Althea. *Foxes.* Crown, 1988.

Byars, Betsy. *Midnight Fox.* Illustrated by Ann Grifalconi. Penguin, 1968.

Chaucer, Geoffrey. *Chanticleer and the Fox.* Illustrated by Barbara Cooney. Crowell, 1982.

Chicken Little. Retold and illustrated by Steven Kellogg. Morrow, 1985.

Johnson, Fred. *The Foxes.* Illustrated by Lorin Thompson and Frank Fretz. National Wildlife, 1973.

LaBonte, Gail. *The Arctic Fox.* Illustrated. Dillon, 1989.

Lavine, Sigmund A. *Wonders of Foxes.* Putnam, 1986.

MacQuitty, Miranda. *Discovering Foxes.* Janet Caukins, ed. Franklin Watts, 1988.

Schnieper, Claudia. *On the Trail of the Fox.* Illustrated. Lerner, 1987.

Critical Thinking Question
Is it possible for the 29 "digger animals" that live in tunnels beneath the tree on the hill to live together in peace under Mr. Fox's plan? Does the story have a fairy tale ending?

Student Activities to Connect Literature and Curriculum

FINE ARTS

1. Construct a large classroom mural using descriptions from *Fantastic Mr. Fox.*

2. Design flannel-board figures and backdrops for retelling the story of Mr. Fox to second-graders.

3. Conduct a *Fantastic Mr. Fox* art contest. The art work that best depicts the personality of one of the story's characters wins.

4. Make Mr. Fox bean bags. Use muslin fabric and permanent marker pens. Styrofoam "peanuts" make good stuffing material and are less expensive and safer than beans.

LANGUAGE ARTS

1. Stage a trial based on the premise that the three farmers destroyed the foxes' home and attempted to murder Mr. Fox and his family. Mr. Fox has been accused of regularly stealing from the farms of Mr. Boggis, Mr. Bunce, and Mr. Bean.

2. Conduct a formal debate based on the following premise: It is appropriate to steal food when the food is used to keep people from starving to death (see p. 45).

WRITING PROMPT

1. Write a newspaper article describing the three farmers going on a fox hunt. Use the following headline:

> Crowds Gather at Crater to See Farmers Capture Fox

MATH

1. "The table was covered with chickens and ducks and geese and hams and bacon, and everyone was tucking in to the lovely food" (p. 58). How many of each item had Mr. Fox stolen? At the current rate of consumption, how much food would be needed each day for all the animals? Construct an illustrated picture graph that shows the needs for a day, a week, a month, and a year at the present rate of consumption. Would the animals need this much food every day? Why or why not?

2. Based on the information about consumption, students may compute the cost of the required food using prices in local stores.

SCIENCE

1. What ecological impact could digging out Mr. Fox have? Why?

2. Do you believe that the farmers could have smelled the way Roald Dahl described them? Why or why not?

3. "Bean never took a bath. He never even washed. As a result, his ear holes were clogged with all kinds of muck and wax and bits of chewing gum and dead flies and stuff like that. This made him deaf" (p. 15). What health practices should Bean be taught? How should people keep themselves clean and in good health? Design an illustrated chart with suggestions for good health care.

4. Provide information about the characteristics, habitat, food, and needs of the following "digger animals" that lived in tunnels under the old tree on the hillside:

   Foxes   Badgers   Moles   Rabbits   Weasels

SOCIAL STUDIES

1. Mr. Fox said, "We will make a little underground village, with streets and houses on each side—separate houses for badgers and moles and rabbits and weasels and foxes. And every day I will go shopping for you all. And every day we will eat like kings" (p. 61).

   Design the ideal village. Present a model layout, including streets, public buildings, private businesses, recreation facilities, and homes to meet the needs of current residents as well as future generations. What type of government would be appropriate? What emergency plan would be enacted if the sound of bulldozers were suddenly heard? What kind of education would be needed?

GEOGRAPHY

1. Using a United States or state map, color areas that provide a tolerable climate, enough trees, and adequate food supplies for this large animal family.

BEYOND THE BOOK

Guided Reading Connections Across a Learning Rainbow: Classic Animal Books

Aesop. *Aesop for Children.* Illustrated by Milo Winter. Macmillan, 1984. Reprint of 1919 ed.

De Brunhoff, Jean. *The Story of Babar.* Illustrated by Jean De Brunhoff. Random House, 1937.

Grahame, Kenneth. *The Wind in the Willows.* Illustrated by Ernest Shepard. Macmillan, 1983.

Lobel, Arnold. *Fables.* Illustrated by Arnold Lobel. Harper & Row, 1980.

Lofting, Hugh. *Doctor Doolittle.* Delacorte Press, 1988.

Milne, A. A. *When We Were Very Young.* Illustrated by Ernest Shepard. Dell, 1980.

Potter, Beatrix. *Tales from Beatrix Potter.* Illustrated by Beatrix Potter. Warne, 1986.

Sendak, Maurice. *Where the Wild Things Are.* Illustrated by Maurice Sendak. Harper & Row, 1984.

White, E. B. *Charlotte's Web.* Illustrated by Garth Williams. Harper & Row, 1952.

Enriching Connections

1. Prepare a reading list of the "100 Best Books Ever Read." Ask all students to list their 10 favorite titles. Present a graph of this information to the library media center specialist for consideration in acquisitions.

2. Establish classroom book clubs around the following genres or subjects:

Animals	Mysteries	Science Fiction	Sports
Fairy Tales	Biography	Picture Books	Nonfiction

FROM ANOTHER POINT OF VIEW

Hastings, Selina. *Reynard the Fox.* Illustrated by Graham Percy. Tambourine, 1991.

Parent-Student Connections

1. With the students, visit the public library to check out books for home reading. Read several classic children's books as a family activity. (See "Guided Reading Connections Across a Learning Rainbow" above.)

2. Discuss the difference between animals in nature, in a circus or zoo, and household pets. Is there any difference in how they eat or survive?

❀   ❀   ❀

RABBIT HILL

Author: Robert Lawson
Illustrator: Robert Lawson
Publisher: Viking, 1944
Suggested Grade Level: 4
Classification: Fiction
Literary Form: Illustrated novel
Theme: Good, old-fashioned values are desirable.

ABOUT THE BOOK

STUDENT OBJECTIVES:

1. From *Rabbit Hill* select 10 animal behaviors that are examples of personification.

2. Adapt and role play six scenes from the book.

3. Compare and contrast *Rabbit Hill* with the following novel about another famous rabbit: Howe, Deborah, and James Howe, *Bunnicula: A Rabbit Tale of Mystery*, Atheneum, 1979.

SYNOPSIS: Little Georgie, the rabbit, was the first to shout the news, "New folks coming into the big house!" There is much excitement when the new owners arrive and begin to put the house aright and replant the garden. All the animal families look forward to prosperous times like those they had in the past.

ABOUT THE AUTHOR-ILLUSTRATOR: Robert Lawson, 1882-1957.

Robert Lawson, like many children's book illustrators, did not plan to become one. Lawson wrote about himself, "I had always had a vague idea that I would like to build bridges, but since I had managed to avoid every form of mathematics, this career did not seem possible" (Press release from Viking Press). Eventually, he studied art at the New York School of Fine and Applied Arts and, because of his aptitude, became an etcher.

Lawson began illustrating books with a commission to illustrate Carl Sandburg's *Rootabaga Stories*. He then created enchanting illustrations for a children's book that would become a classic, *The Story of Ferdinand*. He became well known by writing and illustrating books that retell history through the viewpoint of animal pets of historic figures.

After Lawson's death, *The Horn Book,* a children's literature review magazine, assessed his work as follows: "It is *Rabbit Hill* for which Robert Lawson will be longest remembered, for no one who has read about Little Georgie, Uncle Analdas, and the other animals on the Hill is every likely to forget them or the joy with which they greeted the news that Little Georgie brought."

Robert Lawson was the first recipient of both the Caldecott and Newbery awards, which he won for *They Were Strong and Good* and *Rabbit Hill*, respectively.

SELECTED ADDITIONAL TITLES:

Atwater, Richard, and Florence Atwater. *Mr. Popper's Penguins.* Illustrated by Robert Lawson. Little, Brown, 1938.

Gray, Elizabeth. *Adam of the Road.* Illustrated by Robert Lawson. Viking, 1942.

Lawson, Robert. *Ben and Me.* Illustrated by Robert Lawson. Little, Brown, 1938.

———. *They Were Strong and Good.* Illustrated by Robert Lawson. Viking, 1940.

———. *The Tough Winter.* Illustrated by Robert Lawson. Penguin, 1979.

———. *Watchwords of Liberty: A Pageant of American Quotations.* Illustrated by Robert Lawson. Little, Brown, 1986.

Munro, Leaf. *Story of Ferdinand.* Illustrated by Robert Lawson. Penguin, 1977.

———. *Wee Gillis.* Illustrated by Robert Lawson. Viking, 1985.

USING THE BOOK

Suggested Approach to the Book

Model Lesson

1. Examine the illustrated double-page spread on the title page. List the animals shown. What is the natural habitat of each family? List other animals that could find a comfortable home on the hill.

2. Do the animals who are personified remain true to their animal traits? Why or why not?

3. What does an abandoned farm look like? Describe an abandoned house and a weed-filled garden. Why were these places left without inhabitants?

4. Predict what the family will be like. Design an illustrated family tree for the household.

5. What makes a novel substantially different from a picture book? What are the strengths of each?

6. How many books with animal themes have won the Caldecott or Newbery awards? List them. Is there a significant difference in the types of books receiving each award in the 1930s and 1940s and those receiving the awards since 1980?

7. What kind of soup can you make from cabbage and pea vines? What green vegetable could be substituted for the pea vines? List additional ingredients that would make this a delicious vegetable soup for a class lunch.

Library Media Center Connections

1. Research information about animals that live on a farm or in the nearby woods. What are their needs? Include information about their habitat, shelter, food, and any additional needs. Include the following:

Deer	Foxes	Racoons	Pheasants	Squirrels
Moles	Skunks	Rabbits	Field Mice	Woodchucks
Owls	Bluejays	Crows	Ferrets	

2. Develop a list of nonfiction books in the library media center that contain information about these animals.

Computer Connections

1. Write a letter from Little Georgie to his future grandchildren describing his trip to bring his Uncle Analdas home.

2. Compose a 150-word news story about Little Georgie's accident.

Instructional Materials Connections

1. *They Were Strong and Good.* Filmstrip. Weston Woods, Weston, CT 06880, n.d.

2. *Grow Lab: A Complete Guide to Gardening in the Classroom.* National Gardening Association, 1988.

3. Secure local garden catalogs that list plants, fruits, and vegetables. If possible, invite a city employee who is responsible for plantings in parks and other public areas, including street medians, to speak to the class.

Theme Reading Connections: Rabbits

Adams, Richard. *The Watership Down Film Picture Book.* Macmillan, 1978.

Adler, David. *Bunny Rabbit Rebus.* Illustrated by Madelaine Linden. Harper & Row, 1983.

DeJong, Meindert. *Shadrack.* Illustrated by Maurice Sendak. Harper & Row, 1953.

Harris, Joel. *Jump: The Adventures of Brer Rabbit.* Illustrated by Barry Moser. Harcourt Brace Jovanovich, 1986.

Howe, James. *The Celery Stalks at Midnight.* Illustrated by Leslie Morrill. Atheneum, 1983.

Williams, Margery. *The Velveteen Rabbit.* Illustrated by Michael Hague. Henry Holt, 1983.

Critical Thinking Question
Is *Rabbit Hill* a prototype of an animal utopia? Why or why not? Describe what you need to make your life trouble-free.

Student Activities to Connect Literature and Curriculum

FINE ARTS

1. Father says to Little Georgie before he embarks on a special journey, "Now recite your dogs" (p. 37). Design and illustrate a map of the area where the dogs live.

2. Little Georgie writes an upbeat song about "the new folks coming" (p. 45). Write additional stanzas. What makes a song popular? Why?

3. Draw the living room of Little Georgie's home. Include his family members. Furnish and decorate the room as seen from the viewpoint of a reader. Include a wall of family portraits.

4. Plan a special summer fair to be held at Rabbit Hill one year after the new people arrive. What kind of advertising will be used? Will an admission fee be necessary? How will the residents and community members be involved in the planning, the day's activities, and cleanup? Produce examples of the announcements, program, and menu.

LANGUAGE ARTS

1. Design a set of animal vocabulary flash cards. One side of each card will be a picture of the Rabbit Hill animal. The other side of the card will contain a selection of vocabulary words from *Rabbit Hill*. Vocabulary words may include the following:

Chapter 1: "New Folks Coming"

shiftless	optimistic	felicitous	bountiful
era	indulge	neglected	shingles
depressing	cub	successors	inconsiderate
sumac	bayberry	poison ivy	crabgrass
desolate	shutters	moth-eaten	waddling
squeezed	burrow	slops	hearsay
bluegrass	Kentucky	Connecticut	recollect
Renaissance	sensitive	leeward	offspring

Chapter 2: "Mother Worries"

occurrence	frenzy	unpleasantness	possibility
explosives	untimely	clogged	circumstance
probable	gout	destructive	discipline
pampered	indulgence	feline	fatal
community	gentlemen	distracted	beneficial
acute	edible	extant	invaluable

Chapter 3: "Little Georgie Sings a Song"

nourishing	chirped	warbled	shrilled
mocked	chuckled	scolded	conversation
carelessness	dawdling	recite	foolishness
boredom	prodigious	discouraged	pessimistic

Chapter 4: "Uncle Analdas"

larder	tedious	clamored	jangling
sleigh	cartons	matches	cornstarch
pepper	salt	ginger ale	napkins
pickles	vinegar	apricots	shelves

Chapter 5: "Porkey Sits Tight"

plowed	harrowed raked	generous	
cultivated	fertilized	furrows	buckwheat
adjacent	perilous	extreme	impatient
stubborn	resolved	habitation	ultimatum

Chapter 6: "Moving Vans"

creaked	swayed	rumbled	thicket
ventured	opportunity	character	possession
bulging	occupants	warming	dignified
generous	snares	separate	satisfied

Chapter 7: "Reading Rots the Mind"

movement	surveying	opportunity	gentility
stake	crowbar	hammer	implements
prospecting	ruckus	muskmelon	yawp
mongrel	residents	aristocrats	contradict
radishes	carrots	lettuce	raspberries

Chapter 8: "Willie's Bad Night"

recommends	haste	excitement	gasping
conscious	brilliant	shivering	enormous
delicious	scoundrel	odor	survey
wheeze	scurry	wreckage	poison

Chapter 9: "Dividing Night"

brilliant	rampage	ample	finicky
vegetarians	portion	debate	opinion
majority	privileges	democratic	wrangling
regulations	allotment	banishment	maturity

Chapter 10: "Clouds Over the Hill"

enthusiasm	congenial	outwitted	sorrow
spry	succulent	ecstasy	chatter
bedlam	twittered	incredulous	bandages
congratulations	terrible	waddled	hastened

Chapter 11: "Strain and Strife"

lethargy	housework	chatterers	pleasure
marred	trace	anxiety	irritability
vegetables	controversy	arguments	quarrels
scudding	incessant	suspicion	speculation

Chapter 12: "There Is Enough for All"

swish	sickle	beacon	purr
pool	grain	rakish	appearance
gulping	munching	procession	impressively
resumed	arbor	marauders	wonderment

2. After dividing the class into four teams, conduct a classroom spelling bee using vocabulary words from the book. A challenge may be added by asking for word definitions and usage as well as correct spelling. Correct answers equal two points; wrong answers subtract one point from the score.

3. In cooperative learning groups, prepare a *Rabbit Hill* rebus.

4. Debate in class the statement made by Tim McGrath's grandfather, "reading rots the mind" (p. 71).

5. Before assigning *Rabbit Hill*, explain to the class that one of the main characters is a young, active rabbit named Little Georgie. Using a transparency, cluster descriptions of rabbits using words suggested by the class. Have the class write a one-paragraph description of Little Georgie using as many of the words as appropriate. Repeat the process after reading *Rabbit Hill*, and compare students' work to the first clusters and paragraphs.

6. Write a short story about Rabbit Hill one year later. A celebration has been planned and will include a farm produce exhibit, craft projects, hot-air balloon rides for all, or anything else the students want to include.

WRITING PROMPT

1. Design a newspaper display advertisement for the following statement:

Rabbit Hill Land Plots Now Available for Occupancy

MATH

1. Present a bar graph or pie chart illustrating the number of members in each animal family that lives on Rabbit Hill.

2. Make up math word problems about the amount of food needed for each animal family per day, per week, per month, and per year. Present the answers in a visual format. Based on local prices, calculate the costs of each family's food.

SCIENCE

1. Read the advice given to Little Georgie on running (p. 38). Is this good advice for humans? Why or why not? Give a brief demonstration speech to your physical education class about how to get into good physical condition through exercise. What steps should be made when a person begins a new physical program? Would you rather exercise by running at a track or by going to a health club or school gym to work out on special equipment? Why?

2. Analyze the grasses and crops that the new people planted. What kind of soil additives or fertilizers should be used to insure maximum crop growth and harvest? Are there any insects or animals just as effective and ecologically safer than pesticides?

3. Select grass varieties, food crops, and flower species that are adaptable to your geographic area. Describe the weather and soil conditions that exist locally. If possible, visit a garden, farm, or nursery to see what plants are recommended for local conditions.

4. Present ideas for decorating a winter food tree in the woods for animals.

SOCIAL STUDIES

1. Submit and identify several quilt designs or samples that represent Rabbit Hill lifestyles, social customs, and regional culture. A quilt may be made by the class and auctioned off to purchase library media materials. Check with the site administrator regarding the auction.

2. Illustrate a Rabbit Hill alphabet book with the state flower, tree, and flag, as well as additional regional flowers, trees, and farm produce.

GEOGRAPHY

1. After reading the book, identify the setting of the story. Locate it on a map of the United States. Could Rabbit Hill have been given a setting other than the Danbury area? Why or why not?

2. Draw a plot plan for a neighborhood cooperative garden. What location would you recommend? Why? What prerequisites are necessary in addition to personal safety standards, fencing, water supply, and equipment?

BEYOND THE BOOK

Guided Reading Connections Across a Learning Rainbow: Gardening

Galland, Sarah. *Peter Rabbit's Gardening Book.* Illustrated by Beatrix Potter. Warne, 1983.

Bjork, Christina. *Linnea in Monet's Garden.* Illustrated by Lena Anderson. Raben and Sjogren, distributed by Farrar, Straus & Giroux, 1987.

Burnett, Frances. *The Secret Garden.* Illustrated by Michael Hague. Henry Holt, 1987.

Lofting, Hugh. *Dr. Doolittle's Garden.* Dell, 1988.

Enriching Connections

1. Make a vegetable soup for the class lunch. Give students a copy of the recipe.

2. Plan and prepare a special classroom good-health lunch.

3. Design a board game featuring *Rabbit Hill* animals and farm produce.

4. Bake Honey Bunnies bread (see fig. 4.1 on p. 102).

FROM ANOTHER POINT OF VIEW

Potter, Beatrix. *The Complete Adventures of Peter Rabbit.* Illustrated by Beatrix Potter. Warne, 1985.

Parent-Student Connections

1. Plant a small home garden devoted to flowers and food.

2. Supervise the preparation of one special meal to be planned and prepared by the student with parental participation, if necessary.

3. Recycle family refuse and garbage as part of a community plan.

HONEY BUNNIES
Makes 15 bunnies.

$4\frac{1}{2}$ - 5 cups ROBIN HOOD all-purpose flour
2 packages FLEISCHMANN'S Active Dry or RapidRise Yeast
1 teaspoon salt
$\frac{2}{3}$ cup CARNATION Evaporated Milk
$\frac{1}{2}$ cup each water, honey, and butter or margarine
2 eggs, at room temperature
BAKER'S JOY No Stick Baking Spray
DROMEDARY Raisins
Honey Glaze (recipe follows)

In large bowl, combine $1\frac{1}{2}$ cups flour, undissolved yeast, and salt. Heat evaporated milk, water, honey, and butter until very warm (120° - 130°F). Butter does not need to melt. Gradually add to dry ingredients; beat 2 minutes at medium speed of electric mixer, scraping bowl occasionally. Add eggs and $\frac{1}{2}$ cup flour. Beat 2 minutes at high speed, scraping bowl occasionally. With spoon, stir in enough additional flour to make stiff batter. Place in bowl coated with BAKER'S JOY, and spray top of dough with BAKER'S JOY. Cover tightly with plastic; refrigerate 2 to 24 hours.

On lightly floured surface, divide dough into 15 pieces. Roll each to 20-inch rope. To make bunnies, divide each rope into: 1 (12-inch), 1 (5-inch), and 3 (1-inch) strips. Coil 12-inch strip to make body; coil 5-inch strip to make head; shape remaining 3 strips into ears and tail and attach to body and head. Place bunnies on baking sheets coated with BAKER'S JOY. Cover; let rise in warm, draft-free place until doubled in size, about 20 to 25 minutes.

Bake at 375°F for 12 to 15 minutes or until golden brown. Remove to wire racks. Brush with Honey Glaze while warm. Decorate with raisins for eyes. Brush again with glaze before serving, if desired.

Honey Glaze: Stir $\frac{1}{2}$ cup honey with $\frac{1}{4}$ cup butter over low heat until melted.

Figure 4.1. Honey Bunnies recipe. Reprinted with permission of Fleischmann's Yeast, P.O. Box 7004, San Francisco, CA 94120-7004.

❀ ❀ ❀

Grade Five

OPINIONS

About First Americans Through Legends and Stories

INDIAN CHIEFS

Author: Russell Freedman
Illustrator: Russell Freedman et al.
Publisher: Holiday House, 1987
Suggested Grade Level: 5
Classification: Nonfiction
Literary Form: Photo essay
Theme: American Indians were unfairly chased from their vast, open lands by white settlers and
   European emigrants.

ABOUT THE BOOK

STUDENT OBJECTIVES:

1. Recognize that Native Americans have been poorly treated by the United States government.

2. Propose a plan to restructure Indian reservations in size and to improve the quality of life
    on the reservations.

3. Develop a storytelling program featuring Indian literature for the library media center.

SYNOPSIS: Russell Freedman presents the story of American Indians through the biographies of
   six chiefs: Red Cloud, Satanta, Quanah Parker, Washakie, Joseph, and Sitting Bull.

ABOUT THE AUTHOR: Russell Freedman, 1929- .
   Russell Freedman's parents worked with authors and books. His father was a sales representative
for a book publisher and his mother sold books in a store. Freedman always knew when an author
was coming to dinner because his mother brought home a leg of lamb to be baked and served with
mint jelly!
   Freedman remembers writing comic strips, mysteries, and poetry as a student. Later, he became
a publicity writer for *Kraft Television Theater, Father Knows Best,* and other network television
programs. His first book was *Teenagers Who Made History* (no longer in print), which he wrote after

he learned that a blind 16-year-old, David Abraham, invented the Braille typewriter and that another blind 16-year-old, Louis Braille of France, revised the original 12-dot system to the present 6-dot Braille system. Freedman received the 1988 Newbery award for *Lincoln: A Photobiography* (Clarion Books, 1987) and a 1992 Newbery Honor award for *The Wright Brothers: How They Invented the Airplane* (Holiday House, 1991).

"One of the best things about my work is the opportunity it gives me to explore subjects that, for some reason, excite my curiosity, my enthusiasm, or my concern. Pick a subject, a good subject, and you're sure to find kids who are interested in it."

The author views himself as a storyteller, explaining, "Whatever my subject, I always feel that I have a story to tell that is worth telling. I want to tell it as clearly and simply and effectively as I can, in a way that will stretch the reader's imagination and make that reader care" (Holtze, Sally Holmes, *Sixth Book of Junior Authors and Illustrators,* H. W. Wilson, 1989, pp. 89-91).

SELECTED ADDITIONAL TITLES:

Freedman, Russell. *Animal Superstars: Biggest, Strongest, Fastest, Smartest.* Illustrated. Prentice Hall, 1984.

————. *Buffalo Hunt.* Illustrated with oil paintings. Holiday House, 1988.

————. *Can Bears Predict Earthquakes? Unsolved Mysteries of Animal Behavior.* Illustrated. Prentice Hall, 1982.

————. *Children of the Wild West.* Illustrated. Clarion Books, 1983.

————. *Cowboys of the Wild West.* Illustrated. Clarion Books, 1985.

————. *Immigrant Kids.* Illustrated. Dutton, 1980.

————. *An Indian Winter.* Illustrated by Karl Bodmer. Holiday House, 1992.

————. *Lincoln: A Photobiography.* Illustrated. Clarion Books, 1987.

————. *The Wright Brothers: How They Invented the Airplane.* Photographs by Wilbur and Orville Wright. Holiday House, 1991.

USING THE BOOK

Suggested Approach to the Book

Model Lesson

1. Read the introduction to "War Chiefs and Peace Chiefs." List five facts about American Indian chiefs that you did not know until reading the introduction.

2. What position did the United States government take in regard to Indian lands? Why are representatives of the Sioux tribe shown in a photograph with President Andrew Johnson?

3. "The whites usually applied the word *chief* to all Indian leaders, but Indian society was not that simple." Why? How did a chief become a tribal leader?

4. Examine the photographs of each Indian leader before reading the chapter. Cluster your thoughts about each chief's personality, based on what you see in the picture. Review the clusters after reading the chapter. Did the chief's actions reflect what you thought about his personality, based on his photograph? Does a picture tell a thousand words?

Red Cloud

1. Locate the Powder River area on the classroom floor map. What was Red Cloud's philosophy regarding Indian lands and white lands? How did Red Cloud plan to punish whites again? How did Red Cloud receive his name?

2. Why did the cholera epidemic strike the Indians? Could the same disaster befall explorers of the solar system or ocean today?

3. Identify the Bozeman Trail.

4. What did Red Cloud fear for his tribe? Why was Red Cloud said to be the first and last Indian leader in the West to win a war with the United States? Why was Red Cloud taken on a tour of the weapons arsenal in Washington, D.C.? How did Red Cloud compare the fate of his tribe with the future of the settlers?

Satanta

1. How did the government physician describe Chief Satanta's hospitality?

2. Describe the peace meeting at Medicine Lodge Creek. What kind of gifts were given to the Indians at the Medicine Lodge Creek meetings? Satanta considered himself to be the white man's friend. How did he react at the peace meeting? If you were at the meeting, what would your reaction have been?

3. How did Satanta use his French horn? Describe Satanta's shield, a gift from a famous warrior, Black Horse. What happened to Black Horse? Was the shield magic?

4. What was the fate of Indian leaders Satanta, Satank, and Big Tree at the hands of the United States government? How did the commissioner of Indian affairs try to help Satanta and Big Tree?

5. How was Satanta tortured? What decision would you have made about Satanta if you had been in power?

Quanah Parker

1. Where is the Texas panhandle?

2. Why was Quanah Parker called a half-breed? Why is the term derogatory? Who was Cynthia Ann Parker? What happened to her?

3. Why did buffalo hunters become enemies of the Plains Indians? How many buffalo were killed by white hunters between 1872 and 1874?

4. Describe the Indian defeat at Adobe Wells.

5. Describe the changes in the lifestyle of Quanah Parker when he became a rancher. What made Quanah Parker become a man of peace?

6. The military gave the Comanche permission to hunt buffalo under government supervision in the fall. What did the Indians find on the plains? Why?

Washakie

1. Describe the Shoshoni meeting with the fur trappers. Why did the Shoshoni depend on trappers and traders?

2. How did Pina Quanah become a tribal leader? What is the meaning of the tribal name, Washakie?

3. What occupation did the United States government demand that the Indians pursue? What kind of difficulties did Indians encounter on reservations?

4. Why did the Shoshoni resent sharing their land with an enemy tribe, the Arapaho?

5. What gift did President Andrew Johnson present to Washakie?

6. How did Washakie visualize his life after death?

Joseph

1. When the dying Chief Joseph described his country to his son, Joseph, did he refer to the United States or his Indian country?

2. What does the name Nez Perce mean? What did General Oliver Otis Howard say about removing the Nez Perce tribe to a new reservation? What caused war to come to Joseph and his tribe?

3. Describe the Battle of White Bird Canyon.

4. Why could the Nez Perce tribe claim that they had never tortured prisoners or scalped the dead?

5. What happened to the Indians after the Big Hole battle? Why did Chief Joseph ultimately have to surrender to Colonel Nelson Miles and General Oliver Otis Howard? What was the direct cause of the Indian defeat?

Sitting Bull

1. Describe the childhood of Hunk-es-ni, or Slow.

2. What is a coup stick? How was it used?

3. During battle, how could a chief be identified?

4. What did Sitting Bull tell the reservation Indians about life on a reservation?

5. What is the reputation of George Armstrong Custer? Why is the Battle of Little Bighorn known as Custer's last stand?

6. What was the relationship of Sitting Bull and circus man Buffalo Bill?

7. Why did the Indians lose more than land when they lived on a reservation?

Library Media Center Connections

1. Cooperative learning groups will present an oral report with visual aids on one of the following:

Red Cloud of the Oglala Sioux	Washakie of the Shoshoni
Satanta of the Kiowa	Joseph of the Nez Perce
Quanah Parker of the Comanche	Sitting Bull of the Hunkpapa Sioux

Computer Connections

1. Input information about the six Indian tribes and their chiefs into the class database.

2. Using a word processing program, write a report to the president of the United States recommending possible solutions to the problem of stolen Indian lands. What land could be given to the Indians of your state? Explain how you would provide better education for Indian children.

Instructional Materials Connections

1. *America's Fascinating Indian Heritage.* Reader's Digest, 1991.

2. Artman, John. *Indians: An Activity Book.* Good Apple, 1981.

3. Aten, Jerry. *Americans, Too!* Good Apple, 1982.

4. Bernstein, Bonnie, and Leigh Blair. *Native American Crafts Workshop.* Fearon, 1982.

5. *Children's Atlas of Native Americans.* Rand McNally, 1992.

6. Hook, Jason. *American Indian Warrior Chiefs: Tecumseh, Crazy Horse, Chief Joseph, and Geronimo.* Firebird, 1990.

7. Kindle, Patrick, and Susan Finney. *American Indians.* Illustrated by Ardia Mckay. Good Apple, 1985.

8. Ney, Marian Wallace. *Indian America: A Geography of North American Indians.* Illustrated by Libby Lambert. Cherokee, 1990.

Theme Reading Connections: Indians of North America—Government Relations

Bealer, Alex. *Only the Name Remains: The Cherokees and the Trail of Tears.* Illustrated by William S. Rock. Little, Brown, 1972.

Kelly, Lawrence. *Federal Indian Policy.* Chelsea, 1989.

Marrin, Albert. *Clouds in the West: Indians and Cavalrymen, 1860-1890.* Macmillan, 1984.

> Critical Thinking Question
> What legislation should the United States government have enacted to protect Indian lands? Can any help be given to Indians today?

Student Activities to Connect Literature and Curriculum

FINE ARTS

1. Create a scale model of Satanta's flaming red tipi.

2. Tell the story of your life using Indian symbols on a simulated piece of elk skin.

LANGUAGE ARTS

1. Publish an issue of a classroom newsletter, *The Indian Times,* with special pages on the six Indian chiefs.

2. Imagine that you are Cynthia Ann Parker. Write a letter to President Abraham Lincoln, asking to be returned, along with your child, to your husband's tribe.

3. Prepare a radio news report about the Shoshoni, with Chief Washakie, meeting with fur trappers to sell beaver pelts.

WRITING PROMPT

1. Write a photo feature story for *Newsweek* magazine under the following headline:

> For all Indians, their struggles were a trail of tears.

MATH

1. Design a Westward Ho game.

   What will the game board look like?

   What are the rules and the object of the game?

   What kind of markers are appropriate?

   How will Western dollars be spent?

2. Buffalo Math

> "The buffalo was the biggest animal on the plains ... stood six feet tall at the humped shoulders and weighed a ton or more.... While buffalo were some-what dim-sighted, they could hear the faintest sounds and smell enemies from three miles away" (Freedman, Russell, *Buffalo Hunt*, Holiday House, 1988, p. 12).

Compare the height of a buffalo with the height of each student in the class. What is the ratio of each student's height to that of a buffalo?

> "At one time, perhaps 60 or 70 million buffalo roamed the plains. By the early 1880s, the endless herds had been wiped out. Only a few hundred wild buffalo were still hiding out in remote mountain valleys" (Freedman, Russell, *Buffalo Hunt*, Holiday House, 1988, p. 49).

Present this information in a pictorial graph.

Look at the photograph on page 47 of *Indian Chiefs*. There are about 40,000 hides in the pile. (Note: The Los Angeles County Museum of Natural History taxidermist, Tim Bovard, provided the following information about buffalo hides.)

Dried hides of a buffalo cow weigh about 35 pounds; buffalo bull hides weigh in at 40-50 pounds each. Hides that are green, or not yet cleaned and dried, are 60-75 percent heavier. The weight also varies depending on the season in which the animal is hunted. An animal's fur has a seasonal differential of 10-20 percent, with the winter coat being heaviest.

Using this information, design a math quiz of five word problems. Students should exchange questions with other students several times. Through a process of elimination, declare a student Math Master for math excellence. This may be a cooperative learning project or team challenges at the chalk board.

SCIENCE

1. Indians helped the Pilgrims plant corn and other crops to provide food for survival. What did they use to fertilize the soil? This product is still used today, but in liquid form. What plants use this fertilizer today?

2. Indians did not need or have access to pesticides. Today there is controversy about using pesticides. Why? Could Indians have been the first organic farmers? Could today's farmers return to the Indian methods? What type of fruits and vegetables can be grown in a home garden?

3. List the fruits and vegetables the Indians grew. Which grew underground? Which plants produced a harvest above the ground? Using the newly revised government-approved nutrition standards of five food groups, decide what a well-rounded, nutritious food plan for the Indians would have been.

SOCIAL STUDIES

1. Look at the map of the West in 1840 on page 7 of *Indian Chiefs*. What major Indian tribes are identified on the map? What areas of the map became states? What were the states named and when were they admitted to the Union?

GEOGRAPHY

1. Reproduce the 1840 map of the West (p. 7) as a classroom floor map. Add color to identify areas occupied by various tribes and symbols to identify special places including rivers. Draw in the Oregon and Santa Fe trails.

2. Make a set of colored transparencies recreating the map of the West in 1840 and an overlay map of the United States today. Do not add tribal information, symbols, or Oregon and Santa Fe trails. Student cooperative learning groups may challenge other groups to play I.D. Map. Points are awarded for correct answers to mapping questions; incorrect answers result in losing points.

BEYOND THE BOOK

Guided Reading Connections Across a Learning Rainbow: Indian Biographies

Accorsi, William. *My Name Is Pocahontas.* Holiday House, 1992.

Brown, Marion Marsh. *Sacagawea: Indian Interpreter to Lewis and Clark.* People of Distinction series. Childrens Press, 1988.

———. *Susette La Flesche.* People of Distinction series. Childrens Press, 1992.

Bulla, Clyde R. *Squanto, Friend of the Pilgrims.* Illustrated by Peter Burchard. Harper & Row, 1954.

Capps, Benjamin. *The Great Chiefs.* Silver Burdett, 1975.

D'Aulaire, Ingri, and Edgar D'Aulaire. *Pocahontas.* Doubleday, 1985.

Kvasnicka, Robert M. *Hole-in-the-Day.* American Indian Stories series. Raintree/Steck-Vaughn, 1989.

Lowe, Felix C. *John Ross.* American Indian Stories series. Raintree/Steck-Vaughn, 1990.

McCague, James. *Tecumseh: Shawnee Warrior-Statesman.* Illustrated by Victor Dowd. Garrard, 1970.

McGovern, Ann. *The Defenders.* Scholastic, 1987.

Simon, Charnan. *Wilma P. Mankiller, Chief of the Cherokee.* Childrens Press, 1992.

Wilkie, Katherine E. *Pocahontas: Indian Princess.* Garrard, 1969.

Enriching Connections

1. Assemble a Portrait Gallery of First Americans featuring famous Indian men and women. Art styles and art materials selected by students will provide diverse viewpoints.

FROM ANOTHER POINT OF VIEW

Liptak, Karen. *North American Indian Tribal Chiefs.* Franklin Watts, 1992.

Parent-Student Connections

1. Discuss your family history and diversity. Where did your ancestors live? Were they European immigrants? Did they come from the Pacific Rim? Help your child to develop a family tree. Information about a family's past can be lost and should be shared with the family as its own great story.

❀   ❀   ❀

WATER SKY

Author: Jean Craighead George
Illustrator: Jean Craighead George
Publisher: Harper & Row, 1987
Suggested Grade Level: 5
Classification: Fiction
Literary Form: Novel
Theme: A microscopic examination of Eskimo heritage and culture, with focus on conservation.

ABOUT THE BOOK

STUDENT OBJECTIVES:

1. Differentiate between legend and fact.

2. Analyze the current conservation plan for the Alaskan bowhead whale and recommend additional conservation measures.

3. Write a new Yankee whaler song.

SYNOPSIS: Lincoln Noah Stonewright visits Alaska to stay with a whaler, as his father had done years before. Lincoln's mission is to find his Uncle Jack, who had disappeared two years earlier while working to save the Alaskan bowhead whale.

ABOUT THE AUTHOR-ILLUSTRATOR: Jean Craighead George, 1919- .

Jean Craighead George was born in Washington, D.C. As she grew up, she spent her summers outdoors, studying wildlife. Her experiences as a newspaper reporter, artist, and naturalist strengthened her knowledge of science and nature. She has received two prestigious awards for her work: the 1972 Newbery medal for *Julie of the Wolves,* and a 1959 Newbery Honor medal for *My Side of the Mountain.*

Several of George's works portray the need for ecological balance. Her characters escape from their normal lives but always return home with a greater understanding of nature and of themselves. Her characters feel great pain when they realize that the old way is doomed and, by necessity, time will bring change. She introduced the study of ecology to her readers and makes a strong plea for maintaining the balance of nature. Jean Craighead George may be considered a visionary for her keen insight into the need to preserve natural resources.

George's *Water Sky* characters can be compared to the characters in Elaine Konigsburg's *From the Mixed-Up Files of Mrs. Basil E. Frankweiler* (Macmillan, 1967). The characters leave home, grow, and must return to the modern world. They are changed by their experiences.

SELECTED ADDITIONAL TITLES:

George, Jean Craighead. *The Cry of the Crow.* Harper & Row, 1980.

————. *Julie of the Wolves.* Illustrated by John Schoenherr. Harper & Row, 1972.

————. *My Side of the Mountain.* Dutton, 1975.

————. *One Day in the Alpine Tundra.* Illustrated by Walter Gaffney-Kessel. Thomas Y. Crowell, 1984.

————. *One Day in the Desert.* Illustrated by Fred Brenner. Thomas Y. Crowell, 1983.

————. *One Day in the Prairie.* Illustrated by Bob Marstall. Thomas Y. Crowell, 1986.

————. *River Rats, Inc.* Dutton, 1979.

————. *Who Really Killed Cock Robin?* Dutton, 1971.

USING THE BOOK

Suggested Approach to the Book

Model Lesson

1. Describe the clothing that Kusiq was wearing when he met Lincoln at the airport. Where had Lincoln seen a photograph of Eskimos?

2. Vincent Ologak was once mayor of Barrow, Alaska. What is the land area of Barrow? Is there any other area in the United States that compares in size?

3. Describe a Ski-Doo snow vehicle. While driving through Barrow, what buildings did Kusiq point out to Lincoln? Do the same buildings exist in your hometown? How would they differ from Barrow's? Find out when your school was constructed and how much it cost. How does the cost of the school in Barrow ($73 million) compare to the cost of your school?

4. What is the difference between a qanitchaq and an iglu? What four observations did Lincoln make to himself about the iglu? Who is a tanik? If a tanik is considered to be a friend, what language is spoken?

5. What kind of relationship did Uncle Jack and Lincoln have? Do you have a special relationship with another family member?

6. Explain why Kusiq said that "the whale is our hardware store." What kind of clothing was Lincoln outfitted in for whaling.

7. Why was Lincoln not told that his great-great-grandmother Nora was an Eskimo?

8. What is a water sky? Describe *leads* as the term is used by the Eskimo.

9. What happened to the Yankee whaling ships that were caught in Alaskan waters during the winter? Have you seen any television footage of a ship stranded in Alaska? On the news you may see Coast Guard cutters trying to help a ship escape an ice trap. Why did the Yankee whalers leave Alaska?

Library Media Center Connections

1. Annie told the story of the beginning of the world according to her Eskimo culture. "A wolf had two children, a little girl and a little boy, and these two people multiplied and increased." Arrange for the librarian to present a similar myth, the founding of Rome by the wolf brothers Romulus and Remus.

2. Explain Seward's Folly.

3. What is the world-famous Iditarod Trail Sled Dog Race?

Computer Connections

1. Begin a class database about the 78 currently recognized species of cetaceans. Include the following information:

Classification	Description
Food and Feeding	Habitat

Life History   Behavior

Population   Migration

Instructional Materials Connections

1. *America's Fascinating Indian Heritage.* Reader's Digest, 1991.

2. Artman, John. *Indians: An Activity Book.* Good Apple, 1981.

3. Aten, Jerry. *Americans, Too!* Good Apple, 1982.

4. Bernstein, Bonnie, and Leigh Blair. *Native American Crafts Workshop.* Fearon, 1982.

5. Center for Marine Conservation. *The Ocean Book.* John Wiley, 1989.

6. *Children's Atlas of Native Americans.* Rand McNally, 1992.

7. Kindle, Patrick, and Susan Finney. *American Indians.* Illustrated by Ardia Mckay. Good Apple, 1985.

8. *The Magnificent Whales.* Video. Smithsonian, 1988.

9. Martin, Dr. Anthony R. *Whales and Dolphins.* Portland House, 1990.

10. *Visit with Jean Craighead George.* Video. Dutton, 1992.

11. Waldman, Carl. *Encyclopedia of Native American Tribes.* Illustrated by Molly Braun. Facts on File, 1987.

12. The following are sources of a variety of materials:

    Center for Marine Conservation, 1725 DeSales St., Suite 500. Washington, DC 20036. Regional offices are in Texas, Florida, Virginia, and California.

    Totem Bight State Park. North Tongass Hwy., 10 miles north of Ketchikan, AK 99901.

    Alaskaland Theme Park. Airport and Peger Roads, Fairbanks, AK 99709.

13. A miniature polar-bear puzzle with 14 three-dimensional pieces, or a 10-piece whale family with 5 adults and 5 calves, are available from The Paragon, 89 Tom Harvey Rd., Westerly, RI 02891.

14. The Ecology Kit is a practical exploration of "home activities that can help kids understand and monitor our impact on the world around us." This science kit is one in a series resulting from an Alliance for Science partnership between the Museum of Science (Science Park, Boston, MA 02114) and the Nature Company (750 Hearst Ave., Berkeley, CA 94710).

Theme Reading Connections: Whales

Albert, Burton. *Sharks and Whales.* Illustrated by Pamela Johnson. Putnam, 1989.

Behrens, June. *Whales of the World.* Childrens Press, 1987.

Bender, Lionel. *Whales.* Franklin Watts, 1988.

Bright, Michael. *Saving the Whale.* Franklin Watts, 1987.

Bunting, Eve. *The Sea World Book of Whales.* Harcourt Brace Jovanovich, 1987.

Crump, Donald J., ed. *Whales.* 2 vols. National Geographic, 1990.

Fichter, George. *Whales.* Golden Press, 1990.

Gibbons, Gail. *Whales.* Holiday House, 1991.

Graham, Ada, and Frank Graham. *Whale Watch: An Audubon Reader.* Illustrated by D. D. Tyler. Dell, 1983.

Johnson, Gary. *Whale Song.* Illustrated by Ed Young. Sandcastle, 1992.

Patent, Dorothy. *All about Whales.* Holiday House, 1987.

———. *Whales: Giants of the Deep.* Holiday House, 1984.

Simon, Seymour. *Whales.* Harper & Row, 1989.

Stein, R. Conrad. *The Story of the New England Whalers.* Childrens Press, 1982.

Strachan, Elizabeth. *A Closer Look at Whales and Dolphins.* Franklin Watts, 1986.

Whitfield, Phillip. *Oceans.* Strange and Amazing Worlds series. Marshall Cavendish, 1991.

Critical Thinking Question
"The Eskimo has survived by sharing.... Sharing is born within us as the tusks are born in the walrus. We cannot share chicken and hamburger with all the people. It takes a whale to share" (see p. 47 of *Water Sky*). Do you agree or disagree with this statement? Why? Is there anything people can share today?

Student Activities to Connect Literature and Curriculum

FINE ARTS

1. The bowhead whale was classified and given its name in 1758; the Latin name, *Balaena mysticetus,* translates literally as "moustached sea monster." Before beginning the book, share this information with students and ask them to draw their vision of a bowhead whale. Because of the harsh environment in which the bowhead whale lives, none have survived in captivity.

2. Create a white-on-white view of the town of Barrow, Alaska, as described by Lincoln.

3. Construct an icescape model of the lead in which Nukik was found.

4. Why are Yankee whaler songs described as root music?

LANGUAGE ARTS

1. Design an information brochure describing Alaskan whaling camps.

2. Publish a class newsletter, *The Tundra Times,* using information from *Water Sky* and other reference sources.

WRITING PROMPT

1. Write a human-interest story under the following headline:

> The Eskimo and the Whale Are One

MATH

1. How long would it take to travel by car, at an average speed of 50 miles per hour, from Boston to Anchorage? in winter? in summer? What would be the route and how many miles would be driven? How many air miles are between Boston and Anchorage? What route would you have to fly and how long would the flight take?

2. How did whalers use flat sticks to determine the amount of ice shift or drift? What other measuring devices could be used today? Explain the equipment used in the science camp, including hydrophones, computers, intercom radios, and theodolites.

3. How far is Barrow from the North Pole?

SCIENCE

1. Using a flashlight and a globe, explain why there is a two-and-a-half-month period in Alaska when the sun never sets. What is it like during the winter?

2. Develop a *Whales Are Different* card-game quiz. Use information such as "A big whale needs to eat two tons of brit and krill a day." Have cooperative learning groups construct questions. Develop a gameboard with squares or whale shapes. Have students roll a die and answer questions from cards. A correct answer allows the student to advance his or her game token.

3. Identify the following terms:

Ukpik	High Pressure	Baleen	Iceberg
Icicle	Plankton	Blowhole	Umiak
Siku	Water Sky	Beluga Whales	AiviQ
Bowhead Whales	Guillemot	Puktaaq	Qanitchaq

4. Explain the migration waves of bowhead whales.

5. Using silhouettes of various whale species, identify baleen whales and toothed whales on a flannel board.

6. Construct a large, multisectional mural that identifies sea life at various water temperatures.

7. If you live in an earthquake area, compare an earthquake with the description of pack ice in the following statement: "Although siku had crashed into the sharp-fast ice a mile from Lincoln and Little Owl, the tremor was only now reading the spot where they stood. The

shock waves from the collision were powerful and loud. Lincoln thought he had been thrown off the earth" (see p. 123).

SOCIAL STUDIES

1. Lincoln was the victim of racial abuse when Tigluk said, "Taniks get pushed off the ice.... Watch your step" (see p. 62). Explain racial abuse. Why does it happen? Who is responsible? How can changes be made?

2. "Survival makes the Eskimo the scientists of the north all right. We have to know these things to stay alive" (p. 119). What are examples of this specialized Eskimo knowledge?

GEOGRAPHY

1. Identify the latitude and longitude of the following places:

   Boston, Massachusetts

   Anchorage, Alaska

   Barrow, Alaska

   How many aerial miles are there between each city?

2. Using a map transparency of the area, trace the migration of the bowhead whale from the Bering Sea to Barrow, Alaska. How many miles do they swim?

BEYOND THE BOOK

Guided Reading Connections Across a Learning Rainbow: Eskimos

Aigner, Jean S. *The Eskimo: Arctic.* Chelsea, 1989.

Alexander, Bryan, and Cherry Alexander. *An Eskimo Family.* Lerner, 1985.

Cheney, Cora. *Alaska: Indians, Eskimos, Russians and the Rest.* Putnam, 1980.

Cohlene, Terri. *Ka-Ha-Si and the Loon.* Illustrated by Charles Reasoner. Rourke, 1990.

Gill, Shelley. *The Alaska Mother Goose.* Illustrated by Shannon Cartwright. Paws IV, 1987.

———. *Alaska's Three Bears.* Illustrated by Shelley Gill. Paws IV, 1991.

———. *Kiana's Iditarod.* Illustrated by Shannon Cartwright. Paws IV, 1984.

———. *Mammoth Magic.* Illustrated by Shannon Cartwright. Paws IV, 1986.

———. *Thunderfeet, Alaska's Dinosaurs and Other Prehistoric Critters.* Illustrated by Shannon Cartwright. Paws IV, 1988.

Hahn, Elizabeth. *The Inuit.* Illustrated by Luciano Lazzarino. Native American People series. Rourke, 1990.

Kusugak, Michael Arvaarluk. *Baseball Bats for Christmas.* Illustrated by Vladyana Krykorka. Annick, 1990.

Osinki, Alice. *The Eskimo.* Childrens Press, 1985.

Shemie, Bonnie. *Houses of Snow, Skin and Bone.* Illustrated by Bonnie Shemie. Tundra, 1989.

Smith, J. H. *Eskimos: The Inuit of the Arctic.* Rourke, 1987.

Enriching Connections

1. Make scale-model iglus to simulate snow, animal, and sod housing.

2. Eskimos made black wool blankets decorated with white button designs as a native craft. Create a miniature Eskimo blanket design using black felt squares and pearl buttons.

3. Create a chart with an illustrated bowhead whale in the center. Label the various whale parts used by the Eskimos.

FROM ANOTHER POINT OF VIEW

Paulsen, Gary. *Dogsong.* Bradbury Press, 1985.

Parent-Student Connections

1. Read aloud a book about Alaskan history or the life of Eskimos today.

❀ ❀ ❀

HER SEVEN BROTHERS
&
QUILLWORKER—A Cheyenne Legend

(Note: I prefer to correlate various versions of the same story in an integrated classroom unit. This practice helps students learn to identify and distinguish the dominant characteristics of various writers' and illustrators' works. Many school district master plans reflect new curriculum strategies that bridge social studies, language arts, and fine arts. "Student Activities to Connect Literature and Curriculum" on page 122 is a cooperative learning extension that can be used with both book titles.)

HER SEVEN BROTHERS

Author: Paul Goble
Illustrator: Paul Goble
Publisher: Bradbury Press, 1988
Suggested Grade Level: 5
Classification: American Indian mythology
Literary Form: Picture book
Theme: Long ago, people sought explanations for natural phenomena, such as the sun, moon, and stars, through myths, legends, and fairy tales.

ABOUT THE BOOK

STUDENT OBJECTIVES:

1. Evaluate and summarize 25 Indian myths and legends in print and nonprint format for inclusion in a classroom and library media center study center.

2. Role play the part of the tribe storyteller, as described by Paul Goble, and present a myth or legend to the class.

3. Work in cooperative learning groups to produce a video, a read-along story cassette, or an art project on the following subjects:

Indian Culture	Clothing	Housing
Arts and Crafts	Medicine Men	Fort Laramie
Reservations	General Custer	

SYNOPSIS: A young Cheyenne girl was taught how to decorate clothing with porcupine quills. As she grew up, she became more and more skilled. She made shirts and moccasins for seven brothers whom she had not met and who lived far away. She made a smaller set for the youngest of the seven. The girl left her tribe to find the seven brothers. The myth's extraordinary ending tells how the Big Dipper came to be.

ABOUT THE AUTHOR-ILLUSTRATOR: Paul Goble, 1933- .

Paul Goble is a celebrated illustrator and storyteller. He began life in Surrey, England, where his mother read to him about American Indians. After finishing art studies in England, Goble visited the United States many times. Eventually, he became a resident of the Black Hills of South Dakota.

Goble received national praise and recognition in 1978, when he won the Caldecott award for *The Girl Who Loved Wild Horses*. The book is "a synthesis of many legends." It was written, Goble stated, as "an attempt to express and paint what I believe to be the Native American rapport with nature" (Stott, John C., *Children's Literature from A to Z: A Guide for Parents and Teachers*, McGraw-Hill, 1984). Goble is also an adopted member of the Yakima and Ogalala tribes.

SELECTED ADDITIONAL TITLES:

Goble, Paul. *Buffalo Woman.* Illustrated by Paul Goble. Bradbury Press, 1984.

————. *Death of the Iron Horse.* Illustrated by Paul Goble. Bradbury Press, 1987.

————. *The Gift of the Sacred Dog.* Illustrated by Paul Goble. Bradbury Press, 1984.

————. *The Girl Who Loved Wild Horses.* Illustrated by Paul Goble. Bradbury Press, 1978.

————. *Iktomi and the Boulder: A Plains Indian Story.* Illustrated by Paul Goble. Orchard, 1988.

————. *Star Boy.* Illustrated by Paul Goble. Bradbury Press, 1983.

Goble, Paul, and Dorothy Goble. *Custer's Last Battle.* Illustrated by Paul Goble. Pantheon Books, 1969.

————. *Lone Bull's Horse Raid.* Illustrated by Paul Goble. Bradbury Press, 1973.

USING THE BOOK

Suggested Approach to the Book

Model Lesson

1. Look at the title page. What do you see? What kind of story do you think will be told?

2. Outline the author's statement. Why does he give this information to readers at the beginning of the book? Examine the dates of the reference materials Goble used. What did you find out about his sources? What do the publication dates suggest? Why?

3. Why did Native Americans like to tell stories after dark?

4. Why does the illustrator use pairs of animals? Page through the book and identify the animals used in the illustrations.

5. Explain why the porcupine is important in Indian mythology. Why does he have rings around his body? Describe how dogs are used to carry packets.

6. Why does the girl's mother offer to accompany her for part of the trip? What kind of welcome does the girl receive? What does she do while the six brothers are away?

7. When did you sense that the girl was in extreme danger? How did Goble relate that information to the reader?

Library Media Center Connections

1. Use the library media center catalog to learn what other books or materials about American Indians are available. Compile a list by Dewey number. What other sources of materials are available?

2. Arrange for the class to watch videos, film strips, or electronic-media materials that support the Indian study unit.

3. What books are available for research about the Cheyenne? Are other appropriate materials that contribute information about Indians available?

Computer Connections

1. Using a word processor, write a letter to a pen pal in another class or school. In the letter, retell the Cheyenne myth, *Her Seven Brothers.*

Instructional Materials Connections

1. *America's Fascinating Indian Heritage.* Reader's Digest, 1991.

2. Artman, John. *Indians: An Activity Book.* Good Apple, 1981.

3. Aten, Jerry. *Americans, Too!* Good Apple, 1982.

4. Bernstein, Bonnie, and Leigh Blair. *Native American Crafts Workshop.* Fearon, 1982.

5. *Children's Atlas of Native Americans.* Rand McNally, 1992.

6. Kindle, Patrick, and Susan Finney. *American Indians.* Illustrated by Ardia Mckay. Good Apple, 1985.

7. Spizzirri, Linda, ed. *Plains Indians: An Educational Coloring Book.* Spizzirri, 1981.

8. Thomson, Ruth. *Indians of the Plains.* Franklin Watts, 1991.

9. Waldman, Carl. *Encyclopedia of Native American Tribes.* Illustrated by Molly Braun. Facts on File, 1987.

Theme Reading Connections: Cheyenne

Fradin, Dennis B. *The Cheyenne.* Illustrated. Childrens Press, 1988.

Goble, Paul. *Death of the Iron Horse.* Illustrated by Paul Goble. Bradbury Press, 1987.

Hoig, Stanley. *The Cheyenne.* Illustrated. Chelsea House, 1989.

———. *People of the Sacred Arrow.* Illustrated. Cobblehill, 1992.

Lodge, Sally. *The Cheyenne.* Illustrated. Rourke, 1990.

McGaw, Jessie. *Chief Red Horse Tells About Custer.* Illustrated. Lodestar, 1981.

Myers, Arthur. *The Cheyenne.* Illustrated. Franklin Watts, 1992.

> Critical Thinking Question
> What contributions have American Indians made to our lives?

Student Activities to Connect Literature and Curriculum

FINE ARTS

1. Ask each student to design and construct a model tepee to be included in a diorama of an Indian village. What other items are needed to authenticate the scene?

2. Construct a model travois or a tribal mask.

3. Organize a classroom contest for the model Cheyenne shield with the best design.

LANGUAGE ARTS

1. As a prewriting exercise, outline *Her Seven Brothers.* What is the most important fact? Should the outline follow chronological order? Why or why not?

2. Write an illustrated feature article for *Smithsonian* magazine about General George Custer at Little Bighorn or the use of tribal masks by Indians.

3. Write a new ending for *Her Seven Brothers* or tell the myth from the point of view of the leader of the buffalo herd.

4. Write a Cheyenne tribal myth to explain the sun and the moon as guardians of day and night.

WRITING PROMPT

1. Write a newspaper article announcing that a newly discovered cave contains wall art that has been hidden for years. Use the following headline:

> New Museum Excavation Turns Up Priceless Indian Art

MATH

1. Explain the designs the girl used in creating shirts and moccasins for her seven brothers. Give your own explanation for each design. Write your explanations on notebook paper. Before you begin writing, draw five narrow columns on the left side of the page. The teacher will give your paper to five students, who will judge it with a score from 1 to 5, the latter being the highest. The last student will total the numbers and write their average on the page.

2. Use a grid to design your own Cheyenne art project.

SCIENCE

1. Color clean sand, rock salt, or rice for sand painting.

   Place 1 cup of the selected material in a small container with a tight-fitting lid. Add $\frac{1}{4}$ cup of water and several drops of food coloring to the jar. Tighten the lid and shake until the color is consistent.

   Strain and discard the water. Place the colored material on a cookie sheet lined with paper towels to absorb the moisture. Let the material dry. Repeat the process for each additional color.

   The finished art may be in the form of a sand picture or layered colored sand in a small jar like a baby food or spice container with a tight screw-on lid. Sandpaper makes a suitable background for art projects. Use glue to build up the background and bind the materials to the background material.

SOCIAL STUDIES

1. Prepare a bar graph listing the name of each state and the number of American Indians living on federal reservations and trust lands in each state. Prepare a similar bar graph for information on the number of American Indians living in states without federal reservations and trust lands. Combine the information from both graphs on a third chart of the total number of American Indians. (See the *World Almanac* for data.)

GEOGRAPHY

1. Using salt dough, construct a map detailing Cheyenne territory from 1600 to 1700. (See Lodge, Sally, *The Cheyenne,* Rourke, 1990.)

BEYOND THE BOOK

Guided Reading Connections Across a Learning Rainbow: Indian Legends

Connolly, James E., ed. *Why the Possum's Tail Is Bare: And Other North American Indian Nature Tales.* Illustrated by Andrea Adams. Stemmer, 1985.

DeArmond, Dale. *The Seal Oil Lamp.* Little, Brown, 1988.

Grossman, Virginia. *Ten Little Rabbits.* Illustrated by Sylvia Long. Chronicle, 1991.

Lurie, Alison. *The Heavenly Zoo.* Illustrated by Monika Beisner. Farrar, Straus & Giroux, 1979.

Medearis, Angela Shelf. *Dancing with the Indians.* Illustrated by Samuel Byrd. Holiday House, 1991.

Monroe, Jean Guard, and Ray A. Williamson. *They Dance in the Sky.* Houghton Mifflin, 1987.

Prusski, Jeffrey. *Bring Back the Deer.* Illustrated by Neil Waldman. Harcourt Brace Jovanovich, 1988.

Taylor, C. J. *The Ghost and Lone Warrior.* Tundra, 1991.

Troughton, Joanna. *Who Will Be the Sun?* P. Bedrick, 1985.

Yolen, Jane. *Sky Dogs.* Illustrated by Barry Moser. Harcourt Brace Jovanovich, 1990.

Enriching Connections

1. Debate the question, "Is it the responsibility of the United States government to pay surviving Indians for the land that was taken from them by settlers?"

FROM ANOTHER POINT OF VIEW

Freedman, Russell. *Buffalo Hunt.* Illustrated. Holiday House, 1988.

Parent-Student Connections

1. Visit the local public library and check out books about Native American art, clothing, or legends.

QUILLWORKER—A Cheyenne Legend

Author: Written and adapted by Terri Cohlene
Illustrator: Charles Reasoner
Publisher: Rourke, 1990
Classification: Native American mythology
Literary Form: Illustrated picture book
Theme: Much of our heritage is the folklore, legends, and myths of the First Americans.

ABOUT THE BOOK

STUDENT OBJECTIVES:

1. Create an Indian village detailing the social life and customs of a specific tribe.

2. Write and produce a play about a specific tribe.

3. Evaluate the natural resources that were at one time available to a specific tribe as compared to resources that remain available to that tribe today.

SYNOPSIS: *Quillworker* is a special legend of the Cheyenne tribe, complete with a nonfiction supplement containing photographs, a regional tribal location map, information about its clothing and food, and a chronological summary of important dates in the history of the tribe.

ABOUT THE AUTHOR: Terri Cohlene, 1950- .
Terri Cohlene has written and adapted information about six Indian tribes, including the distinctive lifestyles and beliefs of these First Americans.

ABOUT THE ILLUSTRATOR: Charles Reasoner

Charles Reasoner illustrated many works on American Indians as well as several books by Stephen Cosgrove, including the series Bumble B Bear, published by Price Stern. Several of Reasoner's illustrations appear in *Something about the Author,* vol. 53, pp. 33-36.

SELECTED ADDITIONAL TITLES: American Indian Legend series

Cohlene, Terri. *Clamshell Boy—A Makah Legend.* Illustrated by Charles Reasoner. American Indian Legend series. Rourke, 1990.

————. *Dancing Drum—A Cherokee Legend.* Illustrated by Charles Reasoner. American Indian Legend series. Rourke, 1990.

————. *Ka-Ha-Si and the Loon—An Eskimo Legend.* Illustrated by Charles Reasoner. American Indian Legend series. Rourke, 1990.

————. *Little Firefly—An Algonquian Legend.* Illustrated by Charles Reasoner. American Indian Legend series. Rourke, 1990.

————. *Turquoise Boy—A Navajo Legend.* Illustrated by Charles Reasoner. American Indian Legend series. Rourke, 1990.

USING THE BOOK

Suggested Approach to the Book

Model Lesson

1. What special skills did Quillworker possess?

2. Describe Quillworker's beautiful designs.

3. Why does Quillworker feel that she must prepare seven war shirts?

4. Describe Quillworker's solitary journey. What preparations did she make?

5. Why did Quillworker's mother not interfere with her daughter's plans?

6. What greeting did the Power of Knowing and the Power of Sky-Reaching give?

7. Why did the buffalo herd want Quillworker? What did it do?

8. How did the legend end?

9. Compare and contrast *Quillworker—A Cheyenne Legend* with Paul Goble's *Her Seven Brothers.*

Library Media Center Connections

1. This assignment is suitable for cooperative learning groups. The classroom will host an afternoon Indian legend storytelling program. Other classrooms will be invited to participate in the program. Each cooperative learning group will prepare potlatch gifts for guests visiting its tepee. Have the group prepare an outline on a specific Indian tribe that includes the following:

meaning of tribe name   U.S. map of tribe locations

illustration of tribe housing   samples of art work

illustrations of clothing	tribe time line
chart of men's and women's work	storytelling program

Computer Connections

1. Prepare a flyer and entertainment schedule detailing the Indian legend storytelling program.

Instructional Materials Connection

Mayo, Gretchen. *Star Tales: North American Indan Stories about the Stars*. Walker, 1987.

Shemie, Bonnie. *Houses of Hide and Earth*. Illustrated by Bonnie Shemie. Tundra, 1991.

Weiss, Harvey. *Shelters from Teepee to Igloo*. Illustrated by Harry Weiss. Harper, 1988.

Theme Reading Connection: Stars

Darling, David. J. *The Galaxies: Cities of Stars*. Illustrated by Jeanette Swofford. Dillon, 1985.

———. *The Stars from Birth to Black Hole*. Illustrated by Jeanette Swofford. Dillon, 1985.

Hatchett, Clint. *The Glow-in-the-Dark Night Story Book*. Illustrated by Stephen Marchesi. Random House, 1988.

The Stars. Silver Burdett, 1989.

West, Robin. *Far Out: How to Create Your Own Star World*. Illustrated by Bob Wolf and Diane Wolf. Lerner, 1987.

Zim, Herbert S., and Robert H. Baker. *The Stars*. Rev. ed. Illustrated by James G. Irving. Western, 1985.

Critical Thinking Question
Discuss this quote from *Quillworker*. "Give me your sister or we will kill you all," roared the bull. How would you have reacted in this situation?

Student Activities to Connect Literature and Curriculum

FINE ARTS

1. Construct costumes to be used in a Quillworker play. Paper on rolls or discarded bed sheets make inexpensive costumes.

LANGUAGE ARTS

1. Present a three-scene play starring Quillworker. Scenes are as follows:

   Quillworker and Her Mother

   At the Teepee of Seven Brothers

   Arrival of the Buffalo Herd

WRITING PROMPT

1. You are a traveling photographer who witnessed the buffalo attack. A picture of the destruction will be printed in the *Tombstone Gazette*. Write the story for this headline:

> Photographer Sees Attack of Buffalo Herd

MATH

1. Examines the pictures on pages 20-21. Estimate how many buffalo are in the herd. What would the total weight of the herd be? (A mature buffalo weighed one ton or more.) See Freedman, Russell, *Indian Chiefs*, Holiday House, 1987, p. 47.

SCIENCE

1. Diagram the body of a buffalo. Identify Native American uses of the animal parts.

SOCIAL STUDIES

1. What kind of work did Indian women do? Compare their work with the work women perform in the 1990s.

2. Make a chart identifying the different clothing worn by Indians in the past and today. Give examples for men, women, and children.

GEOGRAPHY

1. Design an imaginary map identifying Quillworker's tribal home and her journey to her seven brothers. Is it possible to illustrate where Quillworker and her brothers lived after the buffalo herd came?

BEYOND THE BOOK

Guided Reading Connections Across a Learning Rainbow: Indian Life

Brandt, Keith. *Indian Homes.* Illustrated by George Guzzi. Troll, 1985.

Green, Rayna. *Women in American Indian Society.* Chelsea House, 1989.

Nashone. *Where Indians Live: American Indian Houses.* Illustrated by Louise Smith. Sierra Oaks Pub., 1989.

Smith, Howard, E. *All About Arrowheads and Spear Points.* Illustrated by Jennifer O. Dewey. Henry Holt, 1989.

Tunis, Edwin. *Indians.* Rev. ed. Illustrated by Edwin Tunis. Reprint of 1959 ed. Harper, 1979.

Wolfson. *American Indian Tools and Ornaments.* McKay, 1981.

Enriching Connections

1. Make Indian jewelry using natural objects including nut shells, polished pieces of wood, dried flowers, and sea shells.

FROM ANOTHER POINT OF VIEW

Taylor, C. J. *The Secret of the White Buffalo.* Illustrated by C. J. Taylor. Tundra, 1993.

Parent-Student Connections

1. Encourage the students to use paper products to make art projects, such as masks, tepees, or a small Indian village. Indian rattles may be constructed by enclosing pebbles in two paper cups that are glued or taped together. Decorate the cups with Indian pictographs before adding the pebbles.

❀   ❀   ❀

TREE IN THE TRAIL

Author: Holling Clancy Holling
Illustrator: Holling Clancy Holling
Publisher: Houghton Mifflin, 1942
Suggested Grade Level: 5
Classification: Fiction
Literary Form: Illustrated historical fiction
Theme: The history of the United States is like a complex puzzle; many parts make up the whole.

ABOUT THE BOOK

STUDENT OBJECTIVES:

1. Examine the Santa Fe Trail from two viewpoints, that of Native Americans and western settlers.

2. Analyze the plight of the American Indian caused by the loss of their lands.

3. Recommend actions to improve the life of American Indians.

SYNOPSIS: For more than 200 years, a cottonwood tree has served as a landmark on the Santa Fe Trail. This tree is a peace symbol for both American Indians and settlers.

ABOUT THE AUTHOR-ILLUSTRATOR: Holling Clancy Holling, 1900-1973.

Holling C. Holling had many interests. He grew up on a Michigan farm. During school vacations, he worked a number of different jobs, including carpenter, grocery clerk, factory worker, and deck hand on ore boats on the Great Lakes.

Holling fell in love with the Southwest and explored on horseback thousands of miles of its plains, deserts, and mountains. His knowledge of the Southwest was enriched by his study of zoology and anthropology as well as his camping and wildlife study.

His eclectic tastes are evident in his detailed drawings and in the technical explanations that accompany them. Lucille Webster Holling assisted her husband in the research and illustrations for *Tree in the Trail.*

SELECTED ADDITIONAL TITLES:

Holling, Holling C. *Minn of the Mississippi.* Illustrated by Holling C. Holling. Houghton Mifflin, 1951.

―――. *Paddle-to-the-Sea.* Illustrated by Holling C. Holling. Houghton Mifflin, 1941.

―――. *Pagoo.* Illustrated by Holling C. Holling. Houghton Mifflin, 1957.

―――. *Seabird.* Illustrated by Holling C. Holling. Houghton Mifflin, 1948.

USING THE BOOK

Suggested Approach to the Book

Model Lesson

1. Why do the color illustrations in this book differ from those of today?

2. What is a sapling? Explain the symbolism of the tree to the young Indian. What other cultures believe that trees are alive and have living spirits? What did the boy do to assist the tree?

3. Why were the Indians walking on buffalo hunts? Describe the buffalo hunt from the eyes of an Indian hunter. Why were the Indians able to trap the buffalo?

4. What was the first item left on the cottonwood tree? Why?

5. After three years, the Indian returns to the tree and makes a prophecy about its future. He says, "Now you look like a person! Yes, you are like a young girl bending forward, sign-talking. One bent arm says 'come to me!' And the other says 'now go that way, toward the setting sun, and take me with you!'" (See chapter 5.) Predict how the tree will go to the setting sun. Use your imagination; no suggestion is too preposterous.

6. How were Indians introduced to horses? How did these animals change the lives of tribe members?

7. What is the purpose of an Indian shield? How did the shield change during three lifetimes?

8. Why was the tree called a bearer of messages? Why did the Hill-of-the-Talking-Tree become known as an island of peace in a land of wars? Was it a magical tree?

9. What did the trappers carry as tickets of safe passage among the Spaniards and Indians? Explain how goods traveled between Mexico and the United States. Was one route easier than another? Describe wagon camps. Why do people still say, "Circle the wagons!"?

10. How did the cottonwood become the post-office tree? How long does a cottonwood tree live?

11. Identify Jed Simpson and Buck Smith. Why did Buck Smith shoot a bullet into the cottonwood tree?

12. Describe the Santa Fe Trail ox yoke.

13. Why did the Indians believe that Peace-Medicine resided in the yoke?

Library Media Center Connections

1. Identify the following:

Travois	Tepee	Earth Lodges	Santa Fe, New Mexico
Cottonwood	Basswood	Taos, New Mexico	
"Fooferaw"	Oak	Independence, Missouri	

2. Under what Dewey decimal classifications can you locate information about Indians? List subject headings that provide information on this subject.

Computer Connections

1. Travel the Oregon Trail using a simulation computer program of the same name, The Oregon Trail, by MECC, available for IBM-compatible and Apple computers from Educational Resources, 1550 Executive Dr., Elgin, IL 60123. Write a review of the program that includes information about the similarities and differences between the Oregon Trail and the Santa Fe Trail.

Instructional Materials Connections

1. *America's Fascinating Indian Heritage.* Reader's Digest, 1991.

2. Artman, John. *Indians: An Activity Book.* Good Apple, 1981.

3. Bernstein, Bonnie, and Leigh Blair. *Native American Crafts Workshop.* Fearon, 1982.

4. Fisher, Leonard Everett. *The Oregon Trail.* Holiday House, 1990.

5. Freedman, Russell. *Buffalo Hunt.* Holiday House, 1988.

6. Kindle, Patrick, and Susan Finney. *American Indians.* Illustrated by Ardia Mckay. Good Apple, 1985.

7. Stone, Lynn. *Back from the Edge: The American Bison.* Rourke, 1991.

8. Invite a Native American who lives in your community to visit your classroom. If you cannot locate someone to serve as a guest speaker, invite a librarian from a public or school library to tell Indian legends in the classroom.

Theme Reading Connections: Indians—Social Life and Customs

Behrens, June. *Powwow.* Childrens Press, 1983.

Brandt, Keith. *Indian Festivals.* Troll, 1985.

———. *Indian Dwellings.* Troll, 1985.

Family, Clan, Nation. Capstone, 1989.

A Feast for Everyone. Capstone, 1989.

Hoyt-Goldsmith, Diane. *Totem Pole.* Photos by Lawrence Migdale. Holiday House, 1990.

Liptak, Karen. *North American Indian Medicine People.* Franklin Watts, 1990.

———. *North American Indian Sign Language.* Franklin Watts, 1990.

———. *North American Indian Survival Skills.* Franklin Watts, 1990.

McGaw, Jessie B. *Chief Red Horse Tells About Custer.* Lodestar, 1981.

Yue, Charlotte. *The Tipi: A Center of Native American Life.* Illustrated by David Yue. Alfred A. Knopf, 1984.

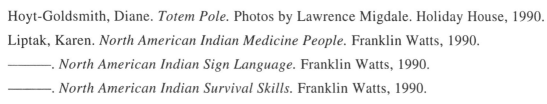

Critical Thinking Question
Explain why the tree in the trail can be called an important observer of American history. Could any tree today be called an important observer of American history?

Student Activities to Connect Literature and Curriculum

FINE ARTS

1. Create an Indian shield using a large wooden ring or bent clothes hanger. Yarn and beads are also needed. Step-by-step directions are given in:

    Coleman, Ann. *Fabrics and Yarns.* Illustrated by Malcolm Walker. Craft Projects series. Rourke, 1990.

2. Draw a picture of the tree as you imagine it would have looked at 28 years of age. Indicate the tree's age by including a drawing of a cross section of its tree rings, each of which indicate one year of life.

3. Construct a scale model of a covered wagon and its 12-animal team.

4. Create a panoramic mural of a journey from Independence, Missouri, to Santa Fe, New Mexico.

5. Present a costume fashion show using miniature paper dolls wearing the period dress of Indians and settlers. An opaque projector may be used to project costumes onto a classroom screen.

LANGUAGE ARTS

1. Make a list of supplies that need to be purchased in Independence, Missouri, for a trip on the Santa Fe Trail. List them in order of importance in case funds are inadequate to purchase all of the supplies.

2. Develop a schedule of activities for one day on the wagon trail.

3. Write daily diary entries about the wagon train trip from Independence, Missouri, to Santa Fe, New Mexico. This activity is suitable for cooperative learning groups.

4. What changes should be made to *Tree in the Trail* to update the information and to make it possible to use a computer in publishing the updated version?

5. Tell the story of *Tree in the Trail* from the viewpoint of a contemporary storyteller. Develop a costume as part of the activity.

6. If you were to become a children's book author, what subject or subjects would you choose to write about? Why?

7. Write and illustrate an Indian legend that explains the role of Thunderbird, Chief of Lightning. How did Thunderbird change the tree? (See chapter 8.)

WRITING PROMPT

1. Write a television story with the following opener:

> Petrified tree found in local excavation site. Historians believe it to be the tree featured in a Santa Fe Trail history book, Holling C. Holling's *Tree in the Trail*.

MATH

1. How many miles did the Santa Fe Trail extend? How many miles was the Oregon Trail? Present your answers in a chart.

SCIENCE

1. Compare and contrast the characteristics and life span of the following trees:

    Cottonwood   Oak   Basswood

2. When you go camping, how do you recognize clean drinking water? The Indians drank upstream of the watering hole used by animals.

SOCIAL STUDIES

1. Design an illustrated time line of the cottonwood tree on the Santa Fe Trail.

2. Write the story of the tree in the trail using Indian sign language.

GEOGRAPHY

1. Mold a physical map of the United States at the time of the Santa Fe Trail with clay or salt dough.

2. Where are buffalo herds found today? Are there any in your state? Describe the Yellowstone National Park buffalo herd. How did bison arrive on Catalina Island off the coast of Southern California?

3. Develop a profile of today's buffalo herds using the following background information:

    In 1905, a small group of individuals formed the American Bison Society. That group and the New York Zoological Society called for bison herds to be established on a few select public lands. With President Theodore R. Roosevelt's help, the government established herds on the following public lands:

Wichita Mountains National Wildlife Refuge, Oklahoma (1907)

National Bison Range, Montana (1908)

Fort Niobrara National Wildlife Refuge, Nebraska (1913)

In 1922 Canada established the magnificent Wood Buffalo National Park, 11 million acres of grassy plains, swamp, and forest. The park's herd now numbers 15,000. (See Stone, Lynn M., *Back from the Edge: The American Bison,* Rourke, 1991, p. 44.)

BEYOND THE BOOK

Guided Reading Connections Across a Learning Rainbow: Indians—Fiction

Banks, Lynne. *The Indian in the Cupboard.* Doubleday, 1982.

Bulla, Clyde R., and Michael Syson. *Conquista!* Illustrated by Ronald Himler. Harper & Row, 1978.

Curry, Jane. *Back in the Beforetime: Tales of the California Indians.* Illustrated by James Watts. Macmillan, 1987.

O'Dell, Scott. *Streams to the River, River to the Sea: A Novel of Sacagawea.* Houghton Mifflin, 1986.

Yellow Robe, Rosebud. *Tonweya and the Eagles.* Illustrated by Jerry Pinkney. Dial, 1991.

Enriching Connections

1. Simulate an Indian village in the classroom for a day.

    Who will be in charge?

    What tribe will be chosen?

    What lessons will be taught to boys? To girls?

    What is appropriate clothing for the day?

    What will the lunch menu be?

    What will students do for recreation?

FROM ANOTHER POINT OF VIEW

Moeri, Louise. *Save the Queen of Sheba.* Dutton, 1981.

Parent-Student Connections

1. Check out several books of Indian legends from the library to read aloud at home.

2. Have Indians been fairly treated in the twentieth century? Is there any present-day prejudice against Indians in the United States?

3. What foods were eaten by the Indians? Prepare several of these items during the week for a family dining experience.

❁   ❁   ❁

DANCING TEEPEES
Poems of American Indian Youth

Author: Virginia Driving Hawk Sneve
Illustrator: Stephen Gammell
Publisher: Holiday House, 1989
Suggested Grade Level: 5
Classification: Poetry
Literary Form: Nineteen selections of traditional Indian poetry are accompanied by rich, pastel-
colored illustrations that enhance the oral tradition through visual imagery.
Theme: "The Indians did not have a written language. They remembered what they heard and
learned that the art of speaking was powerful and gave the words life" (*Dancing Teepees*,
book jacket).

ABOUT THE BOOK

STUDENT OBJECTIVES:

1. Relate to Indian culture through a study of Indian poetry.

2. Interpret the meaning of Indian poetry.

3. Write poetry about one's own culture and heritage.

SYNOPSIS: Sneve selected her materials from the oral tradition as well as contemporary tribal
poetry. The poems span the life of a child from birth through youth.

ABOUT THE AUTHOR: Virginia Driving Hawk Sneve, 1933- .
   Virginia Driving Hawk Sneve was raised on the Rosebud Sioux Reservation in South Dakota.
She has worked as a high-school counselor and a college English teacher; she currently works in the
family antique business in Rapid City, South Dakota.
   Sneve's heritage is reflected in her books. "In my writing, both fiction and nonfiction, I try to
present an accurate portrayal of American Indian life as I have known it. I also attempt to interpret
history from the viewpoint of the American Indian and in so doing, I hope to correct the many
misconceptions and untruths which have been too long perpetuated by non-Indian authors who have
written about us" (*Something About the Author,* vol. 8, p. 193).

ABOUT THE ILLUSTRATOR: Stephen Gammell, 1943- .
   Stephen Gammell has been awarded two Caldecott honor medals for his illustrations in Olaf
Bekers' *Where the Buffaloes Begin* (Warne, 1981) and Cynthia Rylant's *The Relatives Came*
(Bradbury, 1985). When Gammell was growing up, his father was art editor of *Better Homes and
Gardens*, and each night he brought home large selections of art papers and colored pencils. "These
great piles of many thicknesses and colors were better than any toy," Gammell recalls (*Something
About the Author,* vol. 53, p. 51).
   As a child, Gammell was intrigued with illustrations of cowboys and Indians. "Somehow the
memorabilia and romance of Western History has always stayed with me.... An arrowhead, for

instance, is fun to pick up, to play with, to touch, to draw," he said (*Something About the Author,* vol. 53, p. 51).

Gammell's teachers reacted differently than one of Bruce Degen's, illustrator of the Magic School Bus series. One of Degen's teachers let him draw and forgo a scheduled test! Gammell explains, "I tried to get through high school by drawing, too. I'd turn in reports with illustrations, thinking the teacher would be impressed, but, of course, they weren't" (*Something About the Author,* vol. 53, p. 51).

SELECTED ADDITIONAL TITLES: Virginia Driving Hawk Sneve

Sneve, Virginia Driving Hawk. *Betrayed.* Illustrated. Holiday House, 1974.

————. *Jimmy Yellow Hawk.* Illustrated. Holiday House, 1972.

————. *High Elk's Treasure.* Illustrated. Holiday House, 1972.

————. *When Thunder Spoke.* Illustrated. Holiday House, 1974.

SELECTED ADDITIONAL TITLES: Stephen Gammell

Blos, Joan. *Old Henry.* Illustrated by Stephen Gammell. Morrow, 1987.

Cross, Helen R. *The Real Tom Thumb.* Illustrated by Stephen Gammell. Macmillan, 1980.

Gammell, Stephen. *Git Along Old Scudder.* Illustrated by Stephen Gammell. Lothrop, Lee & Shepard, 1983.

Livingston, Myra Cohn. *Thanksgiving Poems.* Illustrated by Stephen Gammell. Holiday House, 1985.

Rylant, Cynthia. *The Relatives Came.* Illustrated by Stephen Gammell. Bradbury Press, 1985.

USING THE BOOK

Suggested Approach to the Book

Model Lesson

1. Identify the illustrator. Have you seen any other books illustrated by him? Name them. Which of his two books became Caldecott honor books? When did he receive these distinguished awards? What are the qualifications governing the Caldecott award?

2. Explain the introduction written by the author.

3. What is a dedication? Read the book's dedication (opposite the table of contents). Who would you dedicate a book to? Why?

4. Examine the table of contents. Are there any terms that you do not understand? List them. Select a poem from the book. Choose one that sounds interesting to you. Which one did you choose? Why? After reading it silently, examine the language. What is the meaning of the poem? Why do you think that?

5. Explain the construction of a tepee. Did all Indians live in teepees?

6. How would you describe the art in *Dancing Teepees*? Is there any pattern to the book's layout? What kind of end papers would be appropriate for this book? Why?

7. What was the significance of the buffalo in the history of the Indians?

Library Media Center Connections

1. Find the copyright information page in the book. Explain the Library of Congress information listed. If you do not understand the information, ask your school librarian or teacher to explain it. Explain why the book might be listed in a library catalog or database as Indian poetry—Collections.

2. Plan an Indian unit for the library. What books should be displayed? List the catalog subjects that could be used to develop a list of available materials. Display student art work, such as posters, dioramas, miniatures, and bulletin board work in the library.

Computer Connections

1. Using a word processor, compose a daily tribal log to accompany *Dancing Teepees*. Class members may work in cooperative learning groups to develop this project. Include information about the roles of men, women, and children in the tribe; food; housing; recreation; legends and myths; hunting; native animals; and clothing. Additional subject listings can be determined from class discussion.

Instructional Materials Connections

1. *America's Fascinating Indian Heritage.* Reader's Digest, 1991.

2. Artman, John. *Indians: An Activity Book.* Good Apple, 1981.

3. Aten, Jerry. *Americans, Too!* Good Apple, 1982.

4. Bernstein, Bonnie, and Leigh Blair. *Native American Crafts Workshop.* Fearon, 1982.

5. *Children's Atlas of Native Americans.* Rand McNally, 1992.

6. dePaola, Tomie. *The Legend of the Bluebonnet: An Old Tale of Texas.* Cassette and filmstrip. Listening Library, n.d.

7. dePaola, Tomie. *The Legend of the Indian Paintbrush.* Cassette and filmstrip. Listening Library, n.d.

8. Henry, Peggy Sue. *Beads to Buckskins.* Jayhawk Rock and Fur Shop, P.O. Box 296, Hill City, KS 67642.

9. Kindle, Patrick, and Susan Finney. *American Indians.* Illustrated by Ardia Mckay. Good Apple, 1985.

10. Klausner, Janet. *Sequoyah's Gift.* HarperCollins, 1993.

11. Spizzirri, Linda, ed. *Plains Indians: An Educational Coloring Book.* Spizzirri, 1981.

12. Weiss, Harvey. *Shelters: From Tepee to Igloo.* Illustrated by Harvey Weiss. Harper & Row, 1988.

13. Waldman, Carl. *Encyclopedia of Native American Tribes.* Illustrated by Molly Braun. Facts on File, 1987.

14. An extensive leather and crafts catalog, including Indian art projects, is available from Tandy Leather Company, 1400 Everman Parkway, Fort Worth, TX 76140.

15. Santa Fe Beading publishes *Easy Jewelry,* a booklet with a number of projects listed. It is available for purchase from Design Originals, 401 No. Bailey-B, Fort Worth, TX 76107.

Theme Reading Connections: Indian Art and Poetry

Baylor, Byrd. *When Clay Sings.* Illustrated by Tom Bahti. Macmillan, 1987.

Gates, Frieda. *North American Indian Masks.* Walker, 1982.

Hoyt-Goldsmith, Diane. *Totem Pole.* Photos by Lawrence Migdale. Holiday House, 1990.

Longfellow, Henry Wadsworth. *Hiawatha's Childhood.* Illustrated by Errol Le Cain. Farrar, Straus & Giroux, 1984.

———. *Hiawatha.* Illustrated by Susan Jeffers. Dial, 1983.

Villasenor, David. *Tapestries in Sand: The Spirit of Indian Sandpainting.* Naturegraph, 1966.

> Critical Thinking Question
> Imagine that you have just learned that your ancestors were Indians. Which tribe would you choose? Why? Does being a member of a minority group change your thinking? What injustices do you believe might have happened to Indians? What are the benefits of tribal membership today? Are there any educational benefits? Would you expect more or less social acceptance in your community? Why?

Student Activities to Connect Literature and Curriculum

FINE ARTS

1. Decorated end papers were not used in this book. Conduct a contest in the classroom to select the most artistic end pages for *Dancing Teepees.* Ask the librarian to glue the winning pages into the library's copy of the book. Students should date and sign their work.

2. Choose one poem and its accompanying art from *Dancing Teepees* and explain how both appealed to you. Draw your own art work to accompany the poem, and display the art work with a hand-written (in ink) copy of the poem on a classroom bulletin board.

3. Construct a life-size Indian mask. Use as many natural materials as possible, including corn husks and cobs; raffia; small sea shells; nuts; and dried beans, peas, and corn.

4. Construct a "Me" totem pole. Some of its materials might include round oatmeal or raisin containers, cardboard tubes, or wooden spools. The totem pole should tell the story of your life.

LANGUAGE ARTS

1. As an introduction to this Native American unit, cluster ideas and descriptive phrases about Indians. Use the information for individual student mind maps (an illustrated map with a central theme and several subjects radiating from one central idea/picture. It might also be described as a visual outline of information).

2. Read aloud the first poem, "The Life of a Man in a Circle." What is the meaning of the circle? Compare the Indian meaning of a circle with the following:

Shakespeare—All the world's a stage

Pioneers—Circling the wagons at night

3. Write an Indian legend based on the picture of the Indian on his horse on the title page of *Dancing Teepees.* What title would you use? Why?

4. Write a class letter to Kate Briggs, Publisher, Holiday House, 18 East 53rd St., New York, NY 10012, describing students' opinions about *Dancing Teepees.* You might also explain how Holiday House books on other Indian subjects are used in your classroom.

WRITING PROMPT

1. Write a one-page feature article under the following title:

```
Author Relates New Information in Dancing Teepees
```

MATH

1. In the past, the United States government made payments to some members of Indian tribes for the loss of their lands. Determine how much money should be paid each person. Choose a specific tribe. Research information about the tribe. See the *World Almanac* for statistics concerning the number of Indians who live both on and off reservation land. The following criteria might apply:

number of living tribe members,

land area taken from the tribe,

land area held now by the tribe, and

compensation for natural resources.

Additional information can be found in "Contemporary Indians: Renaissance of an Ancient People," in Reader's Digest, *America's Fascinating Indian Heritage* (Reader's Digest, 1991). pp. 392-401. This material presents a chronology of American Indian history as well as a discussion of changing national policy and accompanying Indian legislation enacted by the U.S. government.

SCIENCE

1. Explain the process for making colored dyes for decorating clothing and teepees. What meaning was attached to the following colors?

```
Black   Blue   Green   Red   White   Yellow
```

2. What materials were used to make body paint? (See Bernstein, Bonnie, and Leigh Blair, *Native American Crafts Workshop,* Fearon, 1982.)

SOCIAL STUDIES

1. Plan and prepare an Indian luncheon for the classroom. What foods are appropriate? In planning the menu, use the new government-approved food groups. (The revised food groups are as follows: 1. bread, cereals, rice, and pasta; 2. meat, poultry, fish, dried beans and peas, eggs, and nuts; 3. milk, yogurt, and cheese; 4. fruits; 5. vegetables.) Design place mats that may be laminated, and use natural materials in table decorations.

2. Retell Indian legends from the tribes listed in *Dancing Teepees*.

   Establish the mood by turning off the classroom lights, lighting candles, and sitting on the floor on blankets. This atmosphere enhances the presentation of the program.

3. List Indian handicrafts. Which items are sought by collectors? Why?

GEOGRAPHY

1. List the names of Indian tribes represented in this poetry collection. Using a map of North America, label the location of the tribes. Name tribes that might have had commonalities. Why might they have had these things in common?

BEYOND THE BOOK

Guided Reading Connections Across a Learning Rainbow: Indians—Fiction

Baylor, Byrd. *Hawk, I'm Your Brother.* Illustrated by Peter Parnall. Macmillan, 1976.

Dalgliesh, Alice. *The Courage of Sarah Noble.* Illustrated by Leonard Weisgard. Macmillan, 1987.

dePaola, Tomie. *The Legend of the Indian Paintbrush.* Putnam, 1987.

———. *The Legend of the Bluebonnet: An Old Tale of Texas.* Putnam, 1983.

Martin, Bill, and John Archambault. *Knots on a Counting Rope.* Henry Holt, 1987.

Peet, Bill. *Buford the Little Bighorn.* Houghton Mifflin, 1983.

Root, Phyllis. *The Listening Silence.* Illustrated by Dennis McDermott. Harper & Row, 1992.

Yellow Robe, Rosebud. *Tonweya and the Eagles.* Illustrated by Jerry Pinkney. Dial, 1979.

Enriching Connections

1. Select a day in November to celebrate an all-school observation of Indian Day. Include an opening flag ceremony with each class representing a separate tribe. Students may wear banners, stage a march of Indian nations, present a school program, and enjoy a special food services menu.

FROM ANOTHER POINT OF VIEW

Esbensen, Barbara. *The Star Maiden.* Illustrated by Helen Davie. Little, Brown, 1988.

Parent-Student Connections

1. Talk to students about the role of Indians in the United States and prejudice against them today.

2. Read several Indian legends to your family. What makes this literature special? Talk about your family roots and heritage. What makes your family different and unique?

❀   ❀   ❀

By the Light of Flickering Candles

A BOOK OF AMERICANS

Author: Rosemary Benet and Stephen Vincent Benet
Illustrator: Charles Child
Publisher: Henry Holt, 1933
Suggested Grade Level: 5
Classification: Nonfiction
Literary Form: Poetry
Theme:

> "So praise and blame judiciously
> Their foibles and their worth
> The skies they knew were our skies, too
> The earth they found, our earth."

ABOUT THE BOOK

STUDENT OBJECTIVES:

1. Observe the founding and growth of the United States through poetry.

2. Evaluate the role of prominent leaders and their place in American history.

3. Write poetry about contemporary leaders of the United States.

SYNOPSIS: Fifty-five poetry selections represent various individuals and groups of people of the United States. Students will recognize most of the poems, but some may be unfamiliar and will provide an opportunity to understand more of our history through literature.

ABOUT THE AUTHORS: Rosemary Carr Benet, 1898-1962; Stephen Vincent Benet, 1898-1943.
Stephen Vincent Benet, his brother, William Rose Benet, and his sister, Laura Benet, are well-known American poets. Stephen Vincent Benet's home provided a nurturing environment for his poetry. "His father he later remembered as the 'finest critic of poetry' he had ever known and one who taught him 'many things about the writing of English verse, and tolerance, and independence and curiosity of mind' " (*Dictionary of American Biography,* Supplement 3, 1941-1945. Charles

Scribner's Sons, 1973, p. 56). Stephen Benet's special interests were history and folklore. He is best known for *John Brown's Body,* a ballad that received a Pulitzer Prize in 1925. Rosemary Carr Benet preferred that her maiden name always be used along with Stephen's name because she was considered a poet in her own right.

SELECTED ADDITIONAL TITLES:

Benet, Stephen Vincent. *The Devil and Daniel Webster and Other Stories.* Archway, 1972.

USING THE BOOK

Suggested Approach to the Book

Model Lesson

1. Ask students to identify as many people as possible listed in the table of contents. What makes each person famous? Read aloud to the class several selections from the book. Are there any rhyming couplets?

2. Why do you think the authors chose this particular book format? Would you have included other people? Why? What modern leaders are missing?

3. Select a famous person and write a stanza similar to selections in *A Book of Americans.*

4. Can you identify any famous lines of poetry?

5. What subject would you choose to write about in an epic poem? Why?

Library Media Center Connections

1. Ask the librarian to read aloud poetry selections from the following titles:

   Blishen, Edward, ed. *The Oxford Book of Poetry for Children.* Oxford University Press, 1987.

   Ciardi, John. *You Read to Me, I'll Read to You.* Illustrated by Edward Gorey. Harper & Row, 1987.

   Frost, Robert. *Birches.* Illustrated by Ed Young. Henry Holt, 1988.

   Longfellow, Henry Wadsworth. *Paul Revere's Ride.* Illustrated by Nancy W. Parker. Greenwillow Books, 1985.

   Milne, A. A. *Now We Are Six.* Illustrated by Ernest H. Shepard. Dutton, 1988.

   Nash, Ogden. *Custard and Company.* Illustrated by Quentin Blake. Little, Brown, 1985.

   Petersham, Maud, and Miska Petersham. *The Rooster Crows: A Book of American Rhymes and Jingles.* Macmillan, 1987.

   Prelutsky, Jack. *The New Kid on the Block.* Illustrated by James Stevenson. Greenwillow Books, 1984.

   Sendak, Maurice. *Seven Little Monsters.* Illustrated by Maurice Sendak. Harper & Row, 1977.

   Viorst, Judith. *If I Were in Charge of the World and Other Worries.* Illustrated by Lynne Cherry. Macmillan, 1981.

2. Produce a video tape of student poetry readings. Have students dress in appropriate clothing and use the best available materials and stage props as background.

Computer Connections

1. Compile a library media center book of poems written and illustrated by students.

2. Begin a database about the subject Poetry Reading. Include selections from poetry books and anthologies that are recommended by students.

Instructional Materials Connections

1. Aten, Jerry. *America: From Sea to Shining Sea.* Good Apple, 1988.

2. Burda, Margaret. *Amazing States.* Good Apple, 1984.

3. Gordon, Patricia, and Reed Snow. *Kids Learn America!* Williamson, 1991.

4. Lorimer, Larry. *The Julian Messner United States Question and Answer Book.* Messner, 1984.

5. Olsen, Mary Lou. *Presidents of the United States.* Teacher's ed. Garrett Education, 1990.

6. *Pilgrim Quest.* A strategic simulation computer game. National Geographic and Decision Development Corporation.

Theme Reading Connections: Historical Figures and Subjects

Christopher Columbus, 1446?-1506

Adler, David A. *A Picture Book of Christopher Columbus.* Illustrated by John Wallner and Alexandra Wallner. Holiday House, 1991.

Fradin, Dennis. *Columbus Day.* Enslow, 1990.

Fritz, Jean. *Where Do You Think You're Going, Christopher Columbus?* Illustrated by Margot Tomes. Putnam, 1980.

Greene, Carol. *Christopher Columbus: A Great Explorer.* Childrens Press, 1989.

Kent, Zachary. *Christopher Columbus.* World's Great Explorers series. Childrens Press, 1992.

Martin, Susan. *I Sailed with Columbus.* Illustrated by Tom La Padula. Overlook, 1991.

Smith, Barry. *The First Voyage of Christopher Columbus, 1492.* Viking, 1992.

Yolen, Jane. *Encounter.* Illustrated by David Shannon. Harcourt Brace Jovanovich, 1992.

Indians

America's Fascinating Indian Heritage. Reader's Digest, 1991.

Freedman, Russell. *Indian Chiefs.* Holiday House, 1987.

Hook, Jason. *American Indian Warrior Chiefs.* Firebird, 1991.

Upton, Harriet. *Indian Chiefs.* Illustrated by Jerry Harston. Rourke, 1990.

Voight, Virginia. *Massasoit: Friend of the Pilgrims.* Garrard, 1971.

Yolen, Jane. *Sky Dogs.* Illustrated by Barry Moser. Harcourt Brace Jovanovich, 1990.

Hernando De Soto, 1499?-1642

Carson, Robert. *Hernando De Soto: Expedition to the Mississippi River.* Childrens Press, 1991.

Zadra, Dan. *Explorers of America: De Soto.* Creative Education, 1988.

Pocahontas, 1595?-1617

D'Aulaire, Edgar P. *Pocahontas.* Illustrated by Edgar D'Aulaire and Ingri D'Aulaire. Doubleday, 1946.

Fritz, Jean. *The Double Life of Pocahontas.* Illustrated by Ed Young. Putnam, 1983.

Green, Carol. *Pocahontas: Daughter of a Chief.* Childrens Press, 1988.

Santrey, Laurence. *Pocahontas.* Illustrated by David Wenzel. Troll, 1985.

Pilgrims and Puritans, 1620

Bains, Rae. *Pilgrims and Thanksgiving.* Illustrated by David Wenzel. Troll, 1985.

Brown, Margaret W., ed. *Homes in the Wilderness: A Pilgrim's Journal of Plymouth Plantation in 1620, by William Bradford and Others of the Mayflower Company.* Shoe String Press, 1988. Reprint of 1939 ed.

Dalgliesh, Alice. *Thanksgiving Story.* Illustrated by Helen Sewell. Charles Scribner's Sons, 1954.

DeLage, Ida. *The Pilgrim Children on the Mayflower.* Garrard, 1980.

Greene, Carol. *The Pilgrims Are Marching.* Illustrated by Tom Dunnington. Childrens Press, 1988.

Knight, James E. *Sailing to America, Colonists at Sea.* Illustrated by George Guzzi. Troll, 1982.

McGovern, Ann. *The Pilgrim's First Thanksgiving.* Illustrated by Joe Lasker. Scholastic, 1988.

———. *If You Sailed on the Mayflower.* Scholastic, 1969.

Payne, Elizabeth. *Meet the Pilgrim Fathers.* Illustrated by H. B. Vestal. Random House, 1966.

Richards, Norman. *The Story of the Mayflower Compact.* Illustrated by Darrell Wiskur. Childrens Press, 1967.

Sewall, Marsha. *The Pilgrims of Plimoth.* Macmillan, 1986.

Peter Stuyvesant, 1592-1682

Crouse, Anna, and Russel Crouse. *Peter Stuyvesant of Old New York.* Random House, 1963.

Quackenbush, Robert. *Old Silver Leg Takes Over: A Story of Peter Stuyvesant.* Prentice-Hall, 1986.

Captain Kidd, 1650?-1701

Marrin, Albert. *The Sea Rovers: Pirates, Privateers and Buccaneers.* Macmillan, 1984.

McCall, Edith. *Pirates and Privateers.* Illustrated by Felix Palm. Childrens Press, 1980.

McWilliams, Karen. *Pirates.* Franklin Watts, 1989.

French Pioneers, 1534-1759

Sandak, Cass R. *Explorers and Discovery.* Franklin Watts, 1983.

Stein, R. Conrad. *The Story of Marquette and Joliet.* Childrens Press, 1981.

George Washington, 1732-1799

Adler, David. *George Washington: Father of Our Country.* Illustrated by Jacqueline Garrick. Holiday House, 1988.

D'Aulaire, Ingri, and Edgar D'Aulaire. *George Washington.* Doubleday, 1936.

Davidson, Margaret. *The Adventures of George Washington.* Scholastic, 1987.

Falkof, Lucille. *George Washington: First President of the United States.* Garrett, 1989.

Fritz, Jean. *George Washington's Breakfast.* Illustrated by Paul Galdone. Putnam, 1969.

Hilton, Suzanne. *The World of Young George Washington.* Walker, 1987.

Kent, Zachary. *George Washington.* Childrens Press, 1986.

Knight, James E. *The Winter at Valley Forge, Survival and Victory.* Illustrated by George Guzzi. Troll, 1982.

McGovern, Ann. *If You Grew Up with George Washington.* Scholastic, 1985.

McGowen, Tom. *George Washington.* Franklin Watts, 1986.

Rett, Seymour. *Guns for General Washington.* Harcourt Brace Jovanovich, 1990.

Roop, Peter, and Connie Roop. *Buttons for General Washington.* Carolrhoda, 1986.

Siegel, Beatrice. *George and Martha Washington at Home in New York.* Macmillan, 1989.

John Paul Jones, 1747-1792

Brandt, Keith. *John Paul Jones: Hero of the Seas.* Troll, 1983.

Worcester, Donald E. *John Paul Jones.* Houghton Mifflin, 1961.

Zadra, Dan. *Statesmen in America: John Paul Jones.* Creative Education, 1988.

Abigail Adams, 1744-1818

Fradin, Dennis B. *Abigail Adams: Adviser to a President.* Enslow, 1989.

Osborne, Angela. *Abigail Adams.* Chelsea, 1989.

Peterson, Helen S. *Abigail Adams: Dear Partner.* Garrard, 1967.

John Adams, 1735-1826

Fritz, Jean. *Why Don't You Get a Horse, Sam Adams?* Putnam, 1974.

Greenblatt, Miriam. *John Quincy Adams: Sixth President of the United States.* Garrett, 1989.

Kent, Zachary. *John Quincy Adams.* Childrens Press, 1987.

Benjamin Franklin, 1705-1790

Cousins, Margaret. *Ben Franklin of Old Philadelphia.* Random House, 1963.

Fritz, Jean. *What's the Big Idea, Benjamin Franklin?* Putnam, 1982.

Lawson, Robert. *Ben and Me.* Dell, 1973.

Meltzer, Milton. *Benjamin Franklin: The New American.* Franklin Watts, 1988.

Santrey, Laurence. *Young Ben Franklin.* Troll, 1982.

Scarf, Maggie. *Meet Benjamin Franklin*. Random House, 1989.

Stevens, Bryna. *Ben Franklin's Glass Armonica*. Illustrated by Florence Hill. Carolrhoda, 1983.

Stevenson, Augusta. *Benjamin Franklin, Young Printer*. Macmillan, 1983.

Benedict Arnold, 1741-1801

Fritz, Jean. *Traitor: The Case of Benedict Arnold*. Putnam, 1981.

Thomas Jefferson, 1743-1826

Adler, David A. *Thomas Jefferson: Father of Our Democracy*. Holiday House, 1987.

Hargrove, Jim. *Thomas Jefferson*. Childrens Press, 1986.

Hilton, Suzanne. *The World of Young Thomas Jefferson*. Walker, 1986.

Knight, James E. *Journey to Monticello: Traveling in Colonial Times*. Troll, 1982.

Monsell, Helen A. *Thomas Jefferson*. Macmillan, 1989.

Patterson, Charles. *Thomas Jefferson*. Franklin Watts, 1987.

Quackenbush, Robert. *Pass the Quill; I'll Write a Draft: A Story of Thomas Jefferson*. Pippin, 1989.

Smith, Kathie. *Thomas Jefferson*. Messner, 1989.

Stefoff, Rebecca. *Thomas Jefferson: Third President of the United States*. Garrett, 1988.

Alexander Hamilton, 1757-1804

Keller, Mollie. *Alexander Hamilton*. Franklin Watts, 1986.

O'Brien, Steve. *Alexander Hamilton*. Chelsea, 1989.

Johnny Appleseed, 1775-1847

Aliki. *Story of John Chapman*. Prentice-Hall, 1987.

Gleiter, Jan, and Kathleen Thompson. *Johnny Appleseed*. Raintree/Steck-Vaughn, 1986.

Sabin, Lou. *Johnny Appleseed*. Illustrated by Dick Smolinski. Troll, 1985.

Meriwether Lewis, 1774-1809, and William Clark, 1770-1838

Blumberg, Rhoda. *The Incredible Journey of Lewis and Clark*. Lothrop, Lee & Shepard, 1987.

Brown, Marion. *Sacajawea: Indian Interpreter to Lewis and Clark*. Childrens Press, 1988.

Fitz-Gerald, Christine M. *Meriwether Lewis and William Clark: The Northwest Expedition*. Childrens Press, 1991.

McGarth, Patrick. *The Lewis and Clark Expedition*. Silver Burdett, 1985.

Peterson, David, and Mark Coburn. *Meriwether Lewis and William Clark: Soldiers, Explorers and Partners in History*. Childrens Press, 1988.

Sabin, Francine. *Lewis and Clark*. Illustrated by John Lawn. Troll, 1985.

Zadra, Dan. *Explorers of America: Lewis and Clark*. Creative Education, 1988.

Dolly Madison, 1772-1849

Klingel, Cindy. *Women of America: Dolly Madison.* Creative Education, 1987.

James Monroe, 1758-1831

Fitz-Gerald, Christine M. *James Monroe.* Childrens Press, 1987.

Stefoff, Rebecca. *James Monroe: Fifth President of the United States.* Garrett, 1988.

Wetzel, Charles. *James Monroe.* Chelsea, 1989.

John Quincy Adams, 1767-1848

Greenblatt, Miriam. *John Quincy Adams: Sixth President of the United States.* Garrett, 1989.

Kent, Zachary. *John Quincy Adams.* Childrens Press, 1987.

Andrew Jackson, 1767-1845

Csinski, Alice. *Andrew Jackson.* Childrens Press, 1987.

Hilton, Suzanne. *The World of Young Andrew Jackson.* Walker, 1988.

Sabin, Lou. *Andrew Jackson: Frontier Patriot.* Troll, 1985.

Stefoff, Rebecca. *Andrew Jackson: Seventh President of the United States.* Garrett, 1988.

Zachary Taylor, 1784-1850

Collins, David R. *Zachary Taylor: Twelfth President of the United States.* Garrett, 1989.

Kent, Zachary. *Zachary Taylor.* Childrens Press, 1988.

John James Audubon, 1780-1851

Brenner, Barbara. *On the Frontier with Mr. Audubon.* Putnam, 1977.

Daniel Boone, 1735-1820

Brandt, Keith. *Daniel Boone: Frontier Adventures.* Troll, 1983.

Gleiter, Jan, and Kathleen Thompson. *Daniel Boone.* Raintree/Steck-Vaughn, 1984.

Hargrove, Jim. *Daniel Boone: Pioneer Trailblazer.* Childrens Press, 1985.

Lawlor, Laurie. *Daniel Boone.* Whitman, 1989.

May, Robin. *Daniel Boone and the American West.* Franklin Watts, 1986.

Stevenson, Augusta. *Daniel Boone: Young Hunter and Tracker.* Macmillan, 1983.

Zadra, Dan. *Frontiersmen in America: Daniel Boone.* Creative Education, 1988.

Sam Houston, 1793-1863

Fritz, Jean. *Make Way for Sam Houston.* Putnam, 1986.

Gleiter, Jan, and Kathleen Thompson. *Sam Houston.* Raintree/Steck-Vaughn, 1987.

Latham, Jan. *Sam Houston: Hero of Texas.* Garrard, 1985.

Zadra, Dan. *Statesmen in America: Sam Houston.* Creative Education, 1988.

Western Wagons

Lake, A. I. *Women of the West.* Illustrated by Katherine Ace. The Wild West in American History series. Rourke, 1990.

Levine, Ellen. *If You Traveled West in a Covered Wagon.* Illustrated by Charles Shaw. Scholastic, 1986.

Wilder, Laura Ingalls. *West from Home: Letters of Laura Ingalls Wilder, San Francisco 1915.* Harper & Row, 1974.

Clipper Ships and Captains, 1843-1860

McCall, Edith. *Steamboats to the West.* Illustrated by Robert Borja. Childrens Press, 1980.

Stein, R. Conrad. *The Story of the Clipper Ships.* Childrens Press, 1981.

James Buchanan, 1791-1868

Brill, Marlene. *James Buchanan.* Childrens Press, 1988.

Collins, David R. *James Buchanan: Fifteenth President of the United States.* Garrett, 1990.

Crazy Horse, ?-1877

Meadowcroft, Enid. *Crazy Horse: Sioux Warrior.* Garrard, 1965.

Zadra, Dan. *Indians of America: Crazy Horse.* Creative Education, 1987.

Stonewall Jackson, 1824-1863

Fritz, Jean. *Stonewall.* Putnam, 1979.

Abraham Lincoln, 1809-1865

Bulla, Clyde. *Lincoln's Birthday.* Illustrated by Ernest Crichlow. Harper & Row, 1966.

Colver, Anne. *Abraham Lincoln.* Illustrated by William Moyers. Dell, 1981.

D'Aulaire, Ingri, and Edgar D'Aulaire. *Abraham Lincoln.* Doubleday, 1957.

Freedman, Russell. *Lincoln: A Photobiography.* Clarion Books, 1987.

Gross, Ruth. *True Stories about Abraham Lincoln.* Scholastic, 1988.

Hargrove, Jim. *Abraham Lincoln: Sixteenth President of the United States.* Childrens Press, 1988.

Kent, Zachary. *The Story of the Election of Abraham Lincoln.* Childrens Press, 1986.

McGovern, Ann. *If You Grew Up with Abraham Lincoln.* Scholastic, 1985.

Metzger, Larry. *Abraham Lincoln.* Franklin Watts, 1987.

Miller, Natalie. *Story of the Lincoln Memorial.* Childrens Press, 1966.

North, Sterling. *Abe Lincoln: Log Cabin to the White House.* Random House, 1963.

Richards, Kenneth. *The Story of the Gettysburg Address.* Childrens Press, 1969.

Sandburg, Carl. *Abe Lincoln Grows Up.* Illustrated by James Daugherty. Harcourt Brace Jovanovich, 1975.

Stefoff, Rebecca. *Abraham Lincoln: Sixteenth President of the United States.* Garrett, 1989.

Stevenson, Augusta. *Abraham Lincoln: The Great Emancipator.* Illustrated by Jerry Robinson. Macmillan, 1986.

Ulysses S. Grant, 1822-1885

Falkof, Lucille. *Ulysses S. Grant, Eighteenth President of the United States.* Garrett, 1988.

Kent, Zachary. *Ulysses S. Grant.* Childrens Press, 1989.

Viola, Herman. *Ulysses S. Grant.* Chelsea, 1990.

Zadra, Dan. *Statesmen in America: Ulysses S. Grant.* Creative Education, 1988.

Robert E. Lee, 1807-1870

Brandt, Keith. *Robert E. Lee.* Troll, 1985.

Monsell, Helen. *Robert E. Lee: Young Confederate.* Macmillan, 1983.

Weidhorn, Manfred. *Robert E. Lee.* Macmillan, 1988.

Zadra, Dan. *Statesmen in America: Robert E. Lee.* Creative Education, 1988.

David Farragut, 1801-1870

David Farragut. Raintree/Steck-Vaughn, 1989.

Clara Barton, 1821-1912

Bains, Rae. *Clara Barton: Angel of the Battlefield.* Troll, 1982.

Boyston, Helen. *Clara Barton: Founder of American Red Cross.* Random House, 1963.

Kent, Zachary. *The Story of Clara Barton.* Childrens Press, 1987.

Klingel, Cynthia, and Dan Zadra. *Clara Barton.* Creative Education, 1987.

Rose, Mary C. Clara Barton: Soldier of Mercy. Illustrated by E. Harper Johnson. Chelsea House, 1991.

Jesse James, 1847-1882

Ernst, John. *Jesse James.* Prentice-Hall, 1976.

Grover Cleveland, 1837-1908

Collins, David R. *Grover Cleveland: Twenty Second and Twenty Fourth President of the United States.* Garrett, 1988.

Kent, Zachary. *Grover Cleveland: Twenty Second President of the United States.* Childrens Press, 1988.

P. T. Barnum, 1810-1891

Tompert, Ann. *The Greatest Show on Earth: A Biography of P. T. Barnum.* Dillon, 1987.

Wilbur Wright, 1867-1912, and Orville Wright, 1871-1948

Reynolds, Quentin. *The Wright Brothers.* Random House, 1981.

Sabin, Louis. *Wilbur and Orville Wright: The Flight to Adventure.* Troll, 1983.

Sobol, Donald. *The Wright Brothers at Kitty Hawk.* Scholastic, 1987.

Stevenson, Augusta. *Wilbur and Orville Wright: Young Fliers.* Macmillan, 1986.

Robert E. Peary, 1856-1920

Sandak, Cass. *The Arctic and Antarctic*. Childrens Press, 1985.

Stone, Lynn. *The Arctic*. Childrens Press, 1985.

Theodore Roosevelt, 1858-1919

Force, Eden. *Theodore Roosevelt*. Franklin Watts, 1987.

Kay, Helen. *The First Teddy Bear*. Stemmer House, 1985.

Kent, Zachary. *Theodore Roosevelt*. Childrens Press, 1988.

Monjo, F. N. *The One Bad Thing about Father*. Harper & Row, 1987.

Parks, Edd. *Teddy Roosevelt: All-Round Boy*. Macmillan, 1989.

Sabin, Lou. *Teddy Roosevelt, Rough Rider*. Illustrated by Robert Baster. Troll, 1985.

Stefoff, Rebecca. *Theodore Roosevelt, Twenty-Sixth President of the United States*. Garrett, 1988.

Woodrow Wilson, 1856-1924

Collins, David. *Woodrow Wilson: Twenty-Eighth President of the United States*. Garrett, 1989.

Osinski, Alice. *Woodrow Wilson*. Childrens Press, 1989.

United States

America's Historic Places: An Illustrated Guide to Our Country's Past. Reader's Digest, 1988.

Anno, Mitsumasa. *Anno's USA*. Putnam, 1988.

Critical Thinking Question
What is the value of reading and writing poetry?

Student Activities to Connect Literature and Curriculum

FINE ARTS

1. Develop a board game for classroom use with illustrated spaces, action cards, and appropriate markers. Name the game Americans All.

2. For a school library media center display, construct a bulletin-board mural with profiles of historic personalities in uniform dimensions of 11 inches by 14 inches. Each profile should include a statement about the person. Have quiz forms available for other classes to fill out. Paperback books and art supplies are good awards for contest winners.

LANGUAGE ARTS

1. Update *A Book of Americans* as a cooperative learning group project. Brainstorm the names of people and groups who should be included in the updated edition of the book. Divide the selections into units to be written and illustrated. Submit your adaptation to the Editorial Department, Henry Holt, 115 West 18th Street, New York, NY 10011.

2. How would you categorize or classify the people and groups of people included in *A Book of Americans*? Why?

WRITING PROMPT

1. Write the television news announcement under the following headline:

> Publisher Announces Revision of *A Book of Americans* Because of Classroom Writing Project in Local School

2. Write a new introduction for *A Book of Americans* that describes new subjects that have been added to the original book.

3. Plan and present an illustrated oral report about your favorite American.

MATH

1. Using dates in *A Book of Americans*, present a detailed graph showing the increase in population in the United States from its founding to modern times.

SCIENCE

1. What poems relate to science? Why? Which additional men and women of science would you add? What are their contributions to the world of science?

2. Identify medical breakthroughs in treatments and cures that are needed now. Why?

SOCIAL STUDIES

1. Using *The Timetables of History*, detail other events that were taking place throughout the world as America was growing and expanding as a nation. Present the information as a time line comparison table.

GEOGRAPHY

1. On appropriate United States regional map transparencies, label the locations mentioned in the poetry selections.

BEYOND THE BOOK

Guided Reading Connections Across a Learning Rainbow: Poetry Collections

Bayer, Jane A. *My Name Is Alice*. Illustrated by Steven Kellogg. Dial, 1984.

De La Mare, Walter. *Peacock Pie: A Book of Rhymes*. Illustrated by Edward Ardizzone. Faber & Faber, 1988.

de Regniers, Beatrice Schenk, Eva Moore, Mary Michaels White, and Jan Carr, eds. *Sing a Song of Popcorn: Every Child's Book of Poetry*. Rev. ed. Scholastic, 1988.

Livingston, Myra. *Sky Songs*. Illustrated by Leonard Fisher. Holiday House, 1984.

Marsh, James. *Bizarre Birds and Beasts*. Dial, 1991.

Prelutsky, Jack. *The Random House Book of Children's Poetry*. Illustrated by Arnold Lobel. Random House, 1983.

Untermeyer, Louis, ed. *Rainbow in the Sky: Golden Edition*. Illustrated by Reginald Birch. Harcourt Brace Jovanovich, 1985.

Enriching Connections

1. Plan an art fair. Students may display art, music, and written materials in an all-school program. Ribbons may be awarded by a panel of judges for the best entries in each category.

FROM ANOTHER POINT OF VIEW

Prelutsky, Jack. *Ride a Purple Pelican*. Illustrated by Garth Williams. Greenwillow Books, 1986.

Parent-Student Connections

1. Share a variety of poems at a family reading. Include nursery rhymes for younger listeners, as well as selections like the following:

    Atwood, Ann. *Haiku: The Mood of the Earth*. Illustrated by Ann Atwood. Macmillan, 1971.

    Carroll, Lewis. *Jabberwocky*. Illustrated by Jane B. Zalben. Warne, 1977.

    Longfellow, Henry Wadsworth. *Paul Revere's Ride*. Illustrated by Nancy W. Parker. Greenwillow, 1985.

❀ ❀ ❀

SECRET SOLDIER
The Story of Deborah Sampson

Author: Ann McGovern
Illustrator: None
Publisher: Scholastic, 1975
Suggested Grade Level: 5
Classification: Nonfiction
Literary Form: Biography
Theme: People make extraordinary sacrifices for their country in time of war.

ABOUT THE BOOK

STUDENT OBJECTIVES:

1. Compare the uniforms, weapons, equipment, locations of battles, and roles of soldiers of the American Revolution with those of the 1991 Desert Storm (Iraq) conflict. See the CDROM Desert Storm by Warner New Media, available from Educational Resources, 1550 Executive Dr., Elgin, IL 60123.

2. List the wars and conflicts in which the United States has engaged since its founding. Give the reasons for these wars.

3. Develop a Human Rights Peace Plan that will help to avert future wars and conflicts.

SYNOPSIS: This is the story of Deborah Sampson, who was orphaned at the age of five and who became a soldier 13 years later. At the time, only men were allowed to enlist in the army, but this did not stop Deborah. Disguised as a man, she fought for her country for 18 months, until she was wounded during a battle.

ABOUT THE AUTHOR:

Ann McGovern is a well-known contemporary author of many historical books about America's early years. She states, "For my future writing I plan to concentrate on events in our history long ignored and to produce books that reinforce humanitarian values such as love, individuality and honesty to each other" (de Montreville, Doris, and Elizabeth D. Crawford, ed., *The Fourth Book of Junior Authors and Illustrators,* H. W. Wilson, 1978, pp. 242-243).

McGovern believes that her books should show truth. In *If You Lived in Colonial Times*, she explains, "I think it is important to tell it like it was; to show, for example, that the Pilgrims got seasick on the Mayflower and threw up like ordinary folks."

McGovern wrote *Black Is Beautiful* shortly after the death of Martin Luther King. McGovern had attended a rally in New York City where a young man, expressing his anger over the murder of King, said, "Black is beautiful, baby. Know it. Feel it" (*Fourth Book of Junior Authors and Illustrators,* pp. 242-243.)

SELECTED ADDITIONAL TITLES:

McGovern, Ann. *Arrow Book of Poetry.* Scholastic, 1965.

————. *Black Is Beautiful.* Scholastic, 1969.

————. *If You Grew Up with Abraham Lincoln.* Scholastic, 1985.

————. *If You Lived in Colonial Times.* Scholastic, 1969.

————. *If You Sailed on the Mayflower.* Scholastic, 1975.

————. *Shark Lady: The Adventures of Eugenie Clark.* Illustrated by Ruth Chew. Macmillan, 1979.

————. *The Story of Christopher Columbus.* Scholastic, 1963.

————. *The Underwater World of the Coral Reef.* Scholastic, 1977.

————. *Wanted Dead or Alive: The Story of Harriet Tubman.* Scholastic, 1977.

USING THE BOOK

Suggested Approach to the Book

Model Lesson

1. Deborah's mother was forced to give away her five children because of sickness and poverty and the fact that the children's father had drowned in a shipwreck. She could no longer provide for them. Would Deborah's mother have had any other alternatives today?

2. Miss Fuller, Deborah's aunt, took Deborah to live in her home. Why were home-baked cookies and a featherbed of her own special treats for Deborah?

3. Miss Fuller died when Deborah was eight years old. The only home that could be found for her was one in which she had to care for an 80-year-old woman. Deborah had to carry heavy pieces of wood for the fire, wash the clothes, and cook for and feed the elderly woman. Do laws today protect children from such abusive treatment? Was this treatment considered abuse in the 1760s?

4. Deacon Thomas thought that all children needed to learn the value of money. His children and Deborah were given lambs to raise. The money from their sale would be kept by the child. What kind of responsibilities should students have? Should they receive money for chores or should they be given an allowance that is not tied to their chores? Why?

5. The King of England raised money by taxing the colonists. Explain the slogan, No taxation without representation. The king also set the rules for the colonies about hunting, farming, fishing, running businesses, and even about religious worship. What would those rules be today if the United States had a king instead of a president?

6. What did it mean when Deborah Sampson became a free woman in 1778? Women have won many rights. What are they? What responsibilities should go with these rights? "In those days, married women had very few rights" (see p. 27).

7. Deborah Sampson dreamed of a great adventure. What great adventure would you dream about today?

8. "In those days, if a poor man wanted to travel and have adventures, he joined the army" (see p. 28). Is this statement true for men and women today? Explain the differences between then and now.

Library Media Center Connections

1. Assign the following topics to cooperative learning groups to present as oral reports with illustrated support materials:

King George III	Minutemen	Lexington, Massachusetts
Paul Revere	George Washington	Concord, Massachusetts
William Dawes	Tories	Philadelphia, Pennsylvania

Computer Connections

1. Students in cooperative learning groups will prepare a 20-question, true-false or multiple-choice computer test about the life of Deborah Sampson.

2. Use graphics software to design a repetitive quilt pattern.

Instructional Materials Connections

1. Arizzi, Mavis. *Thinking About American History Through Historical Fiction.* Book Lures, 1985.

2. Copeland, Peter. *Early American Trades Coloring Book.* Dover, 1980.

3. Corwin, Judith Hoffman. *Patriotic Fun.* Messner, 1985.

4. Invite a military person and a surgeon to speak to the class about current information on their professions.

Theme Reading Connections: American Revolution

Beatty, Patricia. *Who Comes with Cannons?* Morrow, 1992.

Brown, Drollene. *Sybil Rides for Independence.* Whitman, 1985.

Davis, Burke. *Black Heroes of the American Revolution.* Harcourt Brace Jovanovich, 1976.

Forbes, Esther. *Johnny Tremain.* Illustrated by Lynd Ward. Houghton Mifflin, 1943.

Fritz, Jean. *Can't You Make Them Behave, King George?* Illustrated by Tomie dePaola. Putnam, 1982.

Lawson, Robert. *Mr. Revere and I.* Little, Brown, 1988.

Morris, Richard B. *The American Revolution.* Rev. ed. Illustrated by Leonard Everett Fisher. Lerner, 1985.

Reit, Seymour. *Guns for General Washington—A Story of the American Revolution.* Harcourt Brace Jovanovich, 1990.

Critical Thinking Question
Should women be assigned to battle areas during war? Why or why not?
What role do you think women will play in the military in the twenty-first century?

Student Activities to Connect Literature and Curriculum

FINE ARTS

1. The illustration opposite page 3 shows children asleep in bed and covered with a quilt. Design the pattern for the quilt.

2. Recreate the famous Boston Tea Party as a classroom play.

3. Design a poster to recruit Minutemen.

4. Present an artist's sketch of Deborah Sampson in military uniform (see p. 39). Design a new uniform for today's military personnel, both male and female.

LANGUAGE ARTS

1. Organize a work schedule for Deborah Sampson, who was required to perform the following chores:

   dress, feed, and care for the four boys in the family

   sweep, clean, cook, and carry in water and wood

   help plow the fields and rake the hay

   make everything she needed, including a milking stool

   teach reading to the four boys

2. Deborah Sampson kept a two-page diary. On the right-hand pages she wrote all of her good thoughts and good things she had done; on the left-hand pages she noted all of the things she thought of as bad. The pages on the left side filled up faster! Keep a diary in the same manner and see which pages are used up first.

3. Replicate Deborah Sampson's school room using her curriculum for teaching the lesson. (See pp. 25-26.)

4. Compile a dictionary of student-generated definitions of the following terms:

Tories	Red Coats	Boston Tea Party
Minuteman	Concord, Mass.	Philadelphia, Pa.
Lexington, Mass.	West Point, New York	Continental Army
Robert Shurtliff	Paul Revere	

5. "General Washington began calling for a different kind of soldier. He did not want the old kind of fighting men" (p. 31). Design an enlistment campaign, including pamphlets and posters, that would have helped the first commander-in-chief of the United States secure recruits.

WRITING PROMPT

1. Write brief sketches of Deborah Sampson's life. The sketches should be suitable for inclusion in a contemporary book about her memoirs. This activity is suitable for a class publishing project.

2. Write a feature story about the unusual disguise of Deborah Sampson, beginning with the following comments:

> "Go on! You can do it. Think of the adventures. You want to see rivers and mountains and cities. You want to see Boston" (p. 36).

MATH

1. In early America, the most common beverage was English tea. Conduct a poll to determine the most popular beverage of today. Construct poll questions to include coffee, tea, milk, soda, and others. Present the information, including number of persons polled and the percentage of their choices, using a bar graph or pie chart.

SCIENCE

1. How has the practice of medicine changed since the American Revolution? (See p. 44.) What treatment was available at hospitals for those who had suffered gunshot wounds? How many of us could dig a bullet out of our own leg?

SOCIAL STUDIES

1. Deborah Sampson lived from 1760 to 1827. Draw an illustrated time line for this period, using information about Deborah's life and United States history.

2. The time of *Secret Soldier* is 1765, which is 10 years before the start of the American Revolution. What kind of clothes did adults and children wear? What did their homes look like? Describe the types of transportation that were available.

3. Deborah was excited about visiting the great cities of her time, including Boston, Philadelphia, and New York. Devise a list of great cities today in the United States and what attractions are offered to visitors.

4. Design a pamphlet to be given to today's visitors at Deborah Sampson's former home in Sharon, Massachusetts. What epitaph would you write on her cemetery marker?

GEOGRAPHY

1. Using several transparencies and marking pens, construct maps of the United States, showing the country from 1750 through the 1820s.

2. Develop a classroom patchwork quilt of the United States as it was at the time of Deborah Sampson.

BEYOND THE BOOK

Guided Reading Connections Across a Learning Rainbow: Quilts

Paul, Ann Whitford. *Eight Hands Round—A Patchwork Alphabet.* HarperCollins, 1991.

Johnson, Tony. *The Quilt Story.* Illustrated by Tomie dePaola. Putnam, 1985.

Marsh, Carole. *Let's Quilt Kansas!* Gallopade, 1989. (Computer disk is available.)

———. *Let's Quilt Wyoming!* Gallopade, 1989. (Computer disk is available.)

Enriching Connections

1. Bake several loaves of bread as a classroom project. Some students may wish to churn butter for the bread.

2. Students may enjoy making large pieces of patchwork with pieces of cloth from other sewing projects or discarded garments. The completed fabric can be made into simple clothing, such as aprons, bandannas, scarves, or it can be made into pillow coverings or wall hangings.

3. Hold a classroom tea party. Sample different types of tea. Students may participate by bringing cookies, home made or purchased with the permission of parents. This is an opportunity to discuss manners for various social occasions.

FROM ANOTHER POINT OF VIEW

McGovern, Ann. *Wanted Dead or Alive: The Story of Harriet Tubman.* Scholastic, 1977.

Parent-Student Connections

1. From your local public library check out a family read-aloud book about the colonial or revolutionary periods.

2. Talk about the dangers inherent in civil unrest. In an emergency, what should students do? Give specific instructions.

❀   ❀   ❀

ME AND WILLIE AND PA
The Story of Abraham Lincoln

Author: F. N. Monjo
Illustrator: Douglas Gorsline
Publisher: Simon & Schuster, 1973
Suggested Grade Level: 5
Classification: Nonfiction
Literary Form: Biography
Theme: One viewpoint of American history, the story of family life in the White House from the perspective of Abraham Lincoln's son, Tad.

ABOUT THE BOOK

STUDENT OBJECTIVES:

1. Read and compare and contrast the biographies of three famous people.

2. Prepare 10 questions for interviewing a person on television. The person may have lived in a different era.

3. Discuss unusual ways in which autobiographical and biographical information can be presented in books.

SYNOPSIS: Tad Lincoln narrates the story of life with his famous father and his family. Tad's story includes many historical events.

ABOUT THE AUTHOR: F. N. Monjo, 1924-1978

Ferdinand Monjo's parents immigrated to the United States from Spain in 1850. His father's family became merchant shippers who organized trade with the Eskimos in the arctic; his mother's family owned a plantation in Mississippi. "Hearing my two families discuss the past—often with considerable heat and color—made it clear to me that people like Grant and Lincoln certainly had been flesh and blood creatures" (Holtze, Sally Holmes, ed., *Fifth Book of Junior Authors and Illustrators,* H. W. Wilson, 1983, p. 223).

Monjo's career included 20 years as a children's editor for Golden Press, American Heritage Press, and Harper & Row. Monjo's first book was *Indian Summer* (1968), which received mixed reviews, "including attacks from several fronts for presenting a negative image of American Indians" (*Fifth Book of Junior Authors and Illustrators,* p. 223).

Monjo's narrators were young people who told their historical stories from their viewpoints. He researched each book meticulously, and his stories introduced "unusual or obscure information or events to get to the historical truth." (*Fifth Book of Junior Authors and Illustrators,* pp. 222-223.)

ABOUT THE ILLUSTRATOR: Douglas Gorsline, 1913-1985.

Douglas Gorsline was the first American artist to receive an invitation from China to visit and paint the subjects of his choice. He was an illustrator of adult and children's books, including those written by F. N. Monjo and Clyde Bulla.

SELECTED ADDITIONAL TITLES: F. N. Monjo

Monjo, F. N. *The Drinking Gourd.* Illustrated by Fred Brenner. Harper & Row, 1969.

———. *Indian Summer.* Illustrated by Anita Lobel. Harper & Row, 1968.

SELECTED ADDITIONAL TITLES: Douglas Gorsline

Gorsline, Douglas, and Marie Gorsline. *North American Indians.* Illustrated by Douglas Gorsline. Random House, 1978.

———. *The Night Before Christmas.* Illustrated by Douglas Gorsline. Random House, 1975.

USING THE BOOK

Suggested Approach to the Book

Model Lesson

1. Describe the torchlight processions that went past the Lincoln home on Eighth Street in Springfield, Illinois. During Olympic Games years, there is a day and night torchlight parade. The torch is lit in Greece, and runners carry it to the host nation's Olympic site for the opening of the games. Are any torchlight or candlelight parades held in your area? For what reasons?

2. Why did Lincoln go to the telegraph office for the election results? How do presidents today learn if they are elected?

3. Did Lincoln's "closed mouth" make him a good president? Why or why not?

4. How do official portraits of the president and First Lady of today differ from those of Abraham Lincoln and Mary Todd Lincoln?

5. Why did the Lincoln children call circus people freaks when the children visited the P. T. Barnum's Museum in New York City? Describe the circuses of today. How do they differ from early circuses?

6. What was the meaning of the word *secesh*? (See p. 20.) What did Lincoln say about it? What event marked the beginning of the Civil War?

7. What kind of games did Tad play while living in the White House?

8. Why did Lincoln feel as though he were renting out rooms in one side of a house while the other side of the house was on fire? (See p. 29.)

9. Mama worried about Pa being assassinated. Had any other presidents met that fate?

10. Why did Civil War General Sherman want to be mayor of Galena, Illinois? Why was General Sherman's march to the sea from Atlanta to Savannah so painful for the South?

Library Media Center Connections

1. Have students research and present a miniature model of P. T. Barnum's traveling show. Students should work in cooperative learning groups on this assignment. The following subjects may be explored in the library media center:

Circus History	P. T. Barnum Circus	Circus Acts
Circus Posters	Circus People	Circus Animals
Circus Music	Circus Trains	Circus Big Tops
Circus Vargas	Ringling Brothers	Midgets/Giants

2. Locate illustrations of presidential china patterns. (See *The First Ladies Cook Book*, GMC-Parents Magazine Press, 1982.)

3. Report on the battle of the *Monitor* and the *Merrimac*. Draw pictures of both vessels.

4. Identify the following persons:

Harriet Beecher Stowe	Frederick Douglass	Julia Ward Howe
Simon Legree	Walt Whitman	Stonewall Jackson

Computer Connections

1. Using a word processor, write a letter to Tad Lincoln. Ask questions and express your opinions about life in the White House.

Instructional Materials Connections

1. Blassingame, Wyatt. *Look-It-Up Book of Presidents.* Random House, 1988.

2. Fisher, Leonard Everett. *The White House.* Holiday House, 1989.

3. Klaphtor, Margaret Brown. *The First Ladies.* White House Historical Association, 1987.

4. Freidel, Frank. *The Presidents of the United States of America.* White House Historical Association, 1987.

5. Olsen, Mary Lou. *Presidents of the United States.* Teachers ed. Garrett Education, 1990.

6. Reiter, Edith. *President Games.* Price Stern Sloan, 1987.

7. A three-dimensional jigsaw puzzle of the Capitol in Washington, D.C., is available from The Paragon, 89 Tom Harvey Road, Westerly, RI 02891.

8. Additional materials may be obtained from

   Lincoln Home National Historic Site, Eighth and Jackson, Springfield, IL 62705.

   Gettysburg National Military Park, Route 134, Gettysburg, PA 17325.

   Ford's Theatre, 511 Tenth St. NW, Washington, DC 20004.

   Lincoln Birthplace National Historic Site, Route 31E, Hodgenville, KY 42748.

   Mount Rushmore National Memorial, Route 244, Keystone, SD 57751.

Theme Reading Connections: Abraham Lincoln

D'Aulaire, Ingri, and Edgar D'Aulaire. *Abraham Lincoln.* Doubleday, 1939.

Freedman, Russell. *Lincoln: A Photobiography.* Clarion Books, 1987.

Hargrove, Jim. *Abraham Lincoln: Sixteenth President of the United States.* Childrens Press, 1988.

Kent, Zachary. *The Story of Ford's Theater and the Death of Lincoln.* Childrens Press, 1987.

Metzger, Larry. *Abraham Lincoln.* Franklin Watts, 1987.

Miller, Natalie. *Story of the Lincoln Memorial.* Childrens Press, 1966.

Sandburg, Carl. *Abraham Lincoln Grows Up.* Harcourt Brace Jovanovich, 1975.

Stefoff, Rebecca. *Abraham Lincoln: Sixteenth President of the United States.* Garrett Education, 1989.

> Critical Thinking Question
> Why did John Wilkes Booth believe that he was helping the South by assassinating Abraham Lincoln?

Student Activities to Connect Literature and Curriculum

FINE ARTS

1. Make your version of the official portrait of President Lincoln. Art forms may include collage, mosaic, watercolor, pen and ink, or any art form you select.

2. Make silhouettes of presidents on paper plates.
   For each silhouette, the required supplies include: a paper plate; construction paper; striped gift wrapping paper in red, white, and blue or red markers; foil stars; white glue or glue sticks; and scissors.

   1. Glue striped wrapping paper to the center of a plate. Cover the center of the plate, leaving the rim uncovered.

   2. Cut a silhouette of Lincoln out of black construction paper.

   3. Glue the silhouette slightly to the left of center of the plate.

   4. Decorate the the plate rim with stars or with Lincoln's name.

3. Mrs. Lincoln was "buying silks and velvets and other dress goods and gloves and lace and furniture and china and curtains for the Executive Mansion." Imagine that you are chosen to decorate and furnish the private quarters of the next president and his family. Present art renderings and colors palettes to display your ideas.

   The president has requested the following:

   a personal presidential study

   a personal First Lady's study

   a traditional master bedroom

   extensive closet storage areas

   rooms for teenage children

   an area for 6-year-old twin boys

   a living room with seating for 12

   a formal dining room for 12

   family dining and kitchen areas

   a multimedia viewing room

   a sun room with live plants

4. Each president has his own pattern on china used in the White House. Submit designs that would be appropriate for a new president.

5. Construct a model of a bathing machine. (See p. 30.) What was a lady's bathing suit like in the middle 1800s?

6. Describe the Union and Confederate uniforms. Would they be practical clothing for war today? Why or why not?

7. Construct Lincoln's log cabin using individual papier-mache logs. (For directions, see Corwin, Judith Hoffman, *Patriotic Fun,* Messner, 1985.)

LANGUAGE ARTS

1. Matthew Brady is famous for his photographs of the Civil War. Write an introduction for a display of his works at the Smithsonian Museum in Washington, D.C.

2. Carefully read the material under the heading, About This Story (pp. 88-92). Break the material into a formal outline. Which are the most important facts? Use them as brief headings. List minor material under major topic headings. You do not need to use all the material presented. Be selective in making this brief outline.

3. Present a class debate on the following statement: A woman will be president of the United States in the twenty-first century.

4. Write a feature story about the newly elected sixteenth president of the United States and his wife. Use their formal portraits to illustrate the story.

WRITING PROMPT

1. Write a brief news article under the following headline:

> President Lincoln Sends Message about General Lee:
> PLEASE DON'T LET HIM GET OFF WITHOUT BEING HURT

MATH

1. Construct a chart containing the following information:

   names of presidents in chronlogical order, up to and including Abraham Lincoln

   names of members of the president's family

   number of presidents who served in Congress

   number of years as president

   died in office or number of years lived after leaving office

   Use this information to make statistical statements. What kind of math word problems can be created from the data? Make bar graphs or pie charts to present the information.

SCIENCE

1. What was the disease scarlantina? What is this called today? How is the disease caught, and what medication is used to help people who have it?

SOCIAL STUDIES

1. Design a pictorial time line of transportation from the founding of the United States to the present. Display this project in the library media center, if possible.

2. Why did the newspaper headlines cry, "On to Bull Run"?

3. A Congressman barged into Lincoln's bedroom and requested that the president pardon a soldier who was going to be put to death the next morning for falling asleep on duty. What humorous response did the president give? If you were a military judge faced with this decision, what would you say?

4. Explain the Emancipation Proclamation of January 1, 1863.

5. What role in history did the following people play?

   Robert E. Lee

   "Little Mac" McClellan

   General Burnside

   Ulysses S. Grant

   "Fighting Joe" Hooker

   Jefferson Davis

6. Compare and contrast photographs of the damaged factories of Richmond, Virginia, in the Civil War with photographs of Kuwait's damaged buildings in the Desert Storm conflict of 1991.

GEOGRAPHY

1. Rail transportation was important to the new nation during the presidency of Lincoln. Using a transparency and colored marking pens, outline Lincoln's train trip to Washington from Illinois. Outline the states, mark their capitals, and add illustrations of their famous landmarks and products. Include a schedule of President Lincoln's speeches from the last car in the train.

2. Present a map of the United States at the time of the Civil War. With colored markers, identify the northern and southern states during the Civil War.

3.   Draw a map identifying areas where major Civil War battles were fought.

4.   The White House was located in Washington, D.C. Where was the Confederate White House located?

BEYOND THE BOOK

Guided Reading Connections Across a Learning Rainbow: Circuses

Harkonen, Helen B. *Circuses and Fairs in Art.* Lerner, 1965.

Johnson, John E. *Here Comes the Circus.* Random House, 1985.

Laslo, Cynthia. *The Rosen Photo Guide to a Career in the Circus.* Rosen, 1988.

Moss, Miriam. *Fairs and Circuses.* Franklin Watts, 1987.

Enriching Connections

Plan a Presidents Picnic on the school grounds, and invite parents to join the event. Most food supervisors will plan a special menu for the occasion. Use various theme-related pieces of art, including laminated Americana art placemats. Play a cassette of marching music by John Philip Sousa while walking to and from the playground. (Note: *Stars and Stripes Forever* was written by Sousa.) Uncle Sam hats and red, white, and blue sashes may be made.

FROM ANOTHER POINT OF VIEW

Anderson, LeVere. *Tad Lincoln: Abe's Son.* Garrard, 1971.

Parent-Student Connections

1.   The next time you vote, invite your child to go to the polls with you for a lesson in the essence of democracy.

2.   Discuss with your child the problems of protecting famous people in government, especially presidents, from harm and death.

3.   Supplementary home reading materials:

     Corwin, Judith. *Patriotic Fun.* Messner, 1985.

     The White House: An Historical Guide. White House Historical Association, 1982.

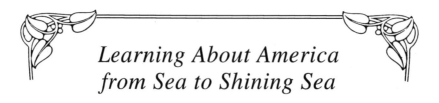

Learning About America
from Sea to Shining Sea

SOMEONE IS HIDING ON
ALCATRAZ ISLAND

Author: Eve Bunting
Publisher: Clarion Books, 1984
Suggested Grade Level: 5
Classification: Fiction
Literary Form: Novel
Theme: Gangs are highly visible in today's society and will retaliate against anyone who threat-
  ens or challenges them.

ABOUT THE BOOK

STUDENT OBJECTIVES:

1. Evaluate the role of gangs in schools today.

2. Determine the benefits and disadvantages of gang membership.

3. Determine a school policy in regard to gang activities on school property and the adjoining
    community.

SYNOPSIS: Danny steps in and helps an old woman who is the victim of a gang attack; the gang is
  determined to have its revenge for the interference.

ABOUT THE AUTHOR: Eve Bunting, 1928- .
  Eve Bunting feels that she is a role model for women who are "middle-aged and starting over"
(Holtze, Sally Holmes, ed., *Fifth Junior Book of Authors and Illustrators,* H. W. Wilson, 1983, pp.
60-61). Bunting had dropped out of college to marry. As her children grew older and her husband
pursued his career, she had the time to explore other fields. The local junior college offered courses

in painting, photography, sewing, and Writing for Publication. Within 12 years, Bunting had written and published 130 books, articles, and short stories.

"I hasten to say that it is my belief that no one can be 'taught to write.' The talent is there, latent or awake. It is a gift, like naturally curly hair or a great sense of humor" (*Fifth Junior Book of Authors and Illustrators*, p. 60). Many of her books are set in Ireland, where Bunting lived 30 years before coming to the United States and where her three children were born.

"I seem to write a lot about birds.... Eagles, hawks, blackbirds, owls, cormorants, parrots ... all of them used in fiction as symbolic of freedom and the unfettering power of love"(*Fifth Junior Book of Authors and Illustrators,* p. 60).

Bunting does not have to force herself to write each day. "I'm doing what I like to do best. I found it. I pursued it. I prospered. Which makes me one of the world's most fortunate women."

(Note: I have attended several conferences at which Eve Bunting has been the featured author. She is a low-key speaker whose demeanor reflects extensive knowledge of her subjects. Bunting shares with her audience her feelings about success as well as her disappointments. The audience keenly felt the writer's disappointment when she told the story of the unsuccessful nomination of *Someone Is Hiding on Alcatraz Island* for the California Young Readers' Medal. Although another of her books, *Face at the End of the World,* later received this coveted award, she was disappointed that her Alcatraz Island novel did not receive it first. Bunting, in her gentle way, explained to the audience that she felt it was one of her best, if not her best, book.)

SELECTED ADDITIONAL TITLES:

Bunting, Eve. *The Day of the Earthlings.* Illustrated. Creative Education, 1978.

———. *Demetrius and the Golden Goblet.* Illustrated by Michael Hague. Harcourt Brace Jovanovich, 1980.

———. *The Great White Shark.* Messner, 1982.

———. *The Happy Funeral.* Illustrated by Mai Vo-Dinh. Harper & Row, 1982.

———. *How Many Days to America? A Thanksgiving Story.* Illustrated by Beth Peck. Clarion Books, 1988.

———. *Just Like Everyone Else.* Illustrated. Creative Education, 1978.

———. *The Mother's Day Mice.* Illustrated by Jan Brett. Clarion Books, 1986.

———. *St. Patrick's Day in the Morning.* Illustrated by Jan Brett. Clarion Books, 1980.

———. *The Sea World Book of Sharks.* Harcourt Brace Jovanovich, 1980.

———. *The Sea World Book of Whales.* Photographs by Flip Nicklin. Harcourt Brace Jovanovich, 1986.

———. *Scary, Scary Halloween.* Illustrated by Jan Brett. Clarion Books, 1986.

———. *Sixth-Grade Sleepover.* Harcourt Brace Jovanovich, 1986.

———. *The Skate Patrol Rides Again.* Illustrated by Don Madden. Whitman, 1981.

———. *The Valentine Bears.* Illustrated by Jan Brett. Clarion Books, 1985.

———. *The Wall.* Illustrated by Ronald Himler. Clarion Books, 1992.

———. *The Wednesday Surprise.* Illustrated by Donald Garrick. Clarion Books, 1989.

USING THE BOOK

Suggested Approach to the Book

Model Lesson

1. What do you think of gangs? How would you feel if you were offered membership in a gang today? Do school activity clubs have an effect on gangs? Why or why not?

2. What weapons were the gang members carrying?

3. Alcatraz Island is well known. Why?

4. Explain why "a person in prison could see paradise, but couldn't get to it" (p. 17). Why did prisoners call an Alcatraz cellblock Broadway? What reason was given for the closing of Alcatraz in 1963? What kind of escape plan would you have tried if you had been in Danny's place?

5. What are Smokey Bear hats? Why were they so named?

6. What advice did Curt give Danny, his friend? Why? (See p. 42.)

7. Why did Danny pick the water tower as his hiding place? What happened to Danny and Biddy? How were they captured? What escape plan did the prisoners devise?

8. Why did Indians take control of the prison in the 1960s? (See p. 81.)

9. Do you think Danny would interfere with a gang activity in the future? What would you do if you were in the same circumstance as Danny?

Library Media Center Connections

1. Compile an alphabetized list of sources about gangs and prisons that are available to students. Ask the librarian if the library needs any additional materials on these subjects.

2. Who were the following special "guests" of Alcatraz Island?

   George "Machine Gun" Kelly

   Robert Stroud

   Al "Scarface" Capone

Computer Connections

1. Use a computer word processing program to produce a student newsletter about student issues. Conduct a student-interest poll and prioritize student opinions. Write an open letter to fellow students about gangs, drug use, or other contemporary issues.

Instructional Materials Connections

1. Invite a police officer to visit the classroom to discuss the role of gangs in your community. What about teenage drug use? Is drug use among students increasing or decreasing? Prepare a list of appropriate questions prior to the officer's visit.

Theme Reading Connections: National Parks

Crump, Donald J., ed. *Adventures in Your National Parks.* National Geographic, 1989.

A Kid's Guide to National Parks. Illustrated by Richard Brown. Harcourt Brace Jovanovich, 1989.

———. *Pathways to Discovery: Exploring America's National Trails.* National Geographic, 1991.

> Critical Thinking Question
> "Who'd think Priest and the rest of the outlaws would have mothers and brothers and stuff, like normal people?" (See p. 9.) Why do kids do things that displease their parents? Do kids today share the same values as their parents? Why or why not?

Student Activities to Connect Literature and Curriculum

FINE ARTS

1. Using soft colors, prepare a cutaway illustration of Fisherman's Wharf, including an underwater view of natural sea life.

2. Divide students into pairs, and seat the pairs back to back. One student will read a description of Cowboy, Maxi, or Jelly Bean. The other student will draw a picture of the character described. (See pp. 5-6.)

3. Using descriptions in the book, draw an aerial view of Alcatraz Island as it is today.

4. Design a tourist brochure for visitors to Alcatraz Island.

LANGUAGE ARTS

1. Do you live in an area that has a pier? If not, have you visited one? Cluster words that describe such a place.

2. In a report to the United States Park Service, recommend other uses of Alcatraz Island.

WRITING PROMPT

1. Imagine that you are being pursued by a gang. Complete the following statement. Describe your personal anxiety.

> "I tried to stay cool and think. But it's hard to stay cool when a gang's after you.... If only I could turn time back to when the Outlaws didn't know that I existed" (p. 1).

2. Write a news article under the following headline:

> Student Trapped on Alcatraz Island by Gang Members

MATH

1. A prison cell was 9 feet by 5 feet. What is the area? Measure the length and width of your bedroom and compute the area. Which has more space, your room or an Alcatraz cell? Use a graph grid to show both measurements.

2. Read your local newspaper for a week. Record on a graph the number of crimes reported each day. Can you determine what crime is the most prevalent?

SCIENCE

1. Why is it 10 degrees colder on Alcatraz Island than in San Francisco?

2. Who discovered "the Rock?" What was it named?

3. Describe Alcatraz Island in scientific terms.

SOCIAL STUDIES

1. Using a map on a transparency and colored marking pens, identify the landmarks of San Francisco. Prepare a script to use in presenting the information to the class as an oral report supplemented with transparencies.

2. Prepare an illustrated time line of Alcatraz Prison.

GEOGRAPHY

1. Construct a United States map and designate National Park locations in each state.

2. Compute the exact mileage from your home town to Alcatraz.

BEYOND THE BOOK

Guided Reading Connections Across a Learning Rainbow: San Francisco

Arnold, Carolyn. *The Golden Gate Bridge.* Franklin Watts, 1986.

Caen, Herb. *The Cable Car and the Dragon.* Illustrated by Barbara Byfield. Chronicle Books, 1986.

Dudman, John. *The San Francisco Earthquake.* Edited by Janet Caulkins. Franklin Watts, 1988.

Haddock, Patricia. *San Francisco.* Dillon, 1989.

Stein, R. Conrad. *The Story of the San Francisco Earthquake.* Childrens Press, 1983.

Yep, Lawrence. *Child of the Owl.* Harper & Row, 1977.

Zibart, Rosemary. *Kidding Around San Francisco: A Young Person's Guide to the City.* John Muir, 1989.

Enriching Connections

1. Present a mock trial in the classroom. Appoint a judge, jury, prosecuting attorney, defense attorney, witnesses, police officers, Coast Guard members, bailiff, and defendant. The charges (trespassing, assault with a deadly weapon, and kidnapping) should be made by the arresting officer at the time the Coast Guard returns the prisoners to San Francisco.

FROM ANOTHER POINT OF VIEW

Barden, Renardo. *Gangs.* Crestwood, 1989.

Parent-Student Connections

1. Discuss gang membership. Is this a problem in your area? What solutions would you recommend? Why?

❀   ❀   ❀

WASHINGTON IRVING'S RIP VAN WINKLE

Author: Retold by Thomas Locker
Illustrator: Thomas Locker
Publisher: Dial, 1988
Suggested Grade Level: 5
Classification: Folklore
Literary Form: Picture book illustrated with oil paintings
Theme: Our world is changing with each generation.

ABOUT THE BOOK

STUDENT OBJECTIVES:

1. Examine the story of Rip Van Winkle through the eyes of various artists.

2. Read five different American folktales.

3. Write and produce a readers theatre script adapted from *Rip Van Winkle.*

SYNOPSIS: After encountering a strange group of men playing ninepins, Rip Van Winkle fell asleep and slumbered for the next 20 years. Upon waking, he returned to his village without being recognized.

ABOUT THE AUTHOR: Washington Irving, 1783-1859.

Washington Irving was one of the first American writers to gain recognition in Europe. He lived during a time in which the United States was developing an art culture of its own. Irving was known for his humorous and satirical essays about New York society. Today, his Knickerbocker Tales provide an important example of New York's folklore.

Irving's *Sketch Book* established the short story as a popular literary form. *Sketch Book* included the original publication of the story of Rip Van Winkle and "The Legend of Sleepy Hollow." Although these stories were set in New York state, they were based on Grimm's fairy tales.

ABOUT THE ILLUSTRATOR: Thomas Locker, 1937- .

Thomas Locker had many gallery showings of his work before he became a children's book illustrator. "I discovered the art form of the picture book while reading to my five sons. I gave it a try as a lark and now I devote most of my time to books.... I see my books as a kind of bridge between generations and a way to bring fine art to the young mind" (Something About the Author, vol. 59, p. 113).

Locker's art is distinctive, with an easily identified focus. Reviewers label it America the Beautiful. His art may be compared with the early American Hudson River school. His work has a soft, natural light and a landscape background that is larger than life.

SELECTED ADDITIONAL TITLES: Washington Irving

Irving, Washington. *Two Tales: Rip Van Winkle and the Legend of Sleepy Hollow.* Illustrated by Barry Moser. Harcourt Brace Jovanovich, 1986.

SELECTED ADDITIONAL TITLES: Thomas Locker

Andersen, Hans Christian. *The Ugly Duckling.* Retold by Marianna Mayer. Illustrated by Thomas Locker. Macmillan, 1987.

Hort, Lenny, retold by. *The Boy Who Held Back the Sea.* Illustrated by Thomas Locker. Dial, 1987.

Locker, Thomas. *Family Farm.* Illustrated by Thomas Locker. Dial, 1988.

———. *The Mare on the Hill.* Illustrated by Thomas Locker. Dial, 1985.

———. *Sailing with the Wind.* Illustrated by Thomas Locker. Dial, 1986.

———. *Where the River Begins.* Illustrated by Thomas Locker. Dial, 1984.

———. *The Young Artist.* Illustrated by Thomas Locker. Dial, 1988.

USING THE BOOK

Suggested Approach to the Book

Model Lesson

1. Look at the opening picture in the book. What is Rip Van Winkle doing? Is the story contemporary or is it set in another time period? What clues to the setting do you see in the art?

2. Why did ghosts of the mountains play tricks on people? What would you do if you met a stranger in the forest and he motioned for you to carry a heavy barrel?

3. Why did Dame Van Winkle embarrass her husband in the inn? Did she have to act in that manner? Should Rip have sold property without discussing the matter with his wife? How has the law changed from the time of Rip?

4. Why did Rip think that the men looked like people he had seen in a painting? How did Rip react to the silent men?

5. Today, substance abuse is a serious problem across the nation. Consider that Rip drank some of the brew when no one was looking. Is it safe to drink or eat unknown liquids or food? Why or why not?

6. What happened to the entrance to the hollow? Why did the strange red, white, and blue flag catch Rip's attention? What would the flag have looked like at the time he fell asleep? Why?

7. How did the illustrator indicate that Rip's house had aged while Rip was sleeping? How did Dame Rip Van Winkle die? How was Rip reunited with his daughter and new grandchild?

8. Why do you think the ghosts of Henry Hudson and his crew return every 20 years? How many years is considered a generation? What do the villagers say about thunder in the hills? How did Rip spend his time after returning home?

Library Media Center Connections

1. Using print and nonprint materials from the library media center, compare and contrast the Hudson River style of art with that of American Impressionists. This activity may be expanded to include additional art styles by assigning different art periods or styles to cooperative learning groups.

2. For an introduction to the people of the Netherlands, the following fiction books are recommended:

DeJong, Meindert. *Wheel on the School*. Illustrated by Maurice Sendak. Harper & Row, 1954.

Dodge, Mary M. *Hans Brinker*. Illustrated by C. L. Baldridge. Putnam, 1963.

Green, Norma. *The Hole in the Dike*. Illustrated by Eric Carle. Harper & Row, 1975.

Krasilovsky, Phyllis. *The Cow Who Fell in the Canal*. Illustrated by Peter Spier. Doubleday, 1985.

Computer Connections

1. Using a word processor, have Rip write a letter to his future descendants describing his 20-year nap.

Instructional Materials Connections

1. Devlin, Harry. *To Grandfather's House We Go: A Roadside Tour of American Homes*. Four Winds Press, 1967.

2. Locker, Thomas. *The Mare on the Hill*. Filmstrip and cassette. Random House, 1986.

3. Locker, Thomas. *Where the River Begins*. Filmstrip and cassette. Random House, 1986.

4. Irving, Washington. *Rip Van Winkle*. Retold by Catherine Storr. Cassette. Raintree/Steck-Vaughn, n.d.

Theme Reading Connections: Henry Hudson, Hudson River

Harley, Ruth. *Henry Hudson*. Troll, 1979.

McNeer, Mayl. *The Hudson: River of History*. Garrard, 1962.

Critical Thinking Question
How interested are you in taking a 20-year nap and waking up in the future? Why or why not?

Student Activities to Connect Literature and Curriculum

FINE ARTS

1. Contrast the illustration of Rip flying the kite with children to an illustration of an adult flying a kite with kids today.

2. Construct a diorama of the village inn that Rip visited with his friends.

3. Construct a Rip Van Winkle "cube of information." Cubes are folded from sturdy paper and each side either has a different picture or some information. (Note: Fold the paper first, then unfold the cube and complete the artwork. Refold for a cube of art and information.)

LANGUAGE ARTS

1. Describe the game of ninepins. What sports activity is played with pins today? In a demonstration speech, outline the game's rules and the skills necessary to play the game.

WRITING PROMPT

1. Imagine that Rip Van Winkle has just awakened after a 20-year sleep and has become famous. Begin your newspaper article with the following words:

> Rip opened his eyes. Where am I?, he wondered.

MATH

1. List and graph the 10 tallest waterfalls in the world. Where are the major waterfalls located in the United States? On a United States map identify the areas in which these waterfalls are located. Are there waterfalls in your state? (See the *World Almanac* for locations of waterfalls.)

SCIENCE

1. Why do the leaves of some trees change colors and fall from the trees during autumn? Explain the word *deciduous*. What scientific term describes trees that do not lose their leaves during a specific season?

2. Explain the scientific process of Rip's gun rusting. Can you remove rust from an item?

3. What is the difference between a waterfall and a cascade?

SOCIAL STUDIES

1. Rip wants to know what happened in his village while he slept. Create an illustrated time line of major events in the United States during the 20 years he slept.

GEOGRAPHY

1. Map the Catskill Mountains and Hudson River areas.

BEYOND THE BOOK

Guided Reading Connections Across a Learning Rainbow: Rip Van Winkle

Chorpenning, Charlotte B. *Rip Van Winkle.* Coach House, 1954.

Gipson, Morrell. *Rip Van Winkle.* Illustrated by Sans Souci. Doubleday, 1984.

York, Carol B. *Rip Van Winkle.* New ed. Troll, 1980.

Enriching Connections

1. Examine the customs of Dutch-Americans, particularly in Pennsylvania. References include:

   Ammon, Richard. *Growing up Amish.* Macmillan, 1989.

   Costabel, Eva D. *The Pennsylvania Dutch: Craftsmen and Farmers.* Illustrated by Eva D. Costabel. Macmillan, 1986.

   Milhous, Katherine. *The Egg Tree.* Illustrated by Katherine Milhous. Macmillan, 1971.

   Olsen, Victoria. *The Dutch-Americans.* Chelsea, 1988.

   Tenzythoff, Gerri. *The Dutch in America.* Lothrop, Lee & Shepard, 1986.

FROM ANOTHER POINT OF VIEW

Irving, Washington. *Rip Van Winkle.* Retold and illustrated by John Howe. Little, Brown, 1988.

Parent-Student Connections

1. Ask the students to practice storytelling by sharing the stories "Rip Van Winkle" and "The Legend of Sleepy Hollow" with the family.

2. Describe various Dutch foods. What part does rice play in the Dutch diet? Include traditional Dutch foods in a home meal.

❀ ❀ ❀

FROM THE MIXED-UP FILES OF MRS. BASIL E. FRANKWEILER

Author: E. L. Konigsburg
Illustrator: E. L. Konigsburg
Publisher: Atheneum, 1967
Suggested Grade Level: 5
Classification: Fiction
Literary Form: Novel
Theme: "Because after a time having a secret and nobody knowing you have a secret is no fun. And although you don't want others to know what the secret is, you want them to at least know you have one."

ABOUT THE BOOK

STUDENT OBJECTIVES:

1. View art works through museum visits, video tapes, and books.

2. Formulate a set of standards for selecting art works to be preserved for future generations.

3. Produce student examples of impressionistic art for a display.

SYNOPSIS: Claudia Kincaid and her brother Jamie run away from home. In her own words, Claudia explains that she is not running FROM home but TO a more interesting place, New York City's Metropolitan Museum of Art.

ABOUT THE AUTHOR-ILLUSTRATOR: E. L. Konigsburg, 1930- .
Elaine Konigsburg has been both a chemist and a high-school science teacher. After her children began school, she turned to writing. Konigsburg was not able to find any stories that took place in suburban America during the 1960s and decided to write about this era. She received the prestigious Newbery award for *From the Mixed-Up Files of Mrs. Basil E. Frankweiler,* and the Newbery honor award at the same time for *Jennifer, Hecate, Macbeth, William McKinley and Me, Elizabeth* (Macmillan, 1967).
"The majority of Konigsburg's characters are on journeys of discovery in which they must come to terms with inner selves and with the people around them" (Stott, Jon C., *Children's Literature from A to Z,* McGraw-Hill, 1984, p. 160). Her books vividly portray the main character maturing and growing up in suburban America.

SELECTED ADDITIONAL TITLES:

Konigsburg, E. L. *A Proud Taste from Scarlet and Miniver.* Macmillan, 1973.

————. *About the B'nai Bagels.* Illustrated by E. L. Konigsburg. Macmillan, 1969.

————. *Jennifer, Hecate, Macbeth, William McKinley and Me, Elizabeth.* Illustrated by E. L. Konigsburg. Macmillan, 1967.

————. *Journey to an Eight Hundred Number.* Macmillan, 1982.

USING THE BOOK

Suggested Approach to the Book

Model Lesson

1. How is the scene set at the opening of *From the Mixed-Up Files of Mrs. Basil E. Frankweiler*?

2. Who is Saxonberg? What interests him, according to Mrs. Frankweiler? Should he have other interests? Why or why not? What interests your own grandparents?

3. What criteria did Claudia use in selecting her brother, Jamie, to run away with her to the museum? Using a cluster format, describe your parents and siblings.

4. What "injustices" did Claudia suffer? Sometimes, doing chores at home can be profitable. How did Claudia benefit from emptying trash cans at home?

5. Why were the runaways safer on the commuter train to New York than they would have been hitchhiking? What is the advantage of being inconspicuous? Where did the Kincaid children hide at closing time? Would that work today? What kind of information would you need to successfully hide overnight in a museum? What kind of security systems are used to protect museums from theft?

6. Mr. Frankweiler earned his fortune through the production of corn oil. Is that a good business today? Why or why not?

7. If you found a candy bar in its original wrapping on a ledge in a museum, would you eat it? Why or why not?

8. Why did Jamie Kincaid sign the post office box rental form as Angelo Michaels, Maiden head, Massachusetts?

9. Claudia wants to return home "different." Have you ever wanted to be perceived as "different" at home or in school? What are the advantages of change? Explain Mrs. Frankweiler's comment, "Claudia was tiptoeing into the grown-up world" (p. 141).

10. Was the book's ending satisfactory? Should Claudia and Jamie be punished? What would happen in your family if you had run away to the museum?

11. If you were Elaine Konigsburg's editor at Atheneum, what location setting would you recommend for her next book?

Library Media Center Connections

1. Using library media center resources, describe Greenwich, Connecticut.

2. What are the attractions of New York City?

3. Identify the following:

Daniel Boone	Henry Hudson	Marie Antoinette
Sarcophagus	Sit Hat-Hor Yunet	English Renaissance
Mastaba	Saris	Michelangelo Buonarroti
Joan of Arc	Clara Barton	Florence Nightingale
Hamlet	Lawrence Olivier	Rolls Royce

Computer Connections

1. Identify what technological systems are replacing card catalogs and check-out procedures in school and public libraries. How would the use of a computer have helped Mrs. Frankweiler?

2. In cooperative learning groups, brainstorm about the needs of your community for a specialized public or private museum. What type of museum is appropriate and what materials might be displayed? Create a program announcing the opening of this new museum in your community.

Instructional Materials Connections

1. Balsamo, Kathy. *Exploring the Lives of Gifted People: The Arts.* Good Apple, 1987.

2. Konigsburg, E. L. *From the Mixed-Up Files of Mrs. Basil E. Frankweiler.* Cassettes. Listening Library, n.d. One Park Ave., Old Greenwhich, CT 06870-1727.

3. *The Lively Art of Picture Books.* Video, n.d. Weston Woods, Weston, CT 06883-9989.

Theme Reading Connections: Museums

Althea. *Visiting a Museum.* Cambridge, 1983.

Cameron, Eleanor. *The Court of the Stone Children.* Dutton, 1973.

Greenwald, Sheila. *The Secret Museum.* Illustrated by Sheila Greenwald. Dell, 1989.

Judson, Bay, et al. *Art Ventures: A Guide for Families to Ten Works of Art in the Carnegie Museum of Art.* Illustrated by Edward Koren. Carnegie Museum of Art, 1987.

Stan, Susan. *Careers in an Art Museum.* Illustrated by Milton J. Blumenfeld. Lerner, 1983.

Waldron, Ann. *True or False? Amazing Art Forgeries.* Hastings, 1983.

Critical Thinking Question
Do you need to learn one new thing each day? Is this a good philosophy? List things you would like to learn more about, including hobbies and sports activities.

Student Activities to Connect Literature and Curriculum

FINE ARTS

1. Draw a cutaway model of Grand Central Station as it might have been in 1967. Write to the New York City Convention and Visitors Bureau (2 Columbus Circle, New York, NY 10019-1823) for information about the station as it is today.

2. Prepare an artist's rendering of the Metropolitan Museum's restaurant and fountain courtyard.

3. Describe Marie Antoinette's bed that was on display in the museum. How does it differ from the styles of furniture that are popular today? Develop a pamphlet on the history of beds.

4. Interpret the design imprinted on the velvet covering on which the statue had stood. Design a stonemason's mark for yourself.

5. Imagine that you are a curator in the Metropolitan Museum. Which area would you choose to supervise? Detail the art materials that would be appropriate for display. Cooperative learning groups can prepare miniature displays of their special interest areas.

6. "Even in this very elegant house of mine, that bathroom is especially grand. All the walls are black marble except for one that is mirrored entirely" (p. 133). Prepare a sketch of this bathroom for future reprints of *From the Mixed-Up Files of Mrs. Basil E. Frankweiler.*

7. How do experts authenticate art?

8. What is the difference between an angel and a cupid? Using a medium of your choice, create an angel.

LANGUAGE ARTS

1. A number of similes and metaphors are used in the book. For example, "Otherwise, Claudia would have worried for fear the driver could hear her heart, for it sounded to her like their electric percolator brewing the morning's coffee" (p. 21). Keep a list of other examples while you are reading the book.

2. Claudia was constantly correcting Jamie's grammar. Keep a list of his grammatical errors. Do you agree with her?

WRITING PROMPT

1. Write a letter home, as Claudia did, explaining that you have not been kidnapped or harmed.

2. Mrs. Frankweiler describes what students would be doing during a museum lecture (p. 35). The student group she described numbered 28. Today's class sizes are larger and sometimes have 36 or more students. Based upon her observations, what would students be doing today? Develop a humorous essay for the student newspaper about this museum field trip.

3. Briefly outline a revised ending for the book.

4. Develop a community handbook about local attractions.

5. Rewrite the chauffeur's report of driving Claudia and Jamie home.

6. Write a news article under the following headline:

> Record Crowd Views Museum "Bargain"

MATH

1. Poll students about their breakfast habits. Ask the following questions:

   What do you eat for breakfast on school days?

   What do you eat for breakfast on weekends?

   If you eat cereal, what is your favorite kind?

   If you could choose what you eat for breakfast on school days, what would you choose?

   Present the results of the survey using graphs and percentages.

2. The Metropolitan Museum receives 26,000 visitors on a Wednesday. The Museum covers 20 acres. If all the people were admitted at one time, how much space would each person have? If more than 250,00 people visit the museum in a week, what is the average daily count?

3. If Jamie and Claudia began with $28.61 and, after breakfast, had $27.11, how much did breakfast cost? Using the cost of breakfast as 20 percent of the day's expenses and lunch and dinner as 80 percent, what amount of money will they spend each day? How long will they be able to stay at the museum before they spend all their money?

4. If the artist Michelangelo was in his early twenties about 470 years before the book was published, how old would he be today?

5. Jamie announced that all his Christmas and birthday presents did not total $225, the auction price of the Angel. To acquire a savings of $225 over 5 years, how much money does he need to receive each year? Assume he will earn 10 percent simple interest on his savings account.

6. Explain the game of War. How could this card game be adapted for math practice exercises? (See p. 11.)

SCIENCE

1. When the two runaways hid on the school bus, "Claudia pretended that she was blind and had to depend upon her senses of hearing, touch, and smell." (See p. 20.) Ask permission to be blindfolded in class for a short period. When the experiment is complete, present notes about the difficulties you encountered. How should blind students be treated in school and in the community?

2. Identify the Neanderthal man. What role has he played in the history of mankind? Where was he discovered? Develop a time line pinpointing his discovery in relation to recorded history. Explain the terms Neanderthal and *Homo sapiens*.

SOCIAL STUDIES

1. If you could visit any city in the world, which one would you choose? What sightseeing attractions would you want to visit? What information do you have about your choice? List 10 books that have information about this city.

GEOGRAPHY

1. Locate the following communities on a map:

   Greenwich, Darien, Stanford, and Farmington, Connecticut

   Port Chester, New York

   Bologna, Italy

BEYOND THE BOOK

Guided Reading Connections Across a Learning Rainbow: Art and Artists

Blizzard, Gladys S. *Exploring Art with Children.* Come Look with Me series. Thomasson-Grant, 1990.

———. *Exploring Landscape Art with Children.* Come Look with Me series. Thomasson-Grant, 1991.

Lipman, Jean. *Calder Creatures.* Dutton, 1985.

Munthe, Nelly. *Meet Matisse.* Little, Brown, 1983.

O'Neil, Zibby. *Grandma Moses: Painter of Rural America.* Illustrated by Donna Ruff. Penguin, 1987.

Turner, Robyn Montana. *Rosa Bonheur.* Portraits of Women Artists for Children series. Little, Brown, 1991.

———. *Georgia O'Keeffe.* Portraits of Women Artists for Children series. Little, Brown, 1991.

Enriching Connections

1. Do you agree "that often the search proves more profitable than the goal"? (See p. 61.)

2. Sculpt an angel from clay.

FROM ANOTHER POINT OF VIEW

Ventura, Piero. *Michelangelo's World.* Putnam, 1989.

Parent-Student Connections

1. Plan to visit a local museum.

2. From the library, check out art books about Michelangelo to share with the family. Explore the works of other well-known artists.

❀ ❀ ❀

CAVE UNDER THE CITY

Author: Harry Mazer
Illustrator: None
Publisher: Harper & Row, 1989
Suggested Grade: 5
Classification: Fiction
Literary Form: Novel
Theme: During financial recessions and depressions, children must accept adult responsibilities and, due to these harsh circumstances, mature quickly.

ABOUT THE BOOK

STUDENT OBJECTIVES:

1. Produce a family budget.

2. Analyze conditions that cause financial downturns.

3. Graph the annual percent change in the consumer index over a period of 10 years. (See the *World Almanac.*)

SYNOPSIS: Twelve-year-old Tolley and his seven-year-old brother live in New York City during the Great Depression. They must take care of themselves due to extenuating family circumstances.

ABOUT THE AUTHOR: Harry Mazer, 1925- .
   Writing was very difficult for Harry Mazer because of his family background. His parents did not write. His relatives were immigrants from Poland and Russia. He feels that he is a writer, not because he does it well, but because he does it poorly. "Whatever I've done as a writer I've done despite the feeling that I have no natural talent. I've never felt articulate or fluent, rarely felt that flow of language that marks the writer." As a boy, he planned to read his way through the library, "starting with the letter A" (Holtze, Sally Holmes, ed., *Fifth Book of Junior Authors and Illustrators*, H. W. Wilson, 1983, p. 203).
   Mazer fell in love with and married Norma Fox. "She loved books, she was beautiful and she wrote," he explained. As the wage earner, he worked as "a longshoreman, a railroad worker, a welder, an iron worker—even an English teacher." His wife asked him what he would do if he could do whatever he wanted. "Be a writer," he said. (*Fifth Book of Junior Authors and Illustrators*, p. 203.)
   Norma and Harry Mazer embarked on a writing program. They were so determined to become writers that they crawled out of bed at 3 a.m. and wrote until their children woke up at 7 a.m. Then Mazer went to work in a factory.
   Their story is one of success after great sacrifice. They have received recognition in the writing field. Harry Mazer, whose characters are exposed to danger but survive in the end, has received numerous awards, including the selection of his book *Snowbound* for an ABC After School Special and selection of four of his books for young adult awards from the American Library Association.

Norma Fox Mazer was named Newbery honor medalist for *After the Rain.* Both authors have written several young adult novels.

SELECTED ADDITIONAL TITLES:

Mazer, Harry. *The Island Keeper.* Dell, 1986.

————. *Snowbound.* Dell, 1986.

USING THE BOOK

Suggested Approach to the Book

Model Lesson

1. Describe the New York City sights mentioned by Tolley Holtz:

Brooklyn	Roxy	Yankee Stadium	Ebbets Field
Downtown	Bronx Zoo	New York Coliseum	

2. Explain Tolley's description of his mother, "but then my mother doesn't like any woman who doesn't go to work or isn't active outside the house" (p. 2).

3. What experience did Tolley have with gangs? How does his view of "talking gangs" differ from today's city gangs?

4. Identify the following:

New York Yankees	Lou Gehrig	President Franklin Roosevelt
Lindbergh baby	Bruno Hauptmann	

5. The father in *Cave Under the City* is a house painter, and the mother works in a dress factory. The dress factory in which Mrs. Holtz sews is described as a sweatshop. What does this mean? Explain what the expression *hard times* means to the family. What expenses are the first to be eliminated when a family has financial difficulties? During the Depression, a family saying was, Electricity costs money. How do people conserve electricity today? How do you repair worn-out shoes when you do not have any money?

6. Describe Bubber's learning difficulties. What could schools do to help him learn?

7. What kind of problems do people who live in apartments have that people who live in single-family homes probably do not have? Are there any advantages to living in an apartment? What is an eviction?

8. Tolley caused a fire in the apartment on Halloween. How did it happen? What should you do if a fire starts in your home?

9. Describe the children's trip to grandmother's apartment? What was the problem? How would you solve it? What would you do if the same thing happened to you?

10. Where did the boys find their cave under the city? What kinds of things did the boys collect for their cave? Would you be able to collect the same things if you were homeless today?

11. Is there ever a time when it is acceptable to steal? Why or why not?

12. Tolley had to nurse his sick brother, who had a serious cold. What did he do? What would you do today?

13. What was the government's answer to the Depression? Would that same program work today? Why or why not? What type of new social program could be enacted if hard times recur?

14. Why do you think the author introduced a new character, Whitey, into the story? What lessons did Whitey teach the brothers about eating in a restaurant during the Depression? Explain the lesson the brothers learned when they tried to sell Ford auto tires to a junk dealer.

15. What was a Camel billboard? What restrictions are placed on cigarette advertisers today?

16. Explain what was happening to Tolley when he said, "I'm walking and dreaming, asleep in my feet. Bubber held my hand and I followed him" (p. 138).

Library Media Center Connections

1. Ask the school library media center librarian to help you find a copy of the "Krazy Kat" and "Little Orphan Annie" comic strips that Tolley read. What are students' favorite comic strips? *The Shadow* and *The Lone Ranger* radio programs were popular during the Depression. Ask the librarian to help you find a cassette recording of the programs.

2. Research information about the abuse and, later, protection of children who worked in sweatshops. What labor laws relate to employment of minors today? What is the minimum wage that can be paid?

Computer Connections

1. Prepare a class cookbook of inexpensive meals and snacks. Criteria for inclusion include price, a variety of food selections, and a balanced diet.

Instructional Materials Connections

1. Mazer, Harry. *Snowbound.* Cassette. Listening Library, n.d.

2. Stein, Conrad R., and Keith Neely. *The Story of Child Labor Laws.* Childrens Press, 1984.

Theme Reading Connections: Finance

Adler, David A. *All Kinds of Money.* Franklin Watts, 1984.

Berry, Joy. *Every Kid's Guide to Making and Managing Money.* Childrens Press, 1987.

———. *What to Do When Your Mom or Dad Says... "Earn Your Allowance."* Living Skills, 1982.

Cantwell, Lois. *Money and Banking.* Franklin Watts, 1984.

Long, J., ed. *Budgeting Know How.* Cambridge, 1987.

Lubov, Andrea. *Taxes and Government Spending.* Lerner, 1989.

Schwartz, David M. *If You Made a Million.* Illustrated by Steven Kellogg. Lothrop, Lee & Shepard, 1989.

Spiselman, David. *A Teenagers Guide to Money, Banking and Finance.* Messner, 1988.

Stine, Jane, and Jovial B. Stine. *Everything You Need to Survive: Money Problems.* Illustrated by Sal Murdocca. Random House, 1983.

Critical Thinking Question
President Franklin Roosevelt stated in his inaugural address in 1933, "The only thing we have to fear is fear itself." How do these words relate to society today? Could the description of hard times apply to today? Explain your answer.

Student Activities to Connect Literature and Curriculum

FINE ARTS

1. Imagine a summertime movie theater that is just like a movie theater, with seats and a screen, but without a roof? Where would an open theater be most practical and useable for most of the year? Create a miniature model of the summertime open-roofed movie house.

2. Present an illustration of a Model A car or a milk wagon.

3. Design a set of picture postcards illustrating New York City; Baltimore, Maryland; or Washington, D.C.

LANGUAGE ARTS

1. Write a television commercial for a hair product used today. Prepare a story board to illustrate the visuals.

2. Imagine that you are an inexperienced writer. What difficulties would you have learning how to write in a professional manner? What would you write? What information would need to be researched? If you had to give up recreation in order to write, what activities would you give up? How much time would you gain?

WRITING PROMPT

1. Develop a diary for Tolley and Bubber. Begin with the following statement:

Nobody knows about what happened to us or where we were. I don't talk about it. It didn't happen to them, and I don't want to hear people making stupid remarks like the only hungry people are too dumb or too lazy to work.

MATH

1. During the Depression, a newspaper cost 2 cents. How much does your community newspaper cost today? What is the percentage increase? Mrs. Holtz owed the grocer $29.24. Using the same percent increase that you used for the newspaper, how much would she owe to the store today? Do grocery stores extend credit to their customers today?

SCIENCE

1. Mother's cough is mentioned several times in the book. What do you think is wrong?

2. What kind of food did the boys eat when they were on their own? Make a complete list of the food. Research the number of calories in each item. How many calories do you need each day? Would the brothers have gained or lost weight? Individual students in cooperative learning groups can scan different chapters of the book for information about what the boys ate.

3. If you had only $100 to feed two people for two weeks, what purchases would you make? Use specific prices, including double-discount coupons and advertised specials from your local market.

SOCIAL STUDIES

1. Construct an economic time line of financial depressions and recessions in the United States. (See *World Almanac*.)

2. List other countries that have had financial depressions and recessions, and list the years of their duration.

GEOGRAPHY

1. How many miles is it from New York City to Baltimore, Maryland; and from New York City to Washington, D.C.?

2. Using the information on page 110, prepare a rough map and memorize the areas on the map. What would a map of your community look like?

BEYOND THE BOOK

Guided Reading Connections Across a Learning Rainbow: Poverty

Coil, Suzanne. *The Poor in America*. Illustrated by Jane Steltenpohl. Messner, 1989.

Kosof, Anna. *Homeless in America*. Kline, M., ed. Illustrated. Franklin Watts, 1988.

Meltzer, Milton. *Poverty in America*. Morrow, 1986.

Enriching Connections

1. Organize a school food and clothing collection drive for poor and homeless people.

FROM ANOTHER POINT OF VIEW

Byars, Betsy. *The Night Swimmers*. Dell, 1981.

Parent-Student Connections

1. Discuss with your child the need to budget an allowance. Recommend a combination of spending and savings. Talk about prioritizing purchases in the family. What bills must be paid first? What percentage of income is used for housing, food, clothing, education, recreation, and other expenses?

2. Have the students plan and prepare an economical family dinner under proper supervision.

❀ ❀ ❀

NIGHT OF THE TWISTERS

Author: Ivy Ruckman
Illustrator: None
Publisher: Harper & Row, 1984
Suggested Grade Level: 5
Classification: Fiction
Literary Form: Novel
Theme: In times of emergency, everyone must show compassion and help where needed. The story is based on a true event, a series of seven tornadoes that struck Grand Island, Nebraska, in 1980.

ABOUT THE BOOK

STUDENT OBJECTIVES:

1. Recognize that emergencies occur and it is important to have plans for school, home, and community.

2. Compile a list of natural disasters common in your area of the country.

3. Prepare and implement a home and school disaster plan.

SYNOPSIS: People of a small town were bound closer together through a common disaster, a night of tornadoes. Knowing emergency procedures was most important for all of the people.

ABOUT THE AUTHOR: Ivy Ruckman, 1931- .

Ivy Ruckman was the seventh and last child in her family. She explains that the advantages of being the youngest outweigh the disadvantages. "What freedom! Until captured by school, I was free as the wind. Leisure and play are important in the development of a writer's imagination" (Holtze, Sally Holmes, ed., *Sixth Book of Junior Authors and Illustrators,* H. W. Wilson, 1989, p. 252).

Ruckman taught high school before becoming a full-time author. She speaks frequently in schools and shares special experiences with her audiences. "I look for a scrawny little girl who can't sit still, whose eyes are neon bright with excitement, and I know she's kin—someone who'd rather read or dream up stories than eat!" (*Sixth Book of Junior Authors and Illustrators,* p. 253).

Night of the Twisters was selected a Junior Literary Guild book and was listed as an Outstanding Science Trade Book for Children in 1984. The story was also serialized in *Cricket,* a children's literary magazine.

SELECTED ADDITIONAL TITLES:

Ruckman, Ivy. *In a Class by Herself.* Harcourt Brace Jovanovich, 1983.

———. *Melba the Brain.* Westminister, 1979.

———. *No Way Out.* Harper & Row, 1988.

———. *What's an Average Kid Like Me Doing Up Here?* Delacorte Press, 1983.

USING THE BOOK

Suggested Approach to the Book

Model Lesson

1. What is a red-letter day? Give examples of red-letter days in your family. Make a chart for your bedroom listing the criteria you have for a red-letter day. How often do you think you will have red-letter days? Make a list of days you would categorize as black-letter days. Ask your parents and grandparents if they remember any black-letter days. Some important dates might be the assassination of President John Kennedy, the invasion of Pearl Harbor, or the 1989 San Francisco earthquake, which occurred during the World Series.

2. Dan Hatch ate Frosty Flakes for breakfast. What do you have for breakfast? Describe a balanced breakfast that includes the new government-approved five food groups.

3. What kind of chores do you do at home? Do you get an allowance or special privileges for doing a good job?

4. Theodor Geisel is the author of a classic Dr. Seuss book, *If I Ran the Zoo* (Random House, 1950). Read the book and give your own version of *If I Ran the World*.

5. Do you have any younger brothers or sisters? What things changed with their arrival in the family? What changes when a parent leaves a job to raise a child? What do you think is the most difficult adjustment? Explain Dan Hatch's comment, "Used to be, we had conversations at the supper table" (p. 23).

6. Why did Dan ask his mom if they had to go to the basement? (See p. 31.) What kind of weather-related emergencies occur in your community?

7. The radio went off the air and the letters *CD* flashed on the television screen. What did the letters mean? After the tornado, Dan could smell gas. What should be done now?

8. Explain why "home base is home base, no matter how much it's been torn up" (p. 139).

9. Predict what the community will be like within one year.

Library Media Center Connections

1. Assign one of the following research topics to cooperative learning groups.

Tornadoes	Storms	Floods	Fires
Earthquakes	Volcanic	Eruptions	

Computer Connections

1. Using a word processor, describe Dan's version of how he steered the police car when the officer was blinded by glass. (See p. 109.)

Instructional Materials Connections

1. Cosgrove, Brian. *Weather*. Eyewitness Book series. Random House, 1991.

2. Cosner, Sharon. *Be Your Own Weather Forecaster*. Messner, 1982.

3. Deery, Ruth. *Earthquakes and Volcanoes*. Good Apple, 1985.

4. Lambert, David, and Ralph Hardy. *Weather and Its Work*. Facts on File, 1985.

5. Markle, Sandra. *Weather, Electricity, Environmental Investigations*. Learning Works, 1982.

6. Meteorology transparencies (6 transparencies with 4 overlays) and meterology study prints (14 cards with text and graphics) are available from Hubbard Scientific, P.O. Box 760 Chippewa Falls, WI 54729-0760.

7. Micallef, Mary. *Floods and Droughts*. Good Apple, 1985.

8. *Water and Weather*. Video. Tell Me Why series. Tornado Tube. (Use two discarded soft-drink 1-liter bottles to create vortex action found in tornadoes and whirlpools.) Both available from Summit Learning, P.O. Box 493D, Ft. Collins, Co 80522.

9. Wilson, Frances. *The Weather Pop-Up Book*. Illustrated by Philip Jacobs. Little Simon, 1987.

10. McVey, Vicki. *The Sierra Club Book of Weatherwisdom*. Illustrated by Martha Weston. Little, Brown, 1991.

11. Weather Kit "introduces you to some of the basic operations—evaporation, wind, humidity, heat retention—through simple hands-on experiments and observations." This science kit is one in a series resulting from an Alliance for Science partnership between the Museum of Science (Science Park, Boston, MA 02114) and the Nature Company (750 Hearst Ave., Berkeley, CA 94710).

Theme Reading Connections: Disasters

Bramwell, Martyn. *Volcanoes and Earthquakes*. Franklin Watts, 1986.

Fradin, Dennis B. *Disaster! Blizzards and Winter Storms*. Childrens Press, 1983.

———. *Disaster! Droughts*. Childrens Press, 1983.

———. *Disaster! Fires*. Childrens Press, 1982.

———. *Disaster! Floods*. Childrens Press, 1982.

———. *Disaster! Volcanoes*. Childrens Press, 1982.

Lauber, Patricia. *Volcano: The Eruption and Healing of Mt. St. Helens*. Bradbury Press, 1986.

Radlauer, Ed, and Ruth Radlauer. *Earthquakes*. Childrens Press, 1987.

Richard, Graham. *The Chernobyl Catastrophe*. Illustrated by Peter Bull. Franklin Watts, 1989.

Scollins, Richard. *The Fire of London*. Illustrated by Richard Scollins. Franklin Watts, 1989.

Simon, Seymour. *Volcanoes*. Morrow, 1988.

Critical Thinking Question
What help was available to tornado victims when President Jimmy Carter promised, "You won't be forgotten"?

Student Activities to Connect Literature and Curriculum

FINE ARTS

1. As a class project, complete a mural in two parts, before and after the tornado.

LANGUAGE ARTS

1. Interview Dan about his actions before, during, and after the tornado. List 20 questions that he should answer.

2. Plan, write, and produce a classroom emergency readiness video.

WRITING PROMPT

1. Explain Dan's statement about taking time to notice, "how beautiful Sand Crane Drive looked in that weird half-light. Up and down the street trees swayed in unison, like dancers in a chorus line. Overhead, clouds boiled so low you could almost jump up and grab them. It was unreal, all the creaking and moaning going on" (p. 31). Write a one-paragraph description of weather conditions you have observed.

2. Write a feature article about one of the victims beginning with the following statement.

> I thought it was the beginning of a nightmare...

MATH

1. Select 10 cities in the United States and record their monthly average temperature with different color markers on a graph. Which one has the warmest temperature? Which city recorded the coldest temperature? What part does geography play in the weather of these 10 cities? (See the *World Almanac*.) Locate the 10 cities on a map.

SCIENCE

1. Explain the formation of a tornado. What is a tornado watch? How long does it last? What preparations should be completed at home before tornado warnings are posted?

2. Compare and contrast the conditions that make up a tornado and a hurricane. Consider size, direction, and velocity.

3. Define hypothermia. How is it treated?

4. Explain the following weather terms:

Small Craft Advisory	Gale Warning	Tropical Storm Warning
Special Marine Warning	Storm Warning	Hurricane Warning

SOCIAL STUDIES

1. Construct a dry marker map of the United States suitable for weather forecasting.

GEOGRAPHY

1. Identify on a map St. Paul, Grand Island, and Danneborg. What is the population of each? What drives the main economy in each area?

BEYOND THE BOOK

Guided Reading Connections Across a Learning Rainbow: Weather Fiction

Barrett, Judith. *Cloudy with a Chance of Meatballs.* Macmillan, 1978.

Bellairs, John. *The Secret of Weatherend.* Illustrated by Edward Gorey. Dial, 1984.

Britain, Bill. *Dr. Dredd's Wagon of Wonders.* Illustrated by Andrew Glass. Harper & Row, 1989.

Enriching Connections

1. Create a game board and question cards combining weather terms and geography information to share with the class.

2. What does a person's food preferences have to do with the weather? Give examples.

FROM ANOTHER POINT OF VIEW

Arnold, Caroline. *Coping with Natural Disasters.* Walker, 1988.

Parent-Student Connections

1. Watch an evening television weather program. Keep a graph of local temperatures for 30 days. What does the data tell you?

2. What books make good reading during inclement weather?

3. Is there any correlation between the weather and music played on the radio? Why or why not?

❀ ❀ ❀

THE WAR WITH GRANDPA

Author: Robert Kimmel Smith
Illustrator: Richard Lauter
Publisher: Delacorte Press, 1984
Suggested Grade Level: 5
Classification: Fiction
Literary Form: Novel
Theme: A family experiences change when another member is added to the living arrangements.

ABOUT THE BOOK

STUDENT OBJECTIVES:

1. Role play family situations.

2. Recommend actions that will create harmony in the family.

3. Describe the plight of older people today and develop a plan to provide aid.

SYNOPSIS: Peter Stokes, a fifth-grader, and his little sister, Jennifer, learn that Grandpa is coming from Florida to live with the family. That's just fine until Peter learns that *his* room will be given to Grandpa and Peter will take the attic guest room. Peter has had only *one* room in his whole life, and he is especially attached to it. From the title of the book, you can guess what happens. Peter goes to war with Grandpa!

ABOUT THE AUTHOR: Robert Kimmel Smith, 1930- .

Robert Kimmel Smith lives in Brooklyn, New York, and is the author of several books. Smith's parents did not encourage him in his career choice, writing. He enrolled in Brooklyn College to become a doctor; instead, he failed every math course. While in the military in Berlin, Germany, Smith began to write. After a career in advertising, he began writing full time. "It was a long and twisting road, filled with frustration, rejection, and disappointment" (Holtz, Sally Holmes, ed., *Sixth Book of Junior Authors and Illustrators,* H. W. Wilson, 1989, p. 283).

His best-known title is *Chocolate Fever,* a story written for his daughter, Heidi. Smith displays a keen insight into his characters. They seem like real people, not artificial book characters.

ABOUT THE ILLUSTRATOR: Richard Lauter, birthdate unavailable.

Richard Lauter has illustrated several books for children, including book jackets for Paula Danziger's *The Divorce Express* (Dell, 1983) and Linda Lewis's first book, *We Hate Everything but Boys* (Pocket Books, 1990).

SELECTED ADDITIONAL TITLES: Robert Kimmel Smith

Smith, Robert Kimmel. *Chocolate Fever.* Dell, 1978.

———. *Jelly Belly.* Dell, 1982.

———. *Mostly Michael.* Delacorte Press, 1987.

USING THE BOOK

Suggested Approach to the Book

Model Lesson

1. Who is telling the story? How do you know? What assignment did Mrs. Klein give to Peter's class?

2. Describe your family. List five positive characteristics of your family.

3. Why does Peter say that he was ashamed of his behavior when his parents told him that he had to give up his room to Grandpa? Explain Dad's statement, "It's not fair that Grandma died. It's not fair that Grandpa is so sad and lonely. Life isn't always fair, Pete" (p. 16). After Peter has moved into the guest room, do you have empathy for him? Why or why not?

4. Do you take lessons in music, dance, or art? If you could take free lessons in anything, what would it be? Why? If other students feel the same way, maybe a plan could be worked out with the city parks and recreation department or another organization to provide lessons.

5. What exceptions to the rule can you find in Pete's promise, "When I grow up and have a kid I will never make him do anything he really does not want to do" (p. 20)?

6. Have you read any books in Pete's favorite series, Encyclopedia Brown and Great Brain? How do you feel about the books? Do other students in the class have any favorite series?

7. What is the importance of 1776 to Peter and his friends, Steve and Billy? Explain the methods of warfare that the boys discuss. Explain Peter's first move in the war against Grandpa. What did he do? What did Grandpa do? What effect did the advice of his friends have on Peter?

8. Describe the events of the war that lead to the story's climax. Would you have done the things Pete did, or do you have other ideas? What part do peer influence and pressure play in the lives of kids today?

Library Media Center Connections

1. Describe the tactics and maneuvers used in the American Revolution. Include art work illustrating battleground conditions. How many people died in the fight for freedom? Compare this early battle for freedom with the 1991 Desert Storm conflict. What were the causes of each war? How did the fighting differ in the two wars?

2. Prepare a grandparents display in the library media center for a special school event.

Computer Connections

1. Use a computer to prepare invitations and programs for a Grandparents Are Special school event.

2. Students will write a special computer message to be given to their guests. They may write poems, essays, or letters appropriate for the occasion.

Instructional Materials Connections

1. Invite an author or artist to visit the classroom. Prepare questions that may be asked during the visit. Ask about materials they use in their work and the difficulties the encounter in creating their work.

2. Smith, Robert Kimmel. *The War with Grandpa.* Cassette. Listening Library, n.d. Available from Listening Library, One Park Avenue, Old Greenwich, CT 06870-1727.

Theme Reading Connections: Grandparents

Ackerman, Karen. *Song and Dance Man.* Illustrated by Stephen Gammell. Alfred A. Knopf, 1988.

Berger, Barbara. *Grandfather Twilight.* Putnam, 1988.

Bunting, Eve. *The Wednesday Surprise.* Clarion Books, 1989.

Carlson, Natalie. *A Grandmother for the Orphelines.* Illustrated by David White. Harper & Row, 1980.

dePaola, Tomie. *Nana Upstairs and Nana Downstairs.* Putnam, 1973.

Martin, Bill, and John Archambault. *Knots on a Counting Rope.* Henry Holt, 1987.

Mazer, Norma. *After the Rain.* Morrow, 1987.

> Critical Thinking Question
> "Grandpa had no life at all. Could you die from being sad? I wondered. Could you?" (See p. 34.) How would you answer Peter's question?

Student Activities to Connect Literature and Curriculum

FINE ARTS

1. Examine the family portrait opposite page 1. Design a collage of your family. Describe your family to the class using a mind map.

2. Design a *War with Grandpa* game. Use a game board, dice, cards, and property such as personal and family items in your game.

3. Construct a shoe-box model of Grandpa's new basement apartment.

LANGUAGE ARTS

1. Poll every student in fifth grade to learn what their favorite five books are. Share this information with fifth-grade teachers, the librarian, and the principal. This list could serve as a recommended-purchase list.

2. Retell an incident from the *War with Grandpa* from Grandpa's viewpoint.

3. Debate the following issue:

> All people should be given a choice to live in government-funded nursing-homes when they reach the age of 65 as compensation for their past service.

WRITING PROMPT

1. Have you ever gone fishing? What is it like? Write a one-page story about participating in your favorite sport or activity. Write in the first person, as Peter did when he wrote the story about *War with Grandpa.*

2. Using the criteria that Mrs. Klein assigned to the class, write "a story about something important that happened to us and to tell it 'true and real' and put in words that people said if we can remember and to put quote marks around them and everything" (p. 1).

3. Write the first paragraph ("lead") of a newspaper article to go with the following headline:

> War with Grandfather Truce Reached by Participants

MATH

1. Discuss in class which 20 occupations are most needed in today's world. Can these occupations be prioritized? Prepare a chart ranking the average salary for each of these occupations.

SCIENCE

1. What is emphysema, the disease that attacked Grandma? What is its cause? What kind of treatment is available today?

2. Trace the technology for making false teeth. Remember that George Washington wore false teeth. When were they invented?

3. Prepare a diagram of your teeth. Using the chart in figure 7.1, draw two half-circles, one for the upper and one for the lower jaw. Work in teams of two to fill out the chart. Students will examine their partners' teeth and mark the chart. Blacken in the diagram for a filled tooth, leave the chart blank for a good tooth, and mark the chart with an X for missing teeth. Small, angled mirrors are needed; they are available from dentists or drug stores. What is the percentage of cavities for the class? Is there a percentage difference between boys and girls?

4. What is the average temperature in Fort Lauderdale, Florida, for each of the four seasons? How does your region compare? If you live in Florida, compare your local temperatures with those of Nome, Alaska.

5. State the latitude and longitude of Fort Lauderdale and of your home town. Locate the place that is exactly halfway around the world from each city. Give the map coordinates for each.

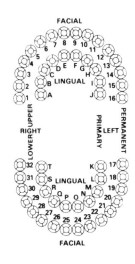

Fig. 7.1. Dental Examination Chart with Juvenile and Adult Diagrams.

SOCIAL STUDIES

1. What is the value of playing Monopoly? Upgrade the board game in terms of money and the cost of property today. What changes would you make? Why? Send your ideas to the company that produces the game: Parker Brothers, Salem, MA, 01970.

2. Ask students to determine their nationality and the geographic roots of their family. Use a world map and flag markers to record the information in class.

3. Today, many people are homeless. Can you recommend any steps or actions to ease their burden? How can students help? Examine the problem, brainstorm solutions, develop a workable plan, and present it to the school principal for approval as a joint project with the school and community.

GEOGRAPHY

1. Before moving to Peter's house, Grandpa had lived in Fort Lauderdale, Florida. List the reasons why he and Grandma had moved there. Prepare a travel brochure about the city and its facilities and activities for visitors. Do you think you would like to live there? Why? Is there another place you would like to live? Why? What makes a town or city a desirable place to live?

BEYOND THE BOOK

Guided Reading Connections Across a Learning Rainbow: Student-Written Books

Baron-Hall, Darla. *Only at the Children's Table.* Raintree/Steck-Vaughn, 1988.

DeWitt, Jamie. *Jamie's Turn.* Raintree/Steck-Vaughn, 1984.

Eldridge, Melinda. *Salcott, The Indian Boy.* Raintree/Steck-Vaughn, 1989.

Estvanik, Nicole B. *The Snowman Who Wanted to See July.* Raintree/Steck-Vaughn, 1989.

Jezek, Alisandra. *Milioli's Orchard.* Raintree/Steck-Vaughn, 1990.

Jin, Sarunna. *My First American Friend.* Raintree/Steck-Vaughn, 1991.

Josephs, Anna Catherine. *Mountain Boy.* Raintree/Steck-Vaughn, 1985.

Klein, David J. *Irwin the Sock.* Raintree/Steck-Vaughn, 1987.

McGuire-Turcotte, Casey A. *How Honu the Turtle Got His Shell.* Raintree/Steck-Vaughn, 1990.

Morgan, Troll. *The Ball, the Book and the Drum.* Raintree/Steck-Vaughn, 1990.

Paulsen, Brendan Patrick. *The Luck of the Irish.* Raintree/Steck-Vaughn, 1988.

Pio, Adam. *The Magic Donkey.* Raintree/Steck-Vaughn, 1989.

Pippin, Christie. *A Very Scraggly Christmas Tree.* Raintree/Steck-Vaughn, 1988.

Reeser, Michael. *Huan Ching and the Golden Fish.* Raintree/Steck-Vaughn, 1988.

Struble, Steve. *To See or Not to See.* Raintree/Steck-Vaughn, 1986.

Troia, Lily. *China Shelf Luxury.* Raintree/Steck-Vaughn, 1990.

Enriching Connections

1. Read aloud and examine the illustrations in one of the Raintree/Steck-Vaughn Publish-a-Book contest winners listed under "Guided Reading Connections across a Learning Rainbow." These books have been written by students for other students. They reflect a wide variety of subjects, cultures, and viewpoints.

2. Submit an entry to this annual Publish-A-Book contest.

3. Ask your parents to help you trace your family tree as far as possible. Create an appropriate illustration of the family tree based on your research. Keep this document for use by other family members.

4. As a community project, plan to visit a retirement home during the year. Take small baskets of treats or present a musical program for the residents to enjoy.

FROM ANOTHER POINT OF VIEW

Greenfield, Howard. *Books: From Writer to Reader.* Crown, 1988.

Parent-Student Connections

1. Read a variety of books and have the students briefly retell the stories.

2. Stop reading a book at the last chapter. Ask how the book should end and why.

3. From the library check out a travel book about Florida. How is this state different from your state? (Note: Students living in Florida may compare their state with Maine.)

❀ ❀ ❀

STUART LITTLE

Author: E. B. White
Illustrator: Garth Williams
Publisher: Harper & Row, 1945
Suggested Grade Level: 5
Classification: Fiction
Literary Form: Fantasy novel
Theme: Physical size is not a deterrent to personal success.

ABOUT THE BOOK

STUDENT OBJECTIVES:

1. Determine the elements of a novel.

2. Outline the plot of a novel.

3. Write a new ending for *Stuart Little.*

SYNOPSIS: Stuart, the youngest child of the Little family, bears a remarkable resemblance to a mouse. He is an example of personification because he has human characteristics.

ABOUT THE AUTHOR: E. B. White, 1899-1985.
E. B. White's first children's book, *Stuart Little,* was written for his six-year-old niece. White worked on the story for 12 years. By the time the work was published, his niece had grown up! *Stuart Little* was followed by *Charlotte's Web* (1952) and *Trumpet of the Swan* (1970). White is known worldwide for his contributions to children's literature, although he wrote only three books.
Many adults knew White's work through his articles and essays in *The New Yorker.* "He is regarded by many as the best essayist of modern time" (*Something about the Author,* vol. 4, pp. 44-45).

ABOUT THE ILLUSTRATOR: Garth Williams, 1912- .
Garth Williams's illustrations have been enjoyed by countless readers. His rich and varied art work has been used in books by many famous authors, including Byrd Baylor, Margaret Wise Brown, Natalie Carlson, Jack Prelutsky, George Selden, Charlotte Zolotow, Else H. Minarik, and E. B. White. Jack Prelutsky's *Ride a Purple Pelican* (1986) was the seventy-fifth book Williams illustrated for other authors.

Williams lived on a farm near Caldwell, New Jersey, as a child. "I was a typical Huckleberry Finn, roaming barefoot around the farm watching the farmer milk the cows by hand, or do his other chores" (*Something About the Author,* vol. 66, p. 230). As a young man, Williams won a sculpting award that provided funds for him to visit art centers of Europe, including Italy, France, and Germany. He was also involved in wartime duties in England and the United States during World War II.

As in many situations, timing played a part. Shortly after the war, Williams decided to become a children's book illustrator. He visited the offices of Harper & Row, which publishes children's books. The children's editor said that a new manuscript would be coming in shortly and he might try his skills on it. E. B. White, who knew Williams when they both worked on *The New Yorker,* penned a note, "Try Garth Williams." Williams's work on the New Yorker was considered to be "too wild and European."

"I found *Stuart Little* more fun to illustrate than Charlotte's Web as there were more moments of fantasy in it... *Stuart* and *Charlotte,* of course, are among my own personal favorites. I feel extremely lucky to be able to share a little of the spotlight of these two books—books I love, admire, envy, and emulate as an author" (*Something About the Author,* vol. 66, p. 232).

Williams's art appears in the revised editions of the Little House series by Laura Ingalls Wilder. Williams visited the locales in which the books were set and met the author and other members of her family. He explains that the illustrations are not representational of what he saw, but viewed through the eyes of Laura. "She understood the meaning of hardship and struggle, of joy and work, of shyness and bravery. She was never overcome by drabness or squalor.... This was the way the illustrator had to follow—no glamorizing for him either; no giving everyone a permanent wave" (*Something About the Author,* vol. 66, p. 232).

SELECTED ADDITIONAL TITLES: E. B. White

White, E. B. *Charlotte's Web.* Illustrated by Garth Williams. Harper & Row, 1952.

————. *Trumpet of the Swan.* Illustrated by Edward Frascino. Harper & Row, 1970.

SELECTED ADDITIONAL TITLES: Garth Williams

Carlson, Natalie. *Family Under the Bridge.* Illustrated by Garth Williams. Harper & Row, 1958.

————. *Happy Orpheline.* Illustrated by Garth Williams. Harper & Row, 1957.

Prelutsky, Jack. *Ride a Purple Pelican.* Illustrated by Garth Williams. Greenwillow Books, 1986.

Selden, George. *Cricket in Times Square.* Illustrated by Garth Williams. Farrar, Straus & Giroux, 1960.

White, E. B. *Charlotte's Web.* Illustrated by Garth Williams. Harper & Row, 1952 .

Wilder, Laura Ingalls. *By the Shores of Silver Lake.* Illustrated by Garth Williams. Harper & Row, 1953.

————. *Farmer Boy.* Illustrated by Garth Williams. Harper & Row, 1953.

USING THE BOOK

Suggested Approach to the Book

Model Lesson

1. Who is Stuart Little? Describe him using a word cluster. How do his parents treat Stuart? Describe him to your parents and ask how they would feel about having Stuart as a son. What kind of childhood did Stuart have? Compare and contrast his childhood with your own. What would be a perfect childhood?

2. Where did the Little family live? Where do you live? If you could, would you change places with Stuart?

3. After Mrs. Little dropped her ring down the drain and was unable to reach it, she asked Stuart to retrieve it. How did Stuart feel about this? What was Stuart's job when someone wanted to play the piano?

4. Why did Mrs. Little tear the nursery rhyme, "Three Blind Mice," from the story book? What change did she make to "The Night Before Christmas?"

5. Describe Stuart's brother, George. What word means someone who puts off doing a task? Learn to spell the word. What kind of friend was Snowball?

6. In cooperative learning groups, retell the story of Stuart the sea captain.

7. Dr. Carey and Stuart felt that most people would not know the difference between the following. Do you?

   Squall and Squid   Jib and Jibe   Luff and Leech

   Deck and Dock   Mast and Mist

8. What is the meaning of each of the following nautical terms:

   Schooner   Headsails   Port Tack   Deck Cleat

   Tramp Steamer   Collision   Halyards   Forestaysail

   Yawing   Helm   Seamanship   Steamship

9. Describe Margalo. Where had she lived before?

10. What is the danger of playing in a refrigerator? What laws have been passed to prevent refrigerator accidents?

11. How did Margalo save Stuart's life? Describe Stuart's search for Margalo. Predict the book's ending.

Library Media Center Connections

1. Research the different kinds of transportation systems in New York, both historical and contemporary. Illustrate the information with a pictorial time line.

2. Pick one New York landmark as your topic for research. Present an oral, three-minute report to the class. Supplementary materials for the presentation may include illustrations on transparencies, diagrams, models, art work, and background music.

Computer Connections

1. Develop a flyer describing events to be held on Stuart Little Day.

2. Using a word processor, write a different last chapter to *Stuart Little*.

Instructional Materials Connections

1. Brown, Richard. *A Kid's Guide to New York City*. Harcourt Brace Jovanovich, 1988.

2. Clinton, Patrick. *The Story of the Empire State Building*. Childrens Press, 1987.

3. Munro, Roxie. *The Inside-Outside Book of New York City*. Putnam, 1985.

4. St. George, Judith. *The Brooklyn Bridge: They Said It Could Not Be Built.* Putnam, 1982.

5. White, E. B. *Stuart Little.* Cassette. Doubleday, n.d.

6. Invite a dental hygienist to the classroom for a lesson on keeping your teeth healthy.

7. Tooth Model. Hubbard Scientific, P.O. Box 760, Chippewa Falls, WI 54729-0760.

8. Crayola Designer Kit for Vehicles. The Paragon, 89 Tom Harvey Road, Westerly, RI 02891.

9. Additional information about New York City may be obtained by writing to the New York City Convention and Visitors Bureau, 2 Columbus Circle, New York, NY 10019-1823.

Theme Reading Connections: Mice—Nonfiction

Bailey, Jill. *Discovering Rats and Mice.* Franklin Watts, 1987.

Burton, Robert. *The Mouse in the Barn.* Gareth Stevens, 1988.

Fischer-Nagel, Heiderose and Andreas Fischer-Nagel. *A Look Through the Mouse Hole.* Illustrated by Heiderose Fischer-Nagel and Andreas Fischer-Nagel. Carolrhoda, 1989.

Fisher, Aileen. *The House of a Mouse.* Harper & Row, 1988.

Harrison, Virginia. *The World of Mice.* Gareth Stevens, 1988.

Silverstein, Alvin, and Virginia Silverstein. *Mice: All about Them.* Harper & Row, 1980.

Wexler, Jerome. *Pet Mice.* Illustrated by Kathleen Tucker. A. Whitman, 1989.

Critical Thinking Question
What clues did E. B. White provide to help you reach a conclusion about the fates of Stuart Little and Margola?

Student Activities to Connect Literature and Curriculum

FINE ARTS

1. Design a commemorative stamp honoring E. B. White. Where should it first be issued? On what date? Why? Plan a formal ceremony for the day of issue.

2. Draw a picture of Stuart's bedroom.

3. Design a wardrobe for Stuart Little. Present color renderings of the wardrobe.

4. Make a model of Stuart's car.

5. Make a model boat for Stuart out of Styrofoam. Styrofoam is easy to cut and floats well. Include a wooden mast and sails made of paper or fabric.

6. Draw a cutaway model of the mouse hole in the Little home.

LANGUAGE ARTS

1. Write the dialogue and present the following scenes as miniplays:

The great sailboat race

Stuart's night vigil over Margola

Dr. Carey presenting the model auto to Stuart

Stuart's day as a substitute teacher

Stuart's visit to the country store in Ames' Crossing

Stuart's visit with a telephone company repairman

2. Compare and contrast the police officers in *Stuart Little* and in *Make Way for Ducklings* (McCloskey, Robert, Viking, 1941). What is the setting of the *Make Way for Ducklings*?

3. Plan a Stuart Little Day for your class. What activities will be scheduled? How will the author and illustrator be honored?

4. Create a flannel-board story to share with primary children. Choose from the following picture books:

Bunting, Eve. *The Mother's Day Mice.* Illustrated by Jan Brett. Clarion Books, 1988.

Cauley, Lorinda B. *The Town Mouse and the Country Mouse.* Putnam, 1984.

Kraus, Robert. *Where Are You Going, Little Mouse?* Illustrated by Jose Aruego and Ariane Dewey. Greenwillow Books, 1986.

Kroll, Steven. *The Biggest Pumpkin Ever.* Illustrated by Jeni Bassett. Holiday House, 1984.

Leonni, Leo. *Frederick.* Pantheon Books, 1967.

Lobel, Arnold. *Mouse Tales.* Harper & Row, 1985.

Mendoza, George. *Henri Mouse.* Illustrated by Joelle Boucher. Penguin, 1986.

Numeroff, Laura. *If You Give a Mouse a Cookie.* Illustrated by Felicia Bond. Harper & Row, 1985.

Potter, Beatrix. *The Tale of Johnny Town-Mouse.* Warne, 1987.

Steptoe, John. *The Story of Jumping Mouse.* Lothrop, Lee & Shepard, 1984.

WRITING PROMPT

1. Prepare a television news release for the following statement:

> Students Say Sub Teacher Stuart Little Is Unusual

MATH

1. What are the 10 tallest buildings in New York City? (See the *World Almanac.*) What are the 10 highest buildings in your community? Use a bar graph and color markers to show the 20 buildings ranked by height.

SCIENCE

1. Mrs. Little had a doctor examine Stuart when he was only one month old because he so small. What did the doctor's examination include? What were his findings? Describe the medical exam and testing required to participate in school sports or camp activities today.

2. Keep a mouse in a cage in the classroom for two weeks. Have students note their visual observations of the animal. Put toys, including a maze, in the mouse's cage.

3. What kind of dental care do all children and students need? How should this care be funded? What preventive care do teeth require? Prepare three illustrated brochures on this subject to hand out to the following groups of students:

Students in Grades 1-3   Students in Grades 4-6   Middle-school Students

4. Using a field guide for birds, identify Margola's species. What other information is available about this species?

5. Devise an exercise program for Stuart and yourself. What exercises are appropriate for both of you? How much should you exercise each week? Include things like recess and walking to school

6. Plan your school lunch menu for a week. If you eat school-prepared food, explain how the new government-approved five food groups are integrated into the plan. If you bring your lunch, develop a menu that provides a nutritious, balanced diet.

SOCIAL STUDIES

1. At the time of Stuart Little's birth, he could have been mailed for the cost of a three-cent, first-class stamp. Using a stamp catalog from the library media center, find out when a first-class stamp could be purchased for three cents. Prepare a chart of the presidential stamp series used at that time. Share the chart with the class. Explain to the class other stamps that were in use at the same time, including air mail, parcel post and commemorative issues. Present an illustrated chart of stamps that are in use today. Compare and contrast their cost and use.

GEOGRAPHY

1. You have just won an art contest, and your prize is a visit to New York. List major landmarks of New York City. Identify their locations on a city map. Which five landmarks would you choose to visit? Why?

2. Prepare a landscape map of Central Park that includes land formations. Use a key or legend to identify areas of the park that have specific uses.

BEYOND THE BOOK

Guided Reading Connections Across a Learning Rainbow: Mice—Fiction

Asch, Frank, and Vladimir Vagin. *Here Comes the Cat.* Scholastic, 1989.

Benchley, Nathaniel. *Feldman Fieldmouse.* Harper & Row, 1971.

Brown, Marcia. *Once a Mouse.* Macmillan, 1982.

Cleary, Beverly. *The Mouse and the Motorcycle.* Illustrated by Louis Darling. Morrow, 1865.

———. *Ralph S. Mouse.* Illustrated by Paul Zelinsky. Morrow, 1982.

Conly, Jane. *Racso and the Rats of NIMH.* Illustrated by Leonard Lubin. Harper & Row, 1988.

Jacques, Brian. *Redwall.* Putnam, 1987.

Lawson, Robert. *Ben and Me.* Little, Brown, 1988.

Moore, Lillian. *I'll Meet You at the Cucumbers.* Illustrated by Sharon Wooding. Macmillan, 1988.

Numeroff, Laura J. *If You Give a Mouse a Cookie.* Illustrated by Felicia Bond. Harper & Row, 1985.

O'Brien, Robert. *Mrs. Frisby and the Rats of NIMH.* Illustrated by Zena Bernstein. Macmillan, 1971.

Steig, William. *Abel's Island.* Farrar, Straus & Giroux, 1985.

Enriching Connections

1. Compare and contrast *Charlotte's Web* and *Stuart Little.*

2. Make mouse bookmarks using grey felt for the body, pink felt for the lining of the ears, small plastic eyes that can be glued on, and a yarn tail.

FROM ANOTHER POINT OF VIEW

Kellogg, Steven. *Island of the Skog.* Dial, 1976.

Parent-Student Connections

1. Read aloud to the family *Charlotte's Web* or *Trumpet of the Swan.*

2. Make a batch of decorated cookies cut in the shape of a mouse.

❀   ❀   ❀

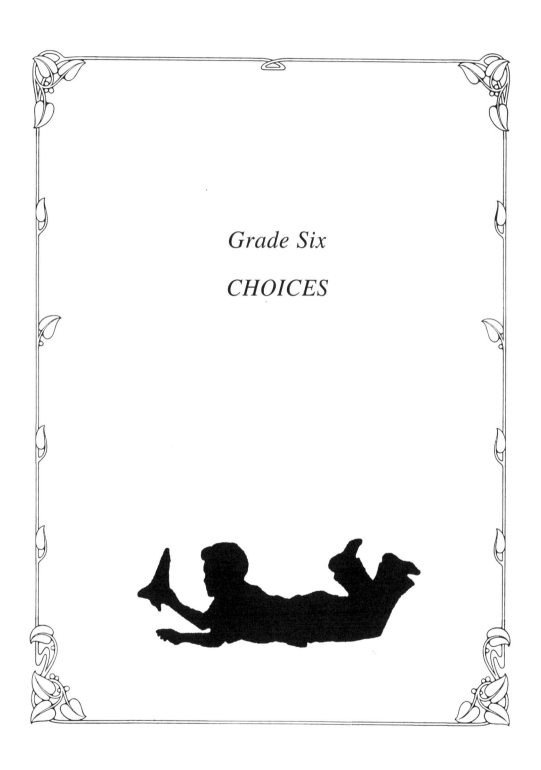

Grade Six

CHOICES

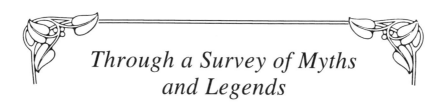

*Through a Survey of Myths
and Legends*

ALADDIN AND THE
WONDERFUL LAMP

Author: Carol Carrick
Illustrator: Donald Carrick
Publisher: Scholastic, 1992
Suggested Grade Level: 6
Classification: Folklore
Literary Form: Picture book
Theme: The good-hearted are always saved from tragedy by a magical force.

ABOUT THE BOOK

STUDENT OBJECTIVES:

1. Explain why many stories are included in the Arabian Nights.

2. Through the book's illustrations, recognize characteristics of Middle East design in buildings, furnishings, clothing, and architecture.

3. Create a modern genie-in-the-lamp story.

SYNOPSIS: Aladdin is befriended by a man whose intentions are not honorable. Aladdin is saved from death in a sealed cave by a genie and his magic lamp.

ABOUT THE AUTHOR: Carol Carrick, 1935- .
    Carol Carrick grew up in a small community on Long Island, New York, where she enjoyed woods, fields filled with wildflowers, and a pond that she studied. Carrick observed various forms of life, including "dragonflies, tadpoles and discarded goldfish" (de Montreville, Doris, and Elizabeth D. Crawford, eds., *Fourth Book of Junior Authors and Illustrators,* H. W. Wilson, 1978, p. 70). This setting nourished her interest in science. She remembers that there was little information available about the care and feeding of baby turtles and tadpoles.

Carrick enjoyed spending summers with her grandmother on the New Jersey shore. Carrick had the entire summer for beach activities and reading books from the library, while most of the other children spent only a week or so in a rented cottage. "Sculpturing sand castles and sea maidens and battling the surf led to dreamy fantasies, heightened by the exotic sights and smells of the boardwalk at night" (*Fourth Book of Junior Authors and Illustrators,* p. 70).

She credits the inspiration for her books about the life cycles of the lobster, sand tiger shark, and octopus to a family move to Martha's Vineyard. "I feel strongly that even if children are just indirectly learning something from us, our books ought to be accurate. Maybe this is the result of my days of frustrated tadpole-raising" (*Fourth Book of Junior Authors and Illustrators*, p. 70).

ABOUT THE ILLUSTRATOR: Donald Carrick, 1929 - 1989.

Like his wife Carol Carrick, Donald Carrick grew up in a natural environment. He lived with his parents on land adjoining the Henry Ford estate in Dearborn, Michigan.

His art background, similar to that of illustrator Gerald McDermott, included study at the Cass Technical High School, Detroit, as well as sign painting. Carrick showed his paintings in several studio exhibits. His interest in illustrating children's books began when Robert Goldston asked Carrick to illustrate a history book for children.

Later, Carrick's editor suggested that he try a book on his own. The book, *The Old Barn*, was done in collaboration with his wife. "I always work from life and like to know as much about a book's subject as possible. A crayfish lived in our turkey roaster while we worked on *The Pond*, two turtles occupied the bathtub for *Turtle Pond*" (*Fourth Book of Junior Authors and Illustrators*, pp. 71-72.).

SELECTED ADDITIONAL TITLES: Carol Carrick and Donald Carrick

Carrick, Carol. *The Accident.* Illustrated by Donald Carrick. Clarion Books, 1976.

————. *Beach Bird.* Illustrated by Donald Carrick. Dial, 1978.

————. *Ben and the Porcupine.* Illustrated by Donald Carrick. Houghton Mifflin, 1985.

————. *The Climb.* Illustrated by Donald Carrick. Houghton Mifflin, 1980.

————. *The Crocodiles Still Wait.* Illustrated by Donald Carrick. Houghton Mifflin, 1980.

————. *Dark and Full of Secrets.* Illustrated by Donald Carrick. Houghton Mifflin, 1984.

————. *Lost in the Storm.* Illustrated by Donald Carrick. Houghton Mifflin, 1974.

————. *Octopus.* Illustrated by Donald Carrick. Houghton Mifflin, 1978.

————. *Old Mother Witch.* Illustrated by Donald Carrick. Houghton Mifflin, 1975.

————. *Patrick's Dinosaurs.* Illustrated by Donald Carrick. Houghton Mifflin, 1983.

————. *Sand Tiger Shark.* Illustrated by Donald Carrick. Houghton Mifflin, 1976.

————. *Sleep Out.* Illustrated by Donald Carrick. Houghton Mifflin, 1973.

————. *Some Friend!* Illustrated by Donald Carrick. Houghton Mifflin, 1979.

————. *Star Rider.* Illustrated by Peter Wilkes. Penguin, 1985.

————. *Stay Away from Simon.* Illustrated by Donald Carrick. Clarion Books, 1985.

————. *Two Coyotes.* Illustrated by Donald Carrick. Houghton Mifflin, 1982.

————. *The Washout.* Illustrated by Donald Carrick. Houghton Mifflin, 1978.

————. *What Happened to Patrick's Dinosaurs?* Illustrated by Donald Carrick. Houghton Mifflin, 1986.

Carrick, Donald. *Harald and the Giant Knight.* Illustrated by Donald Carrick. Houghton Mifflin, 1982.

———. *Milk.* Illustrated by Donald Carrick. Greenwillow Books, 1985.

———. *Morgan and the Artist.* Illustrated by Donald Carrick. Houghton Mifflin, 1985.

Cole, Joanna. *Doctor Change.* Illustrated by Donald Carrick. Morrow, 1986.

Griffith, Helen. *Alex Remembers.* Illustrated by Donald Carrick. Greenwillow Books, 1983.

Hurwitz, Joanna. *Yellow Blue Jay.* Illustrated by Donald Carrick. Morrow, 1986.

USING THE BOOK

Suggested Approach to the Book

Model Lesson

1. How does the architecture pictured on the title pages differ from the architectural style of your home?

2. In the table of contents of *Stories from the Arabian Nights,* retold by Naomi Lewis (Henry Holt, 1987), the story of Aladdin is listed as "The Tale of Ala Al-Din and the Wonderful Lamp." Why is the name Aladdin spelled differently?

3. Look at the clothing that Aladdin and the magician are wearing. How does it differ from contemporary clothing? What kind of feeling is the artist trying to invoke with the selective use of color and shadow?

4. Would you like to live in a city without cars, with your living quarters just a few feet from those of your neighbor? What are the advantages and disadvantages of living so close?

5. Is the story plausible when the magician uses his magic to leave Aladdin trapped inside the cave with the magic lamp?

6. What advice did Aladdin's mother give him about the lamp? What would you have told Aladdin?

7. Why did the sultan order all the people to stay inside behind shutters? Compare the custom of going to the bath then and now. Explore water shortages in drought areas, water purity, and bathing as a ritual.

8. Who is a Grand Vizer? What is the origin of the title?

9. How did Aladdin use the services of the genie? What three wishes would you make today if the genie appeared to you? Why?

10. What is the value of a trade-in program for items that are old or no longer used? What effect would a trade-in program have on the environment?

Library Media Center Connections

1. Ask the library media center specialist to help students find illustrations of other genies in books. Prepare a transparency presentation illustrating the various genies the students located.

2. The Carricks used a particular style of illustration based on an exhibit they had seen at the Metropolitan Museum of Art in New York City. The art works on display were of Suliman the Magnificent, an Ottoman sultan who lived from 1520 to 1566. The Ottoman Empire's primary geographic area is now known as Turkey. Cooperative learning groups will research and write a brief report on one of the following:

Turkish Architecture	Turkish History
Turkish Geography	Turkish Art and Music
Turkish Culture	Turkish Clothing

Computer Connections

1. Using a word processor, organize the story into chapters. Each cooperative learning group will be responsible for a chapter and for preparing a new ending for the story. Class members will vote to select the most unique ending.

Instructional Materials Connections

1. Daniels, Patricia. *Aladdin and the Magic Lamp.* Cassette. Raintree/Steck-Vaughn, 1981.

2. Landes, William-Alan. *Aladdin N' His Magic Lamp.* Rev. ed. (Script). Players Press, 1985. (A teacher's edition is also available.)

3. Jackson, Julia. *Gemstones: Treasures from the Earth's Crust.* Enslow, 1989.

4. Jangl, James F. *Birthstone Coloring Book: Birthstone Legends and other Gem Folklore.* Illustrated by Alda M. Jangl and James F. Jangl. Prisma Press, 1987.

5. Mercer, Ian. *Gemstones.* Franklin Watts, 1987. '

6. O'Neill, Paul. *Gemstones.* Time Life, 1983.

7. Schumann, Walter. *Gemstones of the World.* Sterling, 1977.

8. Swinburne, Laurence, and Irene Swinburne. *The Deadly Diamonds.* Raintree/Steck-Vaughn, 1977.

9. Invite a local jeweler to speak to the class about diamonds and gemstones. Ask the jeweler to bring a gemstone that students may examine during the visit.

10. Patterns for ethnic clothing are available in adult and some children's sizes from The Tauton Press, 63 S. Main Street, P.O. Box 5506, Newton, CT 06740.

Theme Reading Connections: Aladdin

Kimmel, Eric A., retold by. *The Tale of Aladdin and the Wonderful Lamp.* Illustrated by Ju-Hong Chen. Holiday House, 1992.

Lang, Andrew. *Aladdin.* Illustrated by Errol Le Cain. Penguin, 1983.

Lubin, Leonard. *Aladdin and His Wonderful Lamp.* Translated from Arabic by Richard T. Burton. Illustrated by Leonard Lubin. Delacorte Press, 1982.

Mayer, Marianna. *Aladdin and the Enchanted Lamp.* Illustrated by Gerald McDermott. Macmillan, 1985.

Shane, Harold. *Aladdin and the Wonderful Lamp.* Illustrated by Albert Winkler. Society for Visual
Education, 1980.

> Critical Thinking Question
> How do people from many different countries learn the same or similar folk-
> tales, fairy tales, folklore, legends, and myths? Cinderella is a fairy tale that
> has been told all around the world. How many versions exist today? Will the
> story continue to be popular? Why or why not? What is the value of this heri-
> tage? What do you know about your ancestors? How can family histories be
> preserved for future generations?

Student Activities to Connect Literature and Curriculum

FINE ARTS

1. Design trees with colored jewel fruit as part of an art project to illustrate the story of Aladdin.

2. Draw a new interior design for your bedroom using pillows and carpets as illustrated in the
   book. What colors did you select? Why? What design did you select for the carpet designs?

3. Create a roc bird and its egg using papier mache.

4. Construct a diorama of the scene that most intrigues you in *Aladdin and the Wonderful Lamp.*

5. Introduce the class to classical music with the Rimsky-Korsakov composition *Scheherazade.*
   (A recording is available through Rizzol's International Book Store, 3333 Bristol Avenue,
   Costa Mesa, CA 92626.) Queen Scheherazade was the fictitious teller of the stories of the
   Arabian Nights. Use music in the classroom to set the mood for telling stories.

6. Rosenthal China of Germany has in its china pattern catalog a raised relief pattern that
   integrates the visual story of a fairy tale with its musical score. Select a fairy tale and design
   a china service around its theme.

LANGUAGE ARTS

1. Change the setting of the story from historical to contemporary. Change the characters,
   setting, and clothing. What would the new version look like? Why? Have cooperative
   learning groups prepare story boards to use in retelling their versions of the story to the
   class.

WRITING PROMPT

1. Imagine a version of Aladdin in which the magician, instead of meeting Aladdin face-to-
   face, corresponds with him. Complete the letter that begins:

> I have searched the world for my dear brother only to find him dead. Brother
> Mustaph and I found a treasure chest many years ago and I wish to share it
> with you....

MATH

1. Graph the figures for worldwide gold and silver production in 1980 and 1990. The numeric values will be stated in troy ounces. How much is a troy ounce? How much do gold and silver cost today? (See the *World Almanac*.)

SCIENCE

1. "Gemstones are minerals, the fundamental building blocks of the earth. Some materials of biological origins are used as gems and include amber, coral, pearl, shells and jet" (Arem, Joel, *Gems and Jewelry*, Ridge Press, 1975, p. 11). Gemstones come in many colors and degrees of hardness. Illustrate the process of marketing gemstones, from locating deposits, cutting and polishing the stone, and marketing the finished gem. Draw the different types of cuts used for gemstones and describe them in geometric terms.

2. Select from the following topics a subject that you would like to research. Present an oral report with transparencies for visual emphasis:

   Birthstones

   Famous diamonds, including Dresden, Hope, Cullinan I, Sancy, Tiffany, Koh-i-Noor, Cullinan IV, Nassak, Shah, and Florentine

   Corundum group: ruby and sapphire

   Beryl group: emerald and aquamarine

   Chrysoberyl: alexandrite and chrysoberyl cat's eye

   Jade

   Lapis Lazuli

   Malachite

   Opal

   Topaz

   Tourmaline

   Turquoise

   Quartz

SOCIAL STUDIES

1. The Arabian Nights stories evolved over many centuries, and they include materials from the Middle East as well as China and India. Prepare a classroom display of flags of all Middle Eastern countries, India, and China. What do they have in common? What differences can be observed? How do these countries conduct government business with each other today? Why?

2. Draw a family tree to show the relationship of Aladdin and his uncle.

GEOGRAPHY

1. Create maps to accompany the reports generated in the science activities. The maps should show where deposits of each gemstone are located throughout the world.

BEYOND THE BOOK

Guided Reading Connections Across a Learning Rainbow: The Arab World

Arabian Peninsula. Silver Burdett, 1975.

Dutton, Roderic. *An Arabic Family.* Illustrated. Lerner, 1985.

Haskins, Jim. *Count Your Way Through the Arab World.* Carolrhoda, 1987.

Enriching Connections

1. Read 10 stories from the *Arabian Nights or the Thousand and One Nights.* Be prepared to retell one story to the class while comparing and contrasting different elements of it with *Aladdin and His Wonderful Lamp.* You might decide to use a small rug and a cloak and turban as stage props.

2. Compare and contrast one of the most popular stories, "Ali Baba and the Forty Thieves," with *Aladdin and the Wonderful Lamp.*

FROM ANOTHER POINT OF VIEW

Riordan, James. *Tales from the Arabian Nights.* Illustrated by Victor G. Ambrus. Macmillan, 1985.

Parent-Student Connections

1. Visit a museum's mineral collection that includes gemstones. What birthstones represent each month of the year? Which is yours?

2. Identify the countries of the Middle East and compile a list of ideas, products, and other contributions from these nations that have benefitted mankind.

❀ ❀ ❀

THE VILLAGE OF ROUND
AND SQUARE HOUSES

Author: Ann Grifalconi
Illustrator: Ann Grifalconi
Publisher: Little, Brown, 1986
Classification: Folklore
Literary Form: Picture book
Theme: Natural history influences our lives in many ways.

ABOUT THE BOOK

STUDENT OBJECTIVES:

1. Interpret the various living arrangements of an African village.

2. Produce a village of round and square houses.

3. Plan procedures in case there is an emergency in the community.

SYNOPSIS: A storyteller explains how a natural disaster, a volcanic eruption, causes the residents to live in round and square houses.

ABOUT THE AUTHOR-ILLUSTRATOR: Ann Grifalconi, 1929- .
    Ann Grifalconi is an exceptional storyteller and illustrator as evidenced by *The Village of Round and Square Houses.* She has had a deep interest in the African people and their cultures and has traveled to this special village in the remote hills of the Cameroons in Central Africa. "It is almost entirely isolated with no paved roads closer to it than a full eight hours away. Not but the most adventurous visitor would dare risk the steep and bumpy, rocky clay paths leading to the thatch-roofed village that clings to the side of an almost extinct volcano" (p. iv).
    The story of Tos was told to her by a young woman who had grown up in a village of thatched-roof huts. In addition to this work, Grifalconi has illustrated more than 50 books for children.

SELECTED ADDITIONAL TITLES:

Brewton, Sara, and John Brewton. *America Forever New: A Book of Poems.* Illustrated by Ann Grifalconi. Thomas Y. Crowell, 1968.

Byars, Betsy. *The Midnight Fox.* Illustrated by Ann Grifalconi. Penguin, 1981.

Clifton, Lucille. *Everett Anderson's Goodbye.* Illustrated by Ann Grifalconi. Henry Holt, 1983.

Gray, Genevieve. *How Far, Felipe?* Illustrated by Ann Grifalconi. Harper & Row, 1978.

Grifalconi, Ann. *Flyaway Girl.* Illustrated by Ann Grifalconi. Little, Brown, 1992.

———. *Osa's Pride.* Illustrated by Ann Grifalconi. Little, Brown, 1990.

Weik, Mary H. *The Jazz Man.* Illustrated by Ann Grifalconi. Macmillan, 1977.

USING THE BOOK

Suggested Approach to the Book

Model Lesson

1. From whose point of view is the story told? How do you know?

2. What was special about Gran'pa Oma according to the storyteller? What respect was shown to Uncle Domo?

3. How did Gran'ma Tika relax in the evenings? What is the symbolism of the Grandmother and Mother Naka smoking peacefully? How did the villagers hear Naka snoring in her sleep?

4. What did the previous villagers do many years ago when "Old Naka began to groan and rumble and awoke from a long sleep?"

5. Describe the eruption of the volcano. What happened to the people? What directions did the village chief give? What was his plan?

6. How long did Gran'ma Tika say that this lifestyle would last?

Library Media Center Connections

1. Form cooperative learning groups and assign one of the following research topics to each group:

Tornadoes	Storms	Floods	Earthquakes
Volcanoes	Fires	Hurricanes	

Computer Connections

1. Design a form to be used in setting up a classroom database about African folklore. Input data about both print and nonprint materials that are available in your school library media center.

Instructional Materials Connections

1. Deery, Ruth. *Earthquakes and Volcanoes.* Good Apple, 1985.

2. Kramer, Alan. *How to Make a Chemical Volcano and Other Mysterious Experiments.* Franklin Watts, 1989.

Theme Reading Connections: Disasters

Bramwell, Martyn. *Volcanoes and Earthquakes.* Franklin Watts, 1986.

Dineen, Jacqueline. *Volcanoes.* Franklin Watts, 1991.

Fradin, Dennis B. *Disaster! Blizzards and Winter Storms.* Childrens Press, 1983.

———. *Disaster! Droughts.* Childrens Press, 1983.

———. *Disaster! Fires.* Childrens Press, 1982.

———. *Disaster! Floods.* Childrens Press, 1982.

———. *Disaster! Volcanoes.* Childrens Press, 1982.

Lauber, Patricia. *Volcano: The Eruption and Healing of Mt. St. Helens.* Bradbury Press, 1986.

Radlauer, Ed, and Ruth Radlauer. *Earthquakes.* Childrens Press, 1987.

Richard, Graham. *The Chernobyl Catastrophe.* Illustrated by Peter Bull. Franklin Watts, 1989.

Scollins, Richard. *The Fire of London.* Illustrated by Richard Scollins. Franklin Watts, 1989.

Simon, Seymour. *Volcanoes.* Morrow, 1988.

Critical Thinking Question

Who has a better quality of life, the Tos of Africa or you? What are the advantages and disadvantages of each lifestyle? How would you act if, by magic, you were transported to the village of round and square houses?

Student Activities to Connect Literature and Curriculum

FINE ARTS

1. Construct a diorama of Gran'ma Tika's round house. Include family members from the story.

2. Form cooperative learning groups. A U.S. organization has received permission to build a new resort and sports facility in Tos. Conduct an assessment of what future tourists will need, and then design the buildings. Prepare preliminary sketches of activity areas, guest rooms, meeting rooms, and public areas.

3. Imagine that you are a designer who, twice a year, must develop new clothing collections. Design African-influenced wardrobes to be displayed in a fashion show. What will the models wear? Include sketches. What will be the theme of each show? Provide detailed information about the shows in announcements to department-store buyers and newspaper advertisements. How long in advance of the season must each collection preview? Both men's and women's clothing may be shown. What will be your brand name and logo?

LANGUAGE ARTS

1. Write a new African myth or fable explaining the eruption of a volcano or the onset of a drought.

2. Write and illustrate an alphabet book to accompany *The Village of Round and Square Houses.*

3. Using the word-play format of Susan Ramsay Hoguet's *I Unpacked My Grandmother's Trunk* (illustrated by Susan Ramsay Hoguet, Dutton, 1983), play the word game using items that could be brought home from an African trip.

4. Compare and contrast the following books by Ann Grifalconi: *The Village of Round and Square Houses, Osa's Pride,* and *Flyaway Girl.* (For references to *Osa's Pride* and *Flyaway Girl,* see Selected Additional Titles.)

WRITING PROMPT

1. Does anyone at home ask you, "What have you learned today?" Keep a diary for two weeks. Begin each entry with

> Today, I ....

MATH

1. Using information about Africa, develop 10 word problems. Have students exchange lists three times. Unsolved problems may be presented to the class and solved by the students who developed them.

SCIENCE

1. What crops were grown on the farm? Research these crops, including recommended soil preparation, temperatures needed for growth, length of growing season, and crop production.

2. What is a white cassava root and how is it used in fou-fou?

3. Recommend ways to bring water to the arid areas of Africa. Are there any available sources of water in neighboring nations?

SOCIAL STUDIES

1. Mythology attempts to place people in the world. It is common to all cultures. Many stories have been told and written to explain natural phenomena. What other ways can a volcanic eruption be explained?

2. If you were a community trade advisor sent to assist in developing products to be exported from Cameroon to the United States, what products would you recommend? Why?

GEOGRAPHY

1. "I grew up on my grandmother's farm in the village of Tos that lies at the foot of Naka Mountain in the Bameni Hills of west Africa" (p. 2). Can you use this description to locate Tos on a map? Why or why not?

2. Using a classroom globe, identify areas in the world that are on the same latitude or longitude as Cameroon. Explain the physical differences of these regions as indicated by colors used on the map to indicate the regions' topography.

BEYOND THE BOOK

Guided Reading Connections Across a Learning Rainbow: Africa

Central African Republic. Chelsea, 1989.

Musgrove, Margaret W. *Ashanti to Zulu: African Traditions.* Illustrated by Diane Dillon and Leo Dillon. Dial, 1976.

Owoo, Ife. *A Is for Africa: Looking at Africa Through the Alphabet.* Africa World Press, 1992.

Enriching Connections

1. Use a cookbook to find ways to prepare yams and corn. Prepare one dish for a class tasting. Other African dishes may be prepared. Plan a pot-luck lunch for the class. What table decorations and place mats would be appropriate? African musical instruments may be demonstrated.

FROM ANOTHER POINT OF VIEW

Aardema, Verna. *Why Mosquitoes Buzz in People's Ears.* Illustrated by Leo Dillon and Diane Dillon. Dial, 1978.

Parent-Student Connections

1. Talk with your child about what to do in an emergency. What items should be carried in the car (for emergencies on the road) and what supplies should be stored at home? The area of the United States in which you live will dictate the type of emergency plan your family needs. What kind of disasters can happen in your area?

❀ ❀ ❀

THE WEAVING OF A DREAM

Author: Retold by Marilee Heyer
Illustrator: Marilee Heyer
Publisher: Viking Kestrel, 1986
Suggested Grade Level: 6
Classification: Folklore
Literary Form: Picture book
Theme: Story presents elements of love, loyalty, greed, and envy through many rich, detailed examples of imagery.

ABOUT THE BOOK

STUDENT OBJECTIVES:

1. Use the illustrations to identify the geographic setting of the story in *The Weaving of a Dream.*

2. Discover student visitation programs offered by local art galleries, museums, and gardens.

3. Present *The Weaving of a Dream* using color transparencies produced by students with a reading of the story on cassette.

SYNOPSIS: This is an age-old story about a widow and her three sons. She supports the family by weaving brocade pictures. One day at the market, she is enchanted by the beauty of a painting. She purchases the painting and weaves the scene into a brocade picture. After completing her weaving, the wind jerks the brocade from her and carries it far away to Sun Mountain. Each of her three sons goes on a quest to retrieve the brocade. Each must make choices along the way. The legend has a fairy-tale ending.

ABOUT THE AUTHOR-ILLUSTRATOR: Marilee Heyer, 1942- .

This is Marilee Heyer's first children's book. Her art career has included designing scenes for children's shows, including *The Lone Ranger, Journey to the Center of the Earth,* and *The Hardy Boys.* She also served as an associate story-board artist for the movie *Return of the Jedi.* Heyer lives in Southern California.

A review of *The Weaving of a Dream* states, "A breathtaking debut.... Heyer's paintings are replete with stunning detail and lavish color ... a perfect blending of fantasy and reality. Let's hope that this superb book is the first of many" (*Publishers Weekly*, April 26, 1986, p. 69).

SELECTED ADDITIONAL TITLES:

Heyer, Marilee. *The Forbidden Door.* Illustrated by Marilee Heyer. Viking Kestrel, 1988.

USING THE BOOK

Suggested Approach to the Book

Model Lesson

1. The red square on the first page of the story contains a symbol of a bat. What is it called?

2. Examine the double-paged village market scene and explain the advantages and disadvantages of the local market as compared to a modern mall.

3. Look at all of the two-page art spreads (3) in the book. List all of the visual images used in the illustrations. Are there any symbols?

4. What is your perception of the fortune teller?

5. Describe each son's quest. How do they differ?

6. Locate Marilee Heyer's dedication. If you were publishing a book, to whom would you dedicate it? Why?

Library Media Center Connections

1. Research koi (a type of fish) and present a brief, illustrated report, including physical props, such as color transparencies and varieties. Are there any koi that you could observe in your community?

2. Find materials, print and nonprint, illustrating and describing oriental gardens and their design elements. Design a small oriental garden to be constructed as part of a new home. What kinds of plants and garden ornaments would you choose?

Computer Connections

1. Write a letter to your teacher about the book you just finished reading, *The Weaving of a Dream.* What is your favorite part? Who else might enjoy the legend?

2. Develop a class cookbook for distribution at the end of the school year. Include a recipe from each study unit.

Instructional Materials Connections

1. Companies like the Nature Company (750 Hearst Ave., Berkeley, CA 94710) sell samples of inexpensive rocks and minerals, including examples of Chinese jade in various colors and other rock formations.

Theme Reading Connections: Folklore of China

Carpenter, Frances. *Tales of a Chinese Grandmother.* Illustrated by Malthe Hasselriie. Charles Tuttle, 1972.

Demi. *The Artist and the Architect.* Illustrated by Demi. Henry Holt, 1991.

———. *Liang and the Magic Paintbrush.* Illustrated by Demi. Henry Holt, 1980.

———. *The Empty Pot.* Illustrated by Demi. Henry Holt, 1990.

———. *Chingis Khan.* Illustrated by Demi. Henry Holt, 1991.

Dolch, Edward. *Stories from Old China.* Garrard, 1964.

Lattimore, Deborah Nourse. *The Dragon's Robe.* Harper & Row, 1990.

Luenn, Nancy. *The Dragon Kite.* Illustrated by Michael Hague. Harcourt Brace Jovanovich, 1992.

Mosel, Arlene. *Tikki Tikki Tembo.* Illustrated by Blair Lent. Henry Holt, 1968.

Rappaport, Doreen. *The Journey of Meng.* Illustrated by Yang Ming-Yi. Dial, 1991.

Wang, Rosalind C. *The Fourth Question: A Chinese Tale.* Illustrated by Ju-Hong Chen. Holiday House, 1991.

Williams, Jay. *Everyone Knows What a Dragon Looks Like.* Illustrated by Mercer Mayer. Four Winds Press, 1976.

Yep, Lawrence. *The Rainbow People.* Illustrated by David Weisner. Harper & Row, 1989.

> Critical Thinking Question
> List symbols used in the illustrations. Are they important to the plot of the story? To character development? Setting? Why were they used? Explain the purpose of some symbols used in the United States. An example might be the blue-and-white symbol identifying parking spaces for the disabled.

Student Activities to Connect Literature and Curriculum

FINE ARTS

1. Examine the cover art of *The Weaving of a Dream.* Notice the use of a border to extend the story. Border art usually presents other elements of the story or foreshadows action. Select a favorite fairy tale and create a new cover for the book using this style.

2. Compare and contrast the works of illustrators Jan Brett, Trina Schart Hyman, and Marilee Heyer. Carefully examine their use of page borders.

3. Using squares of foam rubber that measure at least 2 inches by 2 inches, construct chops designed as student signatures or insect illustrations. (For detailed illustrations and models of insects, see Owen, Jennifer, *Usborne Mysteries and Marvels of Insect Life,* Usborne-Hayes, 1984.)

4. A chop design may also be created using paper plates. Paint the plate with one color of poster paint. When it has dried, use a pencil to outline the chop design. Paint the design with a second color of paint. When that has dried, paint the plate with a thin mixture of white glue to protect it. A second layer of glue may also be used to provide additional protection.

5. Plan and construct a model of a village market for the focal point of a new shopping mall to be constructed near your home.

6. Hands are difficult to replicate in art. How many art forms can be used to replicate human hands? Present a class exhibit called Hands, and present awards for the most unusual hands, the most natural-looking hands, and the most beautiful hands.

7. Design and make a sheet of wrapping paper using a pattern of Chinese flowers, butterflies, and scrolls.

8. Compare and contrast the use of roses in *The Weaving of a Dream, Beauty and the Beast,* and *The Snow Queen.*

LANGUAGE ARTS

1. Write an information play to celebrate the Chinese New Year. Cooperative learning groups will construct lion's heads or dragon's costumes to wear for the presentation. Play props may include paper lanterns, fans, kites, scroll banners, and additional masks.

2. Using Chinese letters, write your name in ink brush strokes across the top of a piece of construction paper. (See Fisher, Leonard Everett, *Alphabet Art: Thirteen ABC's from around the World,* Four Winds Press, 1978.) Use the remainder of the page to write several paragraphs about the Chinese alphabet.

3. Design and produce a travel brochure for Americans planning to visit China.

WRITING PROMPT

1. The following headline flashes across the newspaper office fax machine. Write a one-page story to accompany it.

Weaving Widow Becomes Millionaire

MATH

1. Chinese paper cutting is a precise art. Using a grid system, create a pattern suitable for a cutout. Using the pattern, develop a cut-out form. The use of small scissors is recommended. (For additional instructions, see Borja, Robert, and Corinne Borja, *Making Chinese Paper-cuts,* Whitman, 1980.)

2. It is believed that the Chinese were flying kites at least 2,500 years ago. The kites were made of silk and included many designs. Construct kites in cooperative learning groups. Give awards for the most original design, the most beautiful design, the funniest kite, and the highest flying kite. (For directions, see Toney, Sara D., "Can a Trash Bag Fly?" in *Smithsonian Surprises, An Educational Activity Book*, Smithsonian, 1985.)

3. According to legend, Tan was delivering a ceramic tile to an emperor. Unfortunately, he fell and the tile broke into seven pieces. Tan could not make the tile whole again. Tangrams are seven-piece puzzles, usually of plastic. Use tangrams in the classroom math program.

4. Read Tompert, Ann, *Grandfather Tang's Story,* illustrated by Robert Andrew Parker, Crown, 1990. Each cooperative learning group will create a tangram using the classroom overhead projector and plastic tangrams. A tangram is composed of seven pieces. Arrange the pieces to resemble a shape. When assembled on the glass plate of an overhead projector, it will become a silhouette.

SCIENCE

1. Draw the life cycle of a silkworm. The illustrator used silkworms as part of the art work on the page picturing the mother admiring a silk scroll.

2. Using an encyclopedia or other reference book, prepare a detailed diagram or science model of a hand. Identify the parts of the hand.

SOCIAL STUDIES

1. You are invited to attend a Chinese school as an exchange student for a month. Describe the housing, clothing, food, schools, music, recreation, and shopping. Prepare a chart for China and the United States listing information that would be helpful for students visiting each other's country through an exchange program.

GEOGRAPHY

1. Create a physical map model of all locations named in the story.

2. Sun Mountain is pictured in the book. Is there any mountain or other land form in the United States that might be as high as Sun Mountain? List the three tallest mountains in the United States. What are the three tallest mountains in the world? (See the *World Almanac.*)

3. Marco Polo, who was from Venice, Italy, was one of China's first European visitors. Read Ceserani, Gian Paolo, *Marco Polo,* illustrated by Piero Ventura, Putnam, 1977.

BEYOND THE BOOK

Guided Reading Connections Across a Learning Rainbow: China

Bailey, Jill. *Project Panda.* Raintree/Steck-Vaughn, 1990.

Fisher, Leonard E. *The Great Wall of China.* Macmillan, 1986.

Fyson, Nance L., and Richard Greenhill. *A Family in China.* Lerner, 1985.

Haskins, Jim. *Count Your Way Through China.* Carolrhoda, 1967.

Hughes, Stanton. *See Inside an Ancient Chinese Town.* Franklin Watts, 1986.

Hung-ying, Liao, and Derek Bryan. *China.* Chelsea, 1988.

Jacobsen P., and P. A. Kristensen. *A Family in China.* Franklin Watts, 1986.

Keeler, Stephen. *Passport to China.* Franklin Watts, 1988.

Kendall, Carol, and Li Yao-wen. *Tales from China.* Clarion Books, 1979.

Sabin, Louis. *Ancient China.* Troll, 1985.

Shui, Amy, and Stuart Thompson. *Chinese Food and Drink.* Franklin Watts, 1987.

Thomson, Peggy. *City Kids in China.* Harper & Row, 1991.

Enriching Connections

1. Read for pleasure 25 fairy tales. List the titles of the 25 selected tales and include several illustrated versions of the same stories.

2. Create a modern quest story based on a newspaper or magazine article, as in the following example:

   A volunteer worker in a Tennessee thrift store purchases an old-fashioned locket because of its unusual design. The locket is not examined for several weeks; then the owner becomes intrigued because the locket cannot be opened.

   The services of a local jeweler are sought. Still the locket cannot be opened. The jeweler sends the watch to a jeweler who specializes in antique jewelry to see if he has any experience working with this type of locket. He does open it through a hidden spring mechanism. Inside is a portrait of Josephine, the wife of the French emperor Napoleon, along with a hand-written letter!

   The quest is on. Is it authentic? How did it get to the thrift shop? Who owned it before? Where has it been all these years? What is its history? Can the information be verified through documentation and library research?

FROM ANOTHER POINT OF VIEW

Baker, Keith. *The Magic Fan.* Illustrated by Keith Baker. Harcourt Brace Jovanovich, 1989.

Parent-Student Connections

1. Visit a garden to view koi (fish), visit a zoo to view pandas, or tour a museum's Chinese art collection.

2. Plan and cook a Chinese meal for the family.

3. Fly a kite.

❋   ❋   ❋

THE TWELVE DANCING PRINCESSES

Author: Retold by Ruth Sanderson
Illustrator: Ruth Sanderson
Publisher: Little, Brown, 1991
Suggested Grade Level: 6
Classification: Folklore
Literary Form: Picture book illustrated with oil paintings
Theme: Fairy tales capture the imagination of young and old. All things are possible.

ABOUT THE BOOK

STUDENT OBJECTIVES:

1. Design a shadow theater for the presentation of *The Twelve Dancing Princesses.* Use a white background with shadow silhouettes.

2. Adapt the fairy tale *The Twelve Dancing Princesses* and present it as a play in the shadow theater.

3. Prepare a video tape presentation about the lives of the Brothers Grimm (Jacob and Wilhelm).

SYNOPSIS: Fairy tales are magical stories of beauty and crisis. A king has 12 daughters who are locked in their bedroom each night, but each morning there are 12 pairs of worn-out dancing slippers outside their door. How can this be?

ABOUT THE AUTHOR-ILLUSTRATOR: Ruth Sanderson, 1951- .
  Ruth Sanderson presently teaches oil painting and book illustration at the Northampton School of Design, Northampton, Massachusetts. She lives in nearby Ware, Massachusetts, her birthplace, and explains that she feels "I have come back to my roots." Art has always been one of Sanderson's

major interests. She enjoys relating her first teaching experience—as a second-grader. "I held an art class for my friends and taught them how to draw horses."

Sanderson has illustrated more than 35 books for children, including classic editions of *Heidi* and *Sleeping Beauty*. She feels it is every artist's dream to illustrate fairy tales. Sanderson prefers to use oils because of the "romantic yet realistic style."

"I gravitated toward illustration, because I like having problems to solve. I prefer developing continuity and pictorial impressions of a manuscript to initiating my own ideas." (*Something About the Author,* vol. 41, pp. 198-204.)

ABOUT THE BROTHERS GRIMM: Jacob Grimm, 1785-1863; Wilhelm Grimm, 1786-1859

Jacob Grimm and Wilhelm Grimm published their first book, *Kinder und Hausmarchen* (*Nursery and Household Tales*), in 1812. The book was criticized as a work of superstition, but it became very popular. Before the work of the Grimm brothers, no scientific research about traditional literature had been undertaken. The first English edition of the Grimms' book, published under the title *German Popular Tales,* translated by Edgar Taylor, was published in 1823. Since that time, the tales have been translated into more than 60 languages.

The Brothers Grimm collected stories in the oral tradition from Germany. Their objective was not to provide interesting fairy tales but to record the stories they heard as a scientific research project. They gathered tales from many sources, including family members, friends, neighbors, and peasants. The goal of their research was to find the origin of the stories.

Although the folklore did not originally focus on children, the tales did become integrated into children's literature and in time were modified to remove some violence and terror-inducing elements.

Some of the artists who have enhanced the stories with illustration include Arthur Rackham, Walter Crane, George Cruikshank, Wanda Gág, Nancy Eckholm Burkert, Adrienne Adams, Mercer Mayer, Michael Hague, Nonny Hogrogian, Lisbeth Zwerger, and Trina Schart Hyman.

SELECTED ADDITIONAL TITLES: Ruth Sanderson

Byars, Betsy. *The Animal, the Vegetable and John D. Jones.* Illustrated by Ruth Sanderson. Delacorte Press, 1982.

Bulla, Clyde R. *The Beast of Lor.* Illustrated by Ruth Sanderson. Thomas Y. Crowell, 1977.

Chittenden, Margaret. *The Mystery of the Missing Pony.* Illustrated by Ruth Sanderson. Garrard, 1980.

Cole, William, ed. *Good Dog Poems.* Illustrated by Ruth Sanderson. Macmillan, 1981.

Farrar, Susan. *Samantha on Stage.* Illustrated by Ruth Sanderson. Dial, 1979.

Gorog, Judith. *Caught in the Turtle.* Illustrated by Ruth Sanderson. Putnam, 1983.

Hall, Lynn. *The Mystery of the Carmel Cat.* Illustrated by Ruth Sanderson. Garrard, 1981.

Hope, Laura. *The Bobbsey Twins: Secret in the Pirate's Cave.* Illustrated by Ruth Sanderson. Wanderer, 1980.

Renner, Beverly. *The Hideaway Summer.* Illustrated by Ruth Sanderson. Harper & Row, 1978.

Roberts, Willo D. *Don't Hurt Laurie!* Illustrated by Ruth Sanderson. Macmillan, 1977.

Simon, Norma, and Caroline Rubin, eds. *We Remember Philip.* Illustrated by Ruth Sanderson. Whitman, 1978.

Sleator, William. *Into the Dream.* Illustrated by Ruth Sanderson. Dutton, 1979.

Spyri, Johanna. *Heidi.* Illustrated by Ruth Sanderson. Alfred A. Knopf, 1984.

Stern, Cecily. *A Different Kind of Gold.* Illustrated by Ruth Sanderson. Harper & Row, 1981.

SELECTED ADDITIONAL TITLES: Jacob Grimm and Wilhelm Grimm

Grimm, Jacob, and Wilhelm Grimm. *About Wise Men and Simpletons: Twelve Tales from Grimm.* Translated by Elizabeth Shub. Illustrated by Nonny Hogrogian. Macmillan, 1986.

————. *Brave Little Tailor.* Illustrated by Mark Corcoran. Troll, 1979.

————. *The Bremen Town Musicians.* Illustrated by Janina Domanska. Greenwillow Books, 1980.

————. *The Elves and the Shoemaker.* Illustrated. Troll, 1981.

————. *Fairy Tales.* Illustrated by Allen Atkinson. Messner, 1982.

————. *Favorite Tales from Grimm.* Retold by Nancy Garden. Illustrated. Macmillan, 1982.

————. *The Fisherman and His Wife.* Translated from German by Randall Jarrell. Illustrated by Margot Zemach. Farrar, Straus & Giroux, 1980.

————. *Grimms' Fairy Tales.* Illustrated by Richard Walz. Golden Books, 1986.

————. *Grimm's Fairy Tales for Young and Old: The Complete Stories.* Translated by Ralph Manheim. Doubleday, 1983.

————. *Hansel and Gretel.* Translated by Elizabeth D. Crawford. Illustrated by Lisbeth Zwerger. Morrow, 1980.

————. *The Little Red Cap.* Illustrated by Lisbeth Zwerger. Picture Book Studio, 1983.

————. *Little Red Riding Hood.* Retold and illustrated by Trina Schart Hyman. Holiday House, 1982.

————. *The Queen Bee.* Illustrated by Phillipe Dumas. Creative Education, 1986.

————. *Rapunzel.* Retold by Barbara Rogasky. Illustrated by Trina Schart Hyman. Holiday House, 1982.

————. *Rapunzel.* Illustrated by Michael Hague. Creative Education, 1986.

————. *Rumpelstiltskin.* Retold and illustrated by Donna Diamond. Holiday House, 1983.

————. *Snow White and the Seven Dwarfs.* Translated from German by Randall Jarrell. Illustrated by Nancy E. Burkert. Farrar, Straus & Giroux, 1972.

USING THE BOOK

Suggested Approach to the Book

Model Lesson

1. If you were a king who locked your daughters in their bedroom each night, and each morning there were 12 pairs of worn-out dancing slippers outside their door, what would you think? Brainstorm and list students' thoughts on the blackboard. How did the princesses escape every night? Where were they going? How were they getting there?

2. As the story is read, begin a list of the characteristics of a fairy tale.

3. Describe the commoner, Michael, who came to the palace to solve the mystery of the worn-out dancing slippers. What magical garment was given to Michael by the elderly lady?

4. How would boys react today if they were described as pretty? (Note: The meanings of words have changed. Can you give examples of words that had different meanings in the past?)

5. Can you think of any occasion when giving money is inappropriate?

6. Is there any significance to the rumbling sound heard when Michael and the 12 princesses returned to the castle?

Library Media Center Connections

1. This project may be completed in cooperative learning groups. Research information about theme amusement parks in the United States. Where are they located? How many theme parks are located in your state? How many visitors do they receive each year? What are the main attractions of each park? How much land area is required for the parks? Why?

Computer Connections

1. Design a flyer that will be mailed to local residents announcing the opening of a fairy tales theme park. The flyer should announce the date of the opening and include a special preview invitation for community members. What will be the cost of admission? Will there be any price reductions within the Twelve Dancing Princesses exhibit?

2. Using a computer-generated form letter, obtain information about various theme parks in the United States. Request that brochures and other promotional materials be sent to the classroom.

Instructional Materials Connections

1. *The Art of Shoes, 1898-1960.* Rizzoli, 1992.

2. Spellman, Linda. *Castles, Codes and Calligraphy.* Learning Works, 1984.

3. Macaulay, David. *Castle.* Houghton Mifflin, 1977.

4. Macaulay, David. *Castle.* Video. Dorset Video, 1977. Barnes and Noble, 124 Fifth Ave., New York, NY 10011.

5. *In the Days of Knights and Kings*, a computer simulation of medieval living, Entrex.

6. A paper model of a medieval castle is available from the Los Angeles County Museum of Art Gift Shop, 5905 Wilshire Blvd., Los Angeles, CA 90036.

Theme Reading Connections: Fiction About Princes and Princesses

Andersen, Hans Christian. *The Princess and the Pea.* Translated by Anthea Bell. Illustrated by Eve Tharlet. Picture Book Studio, 1987.

Bretano, Clemens. *The Legend of Rosepetal.* Illustrated by Lisbeth Zwerger. Picture Book Studio, 1985.

Burnett, Frances H. *A Little Princess.* Scholastic, 1987.

de Saint-Exupery, Antoine. *The Little Prince.* Translated by Katherine Woods. Harcourt Brace Jovanovich, 1968.

Grimm, Jacob, and Wilhelm Grimm. *Twelve Dancing Princesses.* Retold and illustrated by Errol Le Cain. Penguin, 1981.

Helprin, Mark, retold by. *Swan Lake.* Illustrated by Chris Van Allsburg. Houghton Mifflin, 1989.

MacDonald, George. *The Princess and the Goblin.* Illustrated by Jesse W. Smith. Morrow, 1986.

Twain, Mark. *The Prince and the Pauper.* Penguin, 1983.

Critical Thinking Question
The United States and many other nations have a president, but other nations still have a king or queen. Should it be unlawful for royalty to rule a country for life? Should all heads of state be elected by the people in a democratic election? Why or why not?

Student Activities to Connect Literature and Curriculum

FINE ARTS

1. Notice the illuminated letter at the beginning of the story. Find examples of illuminated art in other library books to share with the class. Learn to illuminate the initial letter of your last name or your initials. What print style will you use? What colors of ink and textured paper appeal to you? Students may display their work on the bulletin board.

2. Design 12 modern pairs of dancing shoes for the princesses. Explain why you chose the design. Should shoes be beautiful or comfortable? Compare the styles of men's and women's shoes today.

     (Note: Shoes of other times and countries have become the subject of research and museum displays. An Italian shoemaker, Salvatore Ferragamo, came to the United States to design and make shoes for Hollywood movie stars during the 1930s and 1940s. His family has carried on the family business. His unique shoe collection toured museums in the United States in 1992.)

LANGUAGE ARTS

1. Develop a hypothesis about what happened to all the young men who disappeared when they came to the castle at the king's invitation to solve the mystery of the dance shoes. State your thoughts in a well-written paragraph.

2. Imagine that a local amusement company, Fairy Tales, has decided to add a new area, The Twelve Dancing Princesses, to the theme park. Design a building plan for the new exhibit. What displays would meet the educational criteria required by the board of directors? What dress would employees wear in this section? What souvenirs would be appropriate? What food would be sold? Plan the grand opening of this section, including press releases for newspapers, radio, and television. This activity may be completed in cooperative learning groups.

WRITING PROMPT

1. Use the following headline for the opening news report of a local television station about a princess from a small country in Europe:

> Princess Lina to Wed Palace Gardener Next Month!

MATH

1. Determine the variety and quantity of food that the king and his 12 princesses would consume in one day. Plan the menu and list the main ingredients, then estimate the total quantity required. Make up a palace grocery order and compute the cost for the provisions.

SCIENCE

1. Imagine that you have received a commission from the king to create the magical woods within the castle gardens. What kind of flowers and trees would you select? Draw a landscape plan and label plants and trees that would be included. Balance your selections so that some flowers would be blooming during each of the four seasons. Include an addendum to the plans that includes colored illustrations of the trees and plants listed in alphabetical order.

SOCIAL STUDIES

1. Which countries in the world still have royal families? List the countries and provide the names of the ruler and the immediate royal family. What would be the advantages and disadvantages of being royalty? Design a modern coat of arms for each reigning family. Provide a rationale for your designs.

2. If you had an opportunity to own and live in any castle in the world, which one would you choose? Why? In an oral report, present an illustration of the castle and highlight the special features that appeal to you.

GEOGRAPHY

1. Construct an imaginary, textured map (showing trees, water, buildings, etc.) of places described in the *The Twelve Dancing Princesses.*

BEYOND THE BOOK

Guided Reading Connections Across a Learning Rainbow: Amusements

Anderson, Norma D., and Walter R. Brown. *Ferris Wheels.* Pantheon Books, 1983.

Silverstein, Herma. *Scream Machines: Roller Coasters: Past, Present, and Future.* Walker, 1986.

Van Steenwyk, Elizabeth. *Behind the Scenes at the Amusement Park.* Whitman, 1983.

Enriching Connections

1. Using library reference materials, explain the rites of a coronation and the special clothing worn for the ceremony. Are coronations public or religious ceremonies?

FROM ANOTHER POINT OF VIEW

Grimm, Jacob, and Wilhelm Grimm. *The Twelve Dancing Princesses.* Retold by Marianna Mayer. Illustrated by K. Y. Craft. Morrow, 1989.

Parent-Student Connections

1. If you were a king, would you lock your children in their rooms at night? If the reason was for their safety, what kinds of things might happen that they would need to get out of their rooms? What kind of personal safety should be observed in bedrooms? Is placing decorative iron bars across windows, to stop theft and insure the safety of the residents, a good practice? (Building codes require that iron bars have a quick-release mechanism when they are installed in bedrooms.) Why or why not? This question provides parents an opportunity to discuss emergency situations; what to do and what not to do.

❀ ❀ ❀

SAINT GEORGE AND THE DRAGON

Author: Retold by Margaret Hodges
Illustrator: Trina Schart Hyman
Publisher: Little, Brown, 1984
Suggested Grade Level: 6
Classification: Nonfiction
Literary Form: Legend adapted from Edmund Spenser's *Faerie Queene*
Theme: Good will triumph over evil.

ABOUT THE BOOK

STUDENT OBJECTIVES:

1. Compile a list of legends and folktales by their country of origin.

2. Construct a world map bulletin-board display for the school library media center. On the map, pinpoint the names of the legends and their countries. For example, include Cinderella and all the countries that have a version of this story.

3. Read and orally summarize five folktales and legends.

SYNOPSIS: This story features a segment from the *Fairie Queene* about the famous Red Cross Knight and his battle to slay a vicious dragon that is frightening the people.

ABOUT THE AUTHOR: Margaret Hodges, 1911- .

Margaret Hodges worked in the Carnegie Library in Pittsburgh, serving as a storytelling specialist. Eventually, she became a professor emeritus at the University of Pittsburgh. She has written numerous books for children.

About her work, Hodges says, "My writing falls into three types: real life stories based on the adventures and misadventures of my three sons, and retelling of folk tales and myths in picture book format, and biography written to bring to life a few little-known or disregarded characters who contributed in an important way to history." (*Something About the Author,* vol. 33, p. 97.)

ABOUT THE ILLUSTRATOR: Trina Schart Hyman, 1939- .

Trina Schart Hyman is one of the most prolific contemporary illustrators. She received the Caldecott medal for *St. George and the Dragon.*

The story of the Little Red Riding Hood cape is a part of her being. When Hyman was a child, her mother made a cape for her. In Hyman's mind, the cape bestowed magical powers on her during her imaginary journeys to Grandmother's house, which Hyman enacted in her backyard, accompanied by Tip, her dog and wolf character. "I was Red Riding Hood for a year or more. I think it's a great tribute to my mother that she never gave up and took me to a psychiatrist, and if she ever worried, she has never let me know" (Hyman, Trina Schart, *Self Portrait: Trina Schart Hyman,* Addison-Wesley, 1981).

SELECTED ADDITIONAL TITLES: Margaret Hodges

Hodges, Margaret. *The Avenger.* Macmillan, 1982.

———. *The Fire Bringer: A Paiute Indian Legend.* Illustrated by Peter Parnall. Little, Brown, 1972.

———. *The Kitchen Knight.* Illustrated by Trina Schart Hyman. Holiday House, 1990.

———. *Knight Prisoner: The Tale of Sir Thomas Malory and His King Arthur.* Farrar, Straus & Giroux, 1976.

———. *The Wave.* Illustrated by B. Lent. Houghton Mifflin, 1964.

SELECTED ADDITIONAL TITLES: Trina Schart Hyman

Calhoun, Mary. *Big Sixteen.* Illustrated by Trina Schart Hyman. Morrow, 1983.

Dickens, Charles. *A Christmas Carol.* Illustrated by Trina Schart Hyman. Holiday House, 1983.

Fritz, Jean. *The Man Who Loved Books.* Illustrated by Trina Schart Hyman. Putnam, 1981.

———. *Why Don't You Get a Horse, Sam Adams?* Illustrated by Trina Schart Hyman. Putnam, 1974.

———. *Will You Sign Here, John Hancock?* Illustrated by Trina Schart Hyman. Putnam, 1976.

Gates, Doris. *Two Queens of Heaven: Aphrodite and Demeter.* Illustrated by Trina Schart Hyman. Viking, 1974.

Grimm, Jacob, and Wilhelm K. Grimm. *Little Red Riding Hood.* Illustrated by Trina Schart Hyman. Holiday House, 1982.

———. *Rapunzel.* Retold by Barbara Rogasky. Illustrated by Trina Schart Hyman. Holiday House, 1982.

Hyman, Trina Schart. *How Six Found Christmas.* Illustrated by Trina Schart Hyman. Little, Brown, 1979.

————. *The Sleeping Beauty.* Illustrated by Trina Schart Hyman. Little, Brown, 1977.

Lasky, Katherine. *Night Journey.* Illustrated by Trina Schart Hyman. Penguin, 1986.

Livingston, Myra. *Christmas Poems.* Illustrated by Trina Schart Hyman. Holiday House, 1984.

Pyle, Howard. *King Stork.* Illustrated by Trina Schart Hyman. Little, Brown, 1986.

Rogasky, Barbara, ed. *The Water of Life.* Illustrated by Trina Schart Hyman. Holiday House, 1986.

Sleator, William. *Among the Dolls.* Illustrated by Trina Schart Hyman. Dutton, 1986.

Thomas, Dylan. *A Child's Christmas in Wales.* Illustrated by Trina Schart Hyman. Holiday House, 1985.

Winthrop, Elizabeth. *Castle in the Attic.* Illustrated by Trina Schart Hyman. Holiday House, 1985.

USING THE BOOK

Suggested Approach to the Book

Model Lesson

1. The title page differs in several ways from most books. Why? How does the title page build your anticipation?

2. Why were some knights described as noble? What word would you use to describe knights who were not noble?

3. What foreign word is nearest in meaning to the name of the princess, Una?

4. Why does the old hermit send the knight down to the valley to fight the dragon?

5. Describe the scene when the Red Cross Knight and the princess reach the valley inhabited by the dragon.

6. What happened to the knight each time he was injured? Would you describe his healing as magical?

7. What did the townspeople do when the dragon was slain? Would you have reacted the same way? Why or why not?

8. Explain what it means when an author's work is adapted for television.

Library Media Center Connections

1. Look on the back of the title page. What information can you learn about the book? Using the information, explain what catalog subject headings should be used in the school library media center. Why? Where on the shelves would you find *St. George and the Dragon?*

2. Consult the school library media center catalog for all the books about dragons. Classify and list them for grades 1-3 and grades 4-6.

3. Using print and nonprint materials from the school library media center, compare and contrast another illustrator's work with that of Trina Schart Hyman. Cooperative learning groups may choose from the following list:

CONTEMPORARY ILLUSTRATORS

Mitsumasa Anno	Ludwig Bemelmans	Michael Bond
Raymond Briggs	Marcia Brown	Jean de Brunhoff
Barbara Cooney	Edgar D'Aulaire	Ingri D'Aulaire
Leo Dillon	Diane Dillon	Leonard Everett Fisher
Paul Goble	Michael Hague	Gail Haley
Shirley Hughes	Ezra Jack Keats	Steven Kellogg
Leo Lionni	Arnold Lobel	Mercer Mayer
David Macaulay	Gerald McDermott	Alice Provensen
Martin Provensen	Maurice Sendak	Dr. Seuss
Peter Spier	William Steig	Margot Tomes
Tasha Tudor	Chris Van Allsberg	Brian Wildsmith
Garth Williams		

CLASSIC ILLUSTRATORS

Edmund Dulac	Maxfield Parrish	Beatrix Potter
Howard Pyle	Arthur Rackham	Charles Robinson
Jessie Wilcox Smith	Ernest Shepard	Sir John Tenniel
N. C. Wyeth		

Computer Connections

1. Create a database of books about legends, folklore, dragons, fairies, giants, and monsters. Include the author, title, illustrator, date of publication, and student evaluations of the book. This database can be an ongoing project for students as they explore many reading interests.

2. Using a word processor, adapt for video one of the books illustrated by Trina Schart Hyman.

Instructional Materials Connections

1. Goodall, John S. *The Story of an English Village.* Illustrated by John S. Goodall. Macmillan, 1979.

2. Green, Roger L. *Adventures of Robin Hood.* Penguin, 1985.

3. Greene, Carol. *England.* Enchantment of the World series. Childrens Press, 1982.

4. Haitsch, Bette. *England.* Chelsea House, 1988.

5. Haynes, Sarah, retold by. *Robin Hood.* Illustrated by Patrick Benson. Henry Holt, 1989.

6. Hyman, Trina Schart. *Self Portrait: Trina Schart Hyman.* Illustrated by Trina Schart Hyman. Harper & Row, 1989.

7. Hyman, Trina Schart. *Little Red Riding Hood.* Filmstrip and cassette. Listening Library, 1984.

8. McGovern, Ann. *Robin Hood of Sherwood Forest.* Illustrated by Tracey Sugarman. Scholastic, 1987.

9. Ruby, Jennifer. *Costumes in Context: Medieval Times.* Costume in Context series. Southeastern Book Company, 1990.

10. Spellman, Linda. *Castles, Codes, and Calligraphy.* Learning Works, 1984.

11. Stoor, Catherine, retold by. *Robin Hood.* Raintree/Steck-Vaughn, 1984.

12. Twain, Mark. *The Prince and the Pauper.* Troll, 1989.

Theme Reading Connections: English Folklore

Galdone, Paul. *The Teeny-Tiny Woman.* Illustrated by Paul Galdone. Houghton Mifflin, 1984.

———. *The Three Sillies.* Houghton Mifflin, 1981.

Jacobs, Joseph, ed. *English Fairy Tales.* Illustrated by John D. Batten. Dover, 1990.

Parker, Ed. *Jack and the Beanstalk.* Troll, 1979.

Schmidt, Karen. *The Gingerbread Man.* Scholastic, 1985.

Critical Thinking Question
What are the characteristics of legends, folktales, and fairy tales? Using one of your favorites, explain what things need to happen in the story.

Activities to Connect Literature and Curriculum

FINE ARTS

1. Before reading the book, construct a dummy book and sketch in the border art on your pages. Write one sentence on each page describing the art work. Save the dummy to compare after reading the book. How accurately did Trina Schart Hyman project the author's words?

2. Assign students to work on this task in pairs. Students in each pair will sit back to back. One will describe a dragon and the other will draw and color it from the description. The students will reverse roles by having one describe a knight and his horse while the other draws and colors it.

3. Create a scale-model castle. What style of architecture will you use? Why?

4. Develop a George the Red Cross Knight game with a game board, markers, and two decks of direction cards.

5. Prepare drawings that compare and contrast Chinese and English dragons in children's literature. Explain aloud their differences and similarities.

LANGUAGE ARTS

1. Retell the story of St. George and the Dragon with a different ending.

2. Write another adventure for the Red Cross Knight and the princess.

3. Keep a student-response diary. One column should be brief, interesting quotes from the book, and the other column should contain your responses to the setting, character, or plot.

WRITING PROMPT

1. Send a proclamation throughout the kingdom celebrating the slaying of the dreaded dragon. Begin the announcement with the following words:

Hear Ye! Hear Ye! Be it known that the dragon is dead!

MATH

1. Examine the illustration on page 15. Estimate the height of the horse and Red Cross Knight. What is the ratio of the knight's size to the dragon's size? How tall do you think the dragon is?

2. Create a connect-the-dots picture of a dragon, plotting the dots as points on a graph. Begin numbering the coordinates along the axes with 0,0. First drop in the dots to create the drawing, then list the coordinates used. Exchange lists of coordinates, fill in the dots, and connect them. That would require them to work with the coordinates themselves. They could check their work against the creator's original dot-to-dot graph.

SCIENCE

1. Identify the various kinds of flowers used in the page borders. Use a flower-identification guide as a reference. Also, determine if any of the flowers can grow in your area.

SOCIAL STUDIES

1. Plan a palace celebration to honor George, the Red Knight, and Una, the princess. Make the celebration appropriate for medieval times. (See Aliki, *The Medieval Feast,* illustrated by Aliki, Thomas Y. Crowell, 1983.)

GEOGRAPHY

1. Construct a map of the British Isles. Label major sections and cities on the map.

2. Plan an itinerary for a tour of castles of the British Isles and Europe. Include the Castle of Count Dracula in Transylvania, which is in Romania.

BEYOND THE BOOK

Guided Reading Connections Across a Learning Rainbow: Monsters

Ames, Lee J. *Draw Fifty Beasties: And Yugglies and Turnover Uglies and Things That Go Bump in the Night.* Illustrated by Lee J. Ames. Doubleday, 1988.

Blythe, Richard. *Dragons and Other Fabulous Beasts.* Illustrated by Fiona French and Joann Troughton. Putnam, 1980.

Horton, et al. *Amazing Fact Book of Monsters.* Creative Education, 1987.

Odor, Ruth. *Learning About Giants.* Childrens Press, 1981.

Rawson. *Dragons.* Illustrated. Usborne-Hayes, 1980.

———. *Dragons, Giants and Witches.* Illustrated. Usborne-Hayes, 1979.

Stallman, Birdie. *Learning About Dragons.* Illustrated by Lydia Halverson. Childrens Press, 1981.

Enriching Connections

1. Create a St. George and the Dragon diorama scene in a shoe box.

2. Prepare English trifle for the class. The traditional recipe uses ladyfinger cookies, vanilla custard, fruit, and whipped cream. Line a glass dish with the cookies. Add a layer of custard, canned fruit that has been drained (the traditional fruit is peaches), and whipped cream. When serving, be sure to dip through all layers to include all the delicacies in a serving.

3. Construct dragons using various materials and art techniques.

FROM ANOTHER POINT OF VIEW

Williams, Jay. *Everyone Knows What a Dragon Looks Like.* Illustrated by Mercer Mayer. Four Winds Press, 1976.

Parent-Student Connections

1. Read fairy tales, folktales, and legends aloud to one another. What makes them alike and what makes them different?

2. Explore books about the architecture of castles, including Macaulay, David, *Castle*, Houghton Mifflin, 1977.

❀　❀　❀

In the World of Fantasy

THE WIZARD OF OZ

Author: L. Frank Baum
Illustrator: Michael Hague
Publisher: Henry Holt, 1982
Suggested Grade Level: 6
Classification: Fiction
Literary Form: A fantasy story written almost 100 years ago, but presented with the delightful illustrative touch of Michael Hague
Theme: Some children's stories are timeless and magically open doors to other times, places, characters, and plots. Such is the robust story of Dorothy, Toto, Lion, Scarecrow, Tin Woodman, and the Wizard of Oz.

ABOUT THE BOOK

STUDENT OBJECTIVES:

1. Write, direct, and produce a classroom video of *The Wizard of Oz.*

2. Write a review of the movie, *The Wizard of Oz*, starring Judy Garland as Dorothy.

3. Share the story of *The Wizard of Oz* with younger students as part of a cross-age curriculum assignment. Ways to share the story include flannel-board storytelling, art activities, and oral presentations.

SYNOPSIS: Almost all are familiar with the movie, but how many students have actually savored every word of this classic that has been enriched with such unique illustrations?

In this fantasy story, wolves get their heads whacked off and giant killer bees die because their stingers break off in an attack on the tin woodman. Dorothy flies through space, like many heroines of today, but how many contemporary characters live in Kansas, are swept up by a violent cyclone, and are set down in such a land of wonder?

ABOUT THE AUTHOR: L. Frank Baum, 1856-1919.

Lyman Frank Baum was born in New York into a family of wealth. Baum had many occupations, including managing a chain of theaters, acting, writing plays, and owning a small general store in South Dakota. As a shopkeeper, his business skills were poor and he went bankrupt, partly due to the fact that he had 106 nonpaying customers! Later, he suffered bankruptcy as a newspaper publisher.

Finally Baum reached the decision that he would concentrate on writing to support his wife and family. In 1897 his first book, *Mother Goose in Prose,* was published. Two years later, *Father Goose: His Book,* was published. It met with success and sold more than 60,000 copies.

The Wonderful Wizard of Oz was first published in 1900 after many rejections because it was considered too radical. Finally, to get the book published, Baum and the original illustrator, W. W. Denslow, agreed that they would pay all expenses if the book did not sell! Baum chose to drop the "wonderful" from the title as he preferred *The Wizard of Oz.*

Children begged for more Oz stories. Baum did not intend to write any sequels, but to answer the public interest, he wrote 13 more titles. Eventually, 26 additional Oz books were written by other authors.

Baum was a gentle man who envisioned Oz as a place where American values of freedom and independence flourished. "The City of Oz is a Utopian place where there is no money and no one is rich or poor. Disease does not exist, and people happily balance work and play" (Author notes in Baum, L. Frank, *The Wizard of Oz,* p. 219).

ABOUT THE ILLUSTRATOR: Michael Hague, 1948- .

Michael Hague was born in Los Angeles, California. His British parents had immigrated to the United States after World War II. He was educated in California and graduated with a Bachelor of Fine Arts degree from the Los Angeles Art Center College of Design. After graduating he earned a living working for both a greeting card company and a calendar company.

According to Hague, he has been influenced by divergent styles that include Disney Studios, the Japanese woodblock printers Hiroshige and Hokusai, and artists Arthur Rackham, W. Heath Robinson, N. C. Wyeth, and Howard Pyle. He is an avid collector of their books.

Hague's technique is to draw thumbnail sketches that are subsequently enlarged to full size. Next, the full-size art is finished as a pencil illustration. He then covers his canvas with a neutral wash that uses warm tones, such as ocher, or a cool-color cast made with a bluish wash. When the canvas is dry, Hague colors his work. His last step is to draw in ink lines.

SELECTED ADDITIONAL TITLES: L. Frank Baum

Baum, L. Frank. *Adventures in Oz: Ozma of Oz and Marvelous Land of Oz. The Original Editions Complete and Unabridged.* Dover, 1985.

———. *Dorothy and the Wicked Witch.* Troll, 1980.

———. *Dorothy and the Wizard.* Troll, 1980.

———. *Dorothy and the Wizard in Oz.* Dover, 1984.

———. *Land of Oz.* Illustrated by John R. Neill. Macmillan, 1904.

———. *Marvelous Land of Oz.* Illustrated by John R. Neill. Dover, 1969.

———. *Mother Goose in Prose.* Outlet Book, 1986.

———. *Off to See the Wizard.* Troll, 1980.

———. *Ozma of Oz.* Dover, 1985.

———. *The Pop-Up Wizard of Oz.* Illustrated by Karen Avery. Windmill Books, 1992.

————. *The Wizard of Oz.* Penguin, 1983.

————. *The Wizard of Oz.* Edited by Jean L. Scrocco. Illustrated by Greg Hildebrandt. Unicorn, 1985.

————. *The Wonderful Wizard of Oz.* Illustrated by W. W. Denslow. Dover, 1960.

Baum, Roger S. *The Rewolf of Oz.* Illustrated by Charlotte Hart. Green Tiger Press, 1990.

SELECTED ADDITIONAL TITLES: Michael Hague

Andersen, Hans Christian. *Michael Hague's Favorite Hans Christian Andersen Fairy Tales.* Illustrated by Michael Hague. Henry Holt, 1981.

Burnett, Frances. *The Secret Garden.* Illustrated by Michael Hague. Henry Holt, 1987.

Carroll, Lewis. *Alice in Wonderland.* Illustrated by Michael Hague. Henry Holt, 1985.

Grahame, Kenneth. *The Reluctant Dragon.* Illustrated by Michael Hague. Henry Holt, 1983.

Hague, Kathleen. *Alphabears.* Illustrated by Michael Hague. Henry Holt, 1985.

————. *The Legend of the Veery Bird.* Illustrated by Michael Hague. Harcourt Brace Jovanovich, 1985.

————. *The Man Who Kept House.* Illustrated by Michael Hague. Harcourt Brace Jovanovich, 1981.

————. *Numbears: A Counting Book.* Illustrated by Michael Hague. Henry Holt, 1986.

————. *Out of the Nursery, Into the Night.* Illustrated by Michael Hague. Henry Holt, 1986.

Hague, Kathleen, and Michael Hague. *East of the Sun and West of the Moon.* Illustrated by Michael Hague. Harcourt Brace Jovanovich, 1980.

Hague, Michael. *Michael Hague's World of Unicorns.* Illustrated by Michael Hague. Henry Holt, 1986.

Hague, Michael, comp. *Mother Goose.* Illustrated by Michael Hague. Henry Holt, 1984.

Lewis, C. S. *The Lion, the Witch, and the Wardrobe.* Illustrated by Michael Hague. Macmillan, 1983.

Mayer, Marianna. *The Unicorn and the Lake.* Illustrated by Michael Hague. Dial, 1982.

Tolkien, J. R. R. *The Hobbit.* Illustrated by Michael Hague. Houghton Mifflin, 1984.

Williams, Margery. *The Velveteen Rabbit.* Illustrated by Michael Hague. Henry Holt, 1983.

USING THE BOOK

Suggested Approach to the Book

Model Lesson

1. Examine the book's end papers. What do you see? Make notes of your visual observations.

2. If L. Frank Baum wrote *The Wizard of Oz* in 1900 to please children, what kind of story could an author write today?

3. The wood for the house in Kansas had to be hauled many miles by wagon. Why? List other items that would have been transported by wagon for the new settlers.

4. Baum had been the proprietor of Baum's Bazaar, a small frontier general store that eventually went bankrupt because he could not bring himself to force poor people to pay their bills. Compare Baum's character with that of Mr. and Mrs. Olsen, the owners of the general store in the Little House series. How are they similar and different?

5. Compare the cyclone experiences in *The Wizard of Oz* to the tornado experiences in Chris Van Allsburg's *Ben's Dream* (Houghton Mifflin, 1982).

6. Describe a forest. Why do many fairy tales present the forest as a dark, scary place? Give examples of forests in other fairy tales.

7. If you were a wicked witch in *The Wizard of Oz,* what kind of tricks would you play? What would you do if you were a good witch?

8. What activities would be appropriate for celebrating the death of the Wicked Witch of the West?

9. Is the use of green viewing glasses effective? Why? What color is your favorite? How would Oz look through your colored glasses?

Library Media Center Connections

1. Define fairy tales and folklore. Make a list of 20 titles of each from the school library media center catalog. Name 10 titles of each that you have read and 10 titles that sound interesting to read.

2. What information is found on the reverse of the title page of *The Wizard of Oz*? Where is this information usually located? (Note: Some publishers use the reverse of the title page as part of a double-page illustration. In such cases, the cataloging information appears on the reverse side of the book's last page.)

3. Do animals react to changes in weather? Document the answers with specific citations. (Note: There were many newspaper articles about animals when Hurricane Andrew slashed through Florida in August 1992.)

4. Design five geography circle wheels with spinners. Each wheel will be divided into 10 different color spaces like a pie chart. On each wheel, write the names of ten states and a number representing points. Each spinner is attached with a brad. Spin the wheel. Using a United States map, identify the location of the state selected. Pose trivia questions for students about the state (such as state flower, state bird, and major geographic features). Players who answer correctly score that number of points. The player with the most points at the end of the game is the winner.

5. Research the effects of color on humans and animals, as well as the use and effect of color in advertising. Prepare a portfolio of effective advertisements in both black-and-white and color.

Computer Connections

1. Create a database about book illustrations. Include author, title, and name of the illustrator. Also include a note on the artist's style.

Instructional Materials Connections

1. Fricke, John, Jay Scarfone, and William Stillman. *The Wizard of Oz: The Official 50th Anniversary Pictorial History.* Warner Books, 1989.

2. Scrocco, Jean L., ed. *The Wizard of Oz Frieze.* Illustrated by Greg Hildebrandt. Unicorn, 1986.

3. Tigerman, Tracy, and Margaret McCurry. *Dorothy in Dreamland.* Illustrated by Stanley Tigerman. Rizzoli, 1992.

4. An author information pamphlet is available from the publisher, Henry Holt and Co., 115 West Eighteenth Street, New York, NY 10011.

Theme Reading Connections: Kansas

Fradin, Dennis. *Kansas in Words and Pictures.* Illustrated by Richard Wahl. Childrens Press, 1980.

Marsh, Carole. *Kansas "Jography" A Fun Run Thru Your State.* Gallopade, 1989.

Thompson, Kathleen. *Kansas.* Raintree/Steck-Vaughn, 1987.

Wilder, Laura Ingalls. *Little House on the Prairie.* Rev. ed. Illustrated by Garth Williams. Harper & Row, 1953.

Critical Thinking Question
Should school boards outlaw books and materials that present fairy tales and fantasy? Why or why not?

Student Activities to Connect Literature and Curriculum

FINE ARTS

1. *The Wizard of Oz* can be classified as a circular story in that the characters go on a quest that is resolved after several dangerous confrontations. All the characters return to their beginnings but are changed by their personal growth. Ask students to use stick puppets to illustrate the story in circular form as they read the story. Then have students imitate Michael Hague's technique by making additional detailed drawings to illustrate the story. This is an excellent time to introduce the use of mind mapping in generating possible solutions to problems.

2. The descriptions of Dorothy's home and of her step-parents, Uncle Henry and Aunt Em, are depressing. Draw the setting and characters using a grey wash as the background. Examine the grey art. How could the color be changed to reflect a happy, successful family living on the prairie?

3. Compare and contrast the illustrations of Garth Williams in Laura Ingalls Wilder's *Little House on the Prairie* (Harper & Row, 1953) with Michael Hague's illustrations in *The Wizard of Oz.*

4. What would your home look like if it were lifted off its foundation? Present a three-stage art drawing of your house during a tornado.

5. Draw the forest as described on page 35.

LANGUAGE ARTS

1. Use clustering to gather students' impressions about Dorothy, Toto, and the three new friends who accompany her on her quest. Have students write one paragraph describing each character pictured in the illustration opposite the title page. Are the characters drawn realistically? Is the drawing true to life? Could the illustration be changed in any way?

2. Using a game board and a pie-shaped spinner illustrating the different areas of Oz, construct a Wizard of Oz game. Markers may be illustrations of the main characters, the author, and the illustrator.

3. Using the quick-write technique, describe the chase from the point of view of the Kalidahs. (See p. 58). Invent a new mythological animal that is capable of defeating the Kalidahs.

4. Role play the rafting trip taken by Dorothy and her friends. (See p. 64.)

5. Write a new ending for *The Wizard of Oz*.

6. Design, write, and illustrate an alphabet of fictional animals and beasts using alliteration.

WRITING PROMPT

1. Write a television news story using the following headline:

> Dorothy Gale Returns Home from the Land of Oz

MATH

1. Poll students in other classes. Ask for their favorite illustrated book. Present the results in a bar graph.

SCIENCE

1. You are a city building inspector. What kind of construction engineering would you require for houses built in your area?

2. Design a new item that will scare away animals from farm crops. What would be required to manufacture a large number of the invention? How would you field-test it? How would you conduct a market needs assessment poll?

SOCIAL STUDIES

1. You have decided to build a Land of Oz theme park. In cooperative learning groups, determine the following:

   geographic location for present facilities and future expansion

   theme areas, including restaurants and hotels

   a specialty park logo, and a radio/television/magazine advertising portfolio

   opening ceremonies and special events

   emergency plans, including an evacuation plan

GEOGRAPHY

1. Using a contemporary world map, add the location of the mythical Land of Oz. Define the longitude and latitude of the site. What would be the average monthly temperature? Why? Describe the area's weather.

2. Compare the weather in Kansas with that of your state. What weather tools (such as an almanac and thermometer) do you need?

3. Using a roll of shelf paper or butcher paper, draw the beginning of a crooked, yellow brick road. Have cooperative learning groups draw a section of the road to retell the story or add new adventures.

BEYOND THE BOOK

Guided Reading Connections Across a Learning Rainbow: Art

Locker, Thomas. *The Young Artist*. Dial, 1989.

Stan, Susan. *Careers in an Art Museum*. Lerner, 1983.

Enriching Connections

1. What commercial items would be appropriate to sell in a museum gift shop during a month-long showing of the works of L. Frank Baum?

2. Read about several different editions of *The Wizard of Oz*. Report to the class. Which is your favorite book? Why?

3. Make a list of books you like that are part of a series. Name books that you have read that you would like to see continued as a series.

FROM ANOTHER POINT OF VIEW

Baum, Frank L. *The Wizard of Oz*. Illustrated by Charles Santore. Jelly Bean, 1991.

Parent-Student Connections

1. Arrange for your family to view a video tape of the movie *The Wizard of Oz*. If the movie were filmed today, what modern stars would be asked to play the main roles?

2. What kind of menu would be appropriate for a Wizard of Oz birthday party? What kind of food products have a natural green color? Which foods will be attractive if dyed green with food coloring?

❈   ❈   ❈

JUST SO STORIES

Author: Rudyard Kipling
Illustrator: Safaya Salter
Publisher: Henry Holt, 1987
Suggested Grade Level: 6
Classification: Fiction
Literary Form: Collection of stories
Theme: Early myths and legends answered the human need for explanations about why things happened as well as a reason for the way things were.

ABOUT THE BOOK

STUDENT OBJECTIVES:

1. Survey the works of Rudyard Kipling.

2. Compare these stories with Aesop's animal fables.

3. Revise one Just So story to include contemporary characters, setting, and plot as part of a Rudyard Kipling Day class celebration.

SYNOPSIS: A humanistic collection of stories bridging the world's geographic boundaries.

ABOUT THE AUTHOR: Rudyard Kipling, 1865-1936.

Rudyard Kipling was born in Bombay, India, and lived most of his life in India and England. These two countries served as the inspiration for his writing. Interestingly, he lived in Brattleboro, Vermont, for several years. When you read Kipling's "How the Whale Got His Throat," you'll enjoy references to the Northeast and its special places. The whale acts as a train conductor when he calls out, "Change here for Winchester, Ashuelot, Nashua, Keene, and stations on the Fitchburg Road." All of these are names of places in southern New Hampshire.

Kipling was a journalist as well as an author of children's books. He received the prestigious Nobel Prize for literature in 1907. Kipling's former residence in East Sussex, England, is owned and administered by the National Trust.

ABOUT THE ILLUSTRATOR: Safaya Salter, birthdate unavailable.

Born in Cairo, Egypt, Safaya Salter portrays her rich heritage through art works that include textile designs, oil painting, ceramics, and greeting cards. "Her pictures create their own little worlds—the borders surrounding them both lead into the pictures and cushion the subject from the outside world" (Book jacket).

SELECTED ADDITIONAL TITLES: Rudyard Kipling

Kipling, Rudyard. *The Beginning of the Armadillos.* Illustrated by Lorinda B. Cauley. Harcourt Brace Jovanovich, 1985.

———. *The Beginning of the Armadilloes: A Just So Story.* Illustrated by Charles Keeping. P. Bedrick, 1983.

———. *The Butterfly That Stamped: A Just So Story.* Illustrated by Alan Baker. P. Bedrick, 1983.

————. *The Cat That Walked: A Just So Story.* Illustrated by William Stobbs. P. Bedrick, 1983.

————. *The Crab That Played with the Sea: A Just So Story.* Illustrated by Michael Foreman. P. Bedrick, 1983.

————. *The Elephant's Child.* Illustrated by Lorinda B. Cauley. Harcourt Brace Jovanovich, 1983.

————. *The Elephant's Child.* Illustrated by Louise Brierley. P. Bedrick, 1985.

————. *The Elephant's Child.* Illustrated by Tim Raglin. Alfred A. Knopf, 1986.

————. *How the Camel Got His Hump.* Illustrated by Quentin Blake. P. Bedrick, 1985.

————. *How the Leopard Got His Spots.* Illustrated by Catherine Ebborn. P. Bedrick, 1986.

————. *The Jungle Book.* Doubleday, 1981.

————. *The Jungle Book.* Illustrated by Gregory Alexander. Arcade, 1991.

————. *Just So Stories.* Woodcuts by David Frampton. HarperCollins, 1991.

————. *Rikki-Tikki-Tavi.* Illustrated. Childrens Press, 1982.

————. *Rikki-Tikki-Tavi.* Illustrated by James Hays. Creative Education, 1986.

————. *The Sing-Song of Old Man Kangaroo.* Illustrated by Michael Taylor. P. Bedrick, 1986.

USING THE BOOK

Suggested Approach to the Book

Model Lesson

1. Examine the art on the title page of the book. Describe your emotional reaction to this illustration. What art medium has been used? Examine the publication information on the reverse side of the title page. This British edition was published in cooperation with the National Trust of England, and some of the royalties are being donated to the National Trust. Why is this happening? Do we have a similar organization in the United States? What is the purpose of national trust associations?

2. What happens to the reader, "If you swim to latitude Fifty North, longitude Forty West [that is Magic]"? (See p. 9.)

3. In cooperative learning groups, state the moral of each of the *Just So Stories.*

4. How does the alphabet pictured on page 64 relate to India?

Library Media Center Connections

1. How many Kipling books are in your school library media center collection? Are any nonprint materials available? Compile a list of additional materials that could be used in the study of *Just So Stories.*

2. Compare Kipling's *Just So Stories* with Thatcher Hurd's *Mama Don't Allow* (Harper & Row, 1985).

3. Ask the library media center teacher to display alphabet books from the collection in conjunction with student-produced African alphabet projects.

Computer Connections

1. Develop a computer database about animals included in *Just So Stories*. What information will be collected? What format will be used for data entry? How will students use the database in other classes and other curriculum studies?

Instructional Materials Connections

1. Fisher, Leonard Everett. *Alphabet Art: Thirteen ABCs from around the World.* Four Winds Press, 1978.

2. Jaffrey, Madhur. *Seasons of Splendor: Tales, Myths and Legends from India.* Illustrated by Michael Foreman. Atheneum, 1985.

3. Kamen, Gloria. *Kipling: Storyteller of East and West.* Atheneum, 1985.

4. Kipling, Rudyard. *The Jungle Book.* Paintings by Gregory Alexander. Arcade, 1991.

5. Invite an author or editor to explain the steps in the publication of a book.

Theme Reading Connections: India

Caldwell, John C. *India.* Chelsea House, 1988.

Kanitkar, V. P. *Indian Food and Drink.* Franklin Watts, 1987.

Lerner Publications Company, Department of Geography Staff. *India in Pictures.* Lerner, 1989.

Sarin, Amita V. *India: An Ancient Land, A New Nation.* Dillon, 1984.

Critical Thinking Question
Is the value of maintaining captive animals in zoos and aquariums for the pleasure of visitors and/or for allowing research about endangered species sufficient to justify the cost of maintaining the animals in such environments? Is there an alternative that will be beneficial to the animals and provide a way to ensure the survival of endangered species?

Student Activities to Connect Literature and Curriculum

FINE ARTS

1. Experiment with the border art used in the chapter headings. Design a new chapter heading for your favorite Just So story.

2. What can you learn from the art work on page 10? Would you like to add anything to the picture?

3. In this book, a mariner is a sailor on the ocean. In quilting, a mariner star is symbolized by a star. Design a mariner's star for a jean jacket.

4. Prepare art work that features a recurring pattern with animals hidden in it. Examples can be found in the following:

Demi. *Find Demi's Dinosaurs.* Illustrated by Demi. Grossett & Dunlap, 1989.

Jonas, Ann. *The Trek.* Illustrated by Ann Jonas. Greenwillow Books, 1985.

LANGUAGE ARTS

1. Why does Kipling use highlighted prepositions describing man "on a raft, in the middle of the sea, with ..." (p. 11).

2. Compare and contrast "How the Whale Got His Throat" with Pinocchio's adventure inside the whale (Collodi, Carlo, *The Adventures of Pinocchio,* translated by E. Harden, illustrated by Roberto Innocenti, Knopf, 1988) and William Steig's *Amos and Boris* picture book (Farrar, Straus & Giroux, 1971). Steig's book has beautiful language. Read about Amos's enchanted view of the starry sky before he rolls off his boat and into the ocean.

3. Add another stanza to the poem "How the Camel Got His Hump."

4. Discover the use of rich language in individual Just So stories. List words that are descriptive word forms (see p. 36: "From the crocodile on the banks of the great grey-green greasy Limpopo River...") as well as uncommon proper names. Find examples of similes, metaphors, alliteration, and onomatopoeia.

5. Develop a script to present selected Just So stories as readers theatre.

WRITING PROMPT

1. Who are the "six honest serving men"? How do these names (see p. 37) relate to journalism? Using this format, write an opening paragraph for a newspaper article announcing Kipling's Nobel Prize award in 1907. Use the following headline:

```
Nobel Prize Honors Rudyard Kipling
```

MATH

1. Create a bar graph listing all the animals appearing in *Just So Stories* and showing how many times each animal is mentioned. Compute the number of times each animal is mentioned as a percentage. Which animals are mentioned most often?

SCIENCE

1. Create a diagram of the food chain of life for whales.

2. List the many animals that invited Camel to come out of the Howling Desert and work. What types of environment did the animals need for survival? Was the desert a good home for them? Prepare a chart showing the temperature range in which each species lives.

3. List 25 African animals and their protective camouflage.

4. Are any of the animals mentioned in the text endangered species? If they are, report the ways in which the animals are protected.

SOCIAL STUDIES

1. Describe the Neolithic man. Using an illustrated time line, trace the history of man from this ancient time to today's modern man.

2. Investigate various alphabets used around the world. Which one is the most detailed? Write an alphabet from India or Africa.

3. Plan a Rudyard Kipling Day for the classroom. Include readers theatre, poetry readings, art displays, special food snacks, and background music.

GEOGRAPHY

1. Draw overlay transparency maps of India or Africa that identify the habitats of different animal species.

2. What part does geography and the study of maps play in *Just So Stories*?

BEYOND THE BOOK

Guided Reading Connections Across a Learning Rainbow: Animal Poetry

Armour, Richard. *Have You Ever Wished You Were Something Else?* Childrens Press, 1983.

Gardner, John C. *A Child's Bestiary.* Illustrated by John Gardner and Joel Garner. Alfred A. Knopf, 1977.

Gill, Shelley. *Alaska Mother Goose.* Illustrated by Shannon Cartwright. Paws Four, 1987.

Prelutsky, Jack. *Zoo Doings: Animal Poems.* Illustrated by Paul Zelinsky. Greenwillow Books, 1983.

Enriching Connections

1. Experiment with placing a frame of bars, to look like the wall of a cage, over various animal pictures. Which animals should be in special areas of zoos and aquariums? List current opinions about the roles and responsibilities of animal managers in regard to the animals. What type of activities are used to provide diversion for animals held in captivity?

Special Lesson: Tee-Shirt Art in the Classroom

1. Introduce fabric bonding and tee-shirt painting with this project.

2. Both the tee-shirt and applique fabric must be washed to remove sizing. They must be ironed before beginning the project.

3. A cardboard tee-shirt insert form, which can be purchased from a fabric store, will keep the paint from bleeding through to the other side of the tee-shirt.

4. Visit a local fabric store to see a variety of cotton prints that are available. These colorful designs can be used in many different curriculum areas, including the study of Native Americans, animals, art, botany, the oceans, sports, and cultures of the world. Fabric companies include Alexander Henry, Hoffman, RJR, Concord, Bali Fabrication, Westwood, Erlanger/Blumgart, Sumatra, Tropical Paradise, Tahiti Island Prints, Kaui Cove, and Joe Boxer.

5. To coordinate the fabric with *Just So Stories,* select an African animal or border design.

6. Carefully examine the fabric design and have it cut so that the piece you buy includes the complete pattern or design you will be bonding to the tee-shirt. Most patterns repeat every 12, 15, or 18 inches, so the total yardage to purchase will be 4.5, 9, or 12 inches of fabric ($\frac{1}{8}$, $\frac{1}{4}$, or $\frac{1}{3}$ yard). This should provide fabric for several art projects, if shared.

7. Purchase bonding paper. You may purchase it in a package or in a roll. This material is used to attach the fabric to your project. If lightweight paper is used, the edges of the design will need to be sewn to the tee-shirt, or paint will need to be used to seal the edges and glue the applique to the tee-shirt. The heavier type can be ironed on, and there is no need to seal the edges of the fabric to the tee-shirt. There will be a degree of thickness about the design.

8. Cut the design from the fabric, leaving a $\frac{1}{2}$-inch allowance around all edges.

9. Place the fabric face-down on an ironing board. Examine a sheet of the bonding paper. (There is a smooth side and a textured side. The textured side is the glue surface.) Slide the "back side" of the fabric under the paper. This step is like a sandwich and should be layered as follows: Fabric "right side" or face touching the ironing board, next the bond material, "face down" on top of the fabric.

10. To avoid getting glue on the ironing board, cover it with pieces cut from a brown paper bag. Slit a brown paper bag into flat pieces to cover the area that will be used. Or, cover the ironing board with a teflon sheet, which can be wiped clean with a paper towel after each use.

11. Using sharp applique scissors, trim the $\frac{1}{2}$-inch allowance off the fabric.

12. Heat an iron to medium heat. Place the iron on the bonding paper. Hold the iron in place for a count of 10. Lift the iron and place it on another area. Do not slide the iron across the paper; lift and place it. The glue on the textured side of the bonding paper will adhere to the back of the fabric and the paper will peel off easily. If there are wrinkles or bubbles in the fabric, the iron is too hot. Do a test strip to determine proper temperature for the project.

13. Let the design cool for a few minutes. Then peel off the bonding paper. It will slip off easily.

14. The fabric design now has a glue backing. Be careful not to get glue on the front of the fabric. It is impossible to remove.

15. Place the fabric, right side up, on a tee-shirt. Iron it on with a medium-hot iron using the same 10-count technique.

16. The design may be enhanced using fabric paint. Some fabric paints are shiny, iridescent, or contain glitter; these paints are called Scribbles or Polymark. If you cannot find paint that contains glitter, the glitter can be purchased separately. It can be sifted on while the paint is still tacky. Glitter will not adhere after two hours.

17. The fabric paints are used to seal the edge of the applique. Carefully squeeze a bead around the entire edge of the design. If paints are not used, and the light bonding paper was used, machine stitch around the applique to secure the edges.

18. If desired, highlight the design with paint. Allow the paint to dry for several days before washing or wearing it.

19. Be careful when washing the tee-shirt. Turn it inside out and wash it in cold water. Wash it by hand or on the delicate cycle of a washing machine. Air dry it.

FROM ANOTHER POINT OF VIEW

Kipling, Rudyard. *Just So Stories*. Woodcuts by David Frampton. HarperCollins, 1991.

Parent-Student Connections

1. Read aloud several animal alphabet books.

2. Discuss with the student the difficulties that animals around the world are experiencing as a result of population growth and loss of the natural habitats.

❀ ❀ ❀

BEN'S DREAM

Author: Chris Van Allsburg
Illustrator: Chris Van Allsburg
Publisher: Houghton Mifflin, 1982
Suggested Grade Level: 6
Classification: Fiction
Literary Form: A complex, many-faceted picture book illustrated with carbon pencil drawings.
Theme: Chris Van Allsburg presents a remarkable geography lesson with only 281 words and 17 detailed pictures.

ABOUT THE BOOK

STUDENT OBJECTIVES:

1. Plan, write the text, and illustrate classroom big books.

2. Explore social studies curriculum information about world landmarks.

3. Integrate the works of Chris Van Allsburg and that of other Caldecott Medal winners.

SYNOPSIS: Ben falls asleep to the sound of rain and visits some of the great wonders of the world.

ABOUT THE AUTHOR-ILLUSTRATOR: Chris Van Allsburg, 1949- .
 Chris Van Allsburg was born and raised in Michigan where he attended the University of Michigan. He did additional post-graduate study at the Rhode Island School of Design for a Masters of Fine Arts. Like many other famous children's book illustrators, he did not specifically study for that as a career. His initial art works were sculptures which were met with several successful gallery exhibitions.
 His sculptures were successful, but since his studio and home were far apart, he began to plan his sculptures by using carbon pencil drawings. David Macaulay, a future Caldecott medalist, was a friend and suggested that Van Allsburg allow his wife to show his illustrations to some publishers.

His phenomenal carbon pencil drawings were accepted by Houghton Mifflin and he began work on his first book, *The Garden of Abdul Gasazi.*

Since being published, Van Allsburg has worked with color and oil pastel in addition to the carbon pencil. His works are not specifically created for children and their parents, but "A book won't work if it doesn't even hold my interest for long.... I want to make books that are compelling to read and look at" (Press release from Houghton Mifflin).

Van Allsburg explains that in his art, "I am likely to leave a lot of small details out and create a drawing that ultimately has a touch of the surreal" (Press release).

(Note: One of Van Allsburg's early sculptures was a head of a dog entitled Brancusi's Dog. Van Allsburg did not own a dog, but "his brother-in-law did own an English bull terrier very similar to Fritz. Fritz, the dog, appears at least once in all Van Allsburg's books." (Can you find him?)

SELECTED ADDITIONAL TITLES:

Van Allsburg, Chris. *The Garden of Abdul Gasazi.* Illustrated by Chris Van Allsburg. Houghton Mifflin, 1979.

———. *Jumanji.* Illustrated by Chris Van Allsburg. Houghton Mifflin, 1981.

———. *The Mysteries of Harris Burdick.* Illustrated by Chris Van Allsburg. Houghton Mifflin, 1984.

———. *Polar Express.* Illustrated by Chris Van Allsburg. Houghton Mifflin, 1985.

———. *The Stranger.* Illustrated by Chris Van Allsburg. Houghton Mifflin, 1986.

———. *Two Bad Ants.* Illustrated by Chris Van Allsburg. Houghton Mifflin, 1988.

———. *The Wreck of the Zephyr.* Illustrated by Chris Van Allsburg. Houghton Mifflin, 1983.

———. *The Z Was Zapped.* Illustrated by Chris Van Allsburg. Houghton Mifflin, 1987.

USING THE BOOK

Suggested Approach to the Book

Model Lesson

1. Ask students to make predictions about the book's content from illustrations on the front and back covers.

2. Examine the first two pages of the book. What do you see? How do you feel about rain? Depending on where you live, rain can be a welcome or unwelcome visitor. Explain your answers. Is your community a drought or flood area?

3. Approach *Ben's Dream* with a critical eye and look for his sense of humor in the illustrations. Where has Mom gone? How do you know? What are latchkey students? What should be the rules to be followed when staying home alone?

4. What happens to Ben's house? Could it be a tornado?

5. List the landmarks Ben saw. Which ones would you like to visit if you could select three?

6. What does President Washington say to Ben?

7. How does the story end? Is it fiction or non-fiction literature? Why?

8. Examine the illustration on the back book cover. What country is pictured? Why did you make that choice?

Library Media Center Connections

1. Only one of the Seven Wonders of the World still exists today. Which one is it? Where is it located? How big is it? What material was used for its construction? How many were used? How much does it weigh? How long did it take to build? Approximate the number of workers used. Using answers from the research, construct a crossword puzzle, a board game, or card game for class members to evaluate. (Note: See the *World Almanac.*)

2. Prepare an information list about the Seven Wonders of the United States that you would choose.

3. Answer the following questions using the *Guinness Book of World Records:*

    What is the tallest office building in the world?

    Why are five of the world's tallest structures located in Egypt?

    What is the largest air-supported building in the United States?

    Where is the largest palace in the world?

    What is the largest hotel in the world?

    Where is the largest house in the United States?

    Which home cost the most to build in the United States?

    Where is the longest roller coaster in the world located?

    What is the tallest structure in the world?

    Where is the tallest bridge in the world located?

    Where is the world's longest big ship canal located?

    Where is the largest Lego statue in the world?

    Where is the tallest lighthouse in the United States located?

    What is the name of the largest outdoor stadium in the United States?

    Where is the world's tallest statue?

    How long did it take to carve the tallest Canadian totem pole?

Computer Connections

1. Using a data base program, enter information about the Seven Wonders of the World as well as information about the Seven Wonders of the United States as selected by class members.

2. Design a ballot to be used in conducting a poll among other students in the school to determine which landmarks in the United States should be chosen as the Seven National Wonders Landmarks.

Instructional Materials Connections

1. Chris Van Allsburg, an illustrated information sheet about the author and his works including photographs of his early sculpture works, is available from Houghton Mifflin Company, Children's Books, 2 Park Street, Boston MA 02108.

2. McLeish, Kenneth. *The Seven Wonders of the World*. Illustrated by Sharon Pallent. Cambridge University, 1985.

3. *Guinness Book of World Records 1993*. Facts on File, 1992.

Theme Reading Connections: Dreams

Berger, Barbara. *The Donkey's Dream*. Illustrated by Barbara Berger. Putnam, 1986.

Berry, Joy. *Every Kid's Guide to Understanding Nightmares*. Childrens Press, 1987.

Heyer, Marilee. *The Weaving of a Dream*. Illustrated by Marilee Heyer. Viking Kestrel, 1986.

Mayer, Mercer. *There's a Nightmare in My Closet*. Illustrated by Mercer Mayer. Dial, 1976.

Mayle, Peter. *Sweet Dreams and Monsters: A Beginner's Guide to Dreams and Nightmares and Things That Go Bump Under the Bed*. Illustrated by Arthur Robins. Crown, 1986.

Uchida, Yoshiko. *A Jar of Dreams*. Macmillan, 1985.

Critical Thinking Question
What was the purpose of the Seven Wonders of the World? What usage was planned for them and why were they so large? If they were still in existence, how could they be used today?

Student Activities to Connect Literature and Curriculum

FINE ARTS

1. Artists over the centuries have been considered Masters of certain subjects/techniques. A Japanese artist, Hiroshige, has been acclaimed as the artist who best portrayed rain. Check out from the public library a copy of the *Fifty Three Steps of the Tokaido* and examine his portrayals of rain.

2. Construct a scale model of one of the Seven Wonders of the World or choose a world landmark illustrated in *Ben's Dream* to replicate a scale model.

3. Compose and present a new song listing places that Ben saw in his dream.

4. Write and illustrate original big books for classroom/library use. Two standards are mandatory. Write the text using a minimum of words and illustrate with a carbon pencil.

LANGUAGE ARTS

1. Write diary entries about Ben's trip to world landmarks.

2. Prepare an illustrated brochure for distribution to foreign travelers who will be visiting three natural wonders in the United States: Niagara Falls, the Grand Canyon and Death Valley.

3. Using student-made transparencies, present a travel show to the class about the Seven Wonders of the World. Background music is appropriate in order to develop the flavor of travel.

4. Compare and contrast the following books:

   Van Allsburg, Chris. *Ben's Dream*. Houghton Mifflin, 1982.

   Goodall, John. *The Story of an English Village*. Illustrated by John Goodall. Macmillan, 1979.

   Wiesner, David. *Tuesday*. Illustrated by David Wiesner. Clarion, 1991.

5. Write a letter to the class describing your visit to the Great Pyramid at Ginza with your teacher after winning a prize for designing a new pyramid.

WRITING PROMPT

1. Develop a news story describing your visit to Ginza that will be appropriate for the following headline:

   ┌───┐
   │   Student/Teacher Travel to Great Pyramid, Ginza, Egypt   │
   └───┘

MATH

1. Graph the ratings of the poll that determine the popularity of the Seven Wonders of the United States selected by the students.

2. Prepare a currency converter for a trip to each of the Seven Wonders of the World comparing the value of United States currency to those of foreign countries to be visited.

SCIENCE

1. What are the effects of rain on your community? What is the average amount of rain? How much rain has fallen so far this year? Is it average or below average? Is your community subject to drought or flooding? What happens then? How can emergency plans be made to fit the weather pattern? Keep a rainfall record graph for a month. Explain your observations to the class.

2. Explain why you think that most of the Seven Wonders of the World disappeared. Relate your response to the pollution problems that we have today.

SOCIAL STUDIES

1. Select a report topic from the following list:

Floods	Statue of Liberty	Big Ben
Sydney Harbor Bridge	Sphinx	Acropolis
Golden Gate Bridge	Tornado	Mt. Rushmore
Istanbul	Great Wall of China	Parthenon
Roman Forum	Moscow	Tower of Pisa

GEOGRAPHY

1. What are the Seven Wonders of the World? This information may be integrated through cooperative learning groups in which each has one site to present.

2. Draw an ancient map of the world and label the location of the Seven Wonders. Explain what remains today at each of the sites.

BEYOND THE BOOK

Guided Reading Connections Across a Learning Rainbow: World Landmarks

Anno, Mitsumasa. *Anno's Britain*. Illustrated by Mitsumasa Anno. Putnam, 1985.

———. *Anno's Italy*. Illustrated by Mitsumasa Anno. Putnam, 1984.

Arnold, Caroline. *The Golden Gate Bridge*. Illustrated. Watts, 1986.

Behrens, June. *Miss Liberty: First Lady of the World*. Illustrated. Childrens Press, 1986.

Fisher, Leonard E. *The Great Wall of China*. Illustrated by Leonard E. Fisher. Macmillan, 1986.

———. *The Statue of Liberty*. Illustrated by Leonard E. Fisher. Holiday, 1985.

Lepthien, Emilie U. *Australia*. Childrens Press, 1982.

Macaulay, David. *Pyramid*. Illustrated by David Macaulay. Houghton Mifflin, 1975.

Maestro, Betsy. *The Story of the Statue of Liberty*. Illustrated by Giulio Maestro. Lothrop, 1986.

Munro, Roxie. *The Inside-Outside Book of New York City*. Illustrated by Roxie Munro. Putnam, 1985.

Naylor, Sue. *International Picture Library: The Natural Wonders of the World*. Illustrated with photographs. Dillon, 1985.

Richard, Graham. *Bridges*. Illustrated. Watts, 1987.

St. George, Judith. *The Mount Rushmore Story*. Illustrated. Putnam, 1985.

Stein, R. Conrad. *Greece*. Illustrated. Childrens Press, 1987.

———. *Italy*. Illustrated. Childrens Press, 1983.

Thomsen, Steven. *The Great Pyramid of Cheops*. Capstone Press, 1989.

Turner, Dorothy. *International Picture Library: The Man-Made Wonders of the World*. Illustrated with photographs. Dillon, 1983.

Enriching Connections

1. From the list in Guided Reading Connections Across a Learning Rainbow, select a book illustrated by Anno. How many examples of humor hidden in the illustrations can you identify? List them.

2. Check with students, faculty, and community members to determine if travelers who have visited the landmarks illustrated in *Ben's Dream* are willing to speak to the class. Travel agents are a good resource for this activity.

3. List all Caldecott award-winning books from the first award in 1938 to today. Students will create a new book cover for their favorite winner. The back cover will include a personal review of the book written by the student.

FROM ANOTHER POINT OF VIEW

Cooney, Barbara. *Hattie and the Wild Waves.* Illustrated by Barbara Cooney. Viking, 1990.

Parent-Student Connections

1. Check out from the public library a travel book that has photographs of a world landmark that you like and that is featured in *Ben's Dream.* Share the book with your family.

2. Read Van Allsburg's *The Stranger.* Compare the use of color in the book to the carbon pencil illustrations of *Ben's Dream.* Do you like the carbon pencil drawings used in most of Van Allsburg's books, or do you prefer the use of color in *The Stranger*? Why? What are the advantages of black-and-white illustrations?

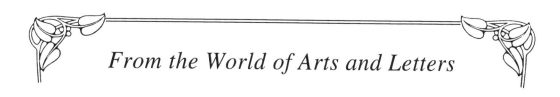

From the World of Arts and Letters

PYRAMID

Author: David Macaulay
Illustrator: David Macaulay
Publisher: Houghton Mifflin, 1975
Classification: Nonfiction
Literary Form: Text with black-and-white drawings
Theme: Step-by-step process of building an ancient Egyptian pyramid.

ABOUT THE BOOK

STUDENT OBJECTIVES:

1. Produce a burial monument suitable for a modern president or ruler.

2. Interpret Egyptian mythology and its relationship to pyramid construction.

3. Role play the building of the pyramid from the viewpoint of the pharaoh and his friend and architect, Mahnud Hotep.

SYNOPSIS: A new pharaoh, beginning to plan for the end of his life on Earth and his ascension to eternal life as a god, builds a pyramid, or a tomb, on the Nile River.

ABOUT THE AUTHOR-ILLUSTRATOR: David Macaulay, 1946- .

David Mccaulay's architectural drawings are complex, easily identifiable, and unique. Technology has fascinated him since his childhood in Burton-on-Trent, England. Fun and play for Macaulay was constructing elevators from cigar boxes, string, and tape as well as designing intricate systems of moving cable cars from bits and pieces of yarn.

Macaulay's formal education includes art instruction, a bachelor's degree in architecture, and postgraduate study at historical sites in Italy. He has worked as an interior designer, a junior-high-school teacher, and as a faculty member at the Rhode Island School of Design. His first book submission was the story of a gargoyle beauty pageant! Fortunately for the artist, his editor liked Macaulay's Notre Dame Cathedral gargoyle picture and sent him to Amiens, France, to make drawings for his first book, *Cathedral*.

All of Macaulay's writings are researched on site. For example, Macaulay climbed the Great Pyramid at Cheops to get a sense of perspective. Architectural works include *City, Castle, Mill, Underground*, and *Unbuilding*. These books can be used by young students as well as college students. *Unbuilding* was so believable that, when it was first published, many readers actually believed that the Empire State Building in New York City would be torn down as discussed in the book.

Macaulay's books have won many awards, including several Caldecott honor awards. *Time* said, "What he draws ... he draws better than any other pen-and-ink illustrator in the world" (de Montreville, Doris, and Elizabeth D. Crawford, *Fifth Book of Junior Authors*, H. W. Wilson, 1978, pp. 199-201).

SELECTED ADDITIONAL TITLES:

Macaulay, David. *BAAA*. Illustrated by David Macaulay. Houghton Mifflin, 1985.

————. *Castle*. Illustrated by David Macaulay. Houghton Mifflin, 1977.

————. *Cathedral: The Story of Its Construction*. Illustrated by David Macaulay. Houghton Mifflin, 1973.

————. *City: A Story of Roman Planning and Construction*. Illustrated by David Macaulay. Houghton Mifflin, 1974.

————. *Mill*. Illustrated by David Macaulay. Houghton Mifflin, 1983.

————. *Unbuilding*. Illustrated by David Macaulay. Houghton Mifflin, 1980.

————. *Underground*. Illustrated by David Macaulay. Houghton Mifflin, 1976.

————. *The Way Things Work*. Illustrated by David Macaulay. Houghton Mifflin, 1988.

USING THE BOOK

Suggested Approach to the Book

Model Lesson

1. What was the occupation of most Egyptians? Why?

2. According to David Macaulay, what were the two goals of most Egyptians? (See the introduction.)

3. What is the difference between a *ba* and a *ka*?

4. Explain the three fundamentals of constructing a pyramid. Why did the funerary complex include a causeway?

5. List some of the workers and artisans needed to work on the pyramid. Explain the gang used in the building process. Did these gang members receive a salary?

6. Describe the tools used in construction and their modern counterparts.

7. Identify various examples of Egyptian architecture.

Library Media Center Connections

1. Research the Seven Wonders of the World. Where were they located? Are any still in existence? If so, what is their condition? Identify their locations on a world map. What would you name the Seven Wonders of the Modern World? Why?

Computer Connections

1. Using a word processor, write a report about the explorations and findings of Howard Carter in 1922 or about Egyptian art or architecture.

Instructional Materials Connections

1. Briquebec, John. *The Ancient World: From the Earliest Civilizations to the Roman Empire.* Historical Atlas series. Warwick, 1990.

2. Conway, Lorraine. *Ancient Egypt.* Illustrated by Linda Akins. Good Apple, 1987.

3. D'Alelio, Jane. *I Know That Building! Discovering Architecture with Activities and Games.* Preservation Press, 1989.

4. Eisen, David. *Fun with Architecture.* (Kit includes 35 rubber stamps students can use to create drawings of buildings.) Metropolitan Museum of Fine Art, New York, 1992.

5. Harris, Geraldine. *Ancient Egypt.* Cultural Atlas for Young People. Facts on File, 1990.

6. Macaulay, David. *Pyramid.* Video. Unicorn, 1988.

7. Munro, Roxie, illus. *Architects Make Zigzags: Looking at Architecture from A to Z.* Preservation Press, 1986.

8. Roehrig, Catharne. *Fun with Hieroglyphs.* (Includes 24 rubber stamps and a book about Egyptian art.) Metropolitan Museum of Fine Art, New York, 1990.

9. Sylvester, Diane, and Mary Wiemann. *Mythology, Archeology, Architecture.* Learning Works, 1982.

10. Additional materials available from the New York Metropolitan Museum of Fine Art, New York, include:

    Pyramids, Mummies and Fun: An Ancient Egyptian Puzzle Book

    The Hieroglyphs Game

    Mummy tin box with 12 decorated hieroglyph pencils

11. An inflatable, heavy-duty vinyl mummy is available from Casual Living, 5401 Hangar Court, P.O. Box 31273, Tampa, FL 33631-3273.

Theme Reading Connections: Egypt

Allen. *Pharaohs and Pyramids.* Usborne-Hayes, 1977.

Caselli, Giovanni. *An Egyptian Craftsman.* Illustrated by Giovanni Caselli. P. Bedrick, 1986.

Clare, John D., ed. *Pyramids of Ancient Egypt.* Living History series. Harcourt Brace Jovanovich, 1992.

Climo, Shirley. *The Egyptian Cinderella.* Illustrated by Ruth Heller. Thomas Y. Crowell, 1989.

Courtaland, Corrine. *On the Banks of the Pharaoh's Nile*. Illustrated by Christian Broutin. Childrens Press, 1988.

Cross, Wilbur. *Egypt*. Illustrated by Childrens Press, 1982.

Department of Geography. *Egypt in Pictures*. Lerner, 1988.

Hart, George. *Ancient Egypt*. Exploring the Past series. Illustrated by Stephen Biesty. Harcourt Brace Jovanovich, 1989.

Kerr, James. *Egyptian Farmers*. Beginning History series. Franklin Watts, 1991.

Kristensen, Preben, and Frona Cameron. *We Live in Egypt*. Franklin Watts, 1987.

Steel, Anne. *Egyptian Pyramids*. Franklin Watts, 1990.

Terzi, Murinella. *The Land of the Pharaohs*. Childrens Press, 1992.

Unstead, R. J. *An Egyptian Town*. Franklin Watts, 1986.

Ventura, Piero. *Journey to Egypt*. Illustrated by Piero Ventura. Franklin Watts, 1986.

Wilkins, Frances. *Egypt*. Chelsea, 1988.

Woods, Geraldine. *Science in Ancient Egypt*. Edited and illustrated by Henry Rasof. Franklin Watts, 1988.

Critical Thinking Question
What can be done to stop the theft of art works and artifacts? What should be done about items taken in the past? What punishment would deter art thieves? Should new laws be enacted to protect national art treasures?

Student Activities to Connect Literature and Curriculum

FINE ARTS

1. Using hieroglyphs, write the initials of your name as an art project.

2. Design a bulletin-board display of the Life of the Egyptians on the Nile River.

3. Have a class contest of making model barges. Select the most unusual, the most beautiful, and the most original of the entries.

4. Create an Egyptian death mask suitable for a pharaoh.

5. Design and produce a travel brochure of historical sights in Egypt.

6. Explore Egypt through art lessons. (See Raphael, Elaine, and Don Bolognese, *Drawing History: Ancient Egypt*, Franklin Watts, 1989.)

7. Prepare a pen-and-ink drawing using an Egyptian theme. What is the strength of black ink on white paper? Which makes a stronger presentation, black ink or color ink? Why?

LANGUAGE ARTS

1. Using student-made transparencies, retell the Egyptian story of the birth of the world. Compare it with the creation myths of Greece, Rome, and China.

2. Create a crossword puzzle about Egypt using these subjects: history, gods and heroes, geography, and art.

3. Describe the building of the pyramid as seen by author David Macaulay. Cooperative learning groups may select from the following sections:

Site selection and foundation preparation

Blueprint

Selection and transportation of materials

Uses of the ramp and pyramid construction

Pyramid architecture

Pharaoh burial ceremony

Pyramids yesterday and today

4. Cluster descriptive words that relate to pyramids. Using some of these words, prepare a quick-write paragraph. Exchange paragraphs with a partner for corrections.

WRITING PROMPT

1. Write an illustrated story about the sacred animals or gods of Egypt. Begin your story with the following:

> It has been many years, but my story has been passed down to me by my father, my father's father, and his father's father. It began when....

MATH

1. Compute the volume of a pyramid. State the mathematical formula. How many jumbo jets could be parked in a pyramid? Meaning is parked on base, not inside. (See the *World Almanac* and McLeish, Kenneth, *The Seven Wonders of the World*, illustrated by Sharon Pallent, Cambridge University Press, 1985.)

2. How did the Egyptians construct pyramids and obelisks?

SCIENCE

1. Write a comprehensive report about the Nile River at the time of the pharaohs and today.

2. Explain the methods used by Egyptians to farm at the time of the pharaohs. Could today's technology provide alternative methods? Why or why not? Compare the crops grown in the United States with those grown in Egypt. What products are exported from each country?

SOCIAL STUDIES

1. Explain the religion of the pharaohs with a chart that outlines its beliefs and superstitions.

2. Play Meet the Press. Each cooperative learning group will choose a god to research. At the end of a set time, each group will answer questions from the class of reporters. Every correctly answered question will be scored two points; incorrect answers will result in a one-point subtraction.

3. Prepare a time line of Egyptian history.

4. Design a modern tomb for a pharaoh.

GEOGRAPHY

1. Construct a topographical map of Egypt. Identify historical sites as well as modern cities.

BEYOND THE BOOK

Guided Reading Connections Across a Learning Rainbow: Fiction About Egypt

Carter, Dorothy S. *His Majesty, Queen Hatshepsut.* Illustrated by Michele Chessare. Harper & Row, 1987.

Ellerby, Leona. *King Tut's Game Board.* Lerner, 1980.

Kalman, Maira. *Hey Willy. See the Pyramids.* Penguin, 1988.

McGraw, Eloise J. *Mara, Daughter of the Nile.* Penguin, 1985.

Peck, Richard. *Blossom Culp and the Sleep of the Death.* Delacorte, 1986.

Snyder, Zilpha K. *The Egypt Game.* Dell, 1986.

FROM ANOTHER POINT OF VIEW

Isaacson, Phillip M. *Round Buildings, Square Buildings and Buildings That Wiggle Like a Fish.* Illustrated by Phillip M. Isaacson. Alfred A. Knopf, 1988.

Enriching Connections

(Note: I like to correlate *Pyramid* with *Myths and Legends of Ancient Egypt* as an integrated classroom unit. Students will be able to see the effects of culture and religion on Egyptians at the time of the pharaohs. Many school districts' master plans reflect new curriculum strategies that bridge social studies, language arts, and fine arts. Activities to Connect Literature and Curriculum are cooperative learning extensions to be used with both book titles.)

❀ ❀ ❀

ANCIENT EGYPT
Myths and Legends of Ancient Egypt

Author: Abigail Frost
Illustrators: Jean Marie Ruffieux, Jean Jacques, and Yves Chagnaud
Publisher: Marshall Cavendish, 1990
Classification: Mythology
Literary Form: Myths and legends told in illustrated format
Theme: People cannot understand everything in the world but will find some explanations through cultural myths.

ABOUT THE BOOK

STUDENT OBJECTIVES:

1. Interpret Egyptian mythology through storytelling.

2. Illustrate the hierarchy of Egyptian gods through a family tree.

3. Recommend specific myths that should be included in the study of Egypt.

SYNOPSIS: Legends and stories of the Egyptian gods and heroes have been retold by word-of-mouth for centuries.

SELECTED ADDITIONAL TITLES: Myths and Legends series

Frost, Abigail. *The Age of Chivalry.* Illustrated by Francis Phillipps. Marshall Cavendish, 1989.

———. *The Amazon.* Illustrated by Jean Torton. Marshall Cavendish, 1989.

———. *The Wolf.* Marshall Cavendish, 1989.

Ragache, Claude-Catherine. *The Creation of the World.* Illustrated. Marshall Cavendish, 1991.

Ragache, Gilles. *Dragons.* Illustrated by Francis Phillipps. Marshall Cavendish, 1991.

Briais, Bernard. *The Celts.* Marshall Cavendish, 1991.

Küss, Danièle. *The Incas.* Marshall Cavendish, 1991.

USING THE BOOK

Suggested Approach to the Book

Model Lesson

1. Explain this statement: "This book is about the stories of the people and gods of Ancient Egypt: a land where you could stand with one foot in a green field and the other in desert sand."

2. Who was the god Ra?

3. Most countries have legends to explain daylight and darkness. Explain the "Barge of the Sun." Who brought the sun in Greek and Roman myths? Compare various cultural legends that involve the sun's arrival each day.

4. Identify the god of all knowledge.

5. Describe the treachery of Seth.

6. Do the gods usually age in myths? Why is Ra described as "a wretched old man hobbled about the heavens almost crippled"? (See p. 20.)

7. What are the responsibilities of Egypt's gods?

8. If you lived in Egypt today, what occupation would you choose? Why?

Library Media Connections

1. Develop a family tree of the Egyptian gods to compare with the gods of Greek mythology.

Computer Connections

1. Using a word processor program, write three paragraphs about each of the following cultures: Egyptian, Roman, and Japanese. If you could choose your nationality, would you be an Egyptian, Roman, or Japanese? Why?

Instructional Materials Connections

(See list at the beginning of *Pyramid* unit.)

Theme Reading Connections: Egypt

Bailey, Catherine. *Pyramid*. History Highlights series. Glouchester, 1989.

Bendick, Jeanne. *Egyptian Tombs*. Illustrated. Franklin Watts, 1989.

Percefull, Aaron W. *The Nile*. A First Book series. Franklin Watts, 1984.

Reeves, Nicholas, and Nan Forma. *Into the Mummy's Tomb*. A Time Quest book. Scholastic/Modern Press, 1992.

Reiff, Stephanie. *Secrets of Tut's Tomb and the Pyramid*. Raintree/Steck-Vaughn, 1977.

Thomsen, Steven. *The Great Pyramid of Cheops*. Illustrated. Inside Story series. Capstone Press, 1989.

Critical Thinking Question
Should the United States budget funds to build a monument to recognize all presidents of this country? Why or why not?

Student Activities to Connect Literature and Curriculum

FINE ARTS

1. Design an elaborate horse cart for transportation of an Egyptian royalty member or military officer. The cart will be drawn by two horses who are also decorated for the event.

2. Present to the class a new design for Egyptian postal stamps and currency.

3. Construct a model of a pyramid.

LANGUAGE ARTS

1. Design an illustrated dictionary of Egypt. Cooperative learning groups may select a section to research and compile.

WRITING PROMPT

1. Use the following introduction for a video production:

Egypt Is the Land of Mysteries...

MATH

1. Develop word problems that compare and contrast monuments of Egypt and the United States.

SCIENCE

1. Many areas of the United States have become disaster areas because of hurricanes, floods, as well as drought. List plants that tolerate high temperatures and need little moisture to grow. Select plants that will grow in Egypt as well as hot areas in the United States. Identify any areas in the United States that has similar temperatures as compared to Egypt.

SOCIAL STUDIES

1. List the sacred animals of Egypt. Write a paragraph to accompany your animal list.

2. Using the Egyptian time line, develop a time line of the United States for comparison. Draw the two on a transparency to present to the class. What kind of background music would be appropriate?

3. Why could the Nile River be called the Highway of Egypt?

GEOGRAPHY

1. Compare the area of the United States and Egypt.

2. What benefits are derived from the Nile and Mississippi Rivers?

BEYOND THE BOOK

Reading Connections Across a Learning Rainbow: Egypt—Kings and Rulers

Payne, Elizabeth. *The Pharaohs of Ancient Egypt*. Illustrated. Random House, 1981.

Rosen, Deborah N. *Anwar el-Sadat: A Man of Peace*. Illustrated. Childrens Press, 1986.

Sullivan, George. *Sadat: The Man Who Changed Middle East History*. Illustrated. Walker, 1981.

FROM ANOTHER POINT OF VIEW

Crump, Donald J., ed. *Mysteries of Ancient Egypt*. National Geographic, 1990.

Parent-Student Connections

1. Using international cookbooks, plan and prepare an Egyptian meal at home.

2. Research Egyptian clothing for men and women.

❀   ❀   ❀

AIDA

Author: Told by Leontyne Price
Illustrators: Leo Dillon and Diane Dillon
Publisher: Harcourt Brace Jovanovich, 1990
Suggested Grade Level: 6
Classification: Nonfiction
Literary Form: Retelling of Verdi's opera, Aida, the story of love between an enslaved Ethiopian princess and an Egyptian general.
Theme: Prejudice has existed for many centuries; it plays a tragic role in world history.

ABOUT THE BOOK

STUDENT OBJECTIVES:

1. Compare and contrast the art work of Diane Dillon and Leo Dillon in *Aida* and Katherine Paterson in *The Tale of the Mandarin Ducks* (Lodestar, 1990).

2. Interpret the story of Aida as a readers theatre presentation.

3. Compare and contrast *Aida* with the tragedies *Romeo and Juliet* and *The Love of a Mexican Prince and Princess*.

SYNOPSIS: It is always difficult for two young people from different backgrounds to overcome their parents' or society's prejudices regarding religion, class, or race. Such situations can cause unresolvable family tragedy.

ABOUT THE COMPOSER: Giuseppe Verdi, 1813-1901.

Verdi based *Aida* on an historical incident, the evidence of which was uncovered during an archaeological excavation in Egypt. The Italian composer wrote what has become one of the best-known operas.

ABOUT THE AUTHOR: Leontyne Price, 1927- .

Leontyne Price received a toy piano for Christmas when she was six years old. She quickly learned that the attention she received when she played it felt good. Her goal, from early childhood, was to perform on stage. Some time later, Price's mother took her to a concert performance by Marian Anderson, a renowned African-American singer. When the singer emerged on stage dressed in an exquisite white gown, Price knew that she wanted to sing also. Price's talent was recognized early, and she earned a scholarship to the Julliard School of Music in New York City. Within three years she was cast in the leading role of Bess in George Gershwin's opera, *Porgy and Bess.*

Price has sung Aida and other roles, including Cleopatra in *Antony and Cleopatra.* Price first sang in *Aida* at the War Memorial Grand Opera House in San Francisco in 1957. "I always felt, while performing *Aida,* that I was expressing all of myself—as an American, as a woman, and as a human being" (Igus, Toyomi, ed., *Great Women in the Struggle*, Book of Black Heroes series, Just Us Books, 1991).

Critics have described Price's soprano voice as one of the great operatic voices of the age. The opera diva has received numerous awards including Grammy Awards, Emmy Awards, the National Medal of the Arts, and the Presidential Medal of Freedom. As a writer, Price was awarded the Coretta Scott King Award for her children's book, *Aida.*

ABOUT THE ILLUSTRATORS: Diane Dillon, 1933 - ; Leo Dillon, 1933- .

The Dillons were married after studying at the Parsons School of Art in New York. Leo grew up in Brooklyn, the son of parents from Trinidad, and Diane grew up in Glendale, California. Early in their careers they produced art work for advertisements, record album covers, magazine illustrations, movie posters, and paperback-book covers.

The Dillons were awarded two Caldecott medals for *Why Mosquitoes Buzz in People's Ears* and *Ashanti to Zulu: African Traditions.* "We wanted to combine realism with the elegance of a fairy tale," and that, in doing research, "we began to appreciate the grandeur of everyday living." (Stott, Jon C., *Children's Literature from A to Z*, McGraw-Hill, 1984, p. 94.)

SELECTED ADDITIONAL TITLES: Diane Dillon and Leo Dillon

Aardema, Verna, retold by. *Who's in Rabbit's House?* Illustrated by Diane Dillon and Leo Dillon. Dial, 1979.

————. *Why Mosquitoes Buzz in People's Ears: A West African Tale.* Illustrated by Diane Dillon and Leo Dillon. Dial, 1975.

Greenfield, Eloise. *Honey, I Love: And Other Poems.* Illustrated by Diane Dillon and Leo Dillon. Harper & Row, 1986.

Hamilton, Virginia. *The People Could Fly.* Illustrated by Diane Dillon and Leo Dillon. Alfred A. Knopf, 1985.

Musgrove, Margaret. *Ashanti to Zulu: African Traditions.* Illustrated by Diane Dillon and Leo Dillon. Dial, 1976.

USING THE BOOK

Suggested Approach to the Book

Model Lesson

1. Describe the home life of Ethiopian Princess Aida. How did her life change when she was captured and taken to Egypt? Does slavery exist in the world today? Why or why not? Explain special privileges granted by Egyptian Princess Amneris to her slave servant, Aida.

2. How does the clothing of an Egyptian princess differ from that of an Ethiopian princess?

3. What conflicts can you recognize in *Aida*?

4. How is the crisis resolved in *Aida*? Is the solution satisfactory? Why or why not?

5. What types of building materials can be identified in the illustrations? What are the characteristics of the materials?

6. If you were in the place of Aida or Radames, would you have made a different decision? Why or why not? Would your family's position or the involvement of a parent be an issue in your decision?

7. What is symbolic about the design of the page borders?

Library Media Center Connections

1. Research the following famous theaters and present a brief oral report using transparencies for visual support. Describe the operas presented in the theaters.

   Arena di Verone, Verona, Italy

   La Scala Opera House, Milan, Italy

   Paris Opera, Paris, France

   Covent Garden, London, England

   Hamburg Staatsoper, Hamburg, Germany

   Vienna Staatsoper, Vienna, Austria

   Metropolitan Opera House, New York City

   Chicago Lyric Opera House, Chicago

Computer Connections

1. Make a database of fine and applied art book references as well as nonprint materials, available in the school library media center.

Instructional Materials Connections

1. Ensor, Wendy-Ann. *Heroes and Heroines in Music.* Cassette. Oxford University Press, 1981.

2. Rosenberg, Jane. *Dance Me a Story—Twelve Tales from the Classic Ballets.* Thames and Hudson, 1985.

3. Tames, Richard. *Giuseppe Verdi.* Lifetimes Series. Franklin Watts, 1991.

Theme Reading Connections: Opera

Barber, Frank G. *Flying Dutchman.* Silver Burdett, n.d.

Carner, Mosco. *Madam Butterfly.* Silver Burdett, n.d.

Englander, Roger. *Opera! What's All the Screaming About?* Walker, 1983.

Gammond, Peter. *The Magic Flute.* Silver Burdett, n.d.

John, Nicholas. *Opera.* Oxford University Press, 1986.

Kerby, Mona. *Beverly Sills: America's Own Opera Star.* Illustrated by Sheila Hamanaka. Penguin, 1989.

Neidorf, Mary. *Operantics with Wolfgang Amadeus Mozart.* Sunstone, 1987.

Storr, Catherine, retold by. *Flying Dutchman.* Raintree/Steck-Vaughn, 1985.

Williams, Sylvia. *Leontyne Price: Opera Superstar.* Childrens Press, 1984.

> Critical Thinking Question
> What is opera? What are the advantages and disadvantages of using opera to tell a story? as a storyteller's tool?

Student Activities to Connect Literature and Curriculum

FINE ARTS

1. Examine the end papers of *Aida.* Can you replicate the art technique? How? Submit examples for a display in the school library media center.

2. Research opera stories that appeal to you. Design miniature theater sets. (Note: Maurice Sendak, the writer and illustrator, enjoys constructing model sets and has produced an opera based on his book *Where the Wild Things Are.*)

3. Construct a pop-up book of *Aida.*

LANGUAGE ARTS

1. Describe Radames, Aida, and Amneris using mind maps.

WRITING PROMPT

1. Write a review of *Aida* for your school newspaper. What information sources would be appropriate? Begin the book review with this statement:

> Ethiopia and Egypt continue war; latest conflicts kill and injure thousands of soldiers from each country! People suffer from hunger, and disease runs rampant throughout both countries.

MATH

1. If you were a modern-day prince or princess and had an allowance of $1 million per year, how would you spend your money? Create a budget listing annual, monthly, and weekly expenditures. If a $1 million allowance is insufficient, how much money would you need? Why? Revise the original budget to reflect the additional funding. Restate the budget in a bar graph or pie chart.

SCIENCE

1. Compare and contrast the weather, land mass, and natural resources of Egypt and Ethiopia. Is there a significant difference? Why or why not?

SOCIAL STUDIES

1. Examine the topography of Egypt and Ethiopia. Would either country benefit from possessing the other country's land? Why are the two countries at war? Are any countries in the Middle East at war today? Taking history into account, predict the future alliances of Middle Eastern countries. Which ones may be friendly? Why? Which ones are likely to go to war? Why? Does geography play any role in alliances?

GEOGRAPHY

1. Construct a floor map of Africa. Determine the kinds of information that can be included about Egypt and Ethiopia.

2. List ways in which Ethiopia and Egypt are geographically alike.

3. In cooperative learning groups, compare and contrast Ethiopia and Egypt. Use the *World Almanac* to gain information about the following:

Population	Population Density	Ethnic Groups
Languages	Geographic Area	Form of Government
Chief Crops	Imports	Exports
Infant Mortality	Education	Number of Hospital Beds

BEYOND THE BOOK

Guided Reading Connections Across a Learning Rainbow: Music

Brownell, David. *Book of Great Composers: Book 1.* Illustrated by Nancy Conkle. Bellerophon Books, 1978.

Ensor, Wendy-Ann. *Heroes and Heroines in Music.* Oxford University Press, 1981.

Peppin and Mundy. *Book of Music and Painting.* Usborne-Hayes, 1980.

Powers, Bill. *Behind the Scenes of a Broadway Musical.* Crown, 1982.

FROM ANOTHER POINT OF VIEW

Prokofiev, Sergei. *Peter and the Wolf.* Illustrated by Jorg Muller. Book and cassette. Alfred A. Knopf, 1986.

————. *Peter and the Wolf Pop-up-Book.* Illustrated by Barbara Cooney. Penguin, 1986.

Enriching Connections

1. Conduct a poll of upper-grade students to determine their favorite singer and favorite song. Report the results in a school library media center display on popular recording artists and their music.

Parent-Student Connections

1. Attend a dance or musical production with your child. Explore various forms of art by visiting a local museum.

❀ ❀ ❀

CITIES
Through the Eyes of Artists

Authors: Wendy Richardson and Jack Richardson
Illustrators: Various artists
Publisher: Childrens Press, 1991
Classification: Nonfiction
Literary Form: Art appreciation
Theme: Artists and other people view cities differently.

ABOUT THE BOOK

STUDENT OBJECTIVES:

1. Examine historical and contemporary portrayals of cities by various artists.

2. Evaluate the environment of the city today and how that environment is changing.

3. Introduce one artist and his or her work by role playing the artist in a videotaped production.

SYNOPSIS: Artists see the world each in their own way. In the introduction, the authors state, "This is a book of pictures about cities. Some of the pictures are old and some of them were made quite recently. They come from all over the world. Some are paintings, some are drawings, some are prints. Some come from books, some are on walls, and some are made to hang on walls. They look very different."

ABOUT THE AUTHORS: Wendy Richardson, birthdate unavailable; Jack Richardson, birthdate unavailable.

No biographical information available.

SELECTED ADDITIONAL TITLES: Wendy Richardson and Jack Richardson

Richardson, Wendy, and Jack Richardson. *Animals: Through the Eyes of Artists.* Childrens Press, 1991.

————. *Entertainment: Through the Eyes of Artists.* Childrens Press, 1991.

————. *Families: Through the Eyes of Artists.* Childrens Press, 1991.

————. *The Natural World: Through the Eyes of Artists.* Childrens Press, 1991.

————. *Water: Through the Eyes of Artists.* Childrens Press, 1991.

USING THE BOOK

Suggested Approach to the Book

Model Lesson

1. Canaletto's name appeared as a member of the Professional Guild of Painters of Venice in 1721. What is the significance of that listing? What is a guild? Name several guilds.

2. Compare and contrast the art of Venice of Canaletto and Patrick Procktor.

3. How does El Greco make viewers look upward in his painting of Toledo, Spain? How does his work make you feel?

4. Where are people in "The Third-Class Carriage" going? What did Honore Daumier think about this mode of transportation?

5. Why is Claude Monet considered an Impressionist? Name other Impressionists?

6. Why did painters choose to paint train stations?

7. If you were an artist, how would you portray work?

8. If you were an artist, how would you present your view of a city? What would be your style? If you were able to be whisked through time and space, what city in *Cities: Through the Eyes of Artists* would you choose to visit? Why?

Library Media Center Connections

1. Choose an artist to research and role play in a classroom video production. The choice may include any of the following:

Canaletto	Patrick Procktor	El Greco
Honore Daumier	Claude Monet	Gino Severini
Ford Madox Brown	Graham Sutherland	L. S. Lowry
Pierre Auguste Renoir	George Wesley Bellows	Fernand Leger

Charles Sheeler	Georgia O'Keeffe	Frank Auerbach
Mario Sironi	Richard Estes	Ken Done
Diego Rivera	Robert (Milton) Rauschenberg	

Computer Connections

1. Design a ballot for students to vote for their favorite artist. As part of the preliminary work, ask students to identify artists whose work they like. Design the ballot with these names in mind, but allow write-in selections.

Instructional Materials Connections

1. Burger, Celia. *Cities and Their People.* Illustrated by Janet Skiles. Good Apple, 1985.

2. Eisen, David. *Fun with Architecture from the Metropolitan Museum of Art.* Thirty-two rubber stamps of parts of buildings. Viking, 1992.

3. Frayling, Christopher, Helen Frayling, and Ron Van Der Meer. *The Art Pack.* Alfred A. Knopf, 1992.
   "A one-of-a-kind art book of pop-up examples using paper engineering ... use of color, line and composition ... and an audio guide to the 20 greatest pictures of all time." Available from Museum of Fine Arts, Catalog Sales, P.O. Box 1044, Boston, Mass. 02120.

4. Gudeman, Janice. *Creative Encounters with Creative People.* Good Apple, 1984.

5. Kinghorn, Harriet, Jacqueline Badman, and Lisa Lewis-Spicer. *Let's Meet Famous Artists.* Denison, 1991.

6. MacDonald, Fiona. *A Nineteenth Century Railway Station.* Illustrated by John James. Inside Story series. P. Bedrick, 1990.

7. McLeish, Kenneth, and Valerie McLeish. *Troll Famous People.* Troll, 1991.

8. Muller, Jorg. *The Changing City.* Illustrated by Jorg Muller. Macmillan, 1977.

9. Provensen, Alice, and Martin Provensen. *Town and Country.* Illustrated by Alice Provensen and Martin Provensen. Crown, 1985.

10. Sattler, Helen R. *Recipes for Art and Craft Materials.* Rev. ed. Illustrated by Marti Shohet. Lothrop, Lee & Shepard, 1987.

11. Striker, Susan. *Anti-Coloring Book of Masterpieces.* Henry Holt, 1982.

Theme Reading Connections: Art

Hargrove, Jim. *Diego Rivera: Mexican Muralist.* Childrens Press, 1990.

Munthe, Nelly. *Meet Matisse.* Little, Brown, 1983.

Newlands, Anne. *Meet Edgar Degas.* J. B. Lippincott, 1988.

Raboff, Ernest. *Albrecht Durer.* J. B. Lippincott, 1988.

———. *Diego Rodriguez de Silva y Velasquez.* J. B. Lippincott, 1988.

———. *Frederic Remington.* J. B. Lippincott, 1988.

———. *Henri Matisse.* J. B. Lippincott, 1988.

———. *Henri Rousseau.* J. B. Lippincott, 1988.

———. *Henri de Toulouse-Lautrec.* J. B. Lippincott, 1988.

———. *Marc Chagall.* Harper & Row, 1988.

———. *Michelangelo Buonarroti.* Harper & Row, 1988.

———. *Paul Gauguin.* J. B. Lippincott, 1988.

———. *Paul Klee.* J. B. Lippincott, 1988.

Turner, Robyn Montana. *Georgia O'Keeffe.* Little, Brown, 1991.

———. *Rosa Bonheur.* Little, Brown, 1991.

Venezia, Mike. *Botticelli.* Childrens Press, 1991.

———. *Da Vinci.* Childrens Press, 1989.

———. *Edward Hopper.* Childrens Press, 1989.

———. *Francisco Goya.* Childrens Press, 1991.

———. *Mary Cassatt.* Childrens Press, 1990.

———. *Michelangelo.* Childrens Press, 1991.

———. *Monet.* Childrens Press, 1990.

———. *Paul Klee.* Childrens Press, 1991.

———. *Picasso.* Childrens Press, 1988.

———. *Rembrandt.* Childrens Press, 1988.

———. *Van Gogh.* Childrens Press, 1988.

Critical Thinking Question
If you were editor of *Cities: Through the Eyes of Artists*, which art work would you select to be on the cover? What criteria would you use? Why?

Student Activities to Connect Literature and Curriculum

FINE ARTS

1. Explain the view painting style of Canaletto. List 10 observations you can make from viewing the painting.

2. Poll students at your grade level to determine their art preferences.

LANGUAGE ARTS

1. Write a brief caption for each example of art in the book.

2. Prepare an outline of a book to be published about your town or city. What will the title be? Will pictures be included? Describe the format. What references and interviews will be included? Why? What special attractions will be highlighted?

WRITING PROMPT

1. Write a book review beginning with the following statement:

> Both famous and unknown artists have different views of *Cities: Through the Eyes of Artists*, which is being released today by Childrens Press.

MATH

1. What is the nationality of each artist? Create a bar graph or pie chart showing the number of artists from each country represented in the book.

SCIENCE

1. Describe the environment of a perfect city. What part would the water supply, sanitation system, air quality, power supply, architecture, modes of transportation, recreation programs, and trees and plants play? These topics can be developed in cooperative learning groups.

SOCIAL STUDIES

1. Create a time line of artists appearing in *Cities: Through the Eyes of Artists*.

2. Design a travel brochure that includes at least five examples of art about cities that would appeal to visitors.

3. Plan an around-the-word tour to visit museums in 10 countries that are pictured in *Cities: Through the Eyes of Artists*.

GEOGRAPHY

1. On a world map, identify the locations of cities pictured in *Cities: Through the Eyes of Artists*.

2. Venice is called The City of Water because of its geographic location. Create a model of Venice today.

3. Select 10 cities from *Cities: Through the Eyes of Artists* and determine the longitude and latitude of each. Do the cities have any geographic characteristics in common? Using a physical map, can you select specific land forms that could support a new city?

BEYOND THE BOOK

Guided Reading Connections Across a Learning Rainbow: Book Making

Gibson, Ray, and Louisa Somerville. *How to Make Pop-Ups.* Usborne-Hayes, 1990.

Hiner, Mark. *Paper Engineering.* Tarquin, 1985.

Irvine, Joan. *How to Make Pop-Ups.* Illustrated by Barbara Reid. Beech Tree, 1991.

Jenkins, Patrick. *Animation.* Addison-Wesley, 1991.

FROM ANOTHER POINT OF VIEW

Ventura, Piero. *Piero Ventura's Book of Cities.* Random House, 1975.

Enriching Connections

1. Read a biography about an artist. Write a personal letter to a friend describing the life of the artist.

2. Experiment with various art mediums to create an original view of a real or imaginary city.

Parent-Student Connections

1. As a family visit an art exhibit or museum. What do you like? Why? Are there any pictures on exhibit like those in *Cities: Through the Eyes of Artists*?

❀   ❀   ❀

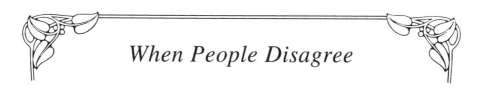

When People Disagree

THE SLAVE DANCER

Author: Paula Fox
Illustrator: None
Publisher: Bradbury Press, 1973
Suggested Grade Level: 6
Classification: Fiction
Literary Form: Historical fiction
Theme: Man's inhumanity to man.

ABOUT THE BOOK

STUDENT OBJECTIVES:

1. Describe the voyage of the slave ship *Moonlight.*

2. Explain the beginnings of slavery in the United States.

3. Recommend an action plan to help people rise above the poverty level.

SYNOPSIS: Jessie Bollier, a poor child from New Orleans, is impressed into service on a slave ship
   to play his fife for the blacks. The slaves are forced to dance to his music as a form of exercise
   so that they will look healthy and sell for higher prices on the slave market.

ABOUT THE AUTHOR: Paula Fox, 1923- .
   New York City, Cuba, London, Paris, Warsaw, and New Hampshire have been home to Paula
Fox. She has worked as a machinist, teacher, reporter, and author. Her books reflect growth and
change in her major characters. They usually return home after a journey, but only after they have
been the victims of some wrongdoing that leaves an indelible mark on them.
   Fox has received several important children's literature awards, including the Newbery medal
in 1974 for *The Slave Dancer* and the Hans Christian Andersen medal in recognition of her
remarkable career. "The question, the central one in each of her books, is how the individual is to
find a meaningful place in the world, one in which he can maintain his integrity while responding to
others" (Stoll, Jon C. *Children's Literature from A to Z*, McGraw-Hill, 1984, p. 115).

SELECTED ADDITIONAL TITLES:

Fox, Paula. *Blowfish Live in the Sea.* Macmillan, 1970.

————. *How Many Miles to Babylon?* Illustrated by Paul Giovanaopoulos. Bradbury Press, 1980.

————. *Maurice's Room.* Illustrated by Ingrid Fetz. Macmillan, 1985.

————. *The Moonlight Man.* Bradbury Press, 1984.

————. *One Eyed Cat.* Illustrated by Irene Trivas. Bradbury Press, 1984.

————. *A Place Apart.* Farrar, Straus & Giroux, 1980.

————. *Portrait of Ivan.* Bradbury Press, 1985.

————. *The Stone-Faced Boy.* Illustrated by Donald A. Mckay. Bradbury Press, 1968.

————. *The Village by the Sea.* Orchard, 1988.

USING THE BOOK

Suggested Approach to the Book

Model Lesson

1. Describe the home of Jessie Bollier.

2. Why was Jessie forbidden by his mother to go to Congo Square?

3. In what ways did Aunt Agatha criticize Jessie's mother? Jessie told his aunt that his mother taught him reading and numbers. Aunt Agatha responded, "But who is to teach you how to think?" (See p. 11.) What is thinking? How do you learn to think? Is thinking the same as using common sense?

4. What is Jessie's pipe? What famous historical painting shows someone playing a fife? Are fifes played today?

5. How long was Jessie told that he would be away on the voyage to Africa?

6. Benjamin Stout told Jessie that he had been pressed too, although he was older. What does *pressed* mean?

7. How much did the captain pay for a slave? What cargo did he carry back to the United States from Cuba?

8. The Captain called Jessie Bollweevil. What did this nickname mean?

9. Explain the flags in the captain's quarters. Were they legal?

10. How did Jessie show man's humanity to man? Was the book's ending a surprise?

Library Media Center Connections

1. Trace the history of New Orleans from its beginnings to today. What would it be like to live there? What kind of work would your parents do? What places would you like to visit? Why?

2. Look at cookbooks that feature food from New Orleans and Louisiana. How does the style of food preparation differ from that used in your home? New Orleans is famous for its Cajun food. Can you describe it?

3. Research information about pirates. Where did they live? What kind of loot did they seek? Name some famous pirates.

4. What was Jessie's family name? Why did he change it? Has your family name been shortened or changed by immigrants to the United States? What is the nationality and meaning of your family name? What reference materials in the school library media center or public library can help you locate additional information?

Computer Connections

1. Using a word processor, write a letter from Jessie to Ras a year after their shipwreck and another letter 50 years later. How would the two boys have changed?

Instructional Materials Connections

1. Meltzer, Milton. *All Times, All People: A World History of Slavery.* Illustrated by Leonard Everett Fisher. Harper & Row, 1980.

2. Meltzer, Milton. *The Black Americans: A History in Their Own Words.* Rev. ed. Thomas Y. Crowell, 1984.

3. Evitts, William J. *Captive Bodies, Free Spirits: The Story of Southern Slavery.* Messner, 1985.

Theme Reading Connections: Slavery

Adler, David A. *A Picture Book of Frederick Douglass.* Illustrated by Samuel Byrd. Holiday House, 1983.

Collier, James, and Christopher Collier. *Jump Ship to Freedom.* Delacorte, 1981.

Smucker, Barbara. *Runaway to Freedom.* Illustrated by Charles Lilly. Harper & Row, 1979.

Stine, Emma G. *The Slave Ship.* Illustrated by David Lockhart. Scholastic, 1988.

Yates, Elizabeth. *Amos Fortune, Free Man.* Illustrated by Nora S. Unwin. Dutton, 1967.

> Critical Thinking Question
> What was the worst thing Jessie saw on the ship? How would you have felt? Could anything be done about the situation?

Student Activities to Connect Literature and Curriculum

FINE ARTS

1. Jessie daydreamed that "Someday, I might become a rich chandler in a fine suit, with a thousand candles to hand if I needed them instead of three grudgingly given stubs. I imagined the splendid house I would live in, my gardens, my carriage and horses" (pp. 12-13). Daydreaming, Jessie didn't pay attention to his route home. What happened? Can it happen today? Why or why not? Present a color-pencil or pen sketch of Jessie with his dream sequence illustrated above his head in a balloon or bubble format.

2. Demonstrate how to play the string game Cat's Cradle.

LANGUAGE ARTS

1. Using the information that is written opposite page 1, create a program for a play, including a summary of three acts and a cast of student actors from your classroom.

2. Debate the following statement: Their own chiefs wanted to sell them as slaves.

3. Compare and contrast the slave trade with today's drug trade. This topic may be assigned to cooperative learning groups to present oral reports using transparencies for statistical information.

WRITING PROMPT

1. Write a book review of *The Slave Dancer* beginning with Jessie's statement:

> "I stepped out of the hut. Daniel had saved my life. I couldn't expect more than that" (p. 121).

MATH

1. Jessie's father died accidentally by drowning. List the eight most common causes of death today. (See the *World Almanac*.) Chart the number of deaths due to each cause for the last five years. Use a different color for each year.

2. What were the 15 leading causes of death in the United States last year? Present the results of your research on a bar graph.

3. Convert the ship's travel speed of 14 knots per hour into miles per hour and kilometers per hour.

SCIENCE

1. Cockroaches are mentioned as a problem on board the *Moonlight*. What other animals on ships spread infectious disease when they leave the ship for land?

2. What are the average temperatures and number of rainy days for New Orleans and Nigeria?

3. Define sailing terms that were used on the *Moonlight*. Have the definitions changed? What navigational instruments were used? What technology has changed the science of sailing? Would you rather be a wind sailor or a high-tech sailor? Why?

SOCIAL STUDIES

1. "There's bits of land like that all over this world. They don't belong to no one. I don't care for the look of them myself. It's not right they should be so empty" (p. 90). Is this statement true today? Why or why not? Identify any island in your area.

GEOGRAPHY

1. Using butcher paper, create a large street map of New Orleans at the time of the slave market. How does it differ today?

2. On a current New Orleans map, find the former location of the slave market at St. Louis and Chartres Streets. (The old slave market is clearly identified on a street map today.)

3. Locate Lake Pontchartrain, Lake Borgne, and Barataria Bay on a map of Louisiana. Imagine that a satellite photograph has been taken. Create an aerial view of New Orleans and its adjoining areas.

4. The Bight of Benin is located at 6.27°N, 5.34°E. What country is this? Describe the country as it is today. What are its natural resources? How do the people earn their living? What is the average income per person? Is this a Third World country? Why or why not? Trace the route of the slave ship from New Orleans, along the coast of Florida, and to Africa, returning to the United States and suffering a shipwreck off the coast of Mississippi.

5. Make a floor-map puzzle of today's African countries. Each puzzle piece should be one country. On the right side of the puzzle piece, mark the country's capital. On the reverse side, list the names of contiguous countries.

BEYOND THE BOOK

Guided Reading Connections Across a Learning Rainbow: Nigeria

Baker, Carol. *A Family in Nigeria.* Lerner, 1985.

Gerson, Mary Joan. *Why the Sky Is Falling.* Little, Brown, 1992.

Musgrove, Margaret W. *Ashanti to Zulu: African Traditions.* Illustrated by Diane Dillon and Leo Dillon. Dial, 1976.

Nigeria. Chelsea, 1988.

Nigeria. Cultures of the World series. Marshall Cavendish, 1993.

Enriching Connections

1. Make an antique-style map showing the route of the final voyage of the *Moonlight.*

2. Draw a map of Jessie's route to New Orleans based on directions Daniel gave Jessie in Mississippi. The map should include thumbnail art sketches to add visual information.

3. Play Moonlight Baby, a Nigerian game.
    Each player brings five small rocks or pebbles.
    One player is selected to be "It." That player leaves the game area.
    One student lies down on the ground, and all the other players outline his or her body with small rocks and pebbles. The student whose form is outlined rises, brushes off debris from the ground to get rid of "evidence," and joins the other players in a circle. "It" returns to the game area and names the student whose form is outlined on the ground. A correct guess earns "It" another turn; an incorrect guess allows someone else to become "It."

FROM ANOTHER POINT OF VIEW

Lester, Julius. *To Be a Slave.* Illustrated by Tom Feelings. Dial, 1968.

Parent-Student Connections

1. Look in a reference book for additional information about the Creole people. How did they get their name? When? Do Creoles still live in New Orleans? What characterizes their style of cooking?

2. Name 10 good things about your home and community. What are 10 interesting facts that you have read about New Orleans?

❁   ❁   ❁

NUMBER THE STARS

Author: Lois Lowry
Illustrator: None
Publisher: Dell, 1989
Suggested Grade Level: 6
Classification: Fiction
Literary Form: Historical novel
Theme: War and its harm to people is without reason.

ABOUT THE BOOK

STUDENT OBJECTIVES:

1. Analyze the effects of World War II on people, including Jewish people.

2. Develop international laws to prevent war.

3. Predict wars that may result because of conditions that exist in the world today.

SYNOPSIS: The lives of two families living in the same building become entwined because of the German invasion of Denmark.

ABOUT THE AUTHOR: Lois Lowry, 1937- .
Lois Lowry grew up as an "army brat," living in many places, including Honolulu and Tokyo. Lowry commented on her four children's influence on her writing, "Their escapades during childhood and adolescence have provided me with enough material to write books for young people for countless years to come" (Holtze, Sally Holmes, ed., *Fifth Book of Junior Authors and Illustrators*, H. W. Wilson, 1983, p. 198).
Lowry's prize possessions include "paintings by artist friends and all the records Billie Holiday ever made. Hanging from my dining room ceiling is a piece of tumbleweed sent to me by young fans in Idaho ... and on top of a lamp in my study a hat, decorated with all the titles of my books given to me by the seventh graders in Boylston, Massachusetts" (*Fifth Book of Junior Authors and Illustrators*, p. 199).
Books that have received special honors include *A Summer to Die, Autumn Street, Anastasia Krupnik,* and *Anastasia Again!*

SELECTED ADDITIONAL TITLES:

Lowry, Lois. *Anastasia Again!* Illustrated by Diane DeGroat. Houghton Mifflin, 1981.

———. *Anastasia, Ask Your Analyst.* Houghton Mifflin, 1984.

———. *Anastasia At Your Service.* Illustrated by Diane DeGroat. Houghton Mifflin, 1982.

———. *Anastasia Has the Answers.* Houghton Mifflin, 1985.

———. *Anastasia Krupnik.* Houghton Mifflin, 1979.

———. *Anastasia On Her Own.* Houghton Mifflin, 1985.

———. *Autumn Street.* Houghton Mifflin, 1980.

———. *The One Hundredth Thing About Carolyn.* Houghton Mifflin, 1985.

———. *A Summer to Die.* Illustrated by Jenni Oliver. Houghton Mifflin, 1977.

USING THE BOOK

Suggested Approach to the Book

Model Lesson

1. Describe the physical appearances of Annemarie and Ellen.

2. What would a resistance newspaper be like? Imagine that the United States is at war with another country. What kind of news articles would be published?

3. What kind of jobs did some of the Danish resistance fighters have?

4. Why were butter and big yellow cupcakes with pink frosting not available?

5. Kirsti begged Annemarie to tell her a fairy tale by Hans Christian Andersen, the most famous Danish fairy storyteller. What stories did he write? When did Andersen live?

6. It was easy for the King of Denmark to visit with his subjects and ride his horse around Copenhagen. In contrast, U.S. presidents are not able to mix freely with the people because of the possibility of an assassination. Why? Explain why all the people of Denmark formed the bodyguard for the king.

7. What happened to the third daughter of the family, Lise?

8. The children were sent on an errand to a thread and button shop. Where would you go to get a new button today? Could you buy just one?

9. The Johansens had potatoes for dinner every night. What food would be most plentiful and served most often in your home if the United States were at war?

10. Why did the Germans give orders to close the stores owned by Jewish people?

11. Why did the Danes destroy their own naval fleet as the German army was approaching? If the United States needed to destroy any of its military supplies, what would be chosen? What can a country do with its nuclear materials, including bombs?

12. Why was the Jewish New Year special for the Rosen family? Why did their religious celebration change?

13. Explain the relocation of people during World War II.

14. How would the story have changed if Annemarie had been caught with Ellen's Star of David hidden in her palm?

15. Why did the publisher of *Number the Stars* use the Jewish Star of David next to each page number of the book? How was the book title chosen?

16. How did Annemarie describe the pride of the people who left Denmark in hopes of finding safety in Sweden?

Library Media Center Connections

1. Prepare a brief oral report about one of the following:

Amalienborg Palace	King Christian X	Copenhagen
Deer Park—Klampenborg	Tivoli Gardens	Kronborg Castle
Danish Royal Family	Danish History	Danish Geography
Danish Smorgasbord	Christmas Plates	Thor, God of Thunder

Computer Connections

1. Prepare an extensive bibliography of war-related materials about countries involved in World War II. Enter the information into a classroom or library database.

Instructional Materials Connections

1. Adler, David. *A Picture Book of Anne Frank.* Illustrated by Karen Ritz. Holiday House, 1993.

2. Corwin, Judith. *Jewish Holiday Fun.* Wanderer, 1987.

3. Emmerich, Elsbeth, with Robert Hall. *My Childhood in Nazi Germany.* Franklin Watts, 1992.

4. Greenberg, Judith E., and Helen Carey. *Jewish Holidays.* Franklin Watts, 1985.

5. Nicholson, Michael, and David Winner. *Raoul Wallenberg: The Swedish Diplomat Who Saved 100,000 Jews from the Nazi Holocaust Before Mysteriously Disappearing.* Edited by Rhoda Sherwood. Gareth Stevens, 1989.

6. Niemark, Anne E. *One Man's Valor: Leo Baeck and the Holocaust.* Lodestar, 1986.

7. Stein, R. Conrad. *Resistance Movements.* Childrens Press, 1982.

8. Turner, Reuben. *Jewish Festivals.* Rourke, 1987.

Theme Reading Connections: Denmark

Andersen, Ulla. *We Live in Denmark.* Franklin Watts, 1984.

James, Alan. *Denmark.* Chelsea, 1988.

Levin, Charlotte R. *Danish Dependencies.* Chelsea, 1989.

Lye, Keith. *Take a Trip to Denmark.* Franklin Watts, 1985.

Scandinavia-American Heritage. Facts on File, 1988.

> Critical Thinking Question
> What is the price of courage in war and in peace? Explain your responses.
> Give examples. How much should people be expected to give of themselves
> in time of war? Why?

Student Activities to Connect Literature and Curriculum

FINE ARTS

1. Kirsti did not like her fish shoes. What product could we substitute for leather today? Present a model drawing of shoe designs and include fabric other than leather.

2. Illustrate Mrs. Johansen's childhood memory of the time she was met by her dog, Trofast, on her way home from school. (See p. 58.) Or, illustrate the house in the woods as seen by Annemarie. (See p. 60.)

3. Create a quilt design using flowers and birds like the one that had been made by Annemarie's great-grandmother. (See p. 65.)

4. Draw a political cartoon about all the Danish butter being relocated to the stomachs of the German army. (See p. 69.)

LANGUAGE ARTS

1. Construct mind maps of the following major characters:

   Annemarie, Ellen, and Kirsti

   parents of the Johansen and the Rosen children

   Peter Neilsen

   Uncle Henrik

2. Role play the scene on the train when two German soldiers ask Mrs. Johansen where she is going with the children.

3. Interview someone in your community who was alive during World War II. Ask the person to tell about rationing stamps, air raids, and Rosie the Riveter.

4. Debate this statement: Men are usually messier than women. (See p. 70.)

5. Write diary entries about the following events. Assume that German soldiers will find the diary and read it; write your entries so that they will not arouse German suspicion.

   stopped by soldiers when the girls were running to practice for the school athletic meet

   Germans searching for the Rosen family

   the train trip to Uncle Henrik's

   the funeral at Uncle Henrik's

6. Write a feature story, to be published after the end of World War II, that describes the funeral and escape to Sweden led by Uncle Henrik and Peter Neilsen.

WRITING PROMPT

1. Write a television story about the lives of brave people who faced fear in many different ways during World War II. Begin with the following quote:

> When they were almost home, Ellen whispered, "I was so scared."

MATH

1. Explain the units of currency used in Scandinavian countries. What is the conversion rate for changing U.S. currency into foreign currency? Which currency, United States or Danish, will purchase the most goods today? Why?

2. Compare the average monthly temperatures in Copenhagen with those in your area. Show the temperatures in graph format.

SCIENCE

1. Explain the Scandinavian Night.

2. Why did the death of a person due to typhus scare the German soldiers?

3. What was the packet that Annemarie carried to her uncle? It looked like a clean handkerchief. Why was it important to drug the baby for the journey?

SOCIAL STUDIES

1. Messages sent during war have had secret meanings. The message to Henrik was a question and a statement "So, Henrik, is the weather good for fishing? I'm sending Inge to you today with the children, and she will bring you a carton of cigarettes." (See p. 53.) Through movies and video tapes, Americans have become more sophisticated, and those messages would not be effective today. Write a message that would be effective today that asks if you can help one person escape in a day or so.

2. In cooperative learning groups, create a time line for the Johansen family, including Lise, Annemarie, and Kirsti, beginning before the occupation of Denmark in World War II. The time line should include key dates in the family's lives (such as births and deaths) as well as major events like the war. (See Grun, Bernard, *The Timetables of History: A Horizontal Linkage of People and Events,* Touchstone, 1982.) A time line of the United States may be researched as a comparison. (See Murphy, Paul C., *Since 1776: A Year-by-Year Timeline of American History,* Price Stern Sloan, 1988.)

3. Using materials from the afterword, briefly list the facts that were incorporated into *Number the Stars.*

GEOGRAPHY

1. Create a secret map of the escape route traveled by Annemarie, Kirsti, Mrs. Johansen, and Ellen Rosen.

BEYOND THE BOOK

**Guided Reading Connections Across a Learning Rainbow:
World War II Fiction**

Anderson, Margaret. *Searching for Shona.* Alfred A. Knopf, 1978.

DeJong, Meindert. *House of Sixty Fathers.* Illustrated by Maurice Sendak. Harper & Row, 1956.

Greene, Betty. *Summer of My German Soldier.* Dial, 1973.

Kerr, Judith. *When Hitler Stole Pink Rabbit.* Putnam, 1972.

Enriching Connections

1. Plan a class Danish smorgasbord for lunch at school. Design and laminate place mats decorated with illustrations of Danish wildflowers.

FROM ANOTHER POINT OF VIEW

Reiss, Johanna. *The Upstairs Room.* Harper & Row, 1972.

Parent-Student Connections

1. Visit the library and check out a Danish cookbook. Suggest that a recipe be selected and prepared as part of the family dinner.

2. Read aloud John Hersey's *Hiroshima* (Random House, 1989), which details the decision made by President Harry Truman to drop the atomic bomb on Japan to hasten the end of World War II.

❀ ❀ ❀

TAKING TERRI MUELLER

Author: Norma Fox Mazer
Illustrator: None
Publisher: Morrow, 1981
Suggested Grade Level: 6
Classification: Fiction
Literary Form: Contemporary novel
Theme: Every person in a family has rights and responsibilities.

ABOUT THE BOOK

STUDENT OBJECTIVES:

1. Analyze the reasons for Terri Mueller's search for identity.

2. Evaluate the losses of each person in this story. In your opinion, did Terri or her mother suffer the most? Why?

3. Recommend nationwide laws and resource agencies that would protect children and parents from similar situations.

SYNOPSIS: Initially, *Taking Terri Mueller* is about a single parent who is raising his daughter. Terri was told her mother had died eight years before. Terri respects her father, feels that he has been a good parent, holds him in deep respect, and loves him. Terri seeks information about her mother so that she can identify with that parent. What did she look like? Do I look like her? The story quickly becomes one of the conflict between father and daughter, as he wants to forget and Terri wants to know.

ABOUT THE AUTHOR: Norma Fox Mazer, 1931- .

Norma Fox Mazer grew up in New York's Adirondack Mountains. Her grandparents were Jewish immigrants from Poland who had started a bakery. She still remembers "walking home from the bakery in the cold blue dusk eating a hot roll.... I played marbles with the boys, read everything possible between covers, and longed for my mother to be more like Marmee in *Little Women* and for myself to have 'adventures' " (Holtz, Sally Holmes, ed., *Fifth Book of Junior Authors and Illustrators*, H. W. Wilson, 1983, pp. 204-5).

"In junior and senior high, I gravitated to the school newspaper. My English composition drew praise. Yet no one ever said to me, as I say now to any aspiring writer, 'Write. Write letters. Keep a journal. Only write something every day. Don't ever write what you think you ought to write, but only what you feel, think and observe for yourself' " (*Fifth Book of Junior Authors and Illustrators*, p. 205).

Mazer believes that her writing career paralleled her children's growth and development. She explains, "I read every day and I write every day—both seem as necessary to my well being as food and sleep. The more I write, the more I understand that I will rarely, if ever, write well enough to please myself, and yet the more I love it and the more privileged I feel to do this as my daily work" (*Fifth Book of Junior Authors and Illustrators*, p. 205).

Mazer has received a Lewis Carroll Shelf Award for *Twelfth of October,* a Christopher award for *Dear Bill, Remember Me?*, an Edgar Allan Poe award for best juvenile mystery for *Taking Terri Mueller,* and a Newbery honor for *After the Rain.*

(Note: It was a pleasure to attend the first summer seminar on children's literature held in 1987 at Columbia University, New York City. Norma Fox Mazer was the afternoon guest of honor for our small group. She told us how she and her husband, Harry Mazer, struggled to get published and how they wrote in the early morning before their children awoke. Mazer shared her thoughts on writing for young adults, explaining that the road to personal success can be a difficult one.

On the flight from Los Angeles to New York, I had prepared for the Columbia seminar by finishing the preconference reading, which included *Taking Terri Mueller.* Reading the story was an emotional experience because of the author's skill in balancing all of the characters in a deep crisis and ending the story on a positive note. I told Mazer that I had big tears in my eyes when I completed the book. Later, a manila envelope was delivered to my home, and inside were autographed copies of Mazer's books.

If children are told that one parent is dead, most will not ask for proof. I recommend that librarians use *Taking Terri Mueller* in a book talk, that teachers integrate it into their classroom reading, that principals recommend the book for curriculum study, and that school boards require that it be an integral part of instruction. This information needs to be put in the hands of upper-elementary and middle-school students in an attempt to stop the separation of children from one parent.)

SELECTED ADDITIONAL TITLES:

Mazer, Norma Fox. *After the Rain.* Morrow, 1987.

———. *Downtown.* Morrow, 1984.

———. *Figure of Speech.* Dell, 1986.

———. *I, Trissy.* Dell, 1986.

———. *Mrs. Fish, Ape and Me, the Dump Queen.* Dutton, 1980.

———. *Three Sisters.* Scholastic, 1983.

USING THE BOOK

Suggested Approach to the Book

Model Lesson

1. Terri's father became sad when he talked about his dead wife. Describe sadness. List things that make you sad. What makes you happy?

2. Terri Mueller thought it was odd that she could not remember what her mother was like. Define her comment, "Sad funny."

3. What was the one family rule for Terri and her father? Would that rule work in your family? What rule would be appropriate for your family?

4. Why did the posters in Terri's room almost always include a house? What are the advantages and disadvantages of moving every six or eight months? Where would you like to move? Why?

5. What is the value of two-parent families? What is the percentage of marriages today that end in divorce? What are some of the ways that divorce affects children?

6. If you were the principal of your school, what kind of assembly programs would you schedule? Why? How do you hold the attention of students during a program?

7. How do you think the Coca-Cola Bottling Company feels about the statement, "Not a *Coke*. They rot your insides." made by Terri's new friend, Shaundra? (See p. 28.) What kind of advertising campaign would succeed with teenagers? List foods that are good and bad for you. Does the quantity eaten make any difference?

8. What did Terri learn from her birth certificate? What is the purpose of this document? How may it be used?

9. Why did Terri think something was wrong when Aunt Vivian came to visit? What conversation did she overhear? Why did Phil tell his sister, Vivian, "You've never betrayed me. You can't now" (p. 60)? If you had been in Vivian's place, what would you have thought? If her father had committed murder, should she protect him? Why or why not? Can you think of *any* circumstance where murder could be justified?

10. Is Terri's breaking into the storage box an invasion of her father's privacy? What reasons did Phil give for taking Terri? What other options might have been available to him?

11. What prompted Terri and Shaundra to hitchhike? Why should neither boys or girls ride with people whom they do not know? List different ideas for the class to discuss.

12. Graffiti was written in the telephone booth outside Azria's Market (p. 103). There are many problems with graffiti and tag gangs today. Some city governments offer rewards to people who give information leading to the arrest of offenders. Some courts require these self-proclaimed artists to paint over their graffiti as part of the punishment. What other restraints could be used?

13. How did Terri use the language of silence against her father? How do you feel when this is used on you?

14. Did Terri make the right decision about going back to her father? What would you have done in the same situation? Why?

Library Media Center Connections

1. Ask the school library media specialist to schedule periodic book talks using library books that need to be introduced to upper-intermediate or middle-school readers. Encourage students to enter the author, title, and a brief summary of the books featured in the book talks into a library media center database. Ask students to rate the book using a system like that used by many professional book critics: five stars for the best book, no stars for the worst book.

Computer Connections

1. Using a word processor, write a critical review of *Taking Terri Mueller*. Select another book, and compare the two regarding how they provide relevant information to readers.

Instructional Materials Connections

1. Fierstein, Jeff. *Kid Contracts.* Good Apple, 1982.

2. Mazer, Norma Fox. *Taking Terri Mueller.* Cassette. Listening Library, n.d.

3. *The World's Children.* 5 vols. Marshall Cavendish, 1988.

4. Terri used the L. L. Bean catalog, which is a well-known mail-order catalog featuring sports clothing and other items. Secure a copy of the catalog and discuss in class the advantages and disadvantages of mail-order shopping. A catalog for classroom use may be obtained by contacting L. L. Bean, Freeport, ME 04033-0001.

Theme Reading Connections: Fiction About Divorce

Angell, Judie. *What's Best for You.* Bradbury Press, 1981.

Cleary, Beverly. *Dear Mr. Henshaw.* Illustrated by Paul O. Zelinsky. Dell, 1984.

Mazer, Harry. *Guy Lenny.* Dell, 1988.

Nixon, Joan L. *Casey and the Great Idea.* Illustrated by Amy Rowen. Scholastic, 1982.

Stolz, Mary. *Go and Catch a Flying Fish.* Harper & Row, 1979.

Talbert, Marc. *Thin Ice.* Little, Brown, 1986.

> Critical Thinking Question
> Explain Terri Mueller's thoughts: "Careful What You Think. Careful What You Ask." Is this good advice? Why or why not?

Student Activities to Connect Literature and Curriculum

FINE ARTS

1. Terri's father had a big toolbox for his work as a carpenter. Toolboxes are used today for storing items and equipment used by hobbyists. Design a toolbox for your hobby. What would be in it? Why?

2. Describe clothes that are manufactured today by Oshkosh B'Gosh. If you were going to design clothing for teenagers, what would you name your company? What would your company logo look like? Prepare sketches of a wardrobe for winter, spring, summer, and fall.

3. Design a model house that you would like to live in. Paint it inside and outside and furnish it as a family home.

LANGUAGE ARTS

1. Terri Mueller's class is going to create a newspaper, which, according to Mr. Higgens, the teacher, is "going to be interesting. Nothing boring for us. Our articles are going to be written with verve, style, and wit" (p. 68). Put out a special newspaper for your grade. Staffing will include an editor, news editors and reporters, sports and column writers, artists and photographers, make-up and display editors, and advertising sales staff. Make the newspaper a very special school event. Develop a campaign promoting its publication. Arrange a delivery schedule. Roll the presses.

2. Pretending that you are Terri Mueller, reply to the letter from Aunt Vivian. (See p. 119.)

WRITING PROMPT

1. Imagine that Terri Mueller, with the permission of both parents, has contracted with a television network to have her story told on a special program for teens. Write a program introduction based on the following statement:

> "My mother," she thought again. "I have a mother. She is somewhere in this world. At this very moment..." (p. 103).

MATH

1. Using overhead transparencies, prepare graphs and charts that reflect statistical information about marriage and divorce. (See the *World Almanac*.)

   How many divorces are granted in your state each year?

   Develop two 10-year graphs, one showing the number of marriages and one showing the number of divorces granted in the United States.

   What was the median age of persons marrying for the first time during each decade between 1890 and 1990?

SCIENCE

1. Compare average temperatures for the various cities in which Terri Mueller lived, including Oakland, California; Richman, Indiana; Wilmington, North Carolina; Niagara Falls, New York; and Ann Arbor, Michigan. What are the average monthly temperatures of each place? What is the daily average temperature? What amount of rainfall does each area receive? Answer these same questions about your community.

SOCIAL STUDIES

1. How did Terri meet new friends when she changed schools so frequently? Does your school have many transient students, or are most students permanent residents? How can your class help newcomers feel welcome? Develop a slide presentation or video to introduce new students to your school. What important information should be included?

GEOGRAPHY

1. How much money per air-mile would Terri pay for her trip to Oakland, California, from Detroit, Michigan? Air fares are now deregulated; consequently, the cost of tickets varies widely. Explain how people on the same airplane in the same class of service pay different rates for the flight. Based on the air fares listed below, determine the cost per air-mile for a round trip from Detroit to Oakland (2,068 miles each way).

Super Saver	$290, round trip
Coach	$840, round trip
Business Class	$670, one way
First Class	$1052, one way

   Plan the route on a map and estimate how much it would cost to drive from Oakland to Detroit and back. Assume your car gets 28 miles per gallon of gas and gasoline costs $1.44 per gallon. Would the mileage be the same by air and auto?

BEYOND THE BOOK

Guided Reading Connections Across a Learning Rainbow: Child Welfare

Berry, Joy. *Every Kid's Guide to Laws That Relate to Kids in the Community*. Childrens Press, 1987.

———. *Every Kid's Guide to the Juvenile Justice System*. Childrens Press, 1987.

Enriching Connections

1. Using the library media center catalog, develop a bibliography of books that interest you. Locate each book in the library media center and choose one for leisure reading. What attracted you to this book? Did the cover art and book flaps promote the book well? What makes a book good?

FROM ANOTHER POINT OF VIEW

Blume, Judy. *It's Not the End of the World.* Bradbury Press, 1972.

Parent-Student Connections

1. Remind the student to ask your permission before accepting a ride in anyone's car. Discourage hitchhiking. Discuss with the student the dangers inherent in hitchhiking.

2. Discuss family rules and why they are necessary. Ask if any other rules could be helpful and why.

❀   ❀   ❀

SO FAR FROM THE BAMBOO GROVE

Author: Yoko Kawashima Watkins
Illustrator: None
Publisher: Lothrop, Lee & Shepard, 1986
Suggested Grade Level: 6
Classification: Fiction
Literary Form: Historical novel
Theme: War changes the lives of many people by forcing them to flee as refugees, seeking safety
  for their families and themselves.

ABOUT THE BOOK

STUDENT OBJECTIVES:

1. Recognize major causes of war throughout history.

2. Interpret the relationship between Koreans and Japanese in 1945.

3. Understand the need for emergency planning in a family.

SYNOPSIS: A family is forced to flee Korea when the communists persecute Japanese living there. Father is a Japanese government official who is in North Korea at the end of World War II. The young son is far from home, working in a munitions factory. Mother and the two daughters, Yoko and Ko, must escape to Japan, which also has been ravaged by war.

ABOUT THE AUTHOR: Yoko Kawashima Watkins, 1934- .

Yoko Kawashima Watkins is married to a U.S. citizen, has four adult daughters, and lives on Cape Cod (on the East Coast of the United States). This is the story of her life; it was her first book. She has overcome language barriers and has shown great determination to write her autobiography with its insightful, painful view of war.

SELECTED ADDITIONAL TITLES:

Watkins, Yoko Kawashima. *Tales from the Bamboo Grove.* Illustrated by Jean Pseng and Mou-Sien Pseng. Bradbury Press, 1992.

USING THE BOOK

Suggested Approach to the Book

Model Lesson

1. Examine the cover of the book. What do you see? What is happening? What kind of feeling is portrayed by the cover artists, Leo Dillon and Diane Dillon?

2. Find Nanam, North Korea, to orient yourself to the starting point journey of the mother and her two daughters. How old are the daughters when they flee their home in the bamboo grove? Who are the other family members? Where are they? Why must the mother leave immediately?

3. What kind of clothes did women and girls wear at the demand of Japanese Prime Minister Tojo? What wartime preparations were being made in school and at home? Why couldn't Hideyo join the student army? How was his failure resolved?

4. Describe the scene at the train station. Cluster your impressions of that awful night.

5. Do people obey the law during war? (See p. 40.) What is the role of the International Red Cross during wartime?

6. Describe the seven days the family spent following the railroad tracks. Compare the provisions that the girls and their mother took (p. 6) with those that Hideyo took (pp. 58-59).

7. On what dates did the United States use atomic bombs on Japan? How many days later did the war end? Name the cities that were bombed.

8. What message did Koyo and Yo leave for their brother on the station post? How did Mother show her age and suffering?

9. "To the light, to the light. At last he reached a small farmhouse, lost all control and collapsed" (p. 100). What happened to Hideyo next?

10. What disappointment met Mother and the daughters in Japan? Why did Mother tell Yoko to save the wrapping cloth?

11. How valuable was a futon to the two sisters? What would you do if you received a futon as a gift today?

Library Media Center Connections

1. Jean Fritz, a popular author, wrote the introduction to *So Far from the Bamboo Grove*. What qualifies her to comment on the story? What books has Fritz written? List the ones you have read. Choose one you have not read to share with the class in a book talk.

2. Research and prepare classroom displays about the following topics:

   Takonoma and Japanese Flower Arrangement

   Calligraphy and Japanese Writing

   Way of Tea and Japanese Ceremonies

   Japanese Musical Instruments

   Japanese Classic Dance

   Japanese Clothing

   Japanese History

   Commodore Matthew C. Perry

   Japanese Architecture

   Japanese Food

Computer Connections

1. Using a word processor, write a letter from Yoko to Corporal Matsumura updating him on the postwar condition of her family and thanking him for saving their lives by warning them to flee Korea.

2. Using *Crossword Puzzle* or similar software, make a puzzle for students to complete after they finish reading *So Far from the Bamboo Grove*.

Instructional Materials Connections

1. Blumberg, Rhoda. *Commodore Perry in the Land of Shogun*. Lothrop, Lee & Shepard, 1985.

2. Fisher, Leonard Everett. *Alphabet Art*. Four Winds Press, 1978.

3. Fisher, Leonard Everett. *Number Art*. Four Winds Press, 1982.

4. Murray, D. M., and T. W. Wong. *Noodle Words: An Introduction to Chinese and Japanese Characters*. Charles Tuttle, 1971.

5. Ottenheimer, Laurence. *Japan: Land of Samurai and Robots*. Young Discovery series. Childrens Press, 1988.

6. Invite an artist to the classroom to demonstrate calligraphy or brush writing.

Theme Reading Connections: Japan

Coates, Bryan E. *Japan.* Bookwright, 1991.

Elkin, Judith. *A Family in Japan.* Lerner, 1987.

Epstein, Sam, and Beryl Epstein. *A Year of Japanese Festivals.* Garrard, 1974.

Greene, Carol. *Japan.* Childrens Press, 1983.

Haskins, Jim. *Count Your Way Through Japan.* Carolrhoda, 1987.

Jacobsen, P., and P. Kristensen. *A Family in Japan.* Franklin Watts, 1984.

Steele, A. *A Samurai Warrior.* Rourke, 1988.

Stefoff, Rebecca. *Japan.* Chelsea, 1988.

> Critical Thinking Question
> Did Mother place too much emphasis on having Yoko attend school when they arrived in Kyoto? " 'You must learn to take likes and dislikes in this world,' Mother told me, drying my wet face" (p. 107). If you were Yoko's mother, what would be your first priority when you reached Kyoto?

Student Activities to Connect Literature and Curriculum

FINE ARTS

1. Illustrate what you think the house so far from the bamboo grove looked like.

2. What is calligraphy? Write your name in calligraphic letters. Make ceramic ink pots as a class art project.

3. Examine several artists' versions of Mount Fuji. Produce a watercolor picture of this famous landmark.

4. Mother directed the daughters to hide in wild irises from the soldiers. Recreate the scene using watercolors. (See p. 23.)

5. Design a name seal that will be made of jade for yourself.

LANGUAGE ARTS

1. One of Yoko's happiest memories of the family home in the bamboo grove was when her father gave her a pair of canaries. As a school assignment, she wrote a story about her birds. What birds are native to your area? Create a story about them. Before you begin writing, be sure you understand their habitat, food, coloration, and survival requirements. Do research in the school library media center to find background materials. Have any stories or legends been written about these native birds? Check the school library media center catalog for fiction. This writing assignment may be completed in cooperative learning groups.

WRITING PROMPT

1. Write Hideyo's story of his flight to Japan. His story may be told only after the war is over. Begin the story when he receives help from strangers, who could be killed for helping him.

> "If he should die or if anyone finds out we have rescued a Japanese Boy, we will be betrayed for prize money and executed" (p. 164).

MATH

1. "Ko counted a little over thirty-six thousand yen—a hundred dollars" (p. 133). What was the conversion rate for one yen?

2. Using information from the mileage key on the two-page map following the title page, how many miles did the family travel from Nanam, Korea, to Kyoto, Japan? How many miles did they travel by train, by foot, and by boat? Can you compute approximately how many miles per hour they covered when walking?

SCIENCE

1. Compare seasonal temperatures and rainfall in Siberia, Manchuria, Korea, and Japan. How do these areas differ from your community? Based on this information, where would you choose to live? Why?

SOCIAL STUDIES

1. Plan a Japanese New Year celebration. Remember that each person becomes one year older on this national birthday holiday in Japan. What food would be appropriate for this celebration in Japan?

GEOGRAPHY

1. Find Korea on the two-page map following the title page. Describe the land formation. What countries are adjacent to Korea? What do you know about these countries? What is the total population of each country? How many square miles are in each country? What is the population density per square mile?

2. Enlarge the two-page map in the front of the book as a model grid map. The map can be a salt-dough project or another type of physical map. On your map, label all the points that are labeled on the book's map. Color your map.

3. Identify the following places:

Manchuria	Vladivostok	Nakhodka	Mount Figi
Seoul	Pusan	Hiroshima	Nagasaki
Kyoto	Tokyo		

BEYOND THE BOOK

Guided Reading Connections Across a Learning Rainbow: Korea

Farley, Carol. *Korea: A Land Divided*. Dillon, 1983.

Haskins, Jim. *Count Your Way Through Korea*. Carolrhoda, 1989.

Kim, Richard E. *Lost Names: Scenes from a Boyhood in Japanese Occupied Korea*. Universe, 1988.

McNair, Sylvia. *Korea*. Childrens Press, 1986.

Moffett, Eileen. *Korean Ways*. Charles Tuttle, 1986.

North Korea. Chelsea, 1988.

South Korea. Chelsea, 1988.

Enriching Connections

1. Compare Korean and Japanese foods using the following cookbooks:
   Chung, Okwha, and Judy Monroe. *Cooking the Korean Way*. Lerner, 1990.
   Weston, Reiko. *Cooking the Japanese Way*. Lerner, 1983.

FROM ANOTHER POINT OF VIEW

Hersey, John R. *Hiroshima*. Random House, 1989.

Parent-Student Connections

1. Visit the library and check out illustrated travel books about Japan and Korea.

2. Explore the folklore of Japan and Korea through collections of fairy tales, including
   Carpenter, Frances. *Tales of a Korean Grandmother*. Charles Tuttle, 1972.
   Sakade, Florence. *Urashima Taro and Other Stories*. Charles Tuttle, 1958.

3. Visit an art museum and view oriental art.

❀　❀　❀

PROFESSIONAL READING

America's Fascinating Indian Heritage. Rev. ed. Reader's Digest, 1991.

Better Homes and Gardens Editors. *Better Homes and Gardens Step-by-Step Kids' Cookbook.* Better Homes and Gardens, 1984.

Briquebec, John. *The Ancient World—From the Earliest Civilizations to the Roman Empire.* Historical Atlas series. Warwick Press, 1990.

Carpenter, Humphrey, and Mari Prichard. *The Oxford Companion to Children's Literature.* Oxford, 1984.

Center for Environmental Education Staff. *The Ocean Book: Aquarium and Seaside Activities and Ideas for All Ages.* Wiley, 1989.

Children's Atlas of Native Americans. Rand McNally, 1992.

Cummins, Julie, ed. *Children's Book Illustration and Design.* PBC International, 1992.

D'Alelio, Jane. *I Know That Building! Discovering Architecture with Activities and Games.* Preservation Press, 1989.

Darling, Harold, and Peter Neumeyer, eds. *Image and Maker.* Green Tiger Press, 1984.

Frickle, John, Jay Scarfone, and William Stillman. *The Wizard of Oz: The Official 50th Anniversary Pictorial History.* Warner, 1989.

Gordon, Patricia, and Reed Snow. *Kids Learn America!* Williamson, 1991.

Grow Lab: A Complete Guide to Gardening in the Classroom. National Gardening Association, 1988.

Grun, Bernard. *The Timetables of History.* Touchstone, 1982.

Haglund, Elaine J., and Marcia L. Harris. *On This Day.* Libraries Unlimited, 1983.

Harris, Geraldine. *Ancient Egypt.* Cultural Atlas for Young People. Facts on File, 1990.

Holtze, Sally Holmes. *Fifth Book of Junior Authors and Illustrators.* H. W. Wilson, 1983.

———. *Sixth Book of Junior Authors and Illustrators.* H. W. Wilson, 1989.

Hopkins, Lee Bennett. *Books Are by People.* Citation Press, 1969.

———. *More Books by More People.* Citation Press, 1974.

Lambert, David, and Ralph Hardy. *Weather and Its Work.* Facts on File, 1985.

Lorimer, Larry. *The Julian Messner United States Question and Answer Book.* Messner, 1984.

Meltzer, Milton. *All Times, All People: A World History of Slavery.* Illustrated by Leonard Everett Fisher. Harper, 1980.

———. *The Black Americans: A History in Their Own Words.* Rev. ed. Crowell, 1984.

Meyer, Susan E. *A Treasury of the Great Children's Book Illustrators.* Abrams, 1983.

Munro, Roxie. *Architects Make Zigzags: Looking at Architecture from A to Z.* Illustrated by Roxie Munro. Preservation Press, 1986.

Murphy, Paul C. *Since 1776.* Price Stern Sloan, 1988.

Olsen, Mary Lou. *Presidents of the United States.* Teacher ed. Garrett Education, 1990.

Poltarnees, Welleran. *All Mirrors Are Magic Mirrors.* Green Tiger Press, 1972.

Sattler, Helen R. *Recipes for Art and Craft Materials.* Rev. ed. Illustrated by Marti Shohet. Lothrop, 1987.

Stott, Jon C. *Children's Literature from A to Z.* McGraw-Hill, 1984.

Thomas, Bob. *Disney's Art of Animation from Mickey Mouse to Beauty and the Beast.* Hyperion, 1991.

Waldman, Carl. *Encyclopedia of Native American Tribes.* Illustrated by Molly Braun. Facts on File, 1987.

Author/Illustrator/Title Index

Subject Index

About the Author

Mary Lou Olsen is a graduate of Marquette University's Journalism Department, Milwaukee, Wisconsin, and received her master's degree in communication from California State University, Fullerton. She has taught in elementary, middle, and high schools in addition to presenting children's literature classes at the university level. Other background experiences include being a library school media specialist and serving as a district librarian.

As a library services-curriculum consultant, she has developed "literature-immersion days" for districts and conferences. These programs serve as a model for implementing strategies that cement literature to curriculum. Emphasis is placed on various strands, including multiculturalism and storytelling, the research process, fine arts, social studies, and science. Mrs. Olsen is the author of *Creative Connections: Literature and the Reading Program, Grades 1-3* (Libraries Unlimited, 1987) and *Presidents of the United States*, Teacher ed. (Garrett Education, 1990).